STUDENT AFFAIRS PRACTICE
IN HIGHER EDUCATION

STUDENT AFFAIRS PRACTICE IN HIGHER EDUCATION
Second Edition

By

Audrey L. Rentz & Associates

C H A R L E S C T H O M A S • P U B L I S H E R , L T D.
Springfield • Illinois • U.S.A.

Published and Distributed Throughout the World by
CHARLES C THOMAS • PUBLISHER, LTD.
2600 South First Street
Springfield, Illinois 62794-9265

© *1996 by* CHARLES C THOMAS • PUBLISHER, LTD.
ISBN 0-398-06658-2 (cloth)
ISBN 0-398-06675-2 (paper)
Library of Congress Catalog Card Number: 96-12918

Printed in the United States of America
SC-R-3

Library of Congress Cataloging-in-Publication Data

Student affairs practice in higher education / edited by Audrey L.
   Rentz. — 2nd ed.
         p.   cm.
      Rev. ed. of: Student affairs functions in higher education. c1988.
      Includes bibliographical references and indexes.
      ISBN 0-398-06658-2. — ISBN 0-398-06675-2 (pbk.)
      1. Student affairs services—United States.   I. Rentz, Audrey L.
   II. Student affairs functions in higher education.
   LB2343.S7936   1996
   378'.194—dc20
                                                    96-12918
                                                       CIP

ABOUT THE AUTHOR

AUDREY L. RENTZ is Professor of Higher Education and Student Affairs at Bowling Green State University (OH). Her educational background includes an A.B. from the College of Mount St. Vincent (Mathematics), an M.S. from The Pennsylvania State University (Counselor Education), and the Ph.D. in Counseling, Personnel Services and Educational Psychology from Michigan State University. Prior to a full-time faculty appointment at Bowling Green, she held positions in student affairs administration in Pennsylvania, Virginia, Michigan and Ohio. She has served on the editorial board of Initiatives (NAWE), and currently with the Journal of College Student Development (ACPA), and the Journal of Psychological Type (APT). Professional association involvements have included several terms on Commission (XII) of ACPA and the Teaching and Research Division of NAWE. Research interests include student affairs practice and history and women in higher education. A recipient of the Philip A. Tripp Distinguished Service Award from OCPA, she is the editor of *Student Affairs: A Profession's Heritage* (1995), and co-author of *Student Affairs Careers: Enhancing the College Experience* (1991) with Gary H. Knock.

ABOUT THE CONTRIBUTORS

D. STANLEY CARPENTER is Professor of Educational Administration at Texas A&M University. He has held positions in Housing (Ogelthorpe University), Fundraising (Texas A&M), and as Dean of Students at the University of Arkansas-Monticello. He coordinates the Student Affairs Administration in Higher Education (SAAHE) Program and is Executive Director of the Association for the Study of Higher Education (ASHE). He holds a B.S. in Mathematics from Tarleton State University, and M.S. in Student Personnel and Guidance from East Texas State University, and the Ph.D. in Counseling and Personnel Services from the University of Georgia. Areas of publication include professionalism and other issues in the field of student affairs.

MICHAEL D. COOMES is an Associate Professor of Higher Education and Student Affairs at Bowling Green State University (OH). He received the B.A. in Education and History from Western Washington University and the Ed.D. in Education from Indiana University

(IA). Previous administrative positions were held at St. Martin's College and Seattle University as Director of Financial Aid. Publication and presentations have emphasized the areas of federal policy process, application of student development to institutional policy and history of student affairs. He is active in ACPA, ASHE, and NASPA.

MICHAEL DANNELLS is an Associate Professor and Coordinator of the College Student Personnel Program at Kansas State University. He received his Ph.D. in College Student Development from the University of Iowa in 1978. He has been an assistant dean of students, a director of residence life, a director of new student programs, and Chair of the Department of Counseling and Educational Psychology at KSU. He is past chair of Commission XII (Professional Preparation) of the American College Personnel Association and is a Director-elect for Commissions of ACPA.

JUDITH J. GOETZ is Senior Associate Director of the Division of Undergraduate Studies at The Pennsylvania State University. She received a B.A. in History from Hamline University, the M.A. in College Student Personnel and M.Ed. in Guidance and Counseling from Bowling Green State University and the Ph.D. in Higher Education Administration from the University of Toledo. Areas of publication and presentations include transitional programs for new first year students, staff development for academic advisers, and the uses of technology in comprehensive advising programs. She is active in NACADA serving as a member of the Commissions for Graduate Student Advising and Advising Undecided Students.

DON HOSSLER is Professor and Chair of the Department of Educational Leadership and Studies at Indiana University. He is the Director of the Center for Postsecondary Research and Planning and teaches courses in student affairs and higher education administration. Research interests include college student development, enrollment management and higher education finance.

JOSH KAPLAN is Director of the Student Health Center at Bowling Green State University (OH). A graduate of Princeton University, he received the M.D. from Downstate Medical Center, State University of New York and is certified by the American Board of Internal Medicine. He has served as president of the Ohio College Health Association and is currently chair of the clinical medicine section of the American College Health Association.

JOANN KROLL is Director of Career Services at Bowling Green State University (OH). She received the B.S. in Marketing from Virginia Commonwealth University and the M.Ed. in Higher Education Administration from Kent State University (OH). She recently received the first College Placement Council Award for Excellence in Educational Programming in Career Planning and Placement. In addition, she has completed consultantships in Russia helping to establish the first Career Service Center and a national network of Career Services professionals. She has authored several book chapters and is a frequent speaker at professional conferences.

CAROLYN L. PALMER is an Associate Professor in the Department of Higher Education and Student Affairs at Bowling Green State University (OH). She received her B.A. from the University of Massachusetts in Human Development, the M.A. from the University of Connecticut in Counseling and the Ph.D. from the University of Illinois in Quantitative and Evaluative Research Methodologies. Recent research interests are in the areas of campus violence, hate speech and hate behaviors, and outcomes assessment in student affairs.

BETTINA C. SHUFORD is a third year doctoral student in Higher Education Administration at Bowling Green State University (OH). She received the B.S. in Psychology from North Carolina Central University and the M.A. in Guidance and Counseling from the University of North Carolina at Greensboro. She has held positions in Residence Life, as an Assistant Dean of Students and Director of Minority Student Affairs at the University of North Carolina at Greensboro. She serves on the NASPA Monograph Advisory Board.

JOHN H. SCHUH is an Associate Vice President for Student Affairs and Professor of Counseling and School Psychology at Wichita State University. Previously he held administrative and faculty assignments at Indiana University and Arizona State University. Schuh is the author, co-author or editor of 125 publications and has received awards from NASPA and ACPA for contributions to the literature and for service from ACPA and ACUHO–I. He has served on the governing boards of ACPA, ACUHO–I, and NASPA. He received a Fulbright fellowship to study higher education in Germany in 1994.

EDWARD G. WHIPPLE is Vice President for Student Affairs at Bowling Green State University (OH). He received the B.A. from Willamette University, the M.A.T. from Northwestern University, and the Ph.D. from Oregon State University. Previous student affairs administrative positions were held at Montana State University-Billings, the University of Alabama, Texas Tech University and Iowa State University.

JEANNE WRIGHT is Health Promotion Coordinator for the Center for Wellness and Prevention and Assistant Professor, College of Health and Human Services at Bowling Green State University (OH). She has been a Registered Nurse since 1974 and received the M.Ed. in Health Education from the University of Toledo.

ELIZABETH YARRIS is an Associate Professor and Psychologist on staff of the Counseling Center at Bowling Green State University (OH). She received the B.S. in Psychology, the M.A. in College Student Personnel and the Ph.D. in Counseling Psychology from the University of Iowa.

PREFACE

Personnel work in a college or university is the systematic bringing to bear on the individual student all those influences, of whatever nature, which will stimulate him and assist him, through his own efforts, to develop in body, mind and character to the limit of his individual capacity for growth, and helping him apply his powers so developed most effectively to the world of work. (Clothier, 1931, p. 10)

Sixty-four years ago, Robert C. Clothier wrote these words to help his colleagues better understand the purpose of the emerging field known then as personnel work. During the past six decades the field has evolved through a number of major transformations reflected in the labels used to describe it. The group of individuals on college and university campuses who have been committed to students' development has been known collectively as personnel work, student personnel work, college student personnel, student development and student affairs. The role and professional practice of student affairs within higher education have been influenced significantly by shifts in philosophy, perceptions of students, strategies, theories, institutional missions, and the nature of American higher education itself. The evolution of student affairs and its practice are the subjects of this book.

Student Affairs Practice in Higher Education is written to serve two audiences: students enrolled in graduate preparation programs who seek to understand the broad nature of student affairs and the specialized arenas in which its practice occurs, and the group of experienced professionals who desire a reference book that describes the trends and patterns that have shaped practice methods and program models. For both groups, a description of contemporary and future issues of importance to student affairs are also provided.

The decision to revise *Student Affairs Functions in Higher Education* (1988) was not one that was undertaken lightly. Initially, it was thought that it would be a difficult task to request previous contributing authors to revisit their original manuscript and prepare a draft of another that was in some ways similar and yet in others, quite different. The inclusion of material that demonstrated the translation of student development

ix

theory to practice in various areas of student affairs would make the book more appealing to its audiences. In addition, I knew that a revised edition must also include a brief history of student affairs, a broader discussion of shifting philosophical perspectives and an attempt to convey the meaning and significance of multicultural affairs and multiculturalism. The overall plan was not difficult to develop, but to complete the total project within a specified number of pages made the task all the more challenging. The contributors, whose names are provided on the preceding pages, graciously agreed to participate. Their collective efforts have, I believe, produced a more substantial and cohesive manuscript that allows the reader to more clearly grasp the nature and importance of significant issues and changes within the evolution of student affairs and its practice.

Writing and editing are skills that I have come to enjoy more and more . . . perhaps because one can develop a sense of confidence and ease when doing so much of both in a concentrated amount of time. Perhaps also because they are one in the same task. When I began my career in student affairs in the mid-1960s, the goal of publishing articles and books was not part of my agenda. As I began the teaching phase of my career at Bowling Green in the mid-1970s, an appreciation of the books available by which the field and its values could be transferred to younger generations began to develop. That appreciation and perhaps the realization that I might contribute to that written knowledge base motivated me to undertake the task of co-editor of the first edition of *Student Affairs Functions in Higher Education* (1988) with the late Gerald L. Saddlemire. That edition has been well received and all of us who contributed to this current volume trust that this edition will be as successful, if not more so.

To graduate students and student affairs professionals, best wishes as your careers unfold.

Audrey L. Rentz
December 15, 1995

CONTENTS

STUDENT AFFAIRS PRACTICE
IN HIGHER EDUCATION

Chapter 1

THE PHILOSOPHICAL HERITAGE OF STUDENT AFFAIRS

STAN CARPENTER

INTRODUCTION

Og, the cave man, had a problem, To be sure, he and his tribe had lots of problems, but this was the most vexing yet. Although he did not know it or even construct the problem that way, the issue really was that his brain was too big and too differentiated. Having a good brain was an advantage and necessary for survival. Og and his people were not very big or very fast compared to other animals. They were not particularly strong or keen of sight, smell, or hearing. But they could think and plan and remember. The problem was that this ability to conceptualize caused them to wonder—to need to know, to speculate, and to be unhappy when they did not have answers. Perhaps it was something poignant, like the death of a child, or just the mundane cycle of the seasons that first elicited a search for a larger meaning to life, but whatever it was, the quest could have soon led to depression, insanity, and death for the members of the tribe and therefore the tribe itself. Thus was philosophy invented or, as some would say discovered, in an attempt to supplant powerlessness with knowledge. It did not matter that the knowledge was "incorrect" (in modern terms)—simply that it explained otherwise terrifyingly uncertain and uncontrollable things like fire and rain, death and birth. It was necessary to have something to believe and to strive to learn more.

Over time a tribal culture developed, encompassing all the beliefs, knowledge, and skills that made the group unique and contributed to survival. The culture was inculcated into the children by formal means and informal in a process of education not materially different than what is in place today. As the tribe became a village, then a city, then a sovereign state, philosophical knowledge grew and differentiated. Eventually, it became necessary to attend to the higher learning of some

3

members to prepare them to lead, to teach, and to press the search for new knowledge. Student affairs professionals are the direct descendants of early educators and, as such, are heir to a long tradition of thinking and writing about educational philosophy. The purpose of this chapter is to examine the impact of philosophy generally and several specific philosophical positions upon higher education and the practice of student affairs work.

WHAT IS PHILOSOPHY?

At first all learning was philosophical. The word "philosophy," from the Greek *philosophia*, literally means love of wisdom or learning. Only in the past 200 years has there occurred a separation of "natural philosophy" (or sciences such as chemistry and physics), "mental philosophy" (or psychology) and "moral philosophy" (political science, economics, and sociology, for example) from the general concept (Brubacher, 1962). For thousands of years, the study of philosophy was the same as advanced learning, a wide-ranging intellectual quest. The knowledge explosion and specialization have changed that, but philosophy is still a broad and deep field.

Philosophy is a poorly understood term. People begin sentences with "My philosophy on that is . . . " and proceed to give unsupported opinions, sometimes inconsistent with their behaviors or facts. Philosophy can be thought of as simply a general approach to the world or it can be a process of disciplined inquiry. Gracia (1992) captured it this way:

> Philosophy may be interpreted . . . :
>   I   . . . as a set of ideas or beliefs, concerning anything, that an ordinary person may hold.
>   II   . . . as view of the world, or any of its parts, that seeks to be accurate, consistent, and comprehensive.
>   III . . . as a discipline of learning.
>   A. Activity whereby a view of the world or any of its parts, that seeks to be accurate, consistent, and comprehensive, is produced.
>   B. Formulation, explanation, and justification of rules to which the production of a view of the world, or any of its parts, that seeks to be accurate, consistent, and comprehensive, is produced (philosophical methodology). (p. 56)

This chapter concerns itself primarily with the second meaning, but also with elements of the third. The reader should be concerned with applying the information presented (meaning II), using the proper methods (meaning III), to modify his/her views (meaning I) in such a way that they are accurate, consistent, and comprehensive.

THE THREE GREAT QUESTIONS OF PHILOSOPHY

Originally, philosophy was concerned with virtually all knowledge, but it has come to consist of three main, very large and important, questions: What is real? How do we know? What is of value?

Ontology

Ontology is also called by some metaphysics (literally "beyond physics"). It is concerned with the ultimate question of existence. Og and his descendants desired to know what was real and what was ephemeral. Is the universe friendly, neutral, or malevolent? Is there order in the universe, or only probabilistic chaos? Is physical existence real or is only our intellect, the goings on in our minds, real? What is life? Is there a God or some other supernatural entity? Is this all there is? Clearly, such questions are overwhelming and demand a systematic and satisfying answer. Just as clearly, they call for speculation, at least, in the early stages of theory building and maybe for a long time after that. Every action taken by an individual, every decision, every thought will be colored by beliefs about the nature of reality.

Ontology can be usefully broken up into other areas of questions (Johnson, Collins, Dupuis, & Johansen, 1969). Anthropology concerns the nature of the human condition. Are people innately good or evil? What is the relation between the mind and the body? Is there a soul or spirit and does it have precedence over the worldly flesh of the body? Do humans have free will? Cosmology involves the study of the nature and origins of the universe including questions about time, space, perceptions, and purpose. Theology considers questions of religion. Is there a God? More than one God? A "good" God or an indifferent one? Is God all-powerful? All-knowing? Some ontological theories depend heavily upon theological theories. Teleology, or the study of purpose in the cosmos, cuts across all of the other areas mentioned. Is the universe a chance event or is there some larger purpose? Much of what troubled Og, and continues to trouble humankind, is the province of ontology.

Epistemology

Questions of ontology, while difficult, are at least straightforward. But how can data be gathered to answer them? Epistemology examines the nature of knowledge itself, sources of knowledge, and the validity of different kinds of knowledge. Generally, knowledge can be gained from sensory perception (empirical knowledge); revelation (knowledge from a supernatural source or being); from an authority or by tradition; reason, logic, or intellect; or by intuition (nonsupernatural insight, not resulting from reason). It is easy to see that all of these sources are subject to criticism. What is truth? Is truth subjective or objective, relative or absolute? Is there truth external to human experience? Can finite beings understand infinite truth?

Different philosophies have very different epistemologies. One fundamental issue is whether truth is unchanging or varies with the situation or the individual. Clearly hinging upon the answer to this question is whether truth can be "discovered" or "constructed". Some philosophers hold that some truths are self-evident and do not need to be proven. These might be called *Truths*. Others reject this notion out of hand, suggesting that there is no truth except that leading from experience and that context is paramount.

Axiology

Speculations and theories about the origin and nature of reality and the ways that knowledge may best be gathered lead quickly to choices. Choices require evaluating options and the third great question of philosophy concerns values. What is good? What is beautiful? Individuals, communities, countries, and societies may develop systems of value based upon their philosophies and tension will develop where these come into conflict. The impact of philosophy on personal and professional behavior is most clear in the process of valuing. What someone believes and thinks is likely, although not certainly, a determinant of action.

Axiology is divided into ethics and aesthetics. Ethics is the study of proper behavioral choices. What is moral? Are ethics contextual or absolute? Is there a connection between what is believed to be right and proper action? Is the good of the societal unit superior to the good of the individual? Who has the right to set ethical standards? Are the laws of society subordinate to the laws of a supernatural entity, such as God? What is the proper relationship between teacher and student? These (and many others) are all questions of ethics. Professions develop more or less enforceable, formal and informal codes of ethics, based upon shared philosophies. It is incumbent upon the practitioner to learn to apply these ethics in such a way that clients are best served and to participate in ongoing dialogue to update the ethics of the profession. Aesthetics involves questions about beauty and art. What is beautiful? Is there some ideal that is impossible to attain? Is beauty affected by individual experience, are there absolute standards, or should experts be called upon to judge what is excellent and what is not? Who is to choose? The phrase "beauty is in the eye of the beholder" suggests that the finger painting of a 4-year-old is beautiful to some, but the world art market suggests otherwise. Aesthetics allows discussion of such choices and values.

Educational Philosophy

Philosophy as a general discipline is often applied to smaller areas. There exists, for example, lively literature on the philosophy of science and the philosophy of law. Similarly, educators need to study educational philosophy to undergird their practice. Because of the unique place of education in the culture, the distinction between the general and the specific is not easy in the case of education. Education is the very transmission of the culture and all accumulated knowledge, in such a way that the student is equipped to continue learning and eventually contribute to the whole. In this sense, education is philosophy in action, a point most clearly made by Dewey (1916) when he defined philosophy as the general theory of education.

The educational implications of assuming that humans must somehow overcome their sensory impressions in order to use their intellect or reason to understand reality, for example, are far-reaching. An alternate view is that experience is the only worthwhile learning. Two different educators, holding such disparate philosophies, would be unlikely to agree on any coherent curriculum. This is just one example of differing viewpoints, taken from epistemology. There are many more epistemological examples available, to say nothing of ontological considerations and questions of value. Obviously, everything done in the name of education has a basis in some philosophical notion and/or "teaches" some philosophical tenet to the student. In a pluralistic society such as the U.S., philosophical differences between and among teacher and student, college and teacher, school and parent, college and society at large, and any permutation of these can and do cause great conflict. This is not necessarily bad, especially at the college and university level where a certain amount of conflict and challenge of views contributes to learning; nevertheless, to the extent that education is an intentional activity, educators and institutions should examine and be aware of their philosophical bases. Practices inconsistent with espoused views and beliefs are confusing at best and may be damaging.

Hence, the study of educational philosophy. Professionals have an obligation to learn and know more than techniques and approaches to problem solving. Only by studying and applying underlying premises and deeply held assumptions can a practitioner of student affairs hope to bring insight to a novel problem, a "different" student, a new situation. If a person holds one view and an institution another, conflict is likely; if neither knows what the other believes, then conflict is certain and may not be easily resolved. Student affairs professionals cannot always tell what an institution truly believes, but they can and should always determine their own educational philosophies.

MAJOR PHILOSOPHICAL SCHOOLS

It will be argued later in this chapter that student affairs and higher education practices are based upon a variety of different philosophies. Therefore, it is necessary to acquaint the reader with a basic understanding of several of the most influential Western schools of thought, since they have had the most impact upon U.S. education. A treatment of Eastern and other thinking is beyond the scope of this book.

Idealism

Plato, in his writing on the thinking of Socrates and through his own work, is generally conceded to have offered the basis of Idealism, the notion that the "real" world is accessible only through reason. The thinking here is that the world as perceived by humans is transient, changeable, always becoming but never quite finished, and hence deceptive. The real world is perfect, not needing and not having physical manifestation. Thus the idea of a chair is more important, a higher order of reality, than the chair which is seen or sat upon. Ontologically, reality depends upon a superordinate Mind which is capable of conceiving Reality in its Ideal state. Humans possess a spark of this Mind and can communicate with the Real world through (and only through) reason and intellect. Material existence, the things of the flesh, inhibit this communication and reason and are not to be trusted. Truth is unchanging and permanent, infinite and ultimately unknowable. Since humans are finite, they can know about the Truth, but can never know all. The ethical goal is to live a moral life, defined as following the will of the Mind or of the universe. Some people (such as teachers, priests, and political leaders) are closer to the Ideal than others and they should be heeded. Beauty is defined as an approximation of the Ideal, usually the Divine.

Idealism allows, almost requires, a supernatural entity and is therefore very compatible with religion. Later thinkers have worked out Idealistic philosophies without the use of a God, but they are largely unsatisfying. Educationally, Idealism posits that each individual should be helped to actualize the spark of the Ideal that is within. However, the test of the actualization is correspondence with the Ideal, much of which has already been "discovered" over the years. Hence, students are taught using materials that have stood the test of time and societal examination. The Great Books are used and the primacy of the state is emphasized. The assumption is that a consensus Ideal is a better approximation than an individual conception. Idealism is one of the cornerstones of a conservative approach to curriculum and education emphasizing essential truths.

Realism

Aristotle was not satisfied with the Platonic view that sensory data were distorted and not to be trusted. He believed instead that observed reality is the only Reality. That is, the universe exists without a mind standing behind it and whether humans perceive it or not. Natural laws are permanent and unchanging and humans can discover them through the use of their minds. If there are things that are not yet understood, then there simply has not been enough research. Truth, then, is external and independent of knowledge. Epistemologically, Realism uses inductive logic. The observer gathers particular bits of knowledge and fits them into theories, propositions, and laws according to the rules of science. Truth is completely knowable and may be judged by its correspondence with reality. Values and beauty have to do with conformance with the Laws of Nature. That is good which allows people to live in accordance with nature, the so-called moral law, and that is beautiful which reflects natural harmony. Human nature is everywhere the same and a distinction is made throughout between the natural and the accidental (Brubacher, 1962). The essential nature of anything does not change, even though some variations may be noted.

Educationally, Realism calls for the student to be acquainted with rational methods of observation and logic. Hence, science and mathematics have a large place in the curriculum. However, the traditional humanities are important as well, because there are natural ways for society to function and the student needs to be made aware of the best thinking to date. Students are not left to learn what they think they want to know, since this would take away time from what they should be learning, what is already known. After all, it is inefficient for students to arrive at their own conclusions about that which is already known, let alone the fact that no one can be expected to contribute to new knowledge without a grounding in research to date. Realism is also, clearly, a foundation for conservative educational thinking, with its reliance upon knowledge external to the student.

Neo-Thomism

St. Thomas Aquinas saw much to like in both Idealism and Realism. On the one hand, Aristotle's ideas were very common sensical and seemed to reflect human experience. On the other hand, it was necessary to bring into account the known (to Roman Catholics like Aquinas) existence of a supernatural being (God). The solution was to combine the two, retaining the duality between mind and body proposed by Plato, but assigning faith a preeminent role over reason. That is, humans were free to observe the material world in scientific, logical ways with the proviso that when reason contradicted the revealed truth of religion, then reason was simply faulty. Much of Realism is inherent in Neo-Thomism, so much that some call this philosophy religious realism (Kneller, 1964). The basic notion is that there is no inherent conflict between faith and reason, so long as it is understood that God is perfect and therefore faith is preeminent. Aquinas lived in the 13th century, the philosophy was originally called Thomism, but his ideas have endured so strongly that the Roman Catholic Church acknowledges this philosophy as its official position (Johnson et al., 1969) and it remains as the basis of much of Catholic education. There are also lay philosophers who subscribe to Neo-Thomism, with their axiology being based upon a rationally derived and unchanging moral law that is not supernaturally based.

Education for Neo-Thomists consists of teaching the perennial truths derived from faith and reason. Because humans have free will, the student must be taught the discipline of learning and encouraged to make good choices. Knowledge and values are permanent and unchanging and the purpose of learning is to live by rational and moral standards. The student is educated in a moral atmosphere that forms the framework for knowledge. Again, it should be clear that established methods and materials form the basis of the curriculum.

Pragmatism

Pragmatism represents a major break with the other philosophies thus far considered in that it rejects the idea of permanent, unchanging truth. Although it has roots in the empiricist tradition, which developed from Realism, Pragmatism, as explicated by Charles Sanders Peirce, John Dewey, and William James, suggests that even so-called natural "laws" are not eternal. Indeed, reality is defined by the interaction of humans with nature. Reality is the sum total of human experience and that is true which is proven useful after a careful investigation and analysis. While nature has an objective, albeit changeable, existence, it has no real meaning except as it relates to human experience. Speculation about the infinite or supernatural is idle, by definition, since it cannot be verified by human means. Pragmatic epistemology does not allow humans to simply make up truth; rather, truth is determined using the experimental method. As a problem is confronted, data are gathered, hypotheses generated, mental testing conducted, and finally solutions implemented. The best or most workable solution is the truth—for these circumstances, using these data collection methods. Given that things change, techniques improve, and different approaches give different answers, this truth is temporary and not absolute. For example, based upon everything scientifically known, the sun will very likely rise in the morning. But it is possible for conditions to change and, therefore, dawn is never a certainty. Values are relative and situational, chosen through a logical process. That does not mean that morality changes willy-nilly, but that there are no absolute precepts, always true and never violated. Morals are not handed down from some higher authority, but rather decided by individuals and groups, by agreement and consensus if possible, in a dynamic process. Pragmatism is thought to require democracy for best use.

The student is thought of as an integrated whole, thoroughly involved in his or her own education. Since experience is the only determiner of reality, the student should be allowed to learn whatever is of interest. Abstract concepts are important, but should be studied later in the education, rather than earlier, so that the student develops a lively style of experiencing and then organizing the experiences from the beginning. This project method should allow for the education of the biological, the psychological, and the social aspects of the student. The teacher or other educator should not be ascendant, but rather facilitative. The curriculum and materials used should be flexible and learner-centered. Readiness and enthusiasm are keys to learning and teaching.

Existentialism

Jean Paul Sartre wrote that "existence precedes essence" (1947, p. 18). This simple phrase is fraught with meaning, implying as it does that the simple fact of being carries with it the awful truth that humans are only and totally what they make of themselves by their own choices. The universe exists and the order that science finds is present, but these facts matter only as backdrop for the confrontation that is inevitable in the life of every person. People find themselves, when they become truly aware of their condition, in an indifferent universe which has no purpose and in which they are doomed to die. Truth is that which each individual concludes in a passionate encounter with the self and the choices available. There is complete freedom because of the indifference of nature, the absence of rules; there is complete responsibility because no one else chooses, or if they do, the individual chooses his/her response. The human condition, searching for meaning in a meaningless world, possessing freedom and aware of finitude, causes *Angst,* or existential dread. Knowledge is gained in an active way, involving both thinking and feeling. Existentialism does not allow detached analysis. Information is less important than what the person does with the data. Values are meaningless unless chosen. However, freedom does not imply anarchy; a commitment to freedom for self leads inevitably to a conception of freedom for all. Responsibility for choices that restrict the freedom of others is its own kind of limit. Too, true freedom is the freedom to commit to others in an authentic relationship. Still, the fundamental value of existentialism is to be true to oneself.

The existentialist educator walks a tightrope between encouraging freedom and bridling immature choices. Students must be confronted with the reality of the human condition and must take responsibility for their choices. The educator must also interact with the students in an authentic way, modeling mature behavior and attending to his/her own growth. The educator stimulates student involvement with learning on a personal level, a commitment to understanding, not to following the crowd or bowing to expert opinion. Every person in any situation is treated with dignity and respect, even if some behaviors are not tolerated. Humanities, literature, art, and history (Kneller, 1964) are heavily utilized since they reflect the struggles of people to understand their own existence. Students also undertake a careful study of traditional knowledge in order to grasp the world in which they live. The student makes the subject matter his/her own by seeking out interpretations (for example, in historical accounts) and considering counter conclusions. Education is an active process and never ends.

A BRIEF PHILOSOPHICAL HISTORY OF HIGHER EDUCATION

The history of higher education is, in some sense, a history of thought and therefore a history of philosophy. This section of the chapter treats philosophical influences upon Western higher education from the Greeks through the present.

As ancient Greece was settled and city-states established, the life of the mind began to take on more importance. The democratic assemblies put a premium on erudition and persuasion. The Sophists, itinerant teachers, were among the first to meet this need. They focused on utilitarian education—they were not concerned about the ends to which logic and rhetorical skills were turned (Domonkos, 1977). This moral relativism caused a counter movement to use the discipline of learning to attain ethical wisdom and absolute truth. Chief among the philosophers engaged in this quest were Socrates and his student Plato. Most importantly, they each established schools for the edification of both teachers and students.

To all intents and purposes, these institutions are the precursors of modern colleges and universities. Plato was an Idealist and believed that only the elite, defined as the intellectually able and educated, should be allowed to rule. Not surprisingly, his notion of education was focused on reason and ideas, a striving for knowledge that was absolute and unchanging. Plato's student Aristotle, on the other hand, did not distrust sensory data, but rather sought to organize it according to logical and scientific principles. Aristotle did believe that truth is unchanging, as seen above in the discussion of Realism, and he advocated a search for the Laws of Nature. These ideas, along with other, minor philosophical schools and some attention to law and medicine, dominated higher education through the fall of Rome.

During the so-called Dark Ages, higher education was essentially the domain of clerics in the Christian West, but there were thriving academic communities among the Jews, Moslems, and the Byzantines. In fact, it is through contact with these other cultures that interest in the ancient Greek philosophies re-emerged to challenge the rather sterile, faith-based notions of the Church hierarchy. The history of all of the early institutions of higher education in the West is too extensive to go into here, but the best of the early universities was the University of Paris, which housed lively philosophical debate around theology and the conflict between religious Idealism and Aristotelian Realism until the University found it necessary to succumb to Church doctrine in order to gain Papal sanction in a struggle against the Parisian authorities. But this debate was not confined to Paris and raged on. St. Thomas Aquinas successfully joined Realism and religion (see above) and his ideas of reason and science as permissible but subservient to faith became the philosophy of the Church and more specifically the universities and schools. Consequently, most of the great discoveries of science for hundreds of years took place independently of the universities, in the academies or as a result of private patrons.

Even the onset of the Reformation, the ecclesiastical revolt against the Roman Catholic Church, did not materially change the philosophy of higher education. Universities were intellectual captives of whomever their sponsors were, whether state governments or state religions, usually both. But the Reformation had allowed the camel's nose under the tent of Catholic theological hegemony. Sect after sect sprang up, eventually leading to the notion that no one group owned the truth. This fertile climate spawned thinkers who came to deny the place of the supernatural in their conceptions of the universe and humankind. Writers and philosophers in this Enlightenment, such as Locke and Voltaire, and the people they influenced, notably Benjamin Franklin and Thomas Jefferson, spoke of inalienable rights and contracts between the rulers and the governed. Effectively, they were seeking the natural laws of society, just as scientists were discovering the natural laws of physics, astronomy, chemistry, and biology. Knowledge and education were becoming too important to be dominated by religious authorities. The power of ideas was beginning to manifest itself.

Still, the colleges and universities were reflective of the society and by and large society was pietistic. If education was too important to be dictated by the church, it was certainly too important to be left to professors, and so there evolved an uneasy equilibrium between lay control and teacher autonomy. In England, higher education was primarily for the elite, intellectually and/or financially, who were being groomed for ecclesiastical and political leadership. They were provided a classical liberal arts education with little science and much orthodox theology. Their spiritual and social progress were monitored as heavily as their intellectual progress. They were taught to strive for the Ideal.

This model of education was lifted whole cloth and set down in the American Colonies. All of the original nine colonial colleges were sectarian, except Penn, and all followed the British model. Standards for behavior, for learning, and for spiritual development were absolute and individuality was not brooked. But new ideas were brewing. In the later part of the colonial period and much more so in the early federal period of the United States, there was a proliferation of colleges, mostly sectarian, but some state sponsored. At first, these were much the same as those that had gone before, but market forces, increased specialization of disciplines, and the onrush of scientific discovery began to engender diversity and differentiation (Potts, 1977). To counter this drift toward the secular, and worse, the nonclassical, the faculty of Yale published the Yale Report in 1828. This was the first formal statement of the philosophy of higher education in the U.S. (Brubacher & Rudy, 1976) and held that the traditional, classical curriculum was the only way to provide higher learning to students because of its emphasis upon mental discipline (based upon faculty psychology) and its steadfast refusal to accord status to the transitory, the ephemeral, the worldly—in other words, economically or scientifically useful knowledge which could be learned elsewhere.

The Yale Report was influential for decades, but its very publication signaled the beginning of the end for strictly Idealist higher education.

Realism, in the form of science, empiricism, and practicality was pushing its way into the curriculum. The latter half of the 19th century saw the advent of the German model university (see next chapter), the bastion of research and academic freedom to teach and to learn. The Morrill Act of 1862 led to the creation of a distinctly U.S. style institution, the land grant university, with its curious combination mission of research, teaching, and service. As secular and current course content displaced religious and ancient knowledge, pressure to focus upon the intellect only increased. The out of class habits of students, the extracurricular activities, the sports they engaged in, these were distractions from the "real" business of education. However, the U.S. was still a moralistic nation and was not about to surrender its young men (and certainly not its young women!) to colleges and universities unconcerned about anything but their minds. Hence, institutions took on obligations that had not existed in other parts of the world, the role of parents without true control, a concern for the out of class behavior of students in ways that were unconnected to the curriculum (as opposed to the earlier British model).

Twentieth Century Philosophical Influences on U.S. Higher Education

As the 20th century began, the hegemony of Realism, embodied as Newtonian science, was cracking as had Idealism before it. To be sure, the receiving of intellectual knowledge was still the primary role of students, but Pragmatism and later Existentialism were making inroads in almost all disciplines and hence working their way into the thinking of those guiding colleges and universities. Until the early 1960s, the dominant philosophical mode for colleges and universities was still a focus upon intellectualism tied to an almost formless attitude of *in loco parentis*.

In many ways, the conflict boiled down to one of epistemology. Is the student to be educated about the truth or does the educated student participate in shaping the truth? Is the content of a liberal education more or less constant or does it change in relation to context?

On the one hand are the essentialists, variously identified as rationalists, rational humanists, neo-humanists, or perennialists, among other labels.

Philosophers and educators in these categories of opinion did not all hold the same beliefs, differing in views about the nature of knowledge, the existence of God, and the importance of reason versus revelation, but they united in their opposition to the corrupting influences of the vocational, the worldly, upon higher education. Veblen's (1918) assertion of the value-free nature of research was one example, but the best known advocates of this position in the early twentieth century were Robert Maynard Hutchins (1936) and Mortimer Adler (1951). Both men extolled the virtues of intellectual excellence to be gained by the assiduous study of the great books, the so-called Western Canon. This kind of study and education were thought to prepare the mind in the best way for any field of endeavor. Indeed, these ideas were timeless and essential. Further, education without moral content was considered useless. Hutchins and Adler were ostensibly secular in their suggestions, but their ideas resonate clearly with the views of the religious perennialists. Truth is something that does not change; it needs to be discovered and once discovered must be learned by each succeeding generation. Ideas that have stood the test of time are to be returned to again and again. Fundamental to this viewpoint is the conception of the mind as separate from the body, knowledge uncontaminated by experience.

On the other hand were the pragmatic naturalists, the experimentalists, the instrumentalists, the progressivists, and the reconstructionists. Such thinkers as John Dewey (1937), Sidney Hook (1946), and Alfred North Whitehead (1929) thought that the split of intellect from the world, of theory from practice, was wrong. Liberal education is and should be based in the context of the time and the place and reason should be informed by passion and emotion. Humans are whole and must be educated as such. Experience and rationality should be used as means rather than ends to help solve the problems of society. Indeed, the reconstructionists dared to dream of utopian goals and sought to involve education in their plans. Truth, in this conception, is something that works, that is meaningful to each individual in different ways.

It is not a long leap from this pragmatic viewpoint to that of existentialism, post-modernism, critical theory, and constructivism (Lincoln, 1989). If knowledge is not external and unchanging, if it is defined as what is workable based upon experience, and if the society is working toward democracy, then who is to define truth? If one conception of truth is just as good as any other, then truth ceases to be universal and becomes intensely individual. Reality is constructed rather than discovered. Not only are the mind and the body not separated, but they are one with context. Pluralism, as opposed to assimilation to the dominant culture, is cultivated and acted upon. As should be immediately clear, these ideas have drastic implications for higher education and student affairs.

Considerations of philosophy were largely settled on the side of the pragmatic by the influx of students after World War II. Returning soldiers had little patience for the parental function of colleges and the nation needed technically trained graduates. The early stirrings of the civil rights movement and the unrest of the '60s refocused the philosophical lens on higher education. For most schools, the parental role perished in the fiery heat of the social revolution of the '60s and the aftershocks in the '70s. Of course, Catholic and many other sectarian institutions continued to adhere to a neo-Thomist view, but in most colleges, students experience a mish-mash of philosophical influences. Colleges are by turns moralistic in some regulations, scientific in some attitudes and services, existential in their assigning of responsibility for learning, and withal pragmatic. The typical institution harbors individuals in important positions, exercising great authority, who firmly believe in each of the major philosophies. And the school which acts consistently on only one of the philosophies is rare and probably sectarian.

EDUCATIONAL PHILOSOPHY AND STUDENT AFFAIRS

For the first two hundred years or so, higher education in the U.S. largely followed an Idealist model. Education was thought of as mental discipline and things of the flesh were to be conquered so they did not get in the way. Young people (students) especially needed help to control their impulses, what with all that energy and all those hormones. Faculty psychology dictated, and spiritual needs reinforced, that students should invest all their resources into training their intellects and moderating their base desires. To this end, educators controlled living and eating arrangements and arranged curricula in such a way as to leave little free time and less discretionary behavior. Since humans were felt to be flawed and incapable of innate understanding of absolute, eternal truths without restraint and focus on reason, colleges took on a parental role.

The explosion of science and specialization, coupled with a growing democratic mindset and the influx of German ideas of higher education, eroded this position by the latter part of the 19th century. In the Realist mode, depending as it did upon the mind-body split articulated by Des Cartes and others, things of the flesh simply did not really matter. Professors and researchers at the new universities were quite simply not interested in anything but knowledge and did not care to participate in students' out of class lives. Again, truth was conceived as external to humans, something to be discovered and understood rationally. Human nature was not thought to be inherently negative or positive, simply not relevant to learning and thinking.

Still, higher education as an institution is known for its inertia and the graduate and research universities required a feeder system of undergraduate colleges. Accordingly, the U.S. developed a model unique in the world. Excellent universities, conducting state of the art research, were joined with undergraduate colleges which continued to follow the British model. U.S. society was not prepared to abandon adolescents to their impulses, even if faculty members felt they had better things to do. The necessity of traveling long distances to attend colleges, the relative youth of American students, the essentially Christian character of the nation, and hundreds of years of tradition in higher education contributed to the need to regulate student conduct on campus. Thus, in rough strokes, was born the student affairs worker.

Philosophically, in loco parentis provided not only a framework for Idealistic rules in order to bring the student into compliance with age old social mores, but also provided an outlet for emotional and psychological needs unmet, and properly so, in the classroom. The roots of the services and control models of student affairs, then, are in the essentialist philosophical tradition. Knowledge is something absolute to which students must accommodate themselves. Since they needed help to do this, and since faculty were increasingly unwilling to provide this help, it was necessary to hire a new kind of educator.

By the beginning of the 20th century, early student affairs workers were filling much of the parental role of the colleges, thereby relieving faculty of the tasks. Colleges and universities were growing and becoming more complex organizationally, requiring administrators and managers, as well. Additionally, psychology was finding its niche as the "science" of human behavior, particularly with the testing movement. The idea was that people were suited to certain careers and that systematic counseling would help with a match. Cowley (1957) held that the field was dominated by these three types of student affairs workers well into the

1950s—humanitarians, administrators, and counselors, each with a role, but rather uncoordinated.

The Student Personnel Point of View (1937)

This confusion about the field and its goals for students is reflected in the first and second statements of the Student Personnel Point of View (American Council on Education, 1937 & 1949). In the 1937 statement, there is a clear emphasis upon coordination with the academic enterprise with the goal of ensuring the maximum improvement of the student, the meeting of potential. Emphasis is also placed upon scientific research to learn how to better serve institutions and students. In fact, the SPPV would be unremarkable philosophically, except for its insistence on the impact of education upon the "whole student." While this is grounded in a rational humanist context, overtones of existentialism and pragmatism are clearly present and the student is presumed to have a role in his/her own education, a radical notion at the time.

The Student Personnel Point of View (1949)

The revised SPPV (A.C.E., 1949) is philosophically much more straightforward in its pragmatic approach. Democracy and social reconstruction are presented as the bases for education. There are nods toward standards of conduct and self-control and the clinical findings of the social sciences are not left out, but problem solving is clearly preferred as a goal. Again, it is noted that the student is responsible for his/her own education but enrichment and facilitation are coming to the fore instead of simply services.

Student Development

The radicalism of the '60s disturbed the uneasy equilibrium that student affairs had reached with the academic establishment. Obviously, societal standards were in flux and could hardly be transmitted wholesale. Students were demanding an increasing amount of attention—the role of education had to shift. The student affairs response was to counsel a focus upon the person rather than the course content. Colleges were to teach students rather than subjects. In fact, the argument went, if the focus is really to be on the whole student, then human development principles must be applied across the curriculum and the extracurriculum (Brown, 1972; Miller & Prince, 1976). Furthermore, the student is in control of what is to be learned and what is to be valued. The university was to be construed as a place where learning was facilitated, where the student learned to make choices and understand that every choice has consequences which must be considered and accepted. *In loco parentis*, dead in a legal sense since the 1960s, died in a practical sense in the 1970s, despite recent attempts to revive it.

The student development model, with its underpinnings in the self-confrontational struggle of existentialism and the utilitarian foundation of pragmatism, changed student affairs practice completely. The merging of the goals of the academic and the "other" education recognizes that, to the student, college is a seamless web of growth and development. All aspects of education are interdependent—one cannot be accomplished without the others being in place. Focus upon the student means that wellness, support for nontraditional students, alcohol awareness, learning assistance, and many other areas are not only just as essential as housing, financial aid, counseling, and student activities, but are crucial if optimum learning is to occur. Educators stop being purveyors and become facilitators and consultants. Colleges do not pronounce appropriate choices for students, but rather propose them for the students to choose from, and sometimes not even that.

A student development focus does not mean that values are abandoned by institutions or student affairs professionals, but that expectations are clearly stated up front in such a way that students can make good choices for themselves. Likewise, science is not forsaken; rather, student development theory is based upon research into developmental psychology, causing some controversy among practitioners who have to reconcile somewhat lockstep conceptualizations with undeniable student uniqueness. Finally, student development capitalizes upon diversity, celebrating and enhancing differences as necessary and educational.

It may seem that existentialism and pragmatism give too much authority to the individual to be used as bases for transmitting a culture. However, pragmatism has a strong emphasis upon the social, with an acknowledgment that the individual lives in a group and that growth for all is a goal. Existentialism emphasizes self confrontation and acceptance of responsibility for choices. This responsibility is understood to include the impact of personal choices upon other, free beings. Rights for one are rights for all and must be respected.

The 1987 NASPA Statement

In 1987, NASPA published "A Perspective on Student Affairs: A Statement Issued on the 50th Anniversary of the Student Personnel Point of View." This paper acknowledged articulately the growing diversity of U.S. higher education, but also strongly emphasized the place of institutional mission in education. Under the label of shared assumptions, the Perspective statement argues for the preeminence of the academic mission for higher education and that student affairs should not compete with, nor substitute for the academic mission. Instead student affairs enhances and supports the principal goals of colleges and universities. Other parts of the statement go on to reiterate the notion of the whole, unique student, the importance of involvement in learning, and the crucial nature of environmental and personal factors in education. Philosophically, the Perspective statement is a mixed bag, with a seeming nod toward Essentialism (the emphasis upon cognitive learning), an expression of Existentialist tenets (worth and uniqueness of the student), and recognition of Pragmatism (importance of involvement, environment, and diversity). This is partially because the statement was not intended to be a philosophical tract, but rather a political statement, and therefore tried to be all things to all people. Still, to the extent that the statement represented the mainstream of student affairs leadership, there was a clear turn toward institutions and academic content as foci, at the expense of emphasis on students and their choices.

The "Reasonable Expectations" Statement

A document entitled "Reasonable Expectations: Renewing the Educational Compact Between Institutions and Students" was published by NASPA in 1995 (Kuh, Lyons, Miller, & Trow, 1995). While not strictly philosophical in tone, it takes the form of an examination of the Pragmatic contract between institutions and their students. The focus is on mutual respect and high expectations going in both directions, with integrity and communication strongly emphasized. There is an Existential recognition of choice and responsibility and a bias toward action and involvement. While the statement is careful to be vague with regard to underlying ontological and epistemological beliefs, presumably so that many and varied institutions are covered, Idealist and Realist educators would be hard pressed to follow all the tenets espoused. Similarly, although the statement is aimed at the broader institution, it is clear that professional student affairs workers are best able to provide the interface called for between the college and students.

The "Student Learning Imperative" (SLI)

The SLI was published by ACPA in 1994. Ostensibly, it is a call to change student affairs practice so that there is more focus on "student learning and personal development" (p. 1). However, the document makes no clear differentiation between these two aims and student development, at one point calling all three terms " . . . inextricable intertwined and inseparable" (p. 1). Philosophically, the statement leans toward the Essentialist, with its insistence upon " . . . educationally-purposeful activities" (p. 2). Presumably, some activities are more important for learning than others and student affairs professionals, along with other institutional agents, know which are which and should guide students accordingly. One way to learn about appropriate activities for students is scientific research. To be sure, process is emphasized, the seamless nature of education as perceived by the student is recognized, and a holistic approach is advocated in the SLI. With all, however, the tone is that student affairs has failed in some way(s) and needs to get on the academic productivity bandwagon and help institutions and students become more efficient learners. Student affairs is relegated to a " . . . complementary mission" (p. 2), involving more emphasis on learning theory and assessment. This is an apparent abrogation of Existentialism as a fundamental base of student affairs practice and pulls back from Pragmatism, as well.

The Search for a Student Affairs Philosophy Goes On

The publication of the SLI is clearly only the latest attempt to codify the philosophical tenets of student affairs. Knock, Rentz, and Penn (1989) detailed significant influences on student affairs' philosophical heritage, arguing that professional practice had moved past Rationalism and Neo-humanism into Pragmatism and Existentialism as the basis of student development. Whitt, Carnaghi, Matkin, Scalese-Love, and Nestor (1990) asserted that emergent paradigm thinking (Lincoln & Guba, 1985) and the complexities of practices and diversity in higher education made a unified philosophy of student affairs impossible to divine—indeed, unwise and inappropriate. Context and cultural considerations should be paramount.

The position here is that sufficient evidence exists to determine that student choice is a *sine qua non* for quality in higher education. Students inarguably make choices as individuals. They decide which classes to attend, what to study, which activities to become involved in and by their choices determine the level of benefit that will be derived from college and its attendant milieu. Students decide which choices work for them, which consequences they are willing to undergo. In short, students are in charge of their own lives. While professional judgment is and should be exercised in matters of curriculum and in student affairs practice, students cannot be coerced to follow such advice. Students create their own meaning based upon their own phenomenological world. This philosophical stance is largely Existentialist, with a generous helping of Pragmatism. But, principally, it revisits the distinction made earlier in this chapter about the nature of truth. It is argued here that truth is largely constructed by individuals rather than located outside human experience, waiting to be discovered or divined or revealed. The goal of student affairs practice is to facilitate the process of collecting information, undergoing experiences, and making meaning by students. Along the way, student affairs professionals may advise, suggest, cajole, and counsel, but they may not live, know, or choose for the students. Nor can any institution.

BUILDING A PERSONAL PHILOSOPHY
OF STUDENT AFFAIRS

Thus far, this chapter has focused on the philosophical heritage of student affairs and higher education and the importance of philosophy in the formulation of policy and programming. It has been argued that the philosophical terrain of colleges and universities is hotly contested and uncertain. In such loosely coupled organizations, multiple missions exist, multiple actors behave with varying motivations, and multiple choices must be made. For the professional to successfully navigate in these seas, he or she must have reference points, guiding stars to chart a course. A knowledge of one's own personal philosophy helps provide such direction.

Questions to be considered in developing or examining a personal and professional philosophy include:

- What is the place of humans in the universe? Are people here to fulfill God's purpose, at the whim of an uncaring supernatural power, as the result of chance, as the ultimate in existence, or does it even matter why? Are people inherently of value or do they need to earn value? Do behaviors matter more than simple existence? Do humans have free choice or is their behavior predetermined by fate, science, or God?
- Does the universe exist in some objective sense external to the understanding of humans? Is reality for any person only what he or she perceives it to be? Is there some larger purpose to creation that is unknown or unknowable?
- Is Truth unchanging and eternal, either in an infinite, supernatural way or an immutable, scientific way? Are there discoverable Laws of nature? Is truth what works or makes sense to individuals or communities or societies? What is the best way to determine truth, the scientific method, experience, reason, or revelation and intuition?
- Are the laws of God more important than the laws of the society or the country? Is the greatest good for the greatest number a measure of behavior or policy? Are individual rights preeminent? Are people free to act in any way that pleases them? Does any person owe any obligation to any other person or state or the world? What is the nature of responsibility?
- Is beauty in the eye of the beholder? Are there objective standards for art or music or love? Do some people know what is best and most beautiful for other people?
- How can cultural standards be best defined? Should children be given instruction on the tried and true best ways to think and live or should they be given the tools of critical thought and left to create their own worlds? Is it better to educate for mastery or understanding or even something else? Do appropriate educational practices differ depending upon the subject matter and the age of the student?

The answers and the search for answers to these and hundreds of other similar questions influence actions, thoughts, and behaviors for everyone every day. Philosophers in all fields of endeavor have tried to create consistent, coherent systems to help with macro and micro decision making, but ultimately it comes down to the individual to choose and to act on the choices. But even the choices that are perceived to be available as options are circumscribed by individual circumstances, education, religion, and custom.

No philosophy or set of beliefs is prescribed here. However, it is strongly urged that every student affairs professional make a continuing and intentional effort to understand his or her own worldview. Expediency and reaction are tempting and too easy. Professionalism demands active thought and thoughtful action.

REFERENCES

Adler, M. J. (1951). Labor, leisure, and liberal education. *Journal of General Education, 6*, 175–184.

American College Personnel Association (ACPA). (1994). *The student learning imperative: Implications for student affairs.* Washington, DC: author.

American Council on Education, Committee on Student Personnel Work. (1937). *The student personnel point of view.* Washington, DC: American Council on Education.

American Council on Education, Committee on Student Personnel Work. (1949). *The student personnel point of view (Rev. Ed.).* Washington, DC: American Council on Education.

Brown, R. D. (1972). *Student development in tomorrow's higher education—a return to the academy.* Washington, DC: American College Personnel Association.

Brubacher, J. S., & Rudy, W. (1976). *Higher education in transition.* New York: Harper & Row.

Brubacher, J. S. (1982). *On the philosophy of higher education.* San Francisco: Jossey-Bass.

Cowley, W. H. (1957). Student personnel services in retrospect and prospect. *School and society,* Jan., 19–22.

Dewey, J. (1916). *Democracy and education.* New York: Macmillan.

Dewey, J. (1937). President Hutchins' proposals to remake higher education. *Social Frontier, 3,* 103–4.

Domonkos, L. S. (1977). History of higher education. In *International Encyclopedia of Higher Education,* pp. 2017–2040. San Francisco: Jossey-Bass.

Gracia, J. J. E. (1992). *Philosophy and its history: Issues in philosophical historiography.* Albany: State University of New York Press.

Hook, S. (1946). *Education for modern man.* New York: Dial.

Hutchins, R. M. (1936). *The higher learning in America.* New Haven, CT: Yale University Press.

Johnson, J. A., Collins, H. W., Dupuis, V. L., & Johansen, J. H. (1969). *Introduction to the Foundations of American Education.* Boston: Allyn and Bacon.

Kneller, G. F. (1964). *Introduction to the philosophy of education.* New York: John Wiley & Sons.

Knock, G. H., Rentz, A. L., & Penn, J. R. (1989). Our philosophical heritage: Significant influences on professional practice and preparation. *NASPA Journal, 27,* (2), 116–22.

Kuh, G., Lyons, J., Miller, T., & Trow, J. A. (1995). *Reasonable expectations: Renewing the educational compact between institutions and students.* Washington, DC: National Association of Student Personnel Administrators (NASPA).

Lincoln, Y. S., & Guba, E. (1985). *Naturalistic inquiry.* Beverly Hills, CA: Sage.

Lincoln, Y. S. (1989). Trouble in the land: The paradigm revolution in the academic disciplines. *Higher education: Handbook of theory and research, 5,* 57–133. New York: Agathon Press.

Miller, T. K., & Prince, J. S. (1976). *The future of student affairs.* San Francisco: Jossey-Bass.

National Association of Student Personnel Administrators (NASPA). (1987). *A perspective on student affairs.* Washington, DC: Author.

Potts, D. B. (1977). 'College Enthusiasm!' as public response, 1800–1860. *Harvard Educational Review, 47,* (1), pp. 28–42.

Sartre, J. P. (1947). *Existentialism.* New York: Philosophical Library.

Veblen, T. (1918). *The higher learning in America.* New York: D. W. Huebsch.

Whitehead, A. N. (1929). *The aims of education and other essays.* New York: Macmillan.

Whitt, E. J., Carnaghi, J. E., Matkin, J., Scalese-Love, P., & Nestor, D. (1990). Believing is seeing: Alternative perspectives on a statement of professional philosophy for student affairs. *NASPA Journal, 27,* (3), 178–84.

Chapter 2

A HISTORY OF STUDENT AFFAIRS

AUDREY L. RENTZ

The student personnel movement constitutes one of the most important efforts of American educators to treat the college and university students as individuals, rather than entries in an impersonal roster. . . . In a real sense this part of modern higher education is an individualized application of the research and clinical findings of modern psychology, sociology, cultural anthropology, and education to the task of aiding students to develop fully in the college environment.

(American Council on Education, 1949, p. 110)

INTRODUCTION

This chapter presents a description of the historical development of student affairs by examining statements of principles and values that guided its practice since its formalization in the early 1930s. Events leading up to the 1870s are thought of as catalysts for the emergence of student personnel work. The material in the chapter is organized according to the perception that the field has experienced three major movements or philosophies reflecting somewhat different orientations towards its mission, its role and practice within the changing context of higher education, and students. Within each movement are one or more significant or essential documents or statements that define, conceptualize or operationalize what we know today as student affairs on college and university campuses. These movements are: student personnel work, student development, and the current evolving emphasis on student learning. Because of the limited nature of this chapter, the reader is encouraged to consult *Student Affairs: A Profession's Heritage* (1994) for a copy of each of the major statements which are only highlighted here.

STUDENT PERSONNEL WORK

An exact date of birth for student affairs remains a matter of opinion. The respected historian, W.H. Cowley, would persuade us that the practice of personnel has a long history and in fact was characteristic of our own college and university system: " . . . what might be called Alma Maternal ministrations to students had characterized the universities of the Middle Ages and had been the most notable element in American higher education up to the time of the Civil war" (as cited in Williamson, 1949, p. 16). For Brubacher and Rudy (1958), a concern for the whole student was sometimes associated with *in loco parentis* and was evident from its practice on the colonial campuses of Harvard, William and Mary, Princeton and Yale in the mid 1600s. In earlier books describing student personnel work, the origin of the field is linked to the work of Frank Parsons (Boston) and Donald G. Paterson (Minneapolis) as well as to the development of the vocational guidance movement in 1908 (Mueller, 1961, Lloyd-Jones & Smith, 1954). Each view, worthy of merit, represents a different professional orientation toward the nature of the field, its mission, and its practice. Many contemporary writers would agree that the first and second decades of the 1900s are generally considered the embryonic period of student personnel work or what we know today as student affairs.

Societal, as well as educational movements generally arise in response to a perceived need or as an attempt to remediate that which is viewed as a negative or undesirable situation or condition. To what need or set of needs were the early proponents of student personnel work responding? What factors helped to create the positions and roles they assumed as the movement grew like topsy on many college and university campuses? More importantly, who were these pioneers? and what did they bring to the evolving field that provided it with strength and a sense of a common purpose or mission?

A knowledge of the evolution of student personnel work as a movement into today's field of student affairs requires a familiarity with the significant events and trends that influenced the context within which it developed, that being American higher education. The catalytic factors that aided the rise of the student personnel work movement are generally considered to be the evolving and changing nature of American society, the expanding focus of higher education, and the differing educational philosophies that shaped higher education's mission.

The prototype institution of the American system of higher education, Harvard, was established in 1636 using European institutions as models: *pro modo Academarium in Anglia* ("according to the manner of universities in England") (Brubacher & Rudy, 1958, p. 3). Curriculum, student discipline, degree requirements and policies were patterned after Emmanuel College, Cambridge University. The early Harvard faculty had an abiding interest in students. For them, the education of the intellect was seen as secondary to the salvation of the individual soul as they labored to achieve the aim of Harvard that "Every one shall consider the mayne End of his life & studyes, to know God & Jesus Christ, which is Eternal life" (Harvard College Records as cited in Brubacher & Rudy, 1958). Faculty interest and commitment to students manifested itself in daily visits to students' rooms, tutoring them in their studies, and praying with them to help maintain them against temptations of sin so that the soon to be gentleman/scholars might serve in the new society as examples of Puritan piety and civility. A somewhat sarcastic view of this early version of personnel work saw it as "a persistent emphasis on extracurricular religion, and also a considerable snooping into the personal lives of the students" (Cowley as cited in Mueller, 1961, p. 51). Subsequent colonial institutions (William and Mary, 1693; and Yale, 1701) replicated the Harvard model. The resulting close relationship between students and faculty, in and out of the classroom, sometimes positive and sometimes negative, remained as one of the unique hallmarks of America's developing system of higher education until the Civil war in the mid-1800s. Events, large and small, both societal and internal to institutions, would change this early profile of American campuses. For example, an internal incident, the Harvard food riot of 1766, sometimes called the butter rebellion, resulted in the dons being less willing to continue to eat and live along side their youthful students. During this outburst, several faculty and students were severely injured and several deaths were recorded. The incident is believed to have been triggered by the presence of rancid butter in the commons and the young male students' repressed volatile behavior. Thus, dramatic changes within society as well as within academic walls would alter previous collegiate traditions, faculty and student roles, and the intimate nature of early educational institutions.

The Expansion of Higher Education

Until the beginning of the 1800s, American institutions of higher education remained predominantly male, private, and residential. Presidents and faculty who were male clerics viewed their roles as paternalistic and acted *in loco parentis.* There was a certain quietude on campuses during those first 150 years. It was soon to be disrupted. Winds of change began to blow through higher education spawned by the turbulence of the societal changes outside its walls. As the young nation grew and developed it changed and so too did higher education institutions as they attempted to respond to the changing economy. The effects of secularization and industrialization were experienced not only outside the ivy-covered walls of the academy, but within as well. Male students attended public colleges and universities which were confirmed by the 1819 decision in the Dartmouth College case and Thomas Jefferson, in 1825, established the University of Virginia as the first state-supported institution. His early attempt to establish student government was also a first, although its subsequent failure was blamed in part on the lack of support from the state legislature and the immaturity of male students (Knock, 1985, p. 15–19). The rise of technical education was embodied in the founding of Rensselear Polytechnic Institute (NY) in 1824 where both "sons and daughters of local farmers and mechanics (would be prepared) in the art of applying science to husbandry, manufactures, and domestic economy" (RPI Annual Register as cited in Brubacher & Rudy, 1958). The traditional, somewhat narrow, liberal arts curriculum of the colonial colleges was in danger of no longer being considered the norm. As the number of new and different institutions grew, many presidents argued about the proper nature of higher education's curriculum. A major contributor to the debate was the president of Yale. President Jeremiah Day issued an authoritative opinion on behalf of his faculty that was known as the Yale Report of 1828. The document, ". . . became a classic statement in defense of the old order" (Rudolph, 1990, p. 130). The case to preserve the classical and narrow curriculum in America "was made with such finality that not until the next generation would another band of reformers assail the old course of study" (Rudolph, p. 131).

Women's Entrance into Higher Education

During this same period, the young nation's needs for teachers at the elementary, secondary, and collegiate level added considerable weight to the previous arguments of women for higher education. The words of President John Adams' wife, Abagail, written in 1776 to her husband as he considered drafts of the Declaration of Independence, were a clarion call to women: "If you complain of neglect of Education in sons, What shall I say with regard to daughters, who every day experience the want of it. With regard to the Education of my own children, I find myself soon out of my depth, and destitute and deficient in every part of Education" (as cited in Solomon, 1985, p. 1). The "years between 1790 and 1850 witnessed a remarkable growth in female schooling and as a result the notion of collegiate study moved from the realm of fantasy to that of real experimentation" (Solomon, 85, p. 14). A college education, closed to women and termed the "forbidden world" (Solomon, 1995, p. 1) was about to change higher education's profile. The new ideal of Republican Motherhood and Christian influences after the Second Great Awakening seemingly justified the education of women (Solomon, 1985). With female boarding schools, academies, and seminaries serving as seeds, women were quick to educate themselves to become teachers and in turn established and taught at colleges for women with a curriculum that varied from containing high school courses to that equal to neighboring male four-year colleges and universities. Mount Holyoke, founded by Mary Lyon in 1836 as a seminary, became one of the earliest single-sex institutions that served as a prototype for the others that followed in the Midwest, Far West, and the South (Solomon, 1985). Other single-sex pioneers were Troy Seminary in Troy (NY) started by Emma Willard in 1821 and Hartford Seminary (CT) established by Catherine Beecher in 1828 (Rudolph, 1990). The pace quickened and in 1836, Georgia Female College (Wesleyan) offered a curriculum that combined secondary and collegiate courses. Mary Sharp College (TN) established in 1853 went one step beyond the usual course offerings with its curriculum that emphasized Latin, Greek, and higher mathematics (Solomon, 1975). In 1837, an alternate form of higher education was possible when in an evangelical community, Oberlin College (OH) became the first undergraduate educational institution to allow four women to enroll as students. Coeducation was now a significant element within American higher education. Once admitted they were able to pursue the traditional baccalaureate degree program or receive a diploma following completion of a special Ladies Course (Rudolph, 1990, p. 311). Women's presence brought with it a new concern. Worried by the perceived problems of having women on Oberlin's predominantly male campus, President Finney said, " . . . you will need a wise and pious matron with such lady assistants as to keep up sufficient supervision" (as cited in Mueller, 1961, p. 53). Informally, the era of the dean of women had begun. Other types of institutions were founded in later years and are described in later sections of this chapter.

The Emergence of Black Institutions

The profile of American higher education changed again with the founding of black institutions in the North. Cheyney College in 1830, and both Lincoln College and Wilberforce University were established in 1856 (Thomas & Hirsch, 1989; Thomas & Hirsch, 1987; Hill, 1984). In the South, black students were hampered in their pursuit of higher education because higher education had been "declared" illegal (Thomas & Hirsch, 1989; Fleming, 1984; Hill, 1984; National Advisory Committee on Black Higher Education and Black Colleges and Universities, 1979). These early historically black institutions served an important function within the larger system of colleges and universities and would serve as models for similar institutions in the years ahead.

The Extracurriculum

Efforts on the part of students to move away from the narrow classical curriculum and the emphasis on piety and discipline led to the creation of debate clubs that evolved into literary societies and later into the fraternity movement. "In a sense, the literary societies and their libraries, the clubs, journals and organizations which compensated for the neglect of science, English literature, history, music, and art in the curriculum — this vast developing extracurriculum was the student response to the classical course of study. It helped to liberate the intellect on the American campus. It was the answer to the Yale Report of 1828, an answer so effective that by the end of the century at Yale itself there would be a real concern over which was really more fundamental, which more important, the curriculum or the extracurriculum" (Rudolph, 1990, p. 144). Between 1825 and 1840, several national Greek-letter social fraternities were created: Kappa Alpha, Theta Delta Chi, Sigma Phi, Delta Phi, Chi Psi and Psi Upsilon (Rudolph, 1990).

Passage of the Morrill Land Grant Acts of 1862 and 1864 led to the creation of the large system of agricultural and mechanical colleges, referred to as "utilitarian institutions" (Mueller, (1961), p. 52). Their curricular offerings combined concentrations in liberal arts with practical education. An extensive elective course system was developed. These legislative acts also required states to either admit black students to existing colleges or to provide separate but equal educational facilities for them. As a result, two systems of higher education, Historically Black and Predominantly White, separate but equal, developed side by side (Taylor, 1993).

The Germanic Influence

The nature of higher education was to change again. A dramatically different educational philosophy that espoused a narrower mission for American higher education emerged in response to society's need for greater numbers of scientifically and technically prepared professionals prepared primarily in the hard sciences: mathematics, physics, astronomy, etc. As more and more American and European faculty educated in German universities taught on American campuses, they introduced a new philosophy and a new concept. They brought with them the concept of academic freedom represented by two words: *lernfreiheit* and *lehrfreiheit.* The first term implied that students were free of administrative control and regulation, could travel from campus to campus, and could live where they chose. The latter term conveyed a faculty member's right to freely engage in research or scientific inquiry and to report findings without fear of reprisals (Rudolph, 1962, p. 412). *Lernfreiheit* was also associated with the philosophical perspective of rationalism or intellectualism, a way of defining the mission of higher education in narrow terms that granted little value to students' personal growth and development. The years when intellectualism was in favor are known as the period of Germanic Influence, approximately 1855 to 1890. Inevitably, faculty and student roles were redefined. Faculty found it necessary and desirable to devote considerable time to the pursuit of scientific research in addition to teaching, and had little concern for student life outside the classroom. The previous interest and value associated with the residential aspect of many colleges and universities all but disappeared. Yale was the only campus to maintain its position of endorsing a residential setting. The quality of student-faculty interactions changed dramatically. Institutional attitudes towards students shifted as well. Earlier handbooks that contained excessively stern rules of student conduct were replaced by thinner pamphlets. The previous definition of the student as adolescent was slowly redefined in adult terms. Male students were perceived capable of solving their own problems, academic, religious and social, as they saw fit. "Overweening paternalism gave way to almost complete indifference" (Cowley, 1937, p. 221). Harvard in 1886 altered its class attendance policies to require only that juniors and seniors pass examinations. Male students left campuses to initiate student-governed off-campus living accommodations; previous debating clubs of the 1700s evolved into literary societies which later became social drinking clubs and then emerged as Greek-letter social fraternities. Intercollegiate athletic programs were initiated with a crew race between Harvard and Yale in 1852 and a football game between Princeton and Rutgers in 1869. Later these programs grew to include baseball and track (Rudolph, 1962; Brubacher & Rudy, 1976). By the 1870s, a major element of higher education had taken form, an array of activities referred to as the era of "the extracurriculum" (Rudolph, 1962).

> In the extracurriculum the college student stated his case for the human mind, the human personality, and the human body, for all aspects of man that the colleges tended to ignore in their single-minded interest in the salvation of souls. In the institutions of the extracurriculum college students everywhere suggested that they preferred the perhaps equally challenging task of saving minds, saving personalities, saving bodies. On the whole the curriculum would still be intact, and compulsory chapel was only beginning to give way. But in the extracurriculum the students erected within the gates a monster. Taming it would now become as necessary a project as the long-delayed reform of the curriculum itself. (Rudolph, p. 155)

The Plurality of Institutions

From the 1850s until the 1870s, a variety of higher education prototypes emerged. They included not only "private women's college," but also "the religiously oriented coeducational college, the private coordinate women's college, the secular coeducational institution, both public and private, and the public single-sex vocational institution" (Solomon, 1985, p. 47). Women's colleges shared a common purpose with previous female seminaries. They perceived their mission to be to educate women so that they might be better prepared to assume their roles within the domestic sphere, as wives and mothers and, only if needed, as school teachers (Solomon, 1985).

Four pioneer public women's colleges were founded in the post-Civil war years: Vassar (NY) in 1865, Wellesley (MA) and Smith (MA) in 1875. Bryn Mawr (PA) in 1884, patterned after Johns Hopkins University, was awarding graduate degrees by 1888 (Rudolph, 1990). All three institutions quickly achieved national status. In addition, the Women's College of Baltimore (MD), opening in 1884 and sponsored by the Methodist Conference, held similarly high standards for academic rigor as its Virginian Presbyterian sponsored neighbor, Randolph-Macon College for Women (VA). The former is known today as Goucher College (Solomon, 1985).

As the 19th century came to a close, several Catholic girls' schools moved toward collegiate status. The Academy of the Sacred Heart at Manhattanville (NY) became a college in 1900 and Washington Trinity College was founded in the same year (Rudolph, 1990). The Catholic system of higher education developed single-sex and later coeducational institutions.

The Early Deans

Presidents of major institutions began to recognize that the new philosophy of intellectualism and its attitude towards students was not leading to desirable ends. Responding to faculty persuasion and parental pressures, Harvard's President Eliot recommended to his Board of Overseers that the prevailing philosophy of impersonalism be challenged and that various policies governing student attendance be reestablished. In 1870, Eliot appointed Professor Ephraim Gurney as the first college dean whose duties were primarily academic. Gurney relieved Eliot of the responsibility for student discipline while maintaining his regular teaching schedule. Later in 1891, when the dean's position was recast into two separate offices, LeBaron Russell Briggs, age 35 and already a respected Professor of English, assumed those duties related to students which were considered nonacademic: discipline, registration and records, and other aspects of students' lives outside the classroom (Brown, 1926). Briggs is generally regarded as the earliest Dean of Students, and the "official sponsor of undergraduates" (Brown, 1926, p. 95; Brubacher & Rudy, 1958; Mueller, 1961). His appointment was part of Eliot's call for a new system of student discipline, a system that would emphasize self-discipline and a developed sense of self responsibility (Morison, 1930). Briggs' attitude toward dealing with student discipline is apparent in the goals he had developed as he assumed the deanship: "(1) To help the student disciplined, and not merely to humiliate him; (2) to make it easy for the faculty to do its work; and (3) to develop a sentiment among the students which would render discipline less and less necessary"

(Brown, 1926, p. 101). In 1897, he organized 60 upperclassmen to assume responsibility for meeting and assisting entering students, "to stand ready in time of need . . . unpretentious counselor(s)" (Brown, 1926, p. 127). Briggs remained in the deanship until his retirement in 1925.

From 1879 to 1930, the undergraduate student body experienced a thirtyfold increase (Brubacher & Rudy, 1958) and many presidents saw the need for an administrator of students; for example, in 1889, President Gilman at Johns Hopkins established the first system of faculty advisers naming Professor E.H. Griffin as the first "chief of the faculty advisers" announcing that "in every institution there should be one or more persons specifically appointed to be counselors or advisers of students" (Cowley, 1949, p. 20). "Everywhere two types of deans made their appearance: 'academic deans' of colleges or special faculties . . . and 'dean of students'—deans of men or women . . . whose concern was with the extracurricular life of undergraduates (Cowley, 1937, pp. 224–225 as cited in Brubacher & Rudy, 1958, p. 322). Presidents were concerned about their ability to continue to administer their institution while assuming responsibility for student life issues, some voiced a concern about women students on their predominantly male campuses, while others spoke out publicly against the previous devaluing of the residential element. President Harper at the University of Chicago was among the first to argue for a return to providing residential facilities. Greek-letter social groups returned to campuses, clubs and student organizations flourished, and the campus "became an arena in which undergraduates erected monuments not to the soul of man but to man as a social and physical being" (Rudolph, 1962, p. 137). Students responded to the earlier narrow curriculum by making their own extracurriculum. Following the years of the Germanic Influence, the extracurriculum came full circle. Administrators wanted it now for students. The effects of the student established extracurriculum were vast:

> The extracurriculum which these young men developed—the agencies of intellect, the deeply embedded social system, the network of organized athletics—would become the repositories of their power. Through the extracurriculum the student arrived at a position of commanding importance in the American college. By opposing the literary societies, journals, and other clubs to the curriculum, by opposing the fraternities to the collegiate way, and by setting up in the athletic hero a more appealing symbol than the pious Christian, the students succeeded,

although not really intentionally, in robbing the college professor of a certain element of prestige and of a sizable area of authority (Rudolph, 1990, p. 157).

The Call for Research on Students

In a bold address in 1899 entitled "The Scientific Study of the Student," University of Chicago President Harper shared his vision of higher education's future. He proclaimed, "in order that the student may receive the assistance so essential to his highest success, another step in the onward evolution will take place. This step will be the scientific study of the student himself . . . provision must be made, either by the regular instructors or by those appointed for the purpose, to study in detail the man or woman to whom instruction is offered" (Cowley as cited in Williamson, 1949, p. 22). In addition to the physical health of the student, Harper proposed five areas of student life in need of study: "(1) his character, (2) his intellectual capacity, (3) his 'special intellectual characteristics,' (4) his special capacities and tastes, and (5) 'the social side of his nature.'" "This feature of twentieth-century education will come to be regarded as of greatest importance, and fifty years hence will prevail as widely as it is now lacking" (Cowley as cited in Williamson, 1949, p. 22). Student affairs would indeed become a significant aspect of and contributor to American campus life.

The Dean of Women

By 1882, increasing numbers of matrons and lady principals succeeded in overseeing coeducational environments to the extent that "relations between them (men and women) are such that there is comparative freedom from the dangers and conditions ordinarily incident to college life" (Holmes, 1939 cited in Mueller, 1961, p. 53). Historians generally credit the hiring of Alice Freeman Palmer at the University of Chicago in 1892 as the appointment of the first Dean of Women. Having agreed to serve part-time as both Dean and Professor of History, Palmer persuaded President Harper to hire her friend, Marion Talbot, as Dean of Women for the University College and Assistant Professor of Domestic Sciences (Solomon, 1980; Talbot, 1925). Talbot replaced Palmer in 1895 as the first full-time Dean of Women (Schwartz, 1995). Educated in Latin, Greek, and modern languages abroad, she received her BA and MA from Boston University, and later a BS from MIT, majoring in sanitation, which later became home economics. In addition, Swarthmore claims a Dean of Women appointment in 1890 (Blackburn, 1969; Fley, 1979). Talbot cofounded the American Association of University Women in 1881 and calling deans together helped establish the National Association of Deans of Women in 1916 (Fley, 1979). She also played a major role in the creation of the American Home Economics Association in 1908. No one could claim that she fit that times' dean stereotype. From the late '20s until the early '30s, she was Acting President of Constantinople Women's College in Turkey (Fley, 1979). These early deans' responsibilities went beyond a charge of supervising women's behavior as they sought to "champion the intellectual and personal ambitions of young women" (Knock, 1985, p. 31). The first MA and Diploma of Dean of Women was granted in 1914 by Teachers College, Columbia University. Women studied the hygiene of childhood and adolescence, biology related to sex education, educational psychology, history of the family, sociology, educational sociology, philosophy of education, management of schools, issues of administration, psychology of religion, and a practicum . . . " (Lloyd-Jones, 1954, p. 262–263).

As undergraduates returned to the campus as residents, their numbers increased and administrative staffs grew in proportion. During the early 1900s, college and university campuses were being served by large numbers of personnel practitioners: deans of men, students, and women; registrars; counselors; vocational guidance counselors; placement counselors; residence hall directors; admissions, food, and health service staffs; and coordinators/advisors of student organizations and activities (Rudolph, 1962). All of these personnel people were committed to providing whatever programs and services were required to help students derive maximum benefit from their collegiate experience, both in and out of the classroom.

The Dean of Men

Although probably not the first dean of men, the appointment of Thomas Arkle Clark as Dean of Undergraduates and Assistant to the President in 1901 led to his serving in that capacity in 1909 at the University of Illinois. A former student of L.R. Briggs at Harvard, Clark's contributions were also primarily in the area of discipline. These student personnel pioneers valued the individuality of each student, were committed to the holistic development of students, and held an unshakeable belief in each student's unique potential for growth and learning. These values and beliefs would become the cornerstones of future statements of the field's mission and goals.

The student personnel movement emerged in part as a reaction against the German-based intellectualism and its resulting impersonal attitude towards students. Developments in the field of psychology created the ability to objectively measure behavior and confirm individual differences and the need of American higher education to maintain a personalized individual relationship with the large number of World War I veterans who enrolled as students.

In 1926, the publication of a report from a study group sponsored by the American Council on Education and directed by L.B. Hopkins "focused national attention upon the importance of (student personnel work) and . . . the need for further research" (American Council on Education, 1937, p. 74). People were talking about and debating the purpose of this new group of college and university personnel officers.

Professional Associations

As small meetings at neighboring campuses brought together student personnel deans to discuss common problems and issues, efforts were made to formalize these conferences within and across state lines resulting in the formation of several professional associations: the early deans of women established the National Association of Women Deans (NAWD) in 1916, which is today's National Association of Women (NAW); the early deans of men convened the National Association of Deans of Men (NADM) in 1919, and in conjunction with the early deans of students, created today's National Association of Student Personnel Administrators (NASPA). In 1924, members from the existing gender specific associations formed the American College Personnel Association (ACPA), and in 1934, the American Personnel and Guidance Association (APGA) was established, which today is the Association for Counseling and Development (Mueller, 1969). For information about professional associations of interest to specialists within student affairs, such as orientation, financial aids, student activities, etc., the reader is advised to consult the appropriate chapter of this book.

In the early 1930s, Chicago's President Harper described the need for "individualized student relationships and predicted that within fifty years the individualization of higher education would be achieved by the appointment of special officers who would devote their attention to the students as men and women rather than as minds merely" (Cowley as cited in Williamson, p. 223). His goal was to be achieved much sooner.

Antecedents of the Student Personnel Point of View

Whenever student personnel professionals gathered to talk about their evolving field, inevitably the conversation included attempts to define it, establish criteria for its practice, and clarify its role on campuses. Seeds of the future Student Personnel Point of View can be found in the following record of a conference of college personnel officers held at Purdue University and Wabash College in 1929, in cooperation with the American Council on Education and the Personnel Research Foundation of New York. J.A. Humphreys (Dean of Personnel Services at Oberlin College) proposed five guiding principles to serve as the basis on which student personnel work should be developed. They were:

1. Personnel work is, and should be, first of all an idea rather than a tangible organization. It stands for individualization in college education. Personnel work among college students consists of those activities or procedures which have as their objective assisting the individual student.
2. The logical outcome of this principle is the idea that there should be brought to bear on all student problems, either individual or group situations, the point of view which concerns itself with the individual student. The application of established policies and the forming of new ones ought to be made with reference to individual needs. After all the college exists for the student and not the student for the college.
3. Specific personnel problems arise out of situations, not out of a clear sky.
4. Every member of the faculty, every administrative officer and assistant is a personnel officer in the sense that responsibility for serving the individual student rests upon all those who come in contact with the students.
5. College personnel work is not an activity set off apart from the educative process of the college. True personnel work functions as a part of the educative process. (Humphreys, 1930, p. 11–12).

Elements of the thoughts above can be found in the classic definition of Clothier (1931) while writing for the Committee on Principles and Functions of the American College Personnel Association:

Personnel work in a college or university is the systematic bringing to bear on the individual student all those influences, of whatever nature, which will stimulate him and assist him, through his own efforts, to develop in body, mind and character to the limit of his individual capacity for growth, and helping him to apply his powers so developed most effectively to the work of the world. (p. 10).

Both the principle of individual differences and the notion that "(p)ersonnel work cannot be departmentalized . . . but must be a leaven throughout the whole college and these influences . . . must be brought to bear by all who come in contact with (the student)" are present in Clothier's statement (p. 10). W.H. Cowley (1936) attempting to bring order to the existing confusion surrounding the amorphous nature of student personnel work provided a review of many of the early definitions in use and concluded that several were too inclusive, while others too restrictive. To separate the new field from guidance and personnel work, an area of some confusion among early practitioners, he offered his own briefer definition: "Personnel work constitutes all activities undertaken or sponsored by an educational institution, aside from curricular instruction, in which the student's personal development is the primary consideration" (p. 65). Establishing student personnel work as an equal to the two main divisions of college and university administration (instructional and operational) on campuses was the view that Lloyd-Jones hoped others would adopt (Lloyd-Jones, 1934, p. 22). Two years later, Cowley (1936) highlighted yet another aspect of student personnel work, the personnel point of view:

> The personnel point of view is a philosophy of education which puts emphasis upon the individual students and his all-round development as a person rather than upon his intellectual training alone and which promotes the establishment in educational institutions of curricular programs, methods of instruction, and extra-instructional media to achieve such emphasis. (p. 69).

Cowley (1949) made an interesting point as he identified the forces that contributed to the rise of the personnel movement. "The usual explanation . . . is that scientific psychology led to the application of research findings to the problems of military, of industry, and of education. . . . But it struck me that for *student* personnel work at least three other considerations were antecedent to scientific psychological research: first, secularization of education; second, the increase in student populations beginning about 1870; and third, the attacks upon the intellectualistic impersonalism imported by American Ph.D.s trained in Germany" (p. 16).

The Student Personnel Point of View (1936)

Numerous definitions and terms were being used interchangeably. An authoritative statement of principles and practice was needed. The

Executive Committee of the American Council on Education (ACE) convened a group of professionals in Washington, DC on April 16–17, 1937 to clarify "the so-called personnel work," the intelligent use of available tools and the development of additional techniques and processes" (ACE, 1937, p. 75). Attending were F.F. Bradshaw, W.H. Cowley, A.B. Crawford, L.B. Hopkins, E. Lloyd-Jones, D.G. Paterson, C.G. Wrenn, and others, with E.G. Williamson serving as chair. Their deliberations resulted in the report entitled "The Student Personnel Point of View." It was the first statement of philosophy, purpose, and methods of practice that clearly established the foundation for the field's future growth and put its emphasis on students. (The reader is encouraged to consult *Student Affairs: A Profession's Heritage* (1995) for the entire 1937 and 1949 documents). It is important to recognize that in the initial paragraph of this 1937 statement, labeled Philosophy, Committee members affirmed the concept of holism as a basic assumption that should guide practice:

> One of the basic purposes of higher education is the preservation, transmission, and enrichment of the important elements of culture—the product of scholarship, research, creative imagination, and human experience. It is the task of colleges and universities so to vitalize this and other educational purposes as to assist the student in developing to the limits of his potentialities and in making his contribution to the betterment of society. This philosophy imposes upon education institutions the obligation to consider the student as a whole—his intellectual capacity and achievement, his emotional make-up, his physical condition, his social relationships, his vocational aptitudes and skills, his moral and religious values, his economic resources, his aesthetic appreciations. It puts emphasis, in brief, upon the development of the student as a person rather than upon his intellectual training alone (ACE, 1937, p. 76).

Twenty-six student personnel services were identified, from interpreting institutional objectives and opportunities to prospective students and their parents to "keeping the student continuously and adequately informed of the educational opportunities and services available to him" (p. 77–79). Coordination was a key concept which the Committee believed should be implemented not only within individual institutions, but also between student personnel work and instruction, between student personnel work and business administration and between higher and secondary education. The communication of information about students, among all those who worked with students, was viewed as beneficial for students.

The Student Personnel Point of View (1949)

In 1949, a revision of the 1937 document was published. This revised statement expanded the goals of higher education to include:

1. Education for a fuller realization of democracy in every phase of living;
2. Education directly and explicitly for international understanding and cooperation;
3. Education for the application of creative imagination and trained intelligence to the solution of social problems and to the administration of publications. (American Council on Education, 1949, p. 108)

From these documents, the set of fundamental assumptions that dictated practice for years was gleaned. Many professionals believed these assumptions represented the *spirit* of student personnel practice. They are: "(1) individual differences are anticipated and every student is recognized as unique; (2) each individual is to be treated as a functioning whole" (Mueller, 1969, p. 56); (3) teaching, counseling, student activities and other organized educational efforts should start realistically from where the individual student is, not from the point of development at which the institution would like to find the hypothetical student; (4) "the individual's current drives, interests, and needs are to be accepted as the most significant factor in developing a personnel program appropriate for any particular campus," (Mueller, 1969, p. 56); and (5) "the student is thought of as a responsible participant in his own development and not as a passive recipient of an imprinted economic, political or religious doctrine or vocational skill" (American Council on Education, 1949, p. 109).

Student Personnel Practice

The movement of student personnel continued to grow during the 1940s and 1950s, aided in part by the post World War II economy and the large numbers of returning veterans who chose to enter higher education. Professionals understood the needs of students, planning and offering services and programs that helped students function effectively in order to benefit from classroom instruction. Practice was dictated by the Student Personnel Point of View; strategies were grounded in the principles of sociology, psychology, philosophy, and anthropology intermingled with educational administration, and guidance. Students were a relatively homogeneous group of individuals. Practitioner roles included caring parent, adviser, and disciplinarian. Students were free to choose to consult and/or use the student services available, or decide to become involved in the programs offered. During this period, professionals debated whether or not the field was secondary to or complementary to the academic mission of the institution. Regardless, the belief was that the extracurriculum provided opportunities for students to learn a variety of skills as they moved toward personal and social maturity. At times, students interacted with professional staff because there was a perception that a particular need existed, adjudicating student conduct violations, for example, or infrequent class attendance. Always the aim was to help students grow and develop as fully functioning human beings.

Following Russia's 1957 launching of Sputnik, the U.S. recognized a new need for scientifically and technically prepared individuals and increased federal funds were channeled into higher education at an unprecedented rate. High school students, who had demonstrated their intellectual abilities and who were encouraged to pursue degrees in the hard sciences, flocked to university campuses. Student enrollments swelled as others, desiring to avoid the military draft linked with the developing Vietnam war, also became full-time students.

STUDENT DEVELOPMENT

Many student personnel administrators found themselves in difficult situations during the 1960s, desiring to serve as advocates for students, sensitive to students' needs to learn about navigating bureaucratic organizations and participation in social causes, while being asked by their presidents to control student behavior. As described in Orientation, students during this period were reacting to a deeper sense of impersonalism invading higher education, which included overcrowding, and the use of new technology to more efficiently process procedures such as class registrations. Undergraduate coursework was viewed as irrelevant to solving major societal issues. "Flower power," "take time to smell the roses," "do not fold, staple or mutilate," and other chants filled the campus air along with shouts of demonstrators protesting the involvement of universities in federally-funded research programs to assist military defense activities. Following the years of turbulence and riots that accompanied student activism and the Civil Rights movement, college and university administrations began to rethink their orientation towards students and the nature of the previous student-institutional relationship. Slowly, institutional perceptions of students changed as well as the roles assumed by student affairs professionals. Concepts of confrontation, *in loco parentis,* and meritocracy were replaced by encounter, collaboration, and egalitarianism. The focus of professional practice moved from reactive to proactive, from an orientation of student services to student development, and the undergraduate years were perceived as a developmental sequence rather than four discrete years. Students were now thought of as adults, albeit as young adults still experiencing a critical period of growth and development. Institutional policies, based on this new view of students, were more liberal. Students were given seats on governing boards and student advisory committees were established in many areas of the campus.

For student personnel itself, by now sometimes called college student personnel, it was also a time of upheaval, turbulence, and confusion. Annual professional conference attendants heard speeches questioning future configurations or even the continued existence of the field. 1964 ACPA President Cowley entreated conferees to support and utilize the newly created organization, the Council of Student Personnel Associations in Higher Education (COSPA), which he hoped would speak for a unified student personnel field. President Barbara Kirk, in 1965, described the field as experiencing an "identity crisis" (Kirk, 1965, 205–206). It was a period of questioning, self-doubt, and concern about the role future student personnel professionals would play in higher education. Adding to the uncertainty was a reordering of priorities by some institutions that suggested that unless student personnel professionals could document their effectiveness with students, future budget allocations would be greatly decreased. Accountability had entered higher education from the corporate world. In his 1966 ACPA Presidential Address, Ralph Berdie responded to the question "What is student personnel work?" by proposing the following:

> (It) is the application in higher education of knowledge and principles derived from the social and behavioral sciences, particularly psychology, educational psychology, and sociology. Accepting this definition student personnel work is different but not apart from other persons in higher education. Neither is it the exclusive responsibility of any one or several groups of persons in colleges and universities. The student personnel worker is the behavioral scientist whose subject matter is the student and whose socio-psychological sphere is the college. . . . A primary purpose . . . is to humanize higher education, to help students respond to others and to themselves as human beings and to help them formulate principles for themselves as to how people should relate to one another, and to aid them to behave accordingly. . . . Another purpose . . . is to individual-

ize higher education. We recognize the presence and significance of individual differences and hope to structure the education of each individual accordingly. (Berdie, 1966, p. 211–212)

COSPA

The efforts of two groups of professionals, who, although meeting independently, focused on the same topic, assessing the status of student personnel work and thinking about its role and mission in the years ahead planted other seeds. One group, composed of representatives of various student personnel associations, was known in 1968 as the Committee on Professional Development of the Council of Student Personnel Associations in Higher Education (COSPA). Their task was to prepare a statement on professional preparation. Committee members (Grant, Saddlemire, Jones, Bradow, Cooper, Kirkbride, Nelson, Page and Riker) concluded that to do so required that they first revisit the SPPV documents of 1937 and 1949. Certain points of view emerged as keystones of the Committee's thinking. Notice the subtle shift from the previous student personnel perspective to what became known as student development:

1. The orientation to student personnel is developmental.
2. Self-direction of the student is the goal of the student and is facilitated by the student development specialist.
3. Students are viewed as collaborators with the faculty and administration in the process of learning and growing.
4. It is recognized that many theoretical approaches to human development have credence, and a thorough understanding of such approaches is important to the student development specialist.
5. The student development specialist prefers a proactive position in policy formulation and decision-making so that a positive impact is made on the change process (1972, p. 385).

Identifying the clientele (students as individuals, groups, or organizations), and the competencies and functions (administrative, instructor, and consultant) of student development specialists, the Committee proposed competencies to be mastered during professional preparation. The former student personnel worker, a generalist, was now considered a specialist. This new professional role implied an area of expertise which could be defined as the process by which development occurs or can be facilitated. See *Student Affairs: A Profession's Heritage* (1994).

Student development became a movement within student affairs in much the same manner as earlier movements. It had its supporters and its detractors. It emerged as a reaction to a perceived negative situation, the devaluing of student personnel on many campuses: " ... The old approach, student personnel work, was subtly or directly denigrated as inappropriate and outmoded" (Bloland, Stamatakos, & Rogers, 1994, p. 6). "This school of thought (student development) quickly captured the imagination of a number of student affairs professionals as a way of adding credibility and validity to the work of administrators and practitioners responsible for organizing, guiding, and facilitating the out-of-class education and development of college students" (Miller, Winston, & Mendenhall, 1983, p. 11).

The T.H.E. Project

The second group was a task force established by ACPA in 1968 that was given the title Tomorrow's Higher Education Project (T.H.E.). The goal of T.H.E. Project was described in the foreword of the resulting monograph by Robert Brown *Tomorrow's Higher Education: A Return to the Academy:*

> The essence of the THE Project is an attempt to reconceptualize college student personnel in a way that will serve to provide a measure of creative input from our profession toward the shaping of higher education in the future. By reconceptualization we mean the systematic reconstruction of our fundamental conceptions as to the specific roles, functions, methods and procedures that will characterize future practice (Brown, 1972, p. i).

Reviewing the literature on the impact of the college experience on students, Brown identified five key student development concepts. These were:

1. Student characteristics when they enter college have a significant impact on how students are affected by their college experience.
2. The collegiate years are the period for many individual students when significant developmental changes occur.
3. There are opportunities within the collegiate program for it to have a significant impact on student development.
4. The environmental factors that hold the most promise for affecting student developmental patterns include the peer group, the living unit, the faculty, and the classroom experience.
5. Developmental changes in students are the result of the interaction of initial characteristics and the press of the environment. (Brown, p. 33–35).

Three families of theories form the basis of this movement: cognitive theories that describe intellectual and moral development; psychosocial theories that describe personal and life cycle development, and the person-environment interaction theories concerned with the ecology of student life (Miller, Winston, & Mendenhall, 1983). From these theory families, three student development principles were extracted: (1) human development is both continuous and cumulative; (2) development is a matter of movement from the simpler to the more complex; and (3) human development tends to be orderly and stage related (1983, pp. 13–14). Publication of Brown's (1972) monograph completed Phase I of the Project. A second group of ten individuals was appointed by ACPA to complete Phase II, model building. This task was completed during a conference in 1974. The model for operationalizing student development which resulted was a process model consisting of three major steps or functions: goal setting, assessment, and strategies for student development. Strategies to facilitate student development, or human growth and development, were teaching, consultation, and milieu management.

By 1976, the concept of student development was defined as "the application of human development concepts in postsecondary settings so that everyone involved can master increasingly complex developmental tasks, achieve self-direction, and become interdependent" (Miller & Prince, 1976, p. 3). Student development educators, the new preferred term over specialists, viewed everyone on campus as members of the academic community. All were perceived as collaborators and learners in the developmental process of growth. The new educator emphasis attempted to place student affairs professionals within the academic side of the institution. Practice strategies were redefined as intentional interventions in students' lives to promote human growth and development. Intentionality implied that goal setting had occurred and was possible because theories described the various developmental processes experienced by college students. Professionals could assess developmental levels (psychosocial, cognitive, . . .) and design environments and interventions (experiences or programs) to help students move along a particular developmental sequence of tasks. Goal setting was now a collaborative effort involving the student. In addition, student development educators were seen as capable of facilitating more effective classroom learning by sharing their process ideas and strategies with faculty to improve teaching. On a broader scale, the aim of higher education was student development.

The 1987 NASPA Statement

During the 1980s, colleges and universities had student affairs staff who implemented either student personnel work or student development, depending on the institution's mission and the orientation of its president. As more and more students emerged from graduate preparation programs that emphasized student development and as professional conferences focused on student development themes, the level of discussion about practice rose again. Student diversity was a key element. Existing theories were not always based on data gathered from diverse student populations. As 1987 approached, fifty years of student affairs practice had been recorded. To commemorate this anniversary of The Student Personnel Point of View, NASPA President Chambers, in 1986, appointed Art Sandeen as Chair of the Plan for a New Century Committee. A month later, the American Council on Education agreed to become involved. Committee members included Allbright, Barr, Golseth, Kuh, Lyons, and Rhatigan. The product was the document "A Perspective on Student Affairs: A Statement Issued at the 50th Anniversary of the Student Personnel Point of View" (1987). Within its pages are basic assumptions and purposes Committee members believed to underlie student affairs practice. These included: "The Academic Mission of the Institution is Preeminent; Each Student is Unique; Each Person Has Worth and Dignity; Bigotry Cannot Be Tolerated; Feelings Affect Thinking and Learning; Student Involvement Enhances Learning; Personal Circumstances Affect Learning; and Out-of-Class Environments Affect Learning" (Sandeen et al., 1987, p. 641–642).

Student Development Practice

Since many of the chapters in this book contain sections by the contributors who discuss the application of student development theory to practice situations in a variety of areas of student affairs, the reader is encouraged to consult particular pages of interest. What is significant to note here is that, during this stage of development of student affairs, practice stressed the assessment of developmental levels as described in the theories of Chickering & Reisser, Perry, Kohlberg, and the later contributions of Helms and Cass, to name just a few. The multiple effects on student growth associated with the interaction between the student and the student's environment were not only recognized and confirmed, but led student development educators to attempt to create positive environments that would provide the appropriate ratio of challenge and support. Theories were not only useful because they provided practitioners with descriptions of student growth, but also because they depicted pathways or road maps of the movement of students toward maturity. Similarly, these theories enhanced student development educators' ability to define goals for their programmatic efforts or intentional interventions. Indeed the whole academic community was viewed as a learning community whose goal was the personal growth and development of all members.

AN EMPHASIS ON STUDENT LEARNING

As with previous movements within student affairs, student development has had its supporters and its critics. An important critique of the movement was prepared by Paul Bloland, Louis Stamatakos and Russell Rogers and is contained within their 1994 monograph, *Reform in Student Affairs: A Critique of Student Development.* "Our argument is not with student development per se. It is rather with our fellow professionals . . . who failed to exercise their critical faculties to raise questions about student development, to slow down the headlong pace of its engulfment of the field of student affairs, and to examine alternatives and options as they presented themselves" (p. x). Essentially these three experienced professionals examined and challenged student development as a reform movement, the application of its theories, and discussed the perceived problems that the use of student development "has created for the field of student affairs" (p. xi). Suggesting a new paradigm, they proposed that "the student affairs profession again take its cue from the central educational mission of higher education and view the learning process as integral to the implementation of that mission" (p. 103). Among their final recommendations are

1. Cease identifying with the student development model as the well-spring or philosophical underpinning of the field of student affairs. . . .
2. Return to the general principles so cogently expressed in the Student Personnel Point of View (ACPA, 1949), clearly placing academic and intellectual development at the center of the student affairs mission.
3. Re-emphasize the primacy of learning as the cardinal value of higher education and employ learning theory, conjointly with student development theory, as an

essential tool for planning experiences and programs that will enhance the learning process.

4. Clearly identify with the institutional educational mission for unless student affairs takes its cue from the mission and goals of higher education, it has no function except the provision of support services; any educational outcomes it may claim are purely accidental. (p. 104)

In 1993, ACPA President Schroeder convened a group of leaders in higher education to consider how the student affairs field might enhance their role relative to student learning and personal development. Members of The Student Learning Imperative Project were A. Astin, H. Astin, P. Bloland, K.P. Cross, J. Hurst, G. Kuh, T. Marchese, E. Nuss, E. Pascarella, A. Pruitt, M. Rooney, and C. Schroeder. Their deliberations produced a document, "The Student Learning Imperative: Implications for Student Affairs" which was "intended to stimulate discussion and debate on how student affairs professionals can intentionally create the conditions that enhance student learning and personal development" (ACPA, 1995, p. 1). In addition, members perceived the present as a period of major transformation precipitated by, in part, the increasing diversity within higher education, eroding public confidence, the effects of accountability being imposed by external constituencies and the importance of positive educational environments. Five characteristics were proposed which Committee members believed student affairs divisions committed to student learning and personal development should exhibit. These were: (1) the student affairs division mission complements the institution's mission, with the enhancement of student learning and personal development being the primary goal of student affairs programs and services; (2) resources are allocated to encourage student learning and personal development; (3) student affairs professionals collaborate with other institutional agents and agencies to promote student learning and personal development; (4) the division of student affairs includes staff who are experts on students, their environments, and teaching and learning processes; and (5) student affairs policies and programs are based on promising practices from the research on student learning and institution-specific assessment data" (p. 2–5).

While many professionals view this new emphasis on student learning, which sometimes also includes the concept of teaching, as a major paradigmatic shift from previous goals and values, others see it as simply another evolutionary stage in the dynamic development of student affairs. Certainly teaching and learning are, and always have been, central to the mission of American higher education. In 1954 Lloyd-Jones and Smith co-authored a major work describing student personnel. Their conceptualization of the field is captured in the book's title, *Student Personnel Work as Deeper Teaching.* In 1972, Brown issued his call for a return to the academy. One wonders about the efficacy of this most recent act of returning to the academy and being so much inside its walls that student affairs professionals may turn their backs on students' growth and development in areas other than intellectual. To do so would certainly be to step away from the core values and beliefs to which the early deans and pioneer practitioners were committed. The debate of student affairs as extracurriculum versus cocurriculum continues and may now extend to the realm of noncurriculum. Will the future hold only services, if students perceive a need, and by students presumed to be more than young adults, yet whose familial and emotional backgrounds signal needs for so much more? Have we come full circle once again in the midst of this period of transition or transformation? Where will we look for the beliefs and values that will form the core of student affairs in the future? . . . to the institution and its mission, to faculty and their values, or to students and their needs? . . . which needs? If we lose sight of the individual student as our focus and weaken our resolve to provide opportunities and guidance for holistic development, who have we become? . . . and why do we exist? Student affairs' future role, its mission and goals continue to be the subject of considerable debate, now as they have been since the early 1900s, 'twas ever thus, and just perhaps, that is not a bad thing after all.

REFERENCES

American Council on Education. "The Student Personnel Point of View," (Originally published in 1937). In A.L. Rentz (Ed.), *Student affairs: A profession's heritage.* (1994). (pp. 66–78). Lanham, MD: University of America Press.

American Council on Education. "The Student Personnel Point of View", (Originally published in 1949). In A.L. Rentz (Ed.), *Student affairs: A profession's heritage.* (1994) (pp. 108–123). Lanham, MD: University of America Press.

Berdie, R. (1966). Student personnel work: Definition and redefinition. *Journal of College Student Personnel, 7,* 131–136.

Blackburn, J.L. (1969). Perceived purposes of student personnel programs by chief student personnel officers as a function of academic preparation and experience. Unpublished doctoral dissertation, Department of Educational Administration, Florida State University.

Bloland, P., Stamatakos, L. C., & Rogers, R. R. (1994). *Reform in student affairs: A critique of student development.* Greensboro: ERIC Counseling and Student Services Clearinghouse.

Brown, R. W. (1926). *Dean briggs.* New York: Harper & Brothers.

Brown, R.D. (1972). Student development in tomorrow's higher education. *Student Personnel Series, No. 16.* Washington: American Personnel and Guidance Association.

Brubacher, J. S., & Rudy, W. (1958). *Higher education in transition.* New York: Harper & Row.

Clothier, R. C. (1931). College personnel principles and functions. In A.L. Rentz (Ed.), *Student affairs: A profession's heritage* (pp. 9–18). Lanham, MD: University of America Press.

Commission of Professional Preparation of COSPA. (1975). Student development services in post secondary education. In A.L. Rentz (Ed.), *Student affairs: A profession's heritage.* (1994) (pp. 428–437). Lanham, MD: University of America Press.

Cowley, W.H. (1936). The nature of student personnel work. In A.L. Rentz (Ed.), *Student affairs: A profession's heritage.* (pp. 43–65). Lanham, MD: University of America Press.

Cowley, W.H. (April, 1937). A preface to the principles of student counseling. The *Educational Record, XVIII, (1),* pp. 217–234.

Cowley, W.H. (1949). Some history and a venture in prophecy. In E.G. Williamson, (ed.), *Trends in student personnel work,* Minneapolis, MN: University of Minnesota Press.

Cowley, W.H., & Williams, D. (1991). *International and historical roots of american higher education.* New York: Garland.

Fleming, J. (1984) *Blacks in college.* San Francisco, CA: Jossey-Bass.

Fley, J. (1979). Student personnel pioneers: Those who developed our profession. *NASPA Journal, 17,* 23–39.

Harper, W.R. (1905). *The trend in higher education.* Chicago, IL: University of Chicago Press.

Hill, S. (1984). The traditionally black institutions of higher education: 1860 to 1982. Washington: U.S. Department of Education.

Holmes, L. (1939). *A history of the position of dean of women in a selected group of co-educational colleges and universities in the united states.* (New York: Teachers College, Columbia University).

Humphreys, J.A. (1930). Techniques of college personnel work. In J.E. Walters, (Ed.), *College Personnel Procedures: Proceedings of Purdue-Wabash Conference of College Personnel Officers.* (pp. 11–13). Lafayette: Purdue University.

Kirk, B. A. (1965). Identity crisis—1965. *Journal of College Student Personnel, 6,* 194–199.

Knock, G.H. (1985). Development of student services in higher education. In M.J. Barr, L.A. Keating, & Associates, *Developing effective student services programs.* San Francisco, CA: Jossey-Bass, Inc.

Lloyd-Jones, E. (1934). Personnel administration. In A.L. Rentz (Ed.), *Student affairs:*

A profession's heritage. (1994). (pp. 19–26). Lanham, MD: University of America Press.

Lloyd-Jones, E. (1949). The beginnings of our profession. In E. G. Williamson (Ed.)., *Student Personnel Work.* (pp. 260–263). Minneapolis, MN: The University of Minnesota Press.

Lloyd-Jones, E., & Smith, M. R. (1954). *Student personnel as deeper teaching.* New York: Harper & Brothers.

Miller, T. K., & Prince, J. S. (1976). *The future of student affairs.* San Francisco: Jossey-Bass.

Miller, T. K., Winston, R. B., Jr., & Mendenhall, W. R. (1983). *Administration and leadership in student affairs.* Muncie, IN: Accelerated Developments.

Morison, S.E. (1930). *The development of Harvard university since the inauguration of President Eliot 1869–1929.* (pp. lxviii–lxix). Cambridge, Harvard University Press.

Mueller, K.H. (1961). *Student personnel work in higher education.* Boston, MA: Houghton Mifflin.

National Advisory Committee on Black Higher Education and Black Colleges and Universities. (1979). *Black colleges and universities: An essential component of a diverse system of higher education.* Washington, DC: Department of Education.

Rentz, A. L., & Saddlemire, G. L. (Eds.). (1994). *Student affairs: A profession's heritage.* Lanham, MD: University Press of America.

Rudolph, F. (1990). *The american college and university: A history.* Athens, GA: University of Georgia Press.

Solomon, B. M. (1985). *In the company of educated women.* New Haven, CT: Yale University Press.

Taylor, T. (1992). The relationship between self-esteem of African-American students and their perception of the environment of their predominately white institution. Unpublished master's thesis, Bowling Green State University, OH.

T.H.E. Phase II Model Building Conference. (1975) A student development model for student affairs in tomorrow's higher education. In A.L. Rentz (Ed.), *Student affairs: A profession's heritage.* (1983). (pp. 410–422). Lanham, MD: University Press of America.

Thomas, G.E., & Hirsch, D.J. (1987). Black institutions in U.S. higher education: Present roles, contributions, future projections. *Journal of College Student Personnel, 27,* 496–503.

Thomas, G. E., & Hirsch, D. J. (1989). Blacks. In A. Levine (Ed.), *Blacks in higher education: Overcoming the odds.* Lanham, MD: University Press of America.

Williamson, E.G. (1949). *Trends in student personnel work.* Minneapolis, MN: The University of Minnesota Press.

Chapter 3

FROM ADMISSIONS TO
ENROLLMENT MANAGEMENT

DON HOSSLER

OVERVIEW

The role of college admissions offices in student affairs has always been clear in formal student affairs documents, but in practice admissions offices are not always housed within student affairs divisions. Both the 1939 Student Personnel Point of View, and the subsequent revision in 1947, place the function of the admissions office within the purview of student affairs. On many campuses, however, the admissions office is located in divisions of academic affairs or institutional advancement. This is unfortunate, because student affairs divisions should be concerned about all aspects of the students' college experience, from the point of initial contact to the point of graduation.

In this chapter, the development of the field of admissions is examined. In addition, this chapter traces the evolution of college admissions to the concept of enrollment management. Admissions offices are primarily interested in attracting and admitting college students, but enrollment management is concerned with the entirety of the college experience. The first part of this chapter defines admissions work and presents a history of the admissions field. The second part of this chapter examines enrollment management and explores it as an organizational concept.

ADMISSIONS

A Definition

Kuh (1977) defines admissions as:

those policies and procedures which provide for students' transitions from secondary to postsecondary education. All admissions policies are based on the inherent belief that the educational experience offered by the institution will benefit certain individuals. Faculty determined admissions policies and academic qualifications, considered the institution's most important expression of educational philosophy, are translated in to action by the admissions office. (p. 6)

The purpose of admissions is to help students make a successful transition from high school to college (Munger and Zucker, 1982) as well as recruiting students for specific colleges and universities (Shaffer and Martinson, 1966). Admissions administrators must be both counselors and marketers, two roles that are sometimes in conflict. Ideally these skills enable admissions officers to help each student to make the best college decision possible while at the same time recruiting students who will be well-suited to the specific institution the admissions officer represents. Like most functional areas in student affairs, the admissions function has a long history in American higher education, although its formal history is relatively short.

A HISTORY OF THE COLLEGE ADMISSIONS OFFICE

Gatekeepers or Salesman— The Image of the Admissions Officer

The history of the field of admissions in American colleges and universities is difficult to unravel because the field has been shaped by two competing images of the admissions officer. On one hand, the image of the admissions officer is that of the "Ivy League" admissions officer who, along with a faculty admissions committee, decides who will receive the coveted offers of admissions on "Bloody Monday."[1] They decide who will be admitted to a small elite group of colleges and universities. The other image, however, is that of the salesman, who attempts to attract prospective students to a college or university so that the institution's budget will be balanced, the doors will be open and the faculty will be happy. Thelin (1982) has described these two contrasting images of the admissions officer as those of gatekeeper and headhunter. Over the last two-hundred years, both images are accurate. It is equally important to note that these competing images may still be accurate for different types of institutions of higher education.

Early American colleges can trace the role of the admissions office to that of the "major beadle" in the medieval university (Smerling, 1960).

---

[1] This is the term used to describe the Monday in April on which all highly selective colleges send out their notices of acceptance or rejection to all applicants.

The "major beadle" was succeeded by the office of the archivist (Lindsay and Holland, 1930) and later by the office of the registrar. The role of faculty members or administrators in these positions was to keep track of student progress while enrolled in college, and to determine whether prospective students—new applicants—had the "right background" for admissions to the institution. For the colonial college, the right background frequently meant that the student could speak the English language with some modicum of proficiency and was of good moral character. At more selective institutions of the time, students were expected to have some knowledge of Latin and Greek (Broome, 1903; Rudolph, 1962). In any case, most early colleges also had preparatory schools attached to them so that students who did not meet the admissions requirements could acquire the necessary skills for admission (Brubacher and Rudy, 1968; Rudolph, 1962).

Not all colleges, however, were able to sit passively and wait for students to arrive for their admissions test. Part of the American dream included equal access to education and upward mobility. During the expansion westward in the Nineteenth Century, every town aspired to greatness. The presence of a college in a town was viewed as a clear signal to current and prospective residents that their town was going to become a major center and a good place to live. As a result colleges were created at a rapid rate. For example, in the early 1870s, England had four universities for a population of 23,000,000. The State of Ohio had 37 colleges for a population of 3,000,000 (Rudolph, 1962, p. 48). Many of these colleges consisted of 1–3 faculty and may not have even had a building. Frequently, the education offered was at the preparatory level.

Even at these early colleges, however, forerunners of the salesman were already hard at work. Frequently a staff consisted of the president and one or two additional faculty. The president taught classes, and in addition, performed all of the roles now associated with positions such as the chief fund raiser, the academic dean, the dean of students, and registrar. Rudolph's history of American higher education (1962) is replete with stories of college presidents traveling through the countryside trying to attract the sons (and it was only *sons* during most of the 18th and 19th centuries) of farmers and the emerging merchant class.

There were simply not enough potential college students to support the large number and variety of colleges established in the United States. As a result, many institutions of higher education had to be creative in devising creative marketing and recruitment strategies. In the middle part of the 19th century, many colleges sold prepaid tuition plans to families. The idea was to attract revenues that could be invested in endowments to support faculty and instruction now, thus reducing current, as well as future instructional costs. Unfortunately, many of these early colleges could not afford to invest the money. They were forced to spend this hard-earned revenue on current expenditures. When the new prepaid students arrived the money was often gone and in some cases the colleges were bankrupt. Institutions such as Dickinson and DePauw lost large amounts of money, more than two dollars for each dollar raised (Rudolph, 1962).

The mass marketing techniques of today are also not entirely new. In 1893, one state university had sufficient funds and political clout to mail brochures describing the virtues of attending the institution to every school superintendent in the state. Superintendents throughout the state were fined $50 if the brochures were not posted in their high schools (Thelin, 1982). The first Dean of Admissions was not appointed until the early part of the 20th century; however, the activities of these struggling colleges to attract students are part of the history of the admissions field.

The Emergence of the Admissions Field

The roles of gatekeeper and salesman continued into the 20th century, even as the professional admissions field began to emerge. Prior to the first Dean of Admissions in the 1920s, two important trends emerged that would shape the role of the admissions officer. Late in the 19th century, many institutions became concerned about the lack of standardization in the preparation of high school students.

In 1870, the University of Michigan, in response to this problem, began to send teams of faculty to visit high schools to improve the level of instruction and articulation between colleges and high schools. Other states followed, and in 1894, the North Central Association was formed to standardize the high school curriculum. Although the University of Michigan was the first university to employ this process, the precedent for regional associations had already been set by the 1880s with the creation of the New England Association of Colleges and Preparatory Schools (Brubacher and Rudy, 1968).

Along with the creation of associations to improve education at the high school level, standardized testing also emerged as a way to improve high school education and to standardize the "chaotic entrance requirements" (Brubacher and Rudy, 1968, p. 245) employed by colleges and universities. The Regents examination created in 1878 was the first such effort. In the 1890s a meeting of the Association of the Colleges and Secondary Schools of the Middle States and Maryland led to the establishment of the College Entrance Examination Board (The College Board). The creation of standardized tests by the College Entrance Examination Board caused many institutions to slowly abandon their own entrance exams and rely on one standardized test.

The emergence of the accreditation associations and standardized testing changed the functions of admissions offices. It became easier to determine who was prepared for college (although the criteria for admissions varied) and to compare the quality of entering students. These changes intensified the debate on institutional quality and prestige and formalized the tension between the role of the gatekeeper and the salesman. It had become possible for admissions officers to use objective criteria to compare not only the number of students enrolled, but the quality of those students enrolled.

The first Deans of Admission were hired in the 1920s, but the practice did not become widespread until the 1930s. During the 1930s, the concept of selective admissions was formally articulated (Thresher, 1966). The concept of selective admissions helped to further entrench the concept of institutional prestige based upon selectivity. As Thelin (1982) notes, the competition for talented students and faculty has always been closely interwoven with institutional prestige.

However, the emergence of elite, highly selective institutions such as Harvard, Yale, and Stanford are still a recent phenomenon. The current image of the admissions gatekeeper as one who sits and selects from among as many as 7–10 applicants for each first year student slot is also a new development. The Depression resulted in a downturn in college applicants. As a result, the 1930s was an era of the salesman and not the gatekeeper. The entry of the United States into World War II also depressed college applications so that it was not really until the 1950s that admissions officers at highly selective institutions were able to truly function as gatekeepers.

With the large numbers of GIs returning to college after World War II and the subsequent rise in enrollments because of the "baby boomers," the 1960s and 1970s are often referred to as the "Golden Age" of American higher education (Jencks & Reisman, 1969). During this era, even some admissions officers at many well-known but less prestigious private colleges and universities, as well as many public institutions were able to function as gatekeepers. Nevertheless, it would be a mistake to think of this as an era of gatekeeping for all admissions officers. The rapid growth of public four-year and two-year colleges had a major influence on admissions officers at smaller and lesser known private institutions. As a result, many private colleges and universities had to actively market themselves and recruit students to maintain enrollments (Thresher, 1966).

The Admissions Officer of Today

By the early 1970s, institutions were preparing for a predicted decrease of traditional age college students that could be as high as 42 percent (Hossler, 1986) before the end of this century. As college administrators shifted from the "bullish" student enrollment market of the 1950s and 1960s to the "bear" market of the 1980s and 1990s, institutions began to look to for-profit businesses for techniques to maintain or increase student enrollments setting the stage for the emergence of the admissions officer of today. The admissions officers of today have, in many cases, become hybrids of both the gatekeeper and the salesman. At nonselective institutions, admissions officers continue to function primarily as salesmen. Nevertheless, even at the most selective institutions, admissions officers have had to be salesmen. This has been necessary to attract a sufficient number of high ability students with all of the other attributes desired by prestigious colleges and universities (geographical representation, minority representation, and music, leadership, athletic, and other special skills).

Thelin (1982) suggests that admissions officers work in the era of marketing. In the 1970s, offices of admissions began to use marketing techniques such as improved publication materials, targeted mailing strategies, and telemarketing techniques to attract larger numbers of students. At the same time, senior level administrators began to use strategic planning techniques, also borrowed from business. Strategic planning incorporates market research so that organizations can better understand their clients and the institution's position in relation to its competitors. This furthered the push toward marketing, but also created the foundation for enrollment management that is discussed later in this chapter.

Marketing techniques require admissions officers to do a better job of tracking and communicating with prospective students. Targeted mailing and telemarketing techniques also require admissions officers who have analytical skills. They need to be able to analyze the background and attitudinal characteristics of students to identify the best potential markets. Personalized communication techniques are also hallmarks of modern marketing techniques. These developments require admissions officers who can use computer assisted technology. For admissions officers serving as salesmen, the adoption of these techniques and skills became essential for institutional well-being. More recently, admissions offices are starting to use CD Roms, the internet, videos, and other techniques to reach out to nontraditional and traditional age students.

In addition to the use of more sophisticated marketing techniques, the 1990s have seen an increased emphasis on the importance of pricing and student financial aid. Ten years ago new marketing techniques such as direct mail and telemarketing were thought to be key to successful student recruitment. Many admissions directors now believe that newly developed analytical approaches to setting tuition costs and to awarding financial aid are the most important elements of successful new student recruitment. Pricing and student aid may have arguably become the most important part of student recruitment. Phrases such as tuition leveraging and high tuition and high aid have become part of the lexicon of admissions work. Many admissions directors report that they now spend more time with vice-presidents of business on financial aid issues than on any other aspect of their job.

The emergence of the modern admissions office, with its emphasis on marketing, computer technology, pricing and student financial aid has separated admissions officers from other student affairs areas that have a stronger counseling or student development orientation. As a result, many professionals in the field of admissions do not think of themselves as student affairs personnel (Hossler, 1986). However, as will be seen in the next section of this chapter, as admissions and student affairs staffs have become part of enrollment management efforts, the connections between admissions and student affairs work are strengthening.

ENROLLMENT MANAGEMENT

An Introduction

As a result of the predicted declines in traditional age college students, college and university administrators became interested in student retention, as well as student recruitment. Student attrition became a frequent topic of inquiry during the late 1970s and 1980s (Bean, 1980; 1983; 1985; 1986; Noel, Levitz and Saluri, 1985; Pascarella, 1985; Pascarella, Duby, Miller, and Rasher, 1981; Pascarella and Terenzini, 1980, 1981; and Tinto, 1987). Student affairs administrators often found themselves assigned the responsibility for developing institutional retention programs.

The converging interests in attracting and retaining new students provided the impetus for the emergence of the enrollment management concept. Enrollment management provided an integrating framework for institutional efforts to more directly influence their student enrollments. On some campuses, the student affairs division began to play key roles in enrollment management activities. Since enrollment management, as a formal concept, is relatively new there is little history to document. In this section, more emphasis will be given to describing and analyzing enrollment management.

A number of conceptual frameworks have been suggested for use as the organizational basis for student affairs divisions (see Delworth and Hanson, 1989). Enrollment management can be viewed as one more framework for organizing student affairs divisions. For this to occur, many student affairs professionals need to become more familiar with the enrollment management concept. The second part of this chapter seeks to: define enrollment management; examine the evolution of enrollment management; discuss enrollment management as a concept; examine enrollment management as a process; present four archetypal enrollment management models; explore the role of student affairs in enrollment management; discuss current trends and ethical issues related to enrollment management; and to consider the professional preparation needs of enrollment managers and the future of enrollment management.

Defining Enrollment Management

In order for student affairs professionals to utilize the enrollment management concept, they must first understand it. On many campuses, the term enrollment management has developed a potent image as a systematic institutional response to issues related to student enrollments. At most institutions, enrollment management has become associated with a diverse set of activities which are being employed by institutions attempting to exert more control over (1) the characteristics of their enrolled student body, or (2) the size of their enrolled student body. In one sense the images of the gatekeeper and salesman are still relevant. However, from an enrollment management perspective, institutions are not only concerned about the characteristics and the total number of new students, but about the characteristics and total number of all enrolled students.

Enrollment management has been defined in many ways, but in each case, students are the fundamental unit of analysis. Enrollment management is not just an organizing concept, it is a process that involves the entire campus. Several definitions of enrollment management have been suggested (Hossler, 1984; Kemerer, Baldridge, and Green, 1982; Muston, 1985).

A definition of enrollment management that synthesizes these previous definitions is presented below:

> Enrollment management is both an organizational concept as well as a systematic set of activities designed to enable educational institutions to exert more influence over their student enrollments. Organized by strategic planning and supported by institutional research, enrollment management activities concern student college choice, transition to college, student attrition and retention, and student outcomes. These processes are studied to guide institutional practices in the areas of new student recruitment and financial aid, student support services, curriculum development and other academic areas that affect enrollments, student persistence, and student outcomes from college. (Hossler, Bean, and Associates, 1990, p. 5)

With this definition of enrollment management, the evolution of this new concept can now be examined. Later in this chapter, process elements of an enrollment management system will be examined, followed by a discussion of organizational models. These sections will further enhance our understanding of enrollment management.

The Emergence of Enrollment Management

The term, and perhaps the concept of, a comprehensive enrollment management system first emerged in 1976. However, as a process, enrollment management had been developing for many years. In fact, an examination of the evolution of offices of admissions and financial aid, along with other areas of student affairs, nonprofit marketing in higher education, research on student college choice, and student persistence demonstrates that enrollment management represented the convergence of developments in each of these areas.

It is difficult to determine whether the competitive nature of college admissions during the last three decades caused the advances made in marketing techniques for higher education or whether the emergence of nonprofit marketing has made possible the increasing sophistication of collegiate recruitment activities. It is equally difficult to determine whether the emergence of differentiated financial aid and pricing activities were the products of competition for students or if research on student college choice and the effects of aid and price on college choice resulted in more effective aid and pricing policies. Additionally, research on student attrition, the impact of college on students, and student-institution fit produced institutional retention programs that are often tailored to meet the needs of specific student populations such as nontraditional adult students, transfer students, or minority students.

It may be difficult to determine the precise genesis of the enrollment management concept. It is clear, however, that the declining numbers of traditional age students, along with the overbuilding of colleges and universities to adapt to the veterans and baby boomers of the 1950s and 60s, created a set of internal and external constraints that required college administrators to be more attentive to student enrollments. Thus, the emergence of the concept of enrollment management has been tied to the environmental press to which institutions of higher education have been forced to respond. What made the enrollment management concept new when it first appeared was not the development of new marketing techniques or new retention strategies. Rather, it was the organizational integration of functions such as academic advising, admissions, financial aid, and orientation into a comprehensive institutional approach designed to enable college and university administrators to exert greater influence over the factors which shape their enrollments.

Research and scholarship in applied fields frequently lags behind new developments in these fields. Scholars and educational observers some-times find themselves in the position of following institutional trends by describing emerging developments, thus formalizing them. In 1976, Maguire used the term enrollment management to describe his efforts to attract and retain students at Boston College (Maguire, 1976). One of the first times the term enrollment management formally appeared in the literature was in a 1980 *College Board Review* article by Kreutner and Godfrey that describes a matrix approach to managing enrollments developed at California State University at Long Beach. These were followed by several books and monographs including: *Strategies for Effective Enrollment Management* (Kemerer, Baldridge and Green, 1982); *Enrollment Management: An Integrated Approach* (Hossler, 1984); *Marketing and Enrollment Management in State Universities* (Muston, 1985); *Creating Effective Enrollment Management Systems* (Hossler, 1986); and *The Strategic Management of College Enrollments* (Hossler, Bean, and Associates, 1990). This formalizing process lent legitimacy to these new ways of influencing enrollments and have been at least partially responsible for the increased interest in the concept of enrollment management.

Institutions such as Boston College, Bradley University, California State University at Long Beach, Carnegie-Mellon University, and North-western University are generally credited as being among the first institu-tions to develop comprehensive enrollment management systems. Even within these there was great variation in the scope and sophistication of their systems. Among these early systems, Hossler (1990) suggested that there are certain common characteristics including:

1. . . . a continual analysis of the institution's image in the student marketplace;
2. . . . attention to the connections between recruitment and finan-cial aid policies;
3. . . . an early willingness to adopt sound marketing principles in their recruitment activities; and
4. . . . a recognition of the importance of gathering and utilizing of information to guide institutional practices and policies.

The concept and process of enrollment management continues to evolve. It appears that as enrollment management systems mature, they continue to focus on marketing and recruitment. In addition, institu-tions begin to give more attention to student retention and student outcomes (Hossler, Bean and Associates, 1990). Undoubtedly enrollment management systems will continue to change and develop in response to the needs of individual institutions.

Enrollment Management as a Concept

To better understand this concept, the metaphor of a lens is a useful way to view enrollment management. There are three lenses that can be used: the organizational lens, the student lens, and the institutional lens. Each one provides a different perspective of enrollment management systems.

The Organizational Lens

Weick (1976) suggests that educational organizations can be described as "loosely coupled." By this he means that administrative and departmental units operate with a great deal of autonomy. Such organizations have difficulty agreeing upon goals, acting consensually, or moving in common directions to achieve organizational purposes. Until the 1980s, the attempts of most colleges and universities to influence their enrollments might be described as loosely coupled. Activities of offices such as orientation, admissions, and financial aid seldom acted in a coordinated fashion and all too often act in ways which are counterproductive.

Examples of loose coupling abound in the anecdotes that can be found at most colleges and universities. At one urban campus that is perceived to be in a threatening neighborhood, the orientation committee sent a notice home about rape prevention to all new students just before they were supposed to sign their housing contracts. On another campus, the financial aid office that waited until May 15th to send their financial aid packages out because it was more efficient. In the meantime, all of the institution's competitors sent their awards out on April 1st. In both cases, the institution experienced enrollment declines.

Although many students of organizational theory in higher education have come to accept loose coupling as normative, the challenge for enrollment managers is to create more tightly coupled systems. The coupling metaphor suggests that one of the goals of enrollment managers is to create a more tightly coupled structure among the offices and administrators who are in a position to influence student enrollments. Although there are a number of organizational models for enrollment management, what may be more important than the specific model that is developed is the degree of communication and cooperation that is created. The organizational lens calls our attention to these issues.

The Student Lens

The student lens provides another perspective on the concept of enrollment management. The student lens attempts to see the college experience from the students' perspective. The student lens is a wide angle lens that views the student experience in its entirety. From the point of initial inquiry, to a student's graduation and career path, the student lens seeks to understand every aspect of the student experience.

The student lens draws primarily on four types of research on college students. It draws on research on student college choice, student persistence, student financial aid, and student outcomes. This knowledge base both provides a basis for policy decisions in areas such as marketing activities, orientation programs, and the activities of the career planning and placement office. Information learned from college student research also raises new questions about students and their experiences with the college that leads to a new round of research, creating an iterative process in which some questions are answered and new ones are raised.

The student college choice research tells enrollment managers why students select one institution over another. It enables campus administrators to determine what prospective students consider important when they select a college or university to attend. During the last decade, the quality and amount of research on student college choice has increased significantly (see for example Hossler, Braxton and Coopersmith, 1989; Litten, 1991; Paulsen, 1990). This line of research has enabled colleges and universities to both improve their marketing techniques as well as make internal changes necessary to enhance their images.

Research on the impact of student financial aid upon college enrollment decisions of students has also grown in sophistication and volume. The work of St. John (1990a, 1990b, 1992, 1993, 1994), Breneman (1994), and Wilcox (1991) among others has demonstrated how students respond to financial aid incentives and to various tuition levels. Some recent works show how institutions can make strategic decisions about both tuition costs and institutional-based financial aid to maximize income (St. John, 1994). These studies have also shifted the focus of enrollment management away from increases in student enrollments to total net tuition revenue.

Student persistence research provides information about students' experiences while they are enrolled. Research-based literature on student retention (see for example Bean 1985, 1986, 1990; Nora, 1990; Pascarella and Terenzini, 1985; Tinto, 1987) can help enrollment managers to understand how the campus enhances student-institution fit and also how fit is affected negatively. Recent financial aid and tuition pricing research has also focused on their impact upon student persistence. Although financial aid and tuition levels do not appear to influence student persistence as much as nonfinancial variables, the growing body of research on this topic suggests that financial incentives also affect student retention. In total, research on student attrition can lead to programmatic interventions to increase student persistence.

Student outcomes research provides information about student growth and maturation during their college experience. It also tracks students after they graduate, tracking the career paths and life-style of alumni. This can be useful information for marketing the institution. Outcomes information can also be used to guide curricular and co-curricular policies. For instance, if institutional outcome studies reveal that most students do not become very involved in campus activities or use the library very much, policies may be developed to increase student use and involvement. Many experts in the area of nonprofit marketing suggest that the colleges and universities must make their products more tangible (Clark and Hossler, 1990). Presenting concrete evidence about the outcomes of college attendance is one way to make colleges and universities more tangible.

The Institutional Lens

The institutional lens is the reverse image of the student lens. Rather than using research to better understand students' experiences, it is used to provide a more accurate picture of the institution. Many college administrators and faculty are unable to see their own institution accurately because they have invested too much of themselves in the campus to be able to acknowledge its shortcomings (and in some cases their own shortcomings). Thus student choice, persistence, and outcomes research can be viewed as a means to see the campus as others perceive it.

Market research may show that prospective students rate residence halls unfavorably when compared to other institutions. Market research may also reveal that currently enrolled students may give a low rating to the quality of instruction in the math department. Some may argue that on "objective criteria" these perceptions are inaccurate. Objectivity, however, is not as relevant as subjective perceptions because students will make decisions to enroll or to persist on the basis of their perceptions. Thus, viewing student research as an institutional lens can become a powerful impetus to cause change. Understanding how prospective and current students view the institution can be extremely useful information for strategic planning and goal setting.

Both the student and institutional lenses are research driven. Effective enrollment management systems are dependent upon a competent institutional research capability. Most large campuses maintain institutional research offices. Smaller campuses may not be able to afford a full-time institutional research office, but they may be able to free a faculty member from full-time teaching in order to conduct some of the necessary research.

The organizational lens, the student lens, and the institutional lens each provide a different perspective on the enrollment management concept. Enrollment management, however, is not only a series of lens, it is also a set of organization activities. It is a process designed to enable institutions to exert more influence over their enrollments.

ENROLLMENT MANAGEMENT AS A PROCESS

To develop a comprehensive enrollment management system, a diverse set of functions and activities must be formally or informally linked. Functional areas ranging from admissions, financial aid, career planning and placement and new student orientation must be linked. Equally important are activities such as student outcome assessments and retention efforts which must be used to inform policy decisions in areas like admissions, financial aid, or curriculum decisions.

Planning and Research

As a process, enrollment management begins with institutional planning. Planning begins with a discussion of the institution's mission statement. Following the institution's mission statement, most authors on strategic planning call for an objective assessment of the external and internal environment (for example see Bean, 1990; Bryson, 1988; Keller, 1984). That is, colleges and universities must carefully assess external social trends, such as reductions in state and federal student financial aid or an increasing number of adults enrolling in higher education, as well as internal strengths and weaknesses such as the need for new buildings on campus, the skills of some administrators, or the lack of an academic major that is popular among high school graduates. Following an environmental assessment, planning involves the development of goals and objectives that take into consideration both the mission of the institution, its strengths and weaknesses, as well as the external environment.

Establishing the effectiveness of enrollment management efforts is not always easy. Several case studies discussing successful efforts on public and private, and two- and four-year campuses are provided in *The Strategic Management of College Enrollments* (Hossler, Bean and Associates, 1990). In these case studies, planning that demonstrates a commitment from senior level administrators, feedback and evaluation, and the effective use of information are identified as essential elements of enrollment management efforts.

A planning process like the one outlined in this chapter cannot be undertaken without institutional research and evaluation capabilities. Information provided by institutional research guides the planning process, as well as policy decisions in areas such as admissions and student retention. Not all campuses are large enough to be able to afford a full-time institutional research office, but even small campuses should have a faculty member or an administrator who conducts institutional research projects. Knowledge gained through institutional research establishes a context for decisions in areas ranging from admissions to student activities.

Attracting Applicants and Matriculants

Information from institutional research efforts will provide needed information; however, marketing and recruitment are typically located in the admissions office. Knowledge of student characteristics helps an admissions office determine what types of potential students are most likely to be interested in coming to the campus. Marketing research can also provide insights into the type information of interest to most students and parents. Tuition levels, or the "sticker price," and targeted financial aid packages play an important role in determining whether a student will apply to an institution and matriculate (St. John, 1994). Indeed, financial aid directors have become key actors in all enrollment management efforts. The financial aid and admissions offices should coordinate financial aid awards with other "courtship" activities in order to attract the quality and number of students the institution is seeking to enroll. The admissions and financial aid offices represent the admissions management subsystem of an enrollment management system.

Influencing the Collegiate Experience

In an enrollment management system, once students arrive on campus, attention shifts to the students' collegiate experiences. The comprehensive nature of enrollment management systems mean that they are concerned with the students' experience during their entire tenure at the institution. An enrollment management system advocates that admissions officers be just as concerned about student-institution fit as they are about the number of students they recruit. Hossler and Bean (1990), for example, suggest that admissions officers be evaluated on the basis of how many matriculants persist rather than on the number of students who are recruited. An enrollment management system encourages student affairs officers to be responsible for creating a more attractive campus environment that will help to retain more students. Astin (1985) recommends that student affairs administrators strive to facilitate student involvement in all facets of the college experience. Faculty also have an impact on students during the college choice process and during the years they spend in college. Academic quality is an important determinant of where students go to college (Hossler, Braxton, and Coopersmith, 1989; Paulsen, 1990), which makes the instructional and research activities of the faculty very important to the ability of institutions to attract students. Pascarella and Terenzini (1991) provide evidence that formal and informal faculty contact has a positive influence on student satisfaction and students' perceptions of the college environment. Both administrators and faculty have roles to play in an enrollment management system.

Orientation

Orientation is the point of transition into the college experience. Orientation programs are an important part of an enrollment management system. They should help students adjust to the intellectual norms, the social norms, and the physical layout of the campus. Pascarella (1985) recommends that orientation be viewed as an opportunity for "anticipatory socialization." Orientation should create new student expectations which more closely approximate campus environment and norms. In this way, students are more likely to find meaning and satisfaction in their collegiate environment (Hossler, Bean and Associates, 1990). Tinto (1987) writes that most students leave during their freshman year. Furthermore, Bean (1985) demonstrates that students whose level of fit is improving during the freshman year are more likely to persist. Orientation can be of help to enhance student-institution fit. Pascarella (1985) reports that participation in orientation has a small, but significant indirect positive effect on student persistence.

Academic Advising

In addition to orientation, academic advising is also important for new students. For many students, their first advising session takes place during orientation. Academic advising is also an excellent place to encourage more student involvement with faculty. Several campuses have begun to take advantage of the linkages between orientation and advising to develop extended orientation/advising programs. "University 101," an orientation and advising course offered at the University of South Carolina, is an example of a linked approach. Using faculty in these extended orientation/advising programs, or in small freshman seminars, can be used to encourage student-faculty interaction.

Course Placement

The first interactions students have with their new environment revolve around academic advising, course placement, and orientation. The diversity of today's college students has resulted in wide variations in student interests, experiences, and skills. This is especially true of two-year colleges and open admission, four-year institutions where some matriculants will enter with minimal academic skills while other new students are eligible for honors programs. This has increased the importance of academic advising and course placement. An enrollment management system should include academic assessment tests to increase the likelihood of appropriate course placement. Helping students to select the courses which will challenge them, but not overwhelm them is a function of orientation and advising during the critical freshman year. Students who do not fare well academically are less likely to persist.

Student Retention

Successful integration into the campus environment should have a positive impact upon student satisfaction and persistence. Student retention research and retention programs should also be part of an enrollment management plan. Unlike functional areas like admissions or orientation, retention is usually not the direct responsibility of one office. Retention cuts across many functional areas and divisions within the institution. Nevertheless, it is precisely because of the many organizational variables which can affect student attrition, that student retention research and programming should be assigned to one administrative office. Retention activities are usually assigned to a committee which insures that retention will not receive adequate attention. As new members rotate in and out of the committee it will be difficult to develop an ongoing set of retention activities. The importance of student attrition in maintaining enrollments requires that it be assigned as the responsibility of a specific office, just as admissions or student activities are the assigned task of identifiable administrators. This will insure that data will be collected and programs will be planned, implemented, and evaluated. The retention officer should not be held personally accountable for attrition rates, the issue is too complex for one office to "control." Nevertheless, creating an administrative office to monitor student attrition and develop retention programs assures that the institution will continue to address student persistence. The retention officer is an integral element of the enrollment management system.

Learning Assistance

Learning assistance offices should also be a part of retention efforts. Many colleges continue to admit underprepared students. In order to help these students succeed academically, campuses have established learning assistance offices. These offices offer a wide range of services including: study skills workshops, reading assistance, writing labs, test-taking workshops, and tutoring in specific subject areas. Professionals in this area are also part of the enrollment management staff. The admissions office usually identifies underprepared students during the admissions process. The admissions office is in the best position to inform the learning assistance office of the particular academic needs of these students. Completing the feedback cycle, learning assistance offices should monitor the academic success of students. This places them in a unique position to provide continual feedback to the admissions office regarding student success. If few underprepared students are succeeding then the institution may not be spending its recruiting and financial aid dollars wisely, or it may not be providing adequate academic support services.

Career Planning and Placement

An important part of the college experience is preparation for a career. Career concerns have become one of the most important considerations for college students from the time they select an institution until the time they graduate. Students are very aware of the competitive nature of the job market. Institutions which are perceived as helping to place their graduates in good jobs after graduation will not only be in a better position to attract new students, but also to retain current students. Part of the job turnover model of student attrition developed by Bean (1990) posits that the practical value of a college degree—the likelihood of getting a desirable job after graduation—has a positive effect in student persistence. A successful career planning and placement office should help students in establishing linkages between their academic and vocational goals. In an enrollment management system, the career planning office should successfully help students secure desirable positions after graduation.

The Role of Other Student Affairs Functions

Career planning, learning assistance, and orientation are part of an array of student affairs found on most campuses. Depending upon whether the campus is residential or not, intramural and intercollegiate athletics, residence life, and greek affairs can greatly enhance the quality of campus life.

In addition to adding to the quality of student life, student participation in intramurals, student government, or fraternities or sororities may also enhance student development and student persistence. Astin (1985), Kuh, Schuh, Whitt and Associates (1991), and Pace (1991) assert that student involvement in co-curricular and extracurricular activities plays an important role in determining the range and quality of student outcomes, as well as influencing student persistence. The work of these researchers suggests that the goals of facilitating student development and managing student enrollments may not be in conflict, but instead mutually reinforcing goals in some areas of student life. The theory of student involvement provides a theoretical basis for strategies to facilitate student development through student involvement. Student affairs officers, through careful planning and evaluation, can develop programs which encourage student involvement in order to enhance development and increase student persistence.

This discussion of enrollment management began with planning and research and then moved to marketing and recruiting students. This was followed by an examination of the student collegiate experience. This brings the discussion to graduation. A comprehensive enrollment management plan, however, does not stop with graduation. This is where enrollment management demonstrates its cyclical nature. Student outcome studies should include regular assessments of alumni. Their experiences and attitudes can provide institutions with useful information about themselves. From an enrollment management systems perspective this brings us back to the imagery of the wide-angle lens which enables us to see and understand the entire collegiate experience.

THE FACULTY ROLE IN ENROLLMENT MANAGEMENT

Faculty play an important role and it is a mistake for any enrollment manager not to consider them. For example, the quality and reputation of faculty members is an important factor in determining where a student will go to college (Hossler, Braxton, and Coopersmith, 1990; Litten, 1991). It is difficult, however, for administrators to speak directly to issues of faculty quality. At best they are likely to be disregarded and at worst administrators will alienate themselves from the faculty and reduce their effectiveness. Faculty, however, should be aware of the impact they have upon student enrollments.

In the areas of marketing and student recruitment, the academic image of an institution and individual majors can determine where students decide to go to college. Marketing research too can be used to create an institutional lens that lets faculty see how they are viewed by prospective students. In some cases, faculty discover that the negative image that students hold of academic programs discourages students from enrolling. Information such as this can create an impetus for changes in academic programs which would be difficult for administrators to require of the faculty.

Student-faculty interaction can have a significant impact on student outcomes and student persistence. Enrollment managers should play an educative role with the faculty in this area. On many campuses the connection between enrollment and institutional health are already understood by the faculty. On these campuses acquainting faculty with research that establishes the impact of faculty upon students and the role of academic programs in college choice is likely to create a receptive audience for enrollment management activities. Many commuter institutions, as well as research universities, however, do not have a strong tradition of faculty involvement with students. At institutions where the faculty are not concerned about student enrollments, it will be more difficult to convince them to seek out more opportunities for student faculty-interaction; yet students at these institutions can also benefit from more contact with faculty.

A COMPREHENSIVE SYSTEM

Successful enrollment management systems must include an organizational structure that enhances communication and cooperation among academic departments and administrative units. For example, a new honors program must be marketed by the admissions office. A new writing test initiated by the faculty will frequently be administered by the academic advising unit which also must then recommend course placements based upon the test results. These are just two examples of the cooperation fostered by an enrollment management system. A sound organizational framework will enable colleges and universities to address both the conceptual and process elements of enrollment management.

Although many campuses appear to be adopting some type of enrollment management system, in many cases the director of admissions is simply taking on a new title while the responsibilities remain the same. Enrollment management involves more than admissions offices or even the addition of financial aid offices.

Hossler, Bean, and Associates (1990) describe four archetypal enrollment management models: the enrollment management committee, the enrollment management coordinator, the enrollment management matrix, and the enrollment management division. Each model has its own strengths and weaknesses and will be briefly described.

The Enrollment Management Committee

The enrollment management committee is often the first step in the creation of an enrollment management system. The committee may begin with a focus on marketing and admissions, student retention, or with a comprehensive view of student enrollments that includes marketing, retention, and monitoring student outcomes. Committee membership usually includes some key faculty members, mid-level administrators like admissions, financial aid, student activities, and perhaps a senior officer, such as the vice president for student affairs, or the vice president of academic affairs.

Most committees begin with unclear goals and are comprised primarily of members who have little knowledge about the complex set of factors that influence student enrollments. In addition, the membership of committees changes regularly, which makes it difficult for them to follow through on any agenda which might develop. Along with these drawbacks, most committees have no formal authority and often have no direct way to influence institutional policy making. Such a description would seem to suggest that the committee approach has little to offer, but this is not necessarily the case.

The committee can be good vehicle for educating a large group of people about enrollment-related issues. Since most members will not have a background in these areas, they start at a basic level and can learn a good deal about such issues as market segments, need versus merit aid, and student persistence. These committee members then become advocates for enrollment related issues and resources. An effective committee can help activate the campus.

The Enrollment Management Coordinator

The enrollment management coordinator is usually a mid-level administrator, often the director of admissions, and has responsibilities for coordinating and monitoring the enrollment management activities of the institution. On many campuses, the term enrollment management is used, but in reality the coordinator is the "admissions manager."

The weaknesses of this approach are that the coordinator seldom has the influence and authority to change administrative practices and procedures. Equally important, the coordinator may be separated by one or more layers of administrative bureaucracy from senior level administrators. As a result, the enrollment management agenda may not be heard by those administrators with the authority to change structures and allocate resources.

Nevertheless, the coordinator's role can be effective if the coordinator is well-respected within the organization. In addition, if the coordinator has a proven record of effectiveness, the coordinator may have needed credibility to be able to exercise leadership in the organization without formal institutional authority.

The Enrollment Management Matrix

In the matrix model, key administrators such as financial aid, career planning, and admissions, who have the most direct influence on student enrollments are brought together regularly under the direction of a senior level vice-president. It is unlikely that all of these middle managers will report directly to this senior administrator. This results in a matrix where some campus managers report to more than one supervisor. The senior level manager functions somewhat like the enrollment management coordinator, because he/she must rely more upon cooperation and persuasion and less upon the organizational hierarchy.

This model has several advantages. For one, a senior level administrator assumes direct responsibility for enrollment management programs. This insures a greater impact on organizational structure and resources and cooperation and communication among appropriate offices will increase. Finally, the head of this matrix will become enmeshed in all elements of an enrollment management system. This process is likely to educate the administrator and create a well informed advocate in senior level administrative circles.

This model also has some disadvantages. In most circumstances, the senior administrator may not have the time that enrollment related issues require. This may cause the system to become ineffective. In addition, this creates a more centralized enrollment management system which may have political reverberations that reduce the effectiveness of enrollment management activities. Finally, the time required to educate the senior level administrator may use valuable time of all of those involved.

The Enrollment Management Division

The enrollment management division is the most centralized enrollment management system. In this model, the major offices connected with enrollment management efforts are brought together under the authority of one senior level administrator. The advantages of such a system appeal to many college and university administrators. Each of the principal components of the system can be directed by one vice-president. Also, cooperation, communication, and resource allocation can be dealt with from a system-wide perspective. In addition, the vice-president speaks with formal authority on enrollment issues in all policy decisions.

The primary problem with this model is that of administrative turf and organizational politics. Rarely do other vice-presidents gladly surrender their control over offices which are part of their responsibilities. On many colleges and universities, philosophical differences make it difficult for areas like career planning or student activities to find themselves reporting to someone who carries the title of enrollment manager. Such a title doesn't sound "very developmental." Even a presidential decision does not easily change existing patterns and politics. In addition to all of the above problems, Leslie and Rhoades (1995) note that the number of administrators at colleges and universities has been increasing for several decades, while the number of faculty members has remained constant. Many faculty are concerned about the growth of administrative "empires" and would react negatively to the creation of a new vice-president. Thus, the potential benefits and liabilities of an enrollment management divisions should be weighed carefully before implementing this model.

Because of the specific needs on each campus, there is no ideal enrollment management system, whether it is directed by a vice-president or a committee. The system that emerges on each campus is usually the product of unique characteristics of each institution. An enrollment management system should adopt a view of the student experience which links new student matriculation, new student adaptation, student persistence, and student outcomes. By closely coupling an array of offices with sound planning and a research and evaluation component, institutions can exert more influence over their enrollments. Nevertheless, they cannot actually "manage" their enrollments. Factors that determine student enrollments are far too complex to really be "managed." Through thoughtful planning and the coordination of programs, however, institutions of higher education can exert more influence over their enrollments. Student affairs professionals can play an integral part of enrollment management efforts.

The Role of Student Affairs

Just as the expertise of a biologist is living organisms, or the professional expertise of a business officer is managing money, the specialized expertise of student affairs personnel should be students. The unit of analysis in student affairs work and enrollment management is students.

In classical models of student affairs organizations, all of the administrative elements of an enrollment management system (excluding curriculum decisions and teaching) fall under the student affairs umbrella. Admissions, financial aid, orientation, career planning and placement, and student activities are traditionally part of student affairs divisions. Although some offices, especially admissions and financial aid, are frequently housed outside of student affairs, there can be little doubt that student affairs professionals can play an important role in an enrollment management system. At Iowa State University and Drake University, the student affairs division is the enrollment management division. On other campuses, student affairs staff members may be responsible for student retention, or for conducting student outcomes research.

Conversely, on some campuses, student affairs divisions have included admissions, financial aid, and registration and records for many years. Oftentimes, these areas have felt unwanted. With the emergence of student development as the "raison d' etre" for most student affairs divisions, these offices sometimes felt unwanted because they did not have a developmental orientation. The enrollment management concept, however, provides an administrative framework that makes these offices an important part of a student affairs division.

Student affairs professionals on some campuses may see the marketing emphasis which accompanies the enrollment management concept as incompatible with a student development perspective. However, if we believe that student development results in increased student growth and satisfaction, then enrollment management and student development need not be in conflict. Marketing efforts grounded in sound student college choice research should help students to better understand the college or university they have chosen to attend, thus enhancing student-institution fit. Increasing student development and involvement should enhance student persistence. The enrollment management concept need not replace existing philosophies for student affairs divisions; it can, in fact, be used along with other frameworks within a comprehensive student affairs division.

CURRENT TRENDS AND ETHICAL ISSUES

There are several current trends and ethical issues in the field of enrollment management. There is growing pressure at both private and public colleges and universities to maintain or increase enrollments. However, the number of new high school graduates is not increasing rapidly and rising tuition costs and stable or declining federal and state financial aid programs make it difficult for institutions to meet their enrollment goals. The pressures on enrollment managers are intensifying. Books and magazines that provide college guidance books and ratings have multiplied dramatically. Like many other areas of American society, there is more interest in ranking all colleges and universities. Many colleges report increased enrollments after being ranked highly in a college rating guide (Shea, 1995) resulting in some colleges withholding information or reporting untruthful information to publishers of guidebooks to make themselves look better. Every campus appears to be interested in moving up in institutional rankings.

During the recruitment process, and after students matriculate, there are also opportunities for unethical practices. During the recruitment process, institutions should be careful to portray the campus accurately. Written publications should accurately describe the location of the campus, the academic offerings, and the nature of the student body. Admissions folklore is replete with stories of admissions representatives that have told prospective students that they could earn a degree in a major that the campus did not even offer, or the campus that used aerial photographs to make a campus that was 45 minutes from the ocean appear as if it was almost "on the beach." Deceptive recruitment is unfair to students and in the long run harms both the institution as well as the entire higher education system. Students and the public can lose confidence in the mission and purpose of American higher education.

A related admissions issue is the admission decision itself. As institutions have had to struggle to maintain enrollments, some institutions have been admitting more underprepared students, along with unprepared foreign students. Unless these institutions have strong academic support systems such as learning support systems, English as a second language, and advising systems in place when students arrive, it is likely that such students will fail academically. In addition, as the competition for admission to elite colleges has intensified, critics have begun to criticize the role that the admissions process plays in social stratification. These critics suggest that elite groups maintain their social and economic status by limiting access to other economic and ethnic groups.

Financial aid is another important area in enrollment management systems. Financial aid offices will sometimes use aid as a recruitment device, offering large sums of nonrenewable money to first-year students. In such cases, the student may not be told that the award in nonrenewable and the student may be unable to return to the same institution the following year because they can no longer afford the tuition costs. The code of ethics of the National Association of Student Financial Aid Administrators advises against such practices, but some institutions continue to do so.

In addition, financial aid and tuition policy issues have become an important part of institutional and public policy debates. As a result of the federal budget deficit and competition for scarce dollars at the state level, federal and state financial aid programs have not been able to keep up with the rapid increases in tuition rates at both public and private colleges and universities. As a result, both public and private colleges are raising tuition and using these funds to provide more institutional financial aid. Winston (1993) has called this the "Robin Hood Strategy." However, many enrollment managers believe that families have hit a price threshold and can no longer afford to pay large increases in tuition. These large tuition increases can result in "sticker prices" that discourage low income students from even applying or aspiring to go to college. Many educational observers fear that student access to higher education is being threatened. This current trend poses serious difficulties for enrollment managers as they attempt to enact policies that are equitable for students of all economic groups while simultaneously attempting to maximize revenues for the institutions they serve. The intersection of tuition policies and financial aid may be the most vexing issue faced by enrollment managers.

The other area rife for unethical practices is the area of student retention programs. Tinto (1987) indicates that for many students who withdraw, the decision to drop out is a positive decision that is in the student's long-term best interests. To the extent to which we use early warning systems and retention programs to try to "talk students into staying," students are not served well. Although enrollment management is a viable concept for student affairs divisions to adopt, student affairs professionals must be careful to carry out their responsibilities with integrity and be sensitive to the potential ethical conflicts.

PREPARATION AND TRAINING

Currently there are no formal preservice training programs specifically designed to prepare enrollment managers. A combination of experiences and coursework, however, would help to prepare professionals who are interested in this field. Coursework that includes the study of the American college student, nonprofit marketing, student attrition, and student development would be useful. Research methods and program evaluation skills are also valuable. In addition, work or internship experiences in admissions, financial aid, orientation, institutional research, and student retention officers would also be useful.

Leadership positions in enrollment management systems typically go to mid-level or senior level administrators. These administrators may have been the senior student affairs officer, director of admissions or financial aid, and occasionally the position is filled by a faculty member or a director of institutional research. Entry level student affairs professionals should attempt to have a range of experiences in the work areas already outlined. The enrollment management concept has gained recognition and acceptance but it continues to be difficult to find professionals with the necessary skills and background. The career opportunities in this area as well as in related entry level areas such as admissions and financial aid should continue to be strong for the foreseeable future. The demand for professionals in new student orientation and student retention is not as strong, but provides a sound background for enrollment managers.

In 1989, when the first edition of this chapter first went into print, the enrollment management concept was too new to make assertive predictions for the future of what was then a new organizational model. However, seven years have passed since then, sufficient time to assess the future of enrollment management. Competition among colleges and universities has not abated. Not all campuses use the term enrollment management as a label to describe their efforts to recruit and retain students, but the use of research and evaluation in admissions, financial aid, and retention programs is widespread and not likely to disappear. Furthermore, organizationally linking, through a matrix model or a more centralized model, such offices as admissions, financial aid, career planning, and other student affairs offices is much more common. Student enrollments account for 60–80 percent of all revenues on most campuses, thus the health and vitality of institutions of higher education is linked to their ability to attract and retain students. Enrollment management, or whatever term is used to label admissions and retention activities, is here for the foreseeable future.

Even student affairs professionals who are not attracted to the concept should be aware of it, because so many of the functional areas within a student affairs division are potentially part of an enrollment management system. In the future, student affairs professionals may find themselves in leadership roles or in support roles on many campuses. Student affairs divisions that choose to become involved with this new concept can be an important element of any enrollment management system.

REFERENCES

Astin, A. W. (1985). *Achieving educational excellence.* San Francisco: Jossey-Bass.

Bean, J. P. (1980). Dropouts and turnover: The synthesis and test of a causal model of student attrition. *Research in Higher Education, 12,* 155–182.

Bean, J. P. (1983). The application of a model of job turnover in work organizations to the student attrition process. *Review of Higher Education, 6,* 129–148.

Bean, J. P. (1985). *The comparative selection effects of socialization and selection on college student attrition.* Paper presented at the Annual Meeting of the American Association of Educational Research, Chicago.

Bean, J. P. (1986). Assessing and reducing attrition. In D. Hossler (Ed.), *New directions in higher education: managing college enrollments.* San Francisco: Jossey-Bass.

Bean, J. P. (1990). Using retention research in enrollment management. In D. Hossler, J. P. Bean (Eds.), *The strategic management of college enrollments.* San Francisco: Jossey-Bass.

Breneman, D. W. (1994). *Liberal arts colleges: Thriving, surviving, or endangered.* Washington, DC: The Brookings Institute.

Broome, E. C. (1903). *A historical and critical discussion of college admissions requirements.* New York: Macmillan.

Brubacher, J. S., & Rudy, W. (1968). *Higher education in transition: A history of American colleges and universities, 1636–1976.* New York: Harper and Row.

Bryson, J. M. (1988). *Strategic planning for public and non-profit organizations: A guide for strengthening and sustaining organizational achievement.* San Francisco: Jossey-Bass.

Clark, C. R., & Hossler, D. (1990). Marketing non-profit organizations. In D. Hossler, J. P. Bean & Associates, *The strategic management of college enrollments.* San Francisco: Jossey-Bass.

Delworth, U., & Hanson, G. (1989). *Student services: A handbook for the profession* (2nd ed.). San Francisco: Jossey-Bass.

Hossler, D. (1984). *Enrollment Management: An Integrated Approach.* New York: The College Board.

Hossler, D. (1986). *Creating effective enrollment management systems.* New York: The College Board.

Hossler, D., Bean, J. P., and Associates. (1990). *The strategic management of college enrollments.* San Francisco: Jossey-Bass.

Jackson, G. (1982). Public efficiency and private choice in higher education. *Educational Evaluation and Policy Analysis, 4*(2), 237–247.

Jencks, C., & Reisman, D. (1969). *The academic revolution.* Garden City, New York: Doubleday.

Keller, G. (1983). *Academic strategy: The management revolution in higher education.* Baltimore: Johns Hopkins University Press.

Kemerer, F. R., Baldridge, J. V., & Green, K. C. (1982). *Strategies for effective enrollment management.* Washington, DC: American Association of State Colleges and Universities.

Kreutner, L., & Godfrey, E. S. (1981, Fall/Winter). Enrollment management: A new vehicle for institutional renewal. *The College Board Review, 6–9,* 29.

Kuh, G. K., Schuh, J., Whitt, E., & Associates. (1991). *Involving colleges: Successful approaches to fostering student learning and development outside of the classroom.* San Francisco: Jossey-Bass.

Kuh, G. D. (1977). Admissions. In W. T. Packwood (Ed.), *College Student Personnel Services.* Springfield, IL: Charles C Thomas.

Leslie, L. L., & Rhoades, G. (1995). Rising administrative costs: Seeking explanations. *Journal of Higher Education, 66*(2), 187–212.

Lindsay, E. E., & Holland, O. C. (1930). *College and university administration.* New York: Macmillan.

Litten, L. H. (1991). *Ivy bound: High ability students and college choice.* New York: The College Board.

Maguire, J. (1976, Fall). To the organized go the students. *Bridge Magazine,* 6–10.

Munger, S. C., & Zucker, R. F. (1982). Discerning the basis for college counseling in the eighties. In W. Lowery and Associates, *College admissions: A handbook for the profession.* San Francisco: Jossey-Bass.

Muston, R. (1985). *Marketing and enrollment management in state universities.* Forest City, IA: The American College Testing Program.

Noel, L., Levitz, R., Saluri, D., & Associates. (1985). *Increasing Student Retention.* San Francisco: Jossey-Bass.

Nora, A. (1990). Campus-based aid programs as determinants of retention among Hispanic community college students. *Journal of Higher Education, 61*(3), 312–331.

Pace, C. R. (1991). *The undergraduates.* Los Angeles: Higher Education Research Institute, University of California at Los Angeles.

Pascarella, E. T., & Terenzini, P. T. (1991). *How college affects students.* San Francisco: Jossey-Bass.

Pascarella, E. T. (1985). *A program for research and policy development on student persistence at the institutional level.* Paper presented at the Second Annual Chicago Conference on Enrollment Management: An Integrated Strategy for Institutional Vitality, sponsored by The Midwest Region of The College Board and Loyola University of Chicago, Chicago, IL.

Pascarella, E. T., Duby, P., Miller, V., & Rasher, S. (1981). Pre-enrollment variables and academic performance as predictors of freshman year persistence, early withdrawal, and stop-out behavior in an urban, non-residential university. *Research in Higher Education, 15,* 329–49.

Pascarella, E. T., & Terenzini, P. T. (1980). Patterns of student-faculty interaction beyond the classroom. *Journal of Higher Education, 48,* 540–52.

Paulsen, M. B. (1990). College Choice: Understanding Student Enrollment Behavior, (Higher Education Report No. 6). Washington, DC: ASHE–ERIC.

Rudolph, F. (1962). *The American college and university: A history.* New York: Vintage Books.

Shaffer, R. F., & Martinson, G. (1966). *Student personnel services in higher education.* New York: Center for Applied Research in Education.

Shea, C. (September 22, 1995). Rankings that roil also gain influence. *The Chronicle of Higher Education,* pp. A53–A54.

Smerling, (1960). The registrar: Changing aspects. *College and University, 35,* 180–186.

St. John, E. P. (1990a). Price response in enrollment decisions: An analysis of the high school and beyond sophomore cohort. *Research in Higher Education, 31*(3), 161–176.

St. John, E. P. (1990b). Price response in persistence decisions: An analysis of the high school and beyond senior cohort. *Research in Higher Education, 31*(3), 161–176.

St. John, E. P. (1992). Changes in institutional pricing behavior during the 1980s: An analysis of selected case studies. *Journal of Higher Education, 63,* 165–187.

St. John, E. P. (1993). Untangling the web: Using price response measures in enroll-ment projections. *Journal of Higher Education, 64,* 676–695.

St. John, E. P. (1990b). Assessing tuition and student aid strategies: Using price-response measures to stimulate pricing alternatives. *Research in Higher Education, 35(3),* 302–334.

The Common Fund. (1992). *A chartbook of trends affecting higher education finance, 1960–1990.* Wesport, CT: The Common Fund Press.

Thelin, J. R. (1982). *Higher education and its useful past: Applied history in research and planning.* Cambridge, MA: Schenkman.

Thresher, B. A. (1966). *College admissions and the public interest.* New York: The College Entrance Examination Board.

Tinto, V. (1987). *Leaving college: rethinking the causes of student attrition.* Chicago: University of Chicago Press.

Weick, K. E. (1976). Educational organizations as loosely coupled systems. *Administrative Science Quarterly, 21*(1), 1–19.

Wilcox, L. (1991). Evaluating the impact of financial aid upon student recruitment and retention programs. In D. Hossler (Ed.), *Evaluating recruitment and retention pro-grams* (New Directions in Institutional Research, No. 70). San Francisco: Jossey-Bass.

Winston, G. C. (1993). Robin Hood in the forests of academe. In M. S. McPherson, M. O. Schapiro, M. O., & G. C. Winston, *Paying the piper: Productivity, incentives, and financing in U.S. Higher Education.* Ann Arbor, MI: University of Michigan Press.

Chapter 4

ACADEMIC ADVISING

JUDITH J. GOETZ

INTRODUCTION

Academic advising is an activity provided by colleges and universities to help their students identify and develop suitable programs of study. An institution's curriculum establishes the context for the activity, its policies and procedures set the guidelines, and various personnel coordinate the delivery systems. The nature of the activity is influenced by such factors as curricular complexity, administrative organization, institutional tradition, and financial resources. Its form may involve an intentional design of advising centers, interactive databases, and special courses. Or, it may be as simple as having faculty approve students' class schedules each semester. Most likely, the activity will have less of the intentional design and more of the idiosyncratic configuration that developed over time to be called "academic advising."

The idea of academic "guidance" began in response to the increasingly complex higher education curriculum that evolved at the end of the 19th century. Prior to this time, academic programs were highly structured, curricular choices were limited, and institutional enrollments were small. As society's need for educated people grew to meet the requirements of advancing technology, colleges and universities broadened their curricula and expanded enrollment opportunities to a wider range of students. The demands placed on higher education today to be cost-effective and efficient in educating an increasingly diverse clientele have placed the activity of academic advising in a unique position to respond again to new challenges.

This chapter addresses the following four areas relevant to the activity of academic advising: historical development, institutional configurations, issues guiding practice, and future considerations.

HISTORICAL DEVELOPMENT

Academic advising is a fairly recent institutionalized term. Early academic guidance focused on faculty interaction with students to discuss curriculum, institutional procedures, course selection, and choice of a field of study (Brubacher & Rudy, 1968; Hardee, 1962, 1970; Kramer & Gardner, 1977, 1983; McKeachie, 1978; Moore, 1967; Rudolph, 1962).

Perhaps the first recognized systems of advising existed at Johns Hopkins University and at Harvard University in the late 1800s (Brubacher & Rudy, 1968; Rudolph, 1962). The Harvard student advising program emphasized faculty helping students "to select those programs which were best suited to their needs and interests" (Brubacher & Rudy, 1968, p. 432).

The Harvard advising plan developed as an outgrowth of the broad curricular experiment of the elective system instituted by President Charles Eliot in the latter part of the 19th century (Brubacher & Rudy, 1968). By 1895, Harvard freshmen were only required to take two English courses and a modern foreign language, with the remaining courses chosen from an array of electives. According to Rudolph (1962), "((t))he creation of a system of faculty advisors at Johns Hopkins and Harvard . . . was apparently the first formal recognition that size and the elective system required some closer attention to undergraduate guidance than was possible with an increasingly professionally-oriented faculty" (p. 460).

The Harvard elective system, as well as similar curricular innovations at other institutions, was in part a reflection of the expansion of knowledge that was occurring in the latter part of the 19th century. This was especially true in the sciences and the newly developing professions, such as social work, education, and economics. According to Wiebe (1967), universities played an important role for the professions with the ". . . power to legitimize, for no new profession felt complete — or scientific — without its distinct academic curriculum" (p. 121).

The expansion of knowledge as embodied in the curriculum required specialists (Light, 1974) who became organized into departments that represented academic disciplines. These affiliations became " . . . the focus of the identity of an academic professional" (Parsons & Platt, 1973, p. 113). Differentiation into academic departments increased the complexity of programs of study and encouraged subject-matter specialization among the faculty (Brubacher & Rudy, 1968; Weaver, 1981).

As the American college and university system adapted to include expanded course offerings, more choice in programs of study, greater diversity of students, and continuing faculty specialization (Levine, 1978), and the concern for educating the "whole student" resulted in the student personnel movement, which attempted to restore the concern of the "old-time college . . . for the non-intellectual side of the student's career" (Brubacher & Rudy, 1968, p. 331). Developments in psychological measurement and new approaches to viewing human behavior and learning laid the groundwork for the task of educational planning and career development. Educational counseling became one area of interest within the broader framework of the expanding area of student personnel (Brubacher & Rudy, 1968).

In addition, concern for student/institution "fit" and the institutional impact on students prompted researchers to examine such issues as the effects of student-faculty interaction on persistence and satisfaction (Astin, 1977; Feldman & Newcomb, 1969; Jacob, 1957; Pascarella, 1980, 1985; Pascarella & Terenzini, 1991; Terenzini, Pascarella, & Lorgan, 1982; Tinto, 1982, 1987; Vreeland & Bidwell, 1966). The issue of student retention has been a key focus for those concerned with one aspect of student-institutional fit, that of academic advising (Carstensen & Silberhorn, 1979; Creamer, 1980; Crockett, 1978b, 1986; Ender, Winston, & Miller, 1982; Glennen, 1976; Habley, 1981). Achieving excellence through involvement, especially through a strong academic advising system, has been a key topic in national studies, such as that produced by the Study Group on the Conditions of Excellence in American Higher Education (1984) and the Carnegie Foundation's investigation of the undergraduate experience (Boyer, 1987).

Two professional associations have developed for educators whose primary concerns include academic advising. In 1971, the Association of Academic Affairs Administrators (ACAFAD) adopted a constitution which included strengthening the quality of higher education by focusing on the individual student and the academic environment. In 1979, the National Academic Advising Association (NACADA) was established as a new organization specifically created to address issues and concerns of practitioners in academic advising. The Association, through the Council for the Advancement of Standards for Student Services/ Development Programs (1986), has prepared standards for academic advising that address such issues as mission, administration, resources, facilities, and ethics. The Association also hosts regional and national meetings.

The American College Testing Program (ACT) has addressed issues related to academic advising by providing training sessions and developing resource materials (Crockett, 1978a, 1979, 1984), as well as by conducting national studies of academic advising (Carstensen & Silberhorn, 1979; Crockett & Levitz, 1984; Habley, 1988, 1993). These efforts have proved useful to practitioners faced with establishing new academic advising programs and enriching existing ones.

In 1981, the term "academic advising" became a descriptor for the Educational Resource Information Center (ERIC) information retrieval system. This recognition of advising as an identifiable programmatic effort brings together, under one rubric, the varied efforts of formal and informal academic planning assistance to students.

INSTITUTIONAL CONFIGURATIONS

Various organizational patterns exist to provide academic advising to students (Habley and McCauley, 1987; King, 1993). As pointed out by Ender, Winston, and Miller (1984) and Grites (1979), no one form of organization exists for all institutions because the individual institutional mission must be considered for the process to be effective.

Although no single program or set of services is appropriate for all institutions, the curriculum, the students, and the structure of procedures and policies are all fundamental to the way an institution defines its advising activity. The curriculum forms the basis for the programs of study, as well as for the array of general education and elective options available to students. The enrollment helps to shape academic programs and services as the institution responds to student enrichment and remediation needs, as well as to student preferences for courses and fields of study. Procedures and policies that govern requirements affect how smoothly students can accomplish their educational goals.

However, the curriculum, the students, and the policy issues do not function independently of one another. The way these factors interact is critical. How the institution responds to these interactions is fundamental to advising because it is through the advising activity that the interactions are unfolded to students.

Colleges and universities with more traditional students and curricula will find that different approaches to advising may be needed than at those institutions with very "career-oriented" students and programs. The multiversities that provide extended curricula may find that different services are required than would be true for those institutions that are smaller, or that have a more restricted purpose in their curricular aims. The sheer size of the enrollment can affect advising services, as can the diversity of preparation of the students. Policies at large institutions may be far more complex and numerous than those at smaller institutions, a factor that often interacts with curricular issues.

DESCRIPTIONS

Early advising programs were developed when the college president selected a core of faculty to aid in the process of providing counsel to students about their academic programs of study (Rudolph, 1962; Brubacher & Rudy, 1968). When Mueller (1961) differentiated advising from counseling, it was to describe advising as more restrictive than counseling, that " . . . the term 'faculty advising' is usually reserved specifically for aiding a student in planning his academic program" (p. 210). Hardee (1962) described faculty advising as a three-part activity of identifying institutional purpose, student purpose, and assisting the student to identify options. Levine (1978) described the purpose of advising as including those areas related to the curriculum, such as course selection, major field requirements, and the area of student performance.

Broader descriptions of academic advising are usually affected by both who does the advising and what constitutes the process. Crookston (1972) approached two relationships possible in the advising encounter: one prescriptive, based on authority, and one developmental, based on personal interaction. He viewed advising as " . . . a teaching function based on a negotiated agreement between the student and the teacher . . . " (p. 17). Borgard (1981) used ideas derived from John Dewey to discuss a philosophy of advising that rests on " . . . the principle that learning begins in experience" (p. 3). He indicated that the advisor should help students to arrange experiences and to assist them in seeing the learning process as "a constant revision through systematic inquiry" (p. 4). Such an approach encourages students to become actively engaged in the learning process, with advisors serving as " . . . the bridge between the student in his present environment and his environments to be" (p. 4).

Borgard noted that the purpose of advising should be to encourage the use of skills derived through content courses as the foundation for " . . . growth both in and out of college" (p. 4).

Winston, Grites, Miller, and Ender (1984) identified four components that characterize academic advising: a teaching-learning activity, a way to stimulate personal and intellectual growth, a support function, and a record keeping function. Crockett (1978b) associated six tasks with academic advising: (1) values clarification and goal identification; (2) understanding the institution of higher education; (3) information giving; (4) program planning that reflects the student's abilities and interests; (5) program assessment; and (6) referral to institutional resources (p. 30). Trombley (1984) found that advising tasks can be classified as technical/ informational, on the one hand, and as interpersonal/developmental on the other. More complex tasks, like helping students define educational goals, result in use of both sets of tasks. Creamer and Creamer (1994) outlined a considerably expanded definition of advising theory and practice using developmental issues that have grown in importance over the years.

Although the scope of academic advising is much broader than issues solely associated with curricular choice, the fundamental expectation is that students will decide from among alternatives the most appropriate direction to take in planning a program of study. Therefore, academic advising is intimately tied to the curriculum, which directly affects such tasks as deciding on a field of study, selecting and monitoring the proper alternatives for required and elective courses, and determining the need for remediation or acceleration in skill components of the major field. Procedures and policies that affect this decision-making process interact with the complexity of the curriculum. The support provided by the institution's academic advising activity will affect how well students can interpret the academic decision-making tasks.

PRACTICE MODELS

Various programmatic options exist as ways of accomplishing advising. Grites pointed out in 1979 that "few theoretical models of the complex process (of advising) exist; rather, descriptions of various advising delivery systems prevail in the literature" (p. 1).

The faculty model of advising exists at some institutions as the only model, and at many institutions as part of other more complex models.

Faculty provide students with an interpretation of their disciplines and an awareness of the institution's policies and procedures that govern degree requirements. Size, and possibly the emphasis on research, may make a difference in the effectiveness of the faculty model. With advising responsibilities, only part of the teaching, research, and service tasks traditionally those of college and university faculties, the institutional mission becomes important in establishing the basis for effectiveness in an all faculty advising model.

Models that incorporate faculty into a larger advising plan often have faculty advising students within the major field of study. These mixed plans may use professional advisors from academic or student affairs units to work with freshmen or special populations, such as undecided students. Colleges and schools within larger universities may have recordkeeping functions within a dean's or departmental office, or may have other personnel handle such matters.

Three studies of academic advising programs undertaken by the American College Testing Program have shown that faculty advising has remained the major pattern for over the years (Carstensen & Silberhorn, 1979; Crockett & Levitz, 1984; Habley, 1993). This decentralized approach of assigning students to faculty advisors supports the curricular influence for advising (Grites, 1979).

Some institutions organize advising around a center, an idea pioneered by community colleges (Grites, 1979; O'Banion, 1971, 1972). The advising center, a centralized approach, combines a number of personnel (faculty, professional advisors, peer advisors) to provide information to students and to assist students with their academic decision-making (Crockett & Levitz, 1984). The advising center may exist for the entire institution, for specific academic units, or for delivering services to special subgroups of students (Crockett & Levitz, 1984; Gerlach, 1983; Grites, 1984; Johnson & Sprandel, 1974; Polson & Jurich, 1979; Spencer, Peterson, & Kramer, 1982). Crockett and Levitz (1984) found that advising the undecided/undeclared major was a primary function of the advising center approach. The advising center has also become a realistic mechanism to handle the large numbers of students (Grites, 1979).

A component of some academic advising models is the formal course, providing to students an extended academic orientation. Often these courses are referred to as freshman seminars, and may be multipurpose courses taught by faculty and/or staff from academic and student affairs. Orientation courses have been used for many years as mechanisms for integrating students into the institutional environment. Higginson, Moore, and White (1981) found that students reported a significant need for academic information as they begin the college experience, a factor still of importance today. Increased emphasis has been placed on the potential for using formal courses as an aid to understanding basic issues and strategies related to advising (Beatty, Davis, & White, 1983; Gardner, 1982; Gardner et al., 1990; Gordon & Grites, 1984).

Conceptual structures that guide administrative models are important to consider. The model credited to the community college (O'Banion, 1972) emphasizes process, or sequencing of events that identify advising as a teaching-learning experience. According to Crockett (1986), advising models such as the one developed by O'Banion should acknowledge that there exists " . . . a logical and sequential set of steps to the advising process" (p. 246–247).

Basically, this early community college model relies on the use of developmental theory as an organizing tool for advising, an idea that has remained a consistent theme for advising over the past several years (Frost, 1991). The notion of "developmental academic advising," as described by Ender, Winston, and Miller (1982) offers " . . . a systematic process based on close student-advisor relationship intended to aid students in achieving educational, career, and personal goals through the utilization of the full range of institutional and community resources" (p. 19). Frequent student-advisor interaction to encourage personal development has been described as a necessary part of an advising program (Greenwood, 1984). Using a framework that addresses the needs of students at various points in their development can provide a way to help students view educational planning as part of a life process.

Both the organizational and the conceptual frameworks for an advising program need support throughout the institution to develop goals, personnel selection, and adequate funding (Frost, 1991; Greenwood, 1984; Hansen & Raney, 1993). The emphasis on coordination among various academic units and student service support areas are important to address, along with a " . . . systematic program of . . . advisement that involves students from matriculation through graduation" (Study Group on the Conditions of Excellence in American Higher Education, 1984, p. 31). These considerations can be highly political, affecting the very nature of the organization. For instance, faculty responsibility for advising students is a long-standing tradition in higher education. However, more complex institutions have turned to nonteaching personnel to assume increasing responsibility for advising. The degree to which an articulated system of advising, using both faculty and staff effectively, can be implemented is an issue that has educational and budgetary implications. Implementing campus-wide models for academic advising can be even more of a challenge because of the cooperation required across constituencies.

STAFFING

The major staffing patterns for college and university advising include faculty, professional staff advisors, and student advisors (Barman & Bansen, 1981; Crockett, 1986; Crockett & Levitz, 1984; Elliott, 1985; Grites, 1979; Habley, 1979; Hardee, 1970; Kramer & Gardner, 1977, 1983; Upcraft, 1971). Various individuals may work independently, or as teams, depending on the degree of centralization (Crockett & Levitz, 1984; Grites, 1979; O'Banion, 1972; chein, Biggers, & Reese, 1986).

Usually faculty will play the key advising role for students who have entered a major field, where the advising tasks will be carried out through the academic department or division housing the appropriate field of study. Often faculty are involved as resource persons in both general and specialized advising centers. They may also serve their academic departments as resources to students seeking information about various fields of study.

Use of professional staff advisors in conjunction with or instead of faculty has taken on increased importance over the years, in part due to the proliferation of information in large institutions, where nonteaching faculty and staff advisors are often found. Professional staff advisors whose full time responsibility is academic advising are usually part of advising centers or specialized academic or support units. These advisors frequently work with those students who have not yet declared majors, helping to identify options and to develop basic curricular plans that can provide a structure to future decisions.

Student, or "peer," advisors can be found at the academic department level as well as in general or specialized advising centers (Schein, Biggers, and Reese, 1986). These students may be graduate or undergraduate students who are integrated into the advising support system. Competency building programs and on-going opportunities to interact with professional staff are extremely important when using students as advisors (Grites, 1984).

APPLICATION OF STUDENT DEVELOPMENT THEORY

The relationship of the individual to the institution can be enriched considerably through the exchange between a student and an academic advisor. An advisor can represent a bridge for the student to the often complicated and complex world of the curriculum, academic requirements, procedures and policies, and the classroom. However, the bridge must be more than informational. It must be conceptual as well.

Research over the years has shown that interaction encourages learning, and that learning can be enriched when the intellectual stage of the individual is acknowledged as fundamental to the meaning-making activity. The idea of developmental academic advising is one that acknowledges the stages of learning, and respects the activity of how individuals come to understand the world around them.

Often the phase of educational exploration that could be identified as "indecision" brings into focus how theory applies to academic advising. When students attempt to sort through potential choices in developing a program of study, their focus may go to previous authorities (family, the media, teachers) to help them decide. Subsequently, the focus may be transferred to current authorities (roommate, advisor, professor) to explore possibilities. Eventually the horizon expands, multiple sources of information are captured, and increasing confidence in the new environment allows for a positioning of oneself into a more relative relationship to the choices available.

What is critical for advisors is the need to acknowledge how the student frames the task of educational exploration and how the student asks the questions relating to the act of deciding. Some students are able to accept "indecision" as a necessary part of learning and frame the educational exploration process accordingly. Other students consider "indecision" not as learning, but as incompetence. These students frame an entirely different educational exploration process. How academic advisors, whether professional staff or disciplinary faculty, frame their relationship to the idea of "indecision," and therefore to the students who have made meaning of "indecision" in a positive or negative way, is a complex advising idea and beyond the scope of this chapter.

ENTRY–LEVEL QUALIFICATIONS

Institutions that employ professional staff advisors in entry-level positions generally require a graduate degree, or specialized experience and training in a specific field relevant to the advising area. Graduate degrees may be in a variety of areas, from general college student development or counseling to specific academic disciplines. Sometimes a degree or coursework relevant to the advising area may be a requirement.

Usually these entry-level advising positions will require familiarity with the institution's policies and procedures as well as the general structure and philosophy of higher education. Experience working with students in a teaching, staff training, or counseling capacity is typically a criterion used as part of the qualifications preferred for entry-level positions. Strong interpersonal skills are important in all types of institutions, and excellent organizational skills are critical in complex settings.

Institutions that implement faculty models for advising incorporate academic advising into the faculty members' usual load of teaching, research, and service responsibilities. Frequently this advising responsibility rests within an academic department or division which determines the role advising plays in relation to promotion and tenure decisions. A beginning faculty member may or may not have assigned advisees, and individuals on research appointments in large institutions may confine their advising responsibilities to graduate students.

ISSUES

How well an advising program works is dependent on many factors. The capacity to respond to student needs means juggling various factors with an effort to integrate the importance of advising into the institutional culture. Responsiveness to student needs is affected by the flexibility of curricular options, the programming to meet the diversified preparation levels of entering students, the availability of information retrieval systems, and the commitment to advising as part of enrollment management concerns.

Any advising program, to be effective, should be structured using some type of organizational plan guided by a statement of purpose (Crockett & Levitz, 1984). Included in such a plan is the issue of identifying, selecting, and training an advising staff (Crockett & Levitz,

1984; Goetz & White, 1986; Gordon, 1980). Building evaluation into the advising program is also an important consideration (Polson & Cashin, 1981), and forms a key part of a reward system frequently found lacking in advising programs (Carstensen & Silberhorn, 1979). The main issue associated with the reward system concern is the degree to which the institutional decision-makers recognize and support the need for a strong advising program. Once such a commitment is made, the organizational factors associated with the development of a coordinated system must be considered, such as the degree to which the advising program will be centralized under a specific academic unit, or the extent of uniformity in the selection and training of the advising staff, or the mechanisms for budget control.

An issue that affects the structure of an advising program is the degree to which the needs of subgroups of students will be addressed through specialized advising. Considerable work has been reported in the literature to determine the best ways to identify and to structure academic advising programs for groups such as academic risk students, minority students, honors students, undecided students, reentry students, women students, and student-athletes (Clayton, 1982; Frost, 1991; Gordon, 1983; Gordon & Steele, 1992; Grites, 1982, 1984; Kerr & Colangelo, 1988; NACADA Journal, 1986; Peterson & McDonough, 1985; Polson, 1989; Smith & Baker, 1987; Titley & Titley, 1980; Ware, Steckler, & Leserman, 1985).

Although the fundamental tasks of identifying and developing an academic program of study are true for all students, special issues may exist in remediation for students with weak backgrounds, or in support for individuals returning to school after an absence who may need careful review of previously acquired college credits. Academic enrichment experiences for honors students may blend the role of faculty mentor and academic advisor. Regulations that apply for academic progress of student-athletes may necessitate specialized training for academic advisors. Continuing research on socialization factors that have an impact on the academic progress of students previously underrepresented in college add dimensions to advising programs that attempt to meet individualized needs of students. Often addressing these issues will have budgetary implications in staffing and training. In some cases, the issue of multiple advisors for a student may result in confusion as to who is performing what function for the student. In other cases, if a student feels that special needs are not being addressed, no advising assistance is sought from anyone.

High student demands on certain curricular areas have forced some institutions to consider the population of students unable to enter the fields of study they desire because of institutional or departmental limitations on enrollment (Gordon & Polson, 1985; Steele, Kennedy, & Gordon, 1993). The implications of student consumerism on curricular demand forces the issue of advising alternatives, with interaction among academic units needed to make information readily available to those students so that contingency plans can be developed and alternative program requirements met.

The way an institution constructs the activity of academic advising should reflect the needs of the students, set in the framework of the institution's mission and resources. How well the institution responds in setting forth this experience will depend on the philosophy toward student learning and the appropriation of financial and human resources. The ability of the institution to provide a multifaceted approach to helping students realize their goals means a broadly-based effort to support a range of options that will help students effectively negotiate the academic experience.

FUTURE CONSIDERATIONS

For some institutions, academic advising is not an organized, well-constructed system, but something that happens when a student wants to register for classes. Increasingly the technology is becoming available for students to bypass even a perfunctory encounter with an advisor. Regardless of an institution's complexity or technological sophistication, the opportunity to have students interact with the institution for the specific purpose of educational planning can add to the value and substance of the academic experience. Five issues seem to be at the forefront for consideration.

1. Perhaps the most far-reaching consideration is how to structure advising so that the activity is clearly defined as to purpose, programmatic options, and desired outcomes in the most efficient and cost-effective way. The degree to which academic advising differs from and is similar to other programs offered to students must be described in a cogent statement of purpose showing the relationship of the activity to the broader institutional mission. A critical part of defining the activity

is establishing assessment mechanisms that are attached to institutional goals and reward systems.

2. A timely issue facing institutions is how to use computer technology to assist in advising, both as a record keeping and data management system for staff and as an interactive and information-retrieval tool for students. With the capacity to provide more and more academic information, some serious reflection is needed about the interpretation of this information to students and staff. Many institutions are developing expert systems and information retrieval models to supplement advising programs (Aitken & Conrad, 1977; Boulet, Barbeau, & Slobodrian, 1990; Grupe & Maples, 1992; Kramer, & Mergerian, 1985; Kramer, Peterson, and Spencer, 1984; Ray, Moore, & Oliver, 1991). Academic advisors can play a critical role in helping institutions to incorporate information technology effectively.

3. With the emphasis on assessment to justify programs and services, collecting information about students prior to entrance and throughout their college years can add significantly to the institutional usefulness of an advising program. For instance, advising tools developed for students which actively engage them in their own program planning, such as feedback of information they have contributed at various points in their academic careers, strengthen the developmental nature of an advising program. In addition, such baseline information can give the institution useful measures for assessment and program planning, such as providing trend data about student academic interests and detailing skill remediation needs for course development.

4. Identifying factors associated with why students select different fields of study (Jackson, Holden, Locklin, & Marks, 1984) can contribute considerably to the advising program. Helping students to develop a perspective of the nature of the curriculum (Ford & Pugno, 1964; Hursh, Haas, & Moore, 1983) can help them to understand better the choices they make. Faculty can play a critical role as resources for this. Academic support areas such as career services also contribute their tools in the advising process by helping students to understand the relationships of educational and career planning.

5. Continuous evaluation of the academic advising program is essential to justify programs that range beyond the minimal record keeping functions of academic advising (Greenwood, 1984). Establishing mechanisms that build student feedback into the evaluation process can keep advisors current to the needs of their constituencies. Demonstrating the

usefulness of advising to the overall aims of the institution comes about through studying multiple measures of effectiveness using broadly designed program evaluation agendas.

REFERENCES

Aitken, C. E., & Conrad, C. F. (1977). Improving academic advising through computerization. *College and University, 53*(1), 115–123.

Anderson, V. (1995). Identifying special advising needs of women engineering students. *Journal of College Student Development, 36*(4), 322–329.

Astin, A. W. (1977). *Four critical years: Effects of college on beliefs, attitudes, and knowledge.* San Francisco: Jossey-Bass.

Barman, C. R., & Benson, P. A. (1981). Peer advising: A working model. *National Academic Advising Association (NACADA) Journal, 1*(20), 33–40.

Baxler Magolda, M. B. (1992). *Knowing and reasoning in college.* San Francisco: Jossey-Bass.

Borgard, J. H. (1981). Toward a pragmatic philosophy of academic advising. *National Academic Advising Association (NACADA) Journal, 1*(1), 1–7.

Boulet, M., Barbeau, L. & Slobodrian, S. (1990). Advisor system: Conception of an intervention model. *Computers in Education, 14*(1), 17–29.

Boyer, E. L. (1987). *College: The undergraduate experience.* New York: Harper & Row.

Braxton, J. M., Duster, M., & Pascarella, E. (1988). Causal modeling and path analysis: An introduction and an illustration in student attrition research. *Journal of College Student Development, 29*(3), 263–272.

Brubacher, J. S., & Rudy, R. (1968). *Higher education in transition.* New York: Harper & Row.

Carstensen, D. J., & Silberhorn, C. A. (1979). *A national survey of academic advising, final report.* Iowa City: American College Testing program.

Clayton, B. (1982). Minority advising resources: An example of consultative services. *National Academic Advising Association (NACADA) Journal, 2*(2), 30–34.

Council for the Advancement of Standards for Student Services/Developmental Programs. (1986). Standards and guidelines for academic advising. *National Academic Advising Association (NACADA) Journal, 6*(2), 63–66.

Creamer, D. G., & Creamer, E. G. (1994). Practicing developmental advising: Theoretical contexts and functional applications. *National Academic Advising Association (NACADA) Journal, 14*(2), 17–24.

Crockett, D. S. (Ed.). (1978a). *Academic advising: A resource document.* Iowa City: American College Testing Program.

Crockett, D. S. (1978b). Academic advising: A cornerstone of student retention. In L. Noel (Ed.), *New directions for student services: No. 3. Reducing the dropout rate* (pp. 29–35). San Francisco: Jossey-Bass.

Crockett, D. S. (Ed.). (1979). *Academic advising: A resource document* (1979 Supplement). Iowa City: American College Testing program.

Crockett, D. S. (1982). Academic advising delivery systems. In R. B. Winston, S. C.

Ender, & T. K. Miller (Eds.), *New directions for student services: No. 17. Developmental approaches to academic advising* (pp. 39–53). San Francisco: Jossey-Bass.

Crockett, D. S. (1984). ACT as a strategic resource in enhancing the advising process. *National Academic Advising Association (NACADA) Journal, 4*(2), 1–11.

Crockett, D. S. (1986). Academic advising. In L. Noel, R. Levitz, D. Saluri, & Associates (Eds.), *Increasing student retention.* San Francisco: Jossey-Bass.

Crockett, D. S., & Levitz, R. (1984). Current advising practices in colleges and universities. In R. B. Winston, Jr., T. K. Miller, S. C. Ender, T. J. Grites, & Associates (Eds.), *Developmental academic advising* (pp. 35–63). San Francisco: Jossey-Bass.

Crookston, B. B. (1972). A developmental view of academic advising as teaching. *Journal of College Student Personnel, 13*, 12–27.

Elliott, E. S. (1985). Academic advising with peer advisors and college freshmen. *National Academic Advising Association (NACADA) Journal, 5*(1), 1–9.

Ender, S. C., Winston, R. B., Jr., & Miller, T. K. (1982). Academic advising as student development. In R. B. Winston, Jr., S. C. Ender, & T. K. Miller, *New directions for student services: No. 17. Developmental approaches to academic advising* (pp. 3–18). San Francisco: Jossey-Bass.

Feldman, K. A., & Newcomb, T. A. (1969). *The impact of college on students.* San Francisco: Jossey-Bass.

Ford, G. W., & Pugno, L. (Eds.). (1964). *The structure of knowledge and the curriculum.* Chicago: Rand McNally.

Frost, S. H. (1991). *Academic advising for student success: A system of shared responsibility* (ASHE–ERIC Higher Education Report No. 3). Washington, DC: George Washington University School of Education and Human Development.

Gardner, J. N. et al. (1990). *Guidelines for evaluating the freshman year experience.* Columbia, SC: Center for the Study of the Freshman Year Experience (ERIC Document Reproduction Service No. ED 334 885).

Gardner, J. N. (1982). *Proceedings of the national conference on the freshman orientation course/freshman seminar concept.* Columbia, SC: University of South Carolina.

Gerlach, M. E. (1983). Academic advising centers. In P. J. Gallagher & G. D. Demos (Eds.). *Handbook of counseling in higher education* (pp. 180–189). New York: Praeger.

Glennen, R. E. (1976). Intrusive college counseling. *The School Counselor, 24*, 48–50.

Goetz, J. J., & White, R. E. (1986). A survey of graduate programs addressing the preparation of professional academic advisors. *National Academic Advising Association (NACADA) Journal, 6*(2), 43–47.

Gordon, V. N. (1980). Training academic advisers: Content and method. *Journal of College Student Personnel, 21*, 334–340.

Gordon, V. N. (1983). Meeting the career needs of undecided honors students. *Journal of College Student Personnel, 24*, 82–83.

Gordon, V. N. (1984). *The undecided college student: An academic and career advising challenge.* Springfield, IL: Charles C. Thomas.

Gordon, V. N. (1992). *Handbook of academic advising.* Westport, CT: Greenwood Press.

Gordon, V. N., & Grites, T. J. (1984). The freshman seminar course: Helping students succeed. *Journal of College Student Personnel, 25*, 315–320.

Gordon, V. N., & Polson, C. L. (1985). Students needing academic alternative advising: A national survey. *National Academic Advising Association (NACADA) Journal, 5*(2), 77–84.

Gordon, V. N., & Steele, G. E. (1992). Advising major-changers: Students in transition. *National Academic Advising Association (NACADA) Journal, 12*(1), 22–27.

Greenwood, J. (1984). Academic advising and institutional goals. In R. B. Winston, Jr., T. K. Miller, S. C. Ender, T. J. Grites, & Associates, *Developmental academic advising* (pp. 64–68). San Francisco: Jossey-Bass.

Grites, T. J. (1979). *Academic advising: Getting us through the eighties (Report No. 7).* Washington, DC: American Association for Higher Education-Educational Resource Information Center.

Grites, T. J. (1981). Being "undecided" might be the best decision they could make. *The School Counselor,* 41–45.

Grites, T. J. (1982). Advising for special populations. In R. B. Winston, Jr., S. C. Ender, & T. K. Miller (Eds.), *New directions for student services: No. 17. Developmental approaches to academic advising* (pp. 67–86). San Francisco: Jossey-Bass.

Grites, T. J. (1984). Noteworthy academic advising programs. In R. B. Winston, Jr., T. K. Miller, S. C. Ender, T. J. Grites, & Associates, *Developmental academic advising* (pp. 469–537). San Francisco: Jossey-Bass.

Grupe, F. H., & Maples, M. (1992). Preadmission student advising: A prototype computerized system. *National Academic Advising Association (NACADA) Journal, 12*(1), 42–47.

Habley, W. R. (1979). The advantages and disadvantages of using students as academic advisors. *National Association of Student Personnel Administrators (NASPA) Journal, 17,* 46–51.

Habley, W. R. (1981). Academic advisement: The critical link in student retention. *National Association of Student Personnel Administrators (NASPA) Journal, 18*(4), 45–50.

Habley, W. R. (1988). *The status and future of academic advising: problems and promise.* Iowa City: American College Testing Program.

Habley, W. R. (1993). *Fulfilling the promise?: Final report: ACT fourth national survey of academic advising.* Iowa City: American College Testing Program.

Habley, W. R., & McCauley, M. E. (1987). The relationship between institutional characteristics and the organization of advising services. *National Academic Advising Association (NACADA) Journal, 7*(1), 1987.

Hansen, G. R., & Raney, M. N. (1993). Evaluating academic advising in a multiversity setting. *National Academic Advising Association (NACADA) Journal, 13*(1), 34–42.

Hardee, M. D. (1962). Faculty advising in contemporary higher education. *Educational Record, 42,* 112–116.

Hardee, M. D. (1970). *Faculty advising in colleges and universities.* Washington, DC: American College Personnel Association.

Higginson, L. C., Moore, L. V., & White, E. R. (1981). A new role for orientation: Getting down to academics. *National Association of Student Personnel Administrators (NASPA) Journal, 19*(1), 21–28.

Hursch, B., Haas, P., & Moore, M. (1983). An interdisciplinary model to implement general education. *Journal of Higher Education, 54*(1), 42–59.

Jackson, D. N., Holden, R. R., Locklin, R. H., & Marks, E. (1984). Taxonomy of vocational interests of academic major areas. *Journal of Educational Measurement, 21*(3), 261–275.

Jacob, P. E. (1957). *Changing values in college.* New York: Harper.

Johnson, J., & Sprandel, K. (1975). Centralized academic advising at the departmental level: A model. *University College Quarterly (Michigan State University), 21*(1), 16–20.

Kerr, B. A., & Colangelo, N. (1988). The college plans of academically talented students. *Journal of Counseling and Development, 67*(1), 42–67.

King, M. C. (Ed.) (1993). *New Directions for Community Colleges: No. 82. Academic advising: Organizing and delivering services for student success.* San Francisco: Jossey-Bass.

Kramer, G. L., & Mergerian, A. (1985). Using computer technology to aid faculty advising. *National Academic Advising Association (NACADA) Journal, 5*(2), 51–61.

Kramer, G. L., Peterson, E. D., & Spencer, R. W. (1984). Using computers in academic advising. In R. B. Winston, Jr., T. K. Miller, S. C. Ender, T. J. Grites, & Associates, *Developmental academic advising* (pp. 226–249). San Francisco: Jossey-Bass.

Kramer, H. C., & Gardner, R. E. (1977). *Advising by faculty.* Washington, DC: National Education Association.

Kuh, G. D., & Andreas, R. E. (1991). It's about time: Using qualitative methods in student life studies. *Journal of College Student Development, 32*(5), 397–405.

Levine, A. (1978). *Handbook of undergraduate curriculum.* San Francisco: Jossey-Bass.

Light, D. (1974). Introduction: The structure of the academic professions. *Sociology of Education, 47,* 2–28.

Love, P. G., Kuh, G. D., MacKay, K. A., & Hardy, C. M. (1993). Side by side: Faculty and student affairs cultures. In G. D. Kuh (Ed.), *Cultural perspectives in student affairs work* (pp. 37–58). San Francisco: Jossey-Bass.

McKeachie, W. J. (1978). *Teaching tips: A guidebook for the beginning college teacher* (7th ed.). Lexington, MA: Heath.

Moore, K. M. (1976). Faculty advising: Panacea or placebo? *Journal of College Student Personnel, 17,* 371–375.

Mueller, K. H. (1961). *Student personnel work in higher education.* Boston: Houghton-Mifflin.

National Academic Advising Association (NACADA) Journal. (1986). Special issue number three: Resources for Advising student-athletes, 6(1), 1–100.

O'Banion, T. (1971). *New directions in community college student personnel programs: No. 15. Student personnel monograph series.* Washington, DC: American College Personnel Association.

O'Banion, T. (1972). An academic advising model. *Junior College Journal, 44,* 62–69.

Padilla, R. V., & Pavel, D. M. (1994). Using qualitative research to assess advising. *The Review of Higher Education, 17*(2), 143–159.

Parsons, T., & Platt, G. M. (1973). *The American university.* Cambridge, MA: Harvard University Press.

Pascarella, E. T. (1980). Student-faculty informal contact and college outcomes. *Review of Educational Research, 50*, 545–595.

Pascarella, E. (1985). College environmental influences on learning and cognitive development: A critical review and synthesis. In J. Smart (Ed.), *Higher education: Handbook of theory and research, Vol. I.* New York: Agathon.

Pascarella, E. T., & Terenzini, P. T. (1991). *How college affects students.* San Francisco: Jossey-Bass.

Peterson, L., & McDonough, E. (1985). Developmental advising of undeclared students using an integrated model of student growth. *National Academic Advising Association (NACADA) Journal, 15*(1), 61–69.

Polson, C. J. (1989). Adult learners: Characteristics, concerns, and challenges to higher education—a bibliography. *National Academic Advising Association (NACADA) Journal, 9*(2), 86–112.

Polson, C. J., & Cashin, W. E. (1981). Research priorities for academic advising: Results of a survey of NACADA membership. *National Academic Advising Association (NACADA) Journal, 1*(1), 34–43.

Polson, C. J., & Jurich, A. P. (1979). The departmental academic advising center: An alternative to faculty advising. *Journal of College Student Personnel, 20*, 249–253.

Ray, H. N., Moore, E. K., & Oliver, J. E. (1991). Evaluation of a computer-assisted advising program. *National Academic Advising Association (NACADA) Journal, 11*(2), 21–27.

Rudolph, R. (1962). *The American college and university.* New York: Random House.

Schein, H., Biggers, D., & Reese, V. (1986). The role of university residence halls in the academic advising process. *National Academic Advising (NACADA) Journal, 6*(2), 1986.

Shaffer, R. H., & Martinson, W. D. (1966). *Student personnel services in higher education.* New York: Center for Applied Research in Higher Education, Inc.

Smith, M. A., & Baker, R. W. (1987). Freshman decidedness regarding academic major and adjustment to college. *Psychological Reports, 61*(3), 847–853.

Spencer, R. W., Peterson, E. D., & Kramer, G. L. (1982). Utilizing college advising centers to facilitate and revitalize academic advising. *National Academic Advising Association (NACADA) Journal, 2*(1), 13–23.

Steele, G. E., Kennedy, G. J., & Gordon, V. N. (1993). The retention of major changers: A longitudinal study. *Journal of College Student Development, 34*, 58–112.

Study Group on the Conditions of Excellence in American Higher Education. (1984). *Involvement in learning: Realizing the potential of American higher education.* Washington, DC: National Institute of Education.

Terenzini, P. T., Pascarella, E. T., & Lorgan, W. G. (1982). An assessment of the academic and social influences on freshman year educational outcomes. *Review of Higher Education, 5*(2), 86–109.

Thomas, R. E., & Chickering, A. W. (1984). Foundations for academic advising. In R. B. Winston, Jr., T. K. Miller, S. C. Ender, T. J. Grites, & Associates, *Developmental Academic Advising* (pp. 89–117). San Francisco: Jossey-Bass.

Tinto, V. (1987). *Leaving college.* Chicago: University of Chicago Press.

Titley, R. W., & Titley, B. S. (1980). Initial choice of college major: Are only the "undecideds" undecided? *Journal of College Student Personnel, 21*(4), 293–298.

Trombley, T. B. (1984). An analysis of the complexity of academic advising tasks. *Journal of College Student Personnel, 25*(4), 234–239.

Upcraft, M. L. (1971). Undergraduate students as academic advisers. *Personnel and Guidance Journal, 49,* 827–831.

Vreeland, R. S., & Bidwell, C. E. (1966). Classifying university departments: An approach to the analysis of their effects upon undergraduates' values and attitudes. *Sociology of Education, 39*(3), 237–254.

Ware, N. C., Steckler, N. A., & Lesterman, J. (1985). Undergraduate women: Who chooses a science major? *Journal of Higher Education, 56,* 73–84.

Weaver, F. S. (1981). Academic disciplines and undergraduate liberal arts education. *Liberal Education,* Summer, 151–165.

Weideman, J. C. (1989). Undergraduate socialization: A conceptual approach. In J. C. Smart, *Higher education: Handbook of theory and research, Vol. 5* (pp. 289–322). New York: Agathon.

Winston, R. B., Jr., Grites, T. J., Miller, T. K., & Ender, S. C. (1984). Epilogue: Improving academic advising. In R. B. Winston, Jr., T. K. Miller, S. C. Ender, T. J. Grites, & Associates, *Developmental academic advising* (pp. 538–550). San Francisco: Jossey-Bass.

Wiebe, R. H. (1967). *The search for order: 1877–1920.* New York: Hill & Wang.

Chapter 5

CAREER SERVICES

Joann Kroll and Audrey L. Rentz

INTRODUCTION

Traditionally, career planning and placement areas have functioned as distinct entities supervised by different student affairs administrators and located in separate offices. The Counseling Center was responsible for career planning activities while the Placement Office was charged with the development of skills associated with the job-search process. Consequently, early writers perceived the Placement Office as business-related and the Counseling Center as clinic-oriented (McLoughlin, 1973). Placement officers were primarily concerned with maintaining relationships with employers, training students to interview effectively, and coordinating efficient on-campus recruitment programs. Career counselors focused their attention on helping students increase their self knowledge and identify occupational goals that fit particular personality traits (Roth, 1994).

Since the early 1900s, placement functions have evolved from a philosophy that stressed job-matching and an assessment of individual needs by trait-and-factor analysis to a more humanistic emphasis on counseling and in the 1980s and 1990s the application of student development theories. Career planning evolved as the popularity of developmental theories describing vocational choice and career search behavior were applied by counselors in the late 1960s and 1970s. Specific stages of the process include self-awareness exploration, occupational exploration, decision-making, preparation and securing employment.

During the late 1960s and early 1970s, many institutions of higher education implemented an organizational model within student affairs that integrated career planning and placement resources. Placement was no longer viewed as an event or a limited matching activity at the end of a student's college career. It was increasingly assumed

108

that deliberate programs of intervention in a student's career development throughout the college years would increase the likelihood that the student would arrive
at the point of placement knowing about his or her preferences, values, abilities,
opportunities; ready to make a commitment to a job search; and having the skills
to do so. (Herr, Rayman & Garis, 1993, p. 4)

Career planning's emergence as an integral part of career development
and its association with lifelong learning began to unite these two closely
related student affairs units.

A new comprehensive Career Center appears to be emerging during
the 1990s. Since the late 1980s, there has been a trend toward merging
cooperative education and internship programs, student employment,
community and service learning programs, and testing coordination
under the umbrella of career services. Thus, the new focus of the Career
Center has become one of coordination of a "centralized collection of
integrated services, functions, programs, and operations that address the
needs of its customers through all phases of career development, college
relations, and recruiting, with an emphasis on experiential learning"
(Shea, 1995, p. 30). Freeman (1994) concluded that career professionals
can best serve students by guiding them through a four-year process
model of career development with the Career Center serving as a link for
involvement and resource identification.

HISTORICAL DEVELOPMENT

Origin of Placement

The development of today's placement office was, at times, attributed
to the activities of three men, each of whom had responsibility for
recruiting, interviewing and employing new personnel in their respective work forces: George Washington, George Steinmetz, and George
Westinghouse (Boynton, 1949; Lansner, 1967). Student affairs professionals, however, generally agree that Oxford University's Committee on
Appointments, created in the 1890s, was the precursor of the modern
American Placement Office (Wrenn, 1951).

During the colonial period, dons frequently assumed responsibility
for assisting male graduates to secure ministerial positions in local churches.
This early placement practice continued until the mission of American

higher education was broadened from an elitist model to that of an egalitarian model.

One of the earliest placement offices in the United States was created and supervised by the chancellor at the University of Nebraska in 1892. Responsibility for the service was assumed by a faculty committee of the Teacher's College in 1907 until a full-time director was appointed in 1912 (Ebel, Noll, & Bauer, 1969). Another early placement office was established at Yale University in 1919 and staffed with professionals trained in vocational guidance who advised and counseled students (Teal & Herrick, 1962). As employer and student needs for services increased, employment offices or bureaus of occupation were established on many campuses. Their goal was to "aid young people in choosing an occupation, preparing themselves for it, and building up a career of efficiency and success" (Brewer, 1942, p. 61). Record keeping was a major function as lists were required of the numbers and types of degrees earned, by whom, and the numbers and types of jobs available.

Significant developments in the vocational guidance movement in the early 1900s had an impact on placement's history. Professionals incorporated into their practice concepts emerging from the vocational guidance movement gaining popularity among psychologists, sociologists and educators. The works of James Cattell, Alfred Binet and Theophile Simon, attempting to assess and predict individual abilities, brought psychological thought in closer communication with the educational process. In Parsons' *Choosing a Vocation*, (1909), the founder of the vocational guidance movement, presented the first major analysis of job-search behavior. He proposed a three part model with decision-making as the central element within the complex process of vocational choice.

> First, a clear understanding of yourself, your aptitudes, abilities, interests, ambitions, resources, limitations, and their qualities. Second, a knowledge of the requirements and conditions of success, advantages and disadvantages, compensations, opportunities, and prospects in different lines of work. Third, true reasoning on the relations of these two groups of facts. (p. 5)

Parsons' triadic model — the individual, the occupation, and the relationship between them — greatly influences the procedures used in career counseling today.

Other changes in Placement Services occurred early in this century. The World War I years were associated with dramatic changes in the evolution of placement services and programs. Manpower demands in the early 1900s and the need to improve the effectiveness of matching individuals to specific jobs provided the impetus for the development of several personnel assessment instruments. An early application of psychometric principles was the Army Alpha General Classification Test. By administering this questionnaire to draftees, the Army more effectively assigned some draftees to leadership and other training specialty programs.

This new and objective method of personnel matching was soon generalized to college and university campuses. Similar surveys were developed to assess the attributes of entering college students. Several years later, the administration of assessment instruments was required during freshman orientation and registration programs. These activities helped new students select courses, preprofessional or technical curricula and undergraduate degree programs.

During the 1920s and 1930s, the placement of graduates required minimal services on the part of many institutions. The availability of jobs following the Stock Market Crash in 1929 and during the Depression of the 1930s was lower than at any previous time in U.S. history. A dramatic reversal occurred after World War II as consumer demands and new technologies created a tremendous need for employees, especially in the manufacturing sector (Lanser, 1967). As a result, 600 employers had established college recruiting programs by the early 1950s (Korvas, 1994). Federal funding for the Vocational Rehabilitation and Educational Counseling Program and the creation of the Veteran's Administration led to a contract in 1944 involving 429 institutions of higher educations agreeing to provide job-related counseling services and programs for returning veterans (Blaska & Schmidt, 1977) re-entering the job market. As the World War II defense economy shifted its focus to the manufacturing of consumer products, the emphasis on industrialization resulted in an increased need for engineers, managers, educators and professionals. As a result, Placement Services witnessed the largest expansion phase within its history (Wrenn, 1951).

Emergence of Career Planning

Starting in the late 1960s, Placement Offices began adding career planning and counseling to their umbrella of services. Many directors of Placement Services changed the title of their functional area to Career Planning and Placement or Career Development Services, symbolizing the increasing popularity of career development (Bishop, 1966). These titles were meant to convey, to members of the campus community, students, their parents and prospective employers, the new importance assigned to career counseling and career planning activities. The significance of this new integration of career planning with placement was characterized in Robb's (1971) statement: "A superb academic program which lacks corollary strength in placement can represent institutional failure to the student who does not receive adequate assistance in working out his career plans" (p. 31). Practitioners believed their function was assisting in the overall education of students rather than to offering a single service in an area separated from the academic mission of the institution (Lorick, 1987). The allocation of resources shifted from an emphasis on campus recruitment toward the goal of dissemination of occupational information and the development of career counseling programs. These programs were designed to help students gain an understanding of self, interests, abilities, values, and needs; determine occupational or career goals; and learn strategies to obtain employment (Stephens, 1970).

During the 1960s, student activism, the Civil Rights Movement, and the Vietnam war had profound effects, not only on students, but college and university administrators as well. A new focus on actualizing one's potential as a goal of life affected basic values and attitudes towards education and the role of work. Education and work were viewed as means of facilitating individual self-expression and self-fulfillment. The decreased need for on-campus recruiting, the reduced popularity and funding of placement activities, and the economic recession forced many directors to operate on reduced budgets.

To achieve the goal of integrating education and the world of employment and to ease an individual's progress through the complex process of job choice and job seeking, interest in studying the behavior of vocational choice increased. Vocational counselors believed that with appropriate motivation, information and assistance, each individual could progress smoothly through the educational process and attain employment that would permit the expression of her or his personality, thus facilitating self-actualization. Career development emerged as the major developmental process that could guide each person through the stages of education to securing employment.

Career development was different because it focused on the decision-maker and the developmental tasks encountered throughout life. The mastery of career development tasks was achieved by completing a five stage process model: (1) self-awareness, (2) occupational exploration, (3) decision-making, (4) preparation, and (5) employment (Issacson, 1977). Assumptions associated with these stages portrayed career development as a dynamic and lifelong process. Skills developed within each stage could be applied repeatedly during a person's lifetime as the individual strives toward the goal of self-actualization. Successful career choices were seen as the fulfillment of a person's self-concept (Scott, 1983).

The first three stages of career development (self-awareness, occupational exploration, and decision-making) became known as career planning. Career planning professionals designed programs to teach skills necessary for the completion of these stages. The awareness stage requires assessing information about the self, including interests, goals, values, attitudes, and motivations. The occupational exploration stage involves learning about the characteristics associated with the multiplicity of occupations, environments and people in the work world. The decision-making stage involves learning the skills needed to examine and select from a variety of variables to achieve a satisfying solution. Workshops and structured credit courses were developed to assist students in learning and applying skills required for the assessment of individual differences, clarification of values, establishing short- and long-range goals, and gaining an understanding of the nature of the world of work.

Models of career planning were based on vocational development theories categorized by their emphasis on one of the following approaches: trait-and-factor analysis, client-centered perspective, psychoanalytic orientation, or a developmental or behavioral viewpoint. Each model assumed a somewhat different view of the individual and suggested different roles for each of the various factors involved in career choice behavior. Common to all career choice models was the continuous nature of decision-making as a behavior "extending from late childhood to at least early adulthood sometimes to mid-life" (Grites, 1981, p. 10).

Shift to Information Integration Paradigm

During the 1980s, several global and national trends began effecting career development in the United States. These trends included: workplace restructuring, changes in working conditions and cultures within our organizations, shifting demographics, rapid technological advancement, rising level of educational attainment of the American populace, an increase in the number of dual career couples or families, and an increasingly global, rather than national economy. As a result of these changes, the definitions of career and career success, and the requirements and expectations placed on those who wish to become or remain viable and productive in the 21st century have changed.

The wave of careerism that swept through higher education in the 1980s as students shifted from learning for learning's sake to equating a college diploma with a ticket to "the good life" is gone. Eight characteristics were identified that differentiate today's college students from previous generations. 1990s students (1) crave variety; (2) demand personal attention; (3) prefer concrete, specific information; (4) want to learn leading edge technology; (5) believe in traditional family goals, once their careers are on track; (6) desire unique, interesting employment; (7) feel emotionally repressed; and (8) tend to postpone commitment (Canon, 1991). Students' tendency to postpone career decisions appears caused by a fear of choosing the wrong path. As a result, "students often . . . wait until their senior year to seek help in career planning, which may [sic] mistakenly view as merely taking an interest inventory, filling out a resume, learning to conduct an interview, and meeting recruiters" (Hansen, 1993, pp. 13–14).

Several authors have advocated that new career service models be adopted (Casella, 1990; Freeman, 1994; Hansen, 1993; Murray, 1993). Hansen (1993) urged career professionals to design new models, theories, and methods of delivery to help students and adults prepare for the changes in their life roles.

> They will need to learn a new process for career planning and decisionmaking, including flexibility in planning for transitions and changes. "What do I want to be?" may be replaced by, "What kinds of life choice experiences do I want to have during my lifetime," "Which of my potentials do I want to develop and implement at what stage and with what kind of help," and "How can my contributions make a positive difference in this society." (p. 19)

Freeman (1994) urged career professionals to move from a reactive strategy offering students a quick fix at the end of their education toward a new paradigm, a four-year career development process model. Using this model, students would be helped to see the transferable essence of their academic experience; gain an increased understanding of self, others, and the world of work; develop skills in listening, assessment of other's needs, relationship-building, negotiation and other relevant areas;

conceptualize a broad range of career possibilities including entrepreneurial opportunities; engage in new experiences to broaden their horizons; participate in all types of experiential learning to acquire a real-world perspective, real-world skills, contacts with future professional colleagues, and access up-to-date technology and business practices; learn how to tap visible and hidden job markets; and take personal responsibility for their lives. Another positive dimension of adopting Freeman's (1994) approach is that career professionals could contribute directly to the instructional process and support faculty by providing students with information about the real-world relevance of knowledge gained in the classroom; identifying real-world resources and experts who can enrich classroom experiences; motivating students to higher levels of achievement; teaching team-building skills used in group projects; and providing students with ideas about how they can use classroom assignments to attain career and academic goals.

Casella (1990) used the term "Career Networking," to define the new fundamental reason for career services' existence. "Our activities rise from our serving new basic concepts that involve information management, connecting, linking, networking, communication, contacts, partnerships, cosponsorships, cooperativeness . . . indeed, such tasks are both our most important services and most effective strategies for delivering them" (p. 33). He viewed the career center as the major intersection where students/alumni, employers, and staff meet to deal with all career matters. Murray (1993) concluded "Networking is a fitting centerpiece for a new career services model, but if we want students to see us as key players, we will have to find new ways to help them network" (p. 31).

MISSION

In 1986, the Council for the Advancement of Standards, a consortium of twenty-one professional associations in higher education, attempted to standardize student affairs practice. A set of criteria was proscribed in *Guidelines for Student Services/Development Programs* for evaluating services or programs. The Council defined the primary purpose of Career Planning and Placement as aiding "students in developing, evaluating, and effectively implementing career plans" (p. 15). Specifically, the Council recommended that career planning and placement programs assist students to "(1) engage in self-assessment, (2) obtain occupational information, (3) explore the full range of employment opportunities and/or graduate study, (4) present themselves effectively as candidates, and (5) obtain optimal placement in employment or further professional preparation" (p. 15). To achieve this mission, the Council developed a list of behavioral objectives for each of the two major program emphases: (1) career counseling and (2) placement counseling and referral programs. Students involved in career counseling should be assisted in analyzing their own interests, aptitudes, abilities, previous work experience, personal traits, and desired life style to understand better the interrelationship between self-awareness and career choice. Additionally, they should be helped to obtain occupational information including exploratory experiences such as cooperative education, internships, externships, and summer and part-time employment; to make reasoned, well-informed career choices that are not based on race/sex stereotypes; and set short- and long-range goals (Council for the Advancement of Standards, 1986). Programs focusing on placement counseling and referral should be designed to assist students as they learn to

> (1) clarify objectives and establish goals; (2) explore the full range of life/work possibilities including graduate and professional preparation; (3) prepare for the job search or further professional preparation; (4) present themselves effectively as candidates for employment or further study; and (5) make the transition from education to the world of work. (p. 15)

Several authors offered an expanded view of the overall mission for career services. A truly comprehensive career guidance program in higher education should provide assistance in (1) selection of a major field of study; (2) self-assessment and self-analysis; (3) understanding the world of work; (4) decision making; (5) accessing the world of work; and (6) meeting the unique needs of various subpopulations (Herr and Cramer, (1992). Leape (1992) proposed that the mission for a career planning office in a liberal arts college or university be

> (1) to teach students how to begin to identify career preferences by thinking evaluatively about educational and work experiences; (2) to assist students in gathering information about careers and about themselves; (3) to encourage students to engage in new experiences through college activities, public service, and international experience; (4) to help students develop an understanding of career development and decision making; (5) to instruct students in researching employers and presenting themselves as applicants; (6) to teach students how to research graduate schools and fellowships and how to be competitive applicants; and (7) to facilitate and support students' transitions from college to work. (p. 108)

Freeman (1994) identified three distinct missions for the college placement center which are (1) translation—helping students establish an identity based on the transferable essence of their total life experiences, synthesize and recognize patterns of strengths, and see possibilities in new ways; (2) empowerment—helping students take effective action in approaching others and building long-term relationships; and (3) facilitation—helping students identify and approach others before the job search is initiated, and continue to approach others once the job search is underway. Each mission interacts with three strategies: (1) proactive—helping students explore the unknown by obtaining advice, building relationships, and taking the initiative in career and job search; (2) reactive—helping students express their career interests using employers' stated requirements, find job postings that are of interest to them, be responsive to employer needs in a personal way, and avoid being eliminated from consideration; and (3) interactive—helping students learn to manage the relationship between their personal needs and the needs of employers and others (Freeman, 1994). He concluded that the principal mission of the college placement center is to "help its clients develop a message, empower them to act, and facilitate effective action on their part … " (Freeman, 1994, p. 72).

TYPES OF SERVICES

Throughout its long history, Placement officials and now Career Services professionals have provided students with a variety of services to help them during the process of choosing and working toward career goals. The College Placement Council, surveying Career Services Directors for the past twenty years, found support for these services: (1) career counseling; (2) occupational and employer information library; (3) placement of graduates into positions of full-time employment; (4) on-campus interviewing; (5) placement of alumni; (6) resume referral; (7) cooperative education, internship, and other experiential programs; (8) credential services; (9) resume booklets; (10) vocational testing; (11) placement of graduates into graduate school; (12) computerized data bases; (13) career planning or employment readiness courses for credit; (14) academic counseling; (15) dropout prevention and counseling; and (16) transfer of associate-degree students to four-year institutions (College Placement Council, 1994). Data from the 1993 survey reflected increases in sponsorship of services offering placement of students in part-time and summer employment; placement of alumni; resume referral; and cooperative education, internship, or other experiential programs. Of these, cooperative education, internship, or other experiential programming experienced the greatest overall increase, up 42.3 percentage points, compared with the 1975 data (College Placement Council, 1994).

While thorough discussion of each service is beyond the scope of this chapter the following essential areas are described: (1) on-campus recruitment; (2) career days and job fairs; (3) resume referrals and computerized services; (4) credential files; (5) occupational and employer information libraries; (6) computer-assisted career guidance systems; and (7) educational programs.

On-campus Recruiting Services

On-campus recruiting has a long tradition at many colleges and universities and is perhaps the most visible program provided by Career Services, particularly for students majoring in business, engineering, science, and education. It offers students opportunities to interview with prospective employers from a wide variety of businesses, industries, nonprofit organizations, human service agencies, public schools, and government agencies.

Career centers employ many procedures for scheduling on-campus interviews. Often, employers are permitted to prescreen resumes and select candidates for half or all of their on-campus interviews. In the last several years, the traditional walk-in or "first-come, first-served" approaches and computerized bidding or lottery systems have given way to on-line scheduling systems which allow students to arrange interviews through a campus computer network. Van De Weert and Baumgartner (1992) describe an innovative approach employed at Kent State University where students, guided through voice menus, request interviews using a touch-tone telephone.

Generally 30 minutes long, the on-campus interview is designed to help the recruiter gather information about the student's career goals, academic preparation, co-curricular activities, relevant work experiences, and job-related skills. A typical on-campus interview is segmented into a three-stage process: (1) planning; (2) conducting; and (3) evaluating. During the initial stage, prior to the actual interview, the interviewer decides which information from the student's resume will be explored, which criteria will be used to evaluate the student, and which questions will be asked of the student. During the conducting stage, once the student is comfortable in the interview situation, the recruiter explains the procedure and clarifies incomplete data from the resume. One of four interviewing techniques is used to gather needed information: open-ended questions designed to encourage expansive responses, asking closed-ended questions to limit responses, using silence to allow the student the opportunity to formulate a response before sharing it, and encouraging comments to help the student feel at ease and willing to respond freely and fully. After the interview, the recruiter evaluates the candidate's responses based on the criteria selected in the planning stage.

Traditionally, on-campus recruiting has been seen as an efficient and cost effective method of bringing recruiters and student applicants together. In recent years, however, there has been considerable discussion regarding the viability of campus recruiting (Hauser, 1990; Langdon, 1990; Gingrich, 1990; Weatherall, 1990).

Proponents report various benefits of campus recruiting programs to students, employers, faculty, and the university. Gingrich (1990) argues that on-campus recruiting programs work because they provide a structured and easily identifiable link between education and industry where the student is the primary concern. For students, an opportunity to meet with college recruiters throughout their last year of study often motivates them to begin searching for employment six to nine months before graduation. Participating in the program encourages their examining career objectives, researching of organizations, writing of resumes, polishing of interviewing skills, and learning to negotiate the campus recruitment systems on their campuses. Weatherall (1990) concludes that campus recruiting has survived because it works by fostering an open process where students have access to national recruiters regardless of students' family connections or socioeconomic background. Chesler (1995), at the University of Pittsburgh, reported that graduates from the College of Arts and Sciences who accessed their first jobs through Career Services started working sooner, in jobs that paid more, and experienced less job-turnover than graduates who obtained their jobs from any other source.

In addition to providing graduates an opportunity to interview for employment, an on-campus recruitment program, "provides personalized face-to-face contacts between educators and employers . . . " (Gingrich, 1990, p. 66). Through interactions with human resource professionals and managers interviewing on campus, Career Services staff and faculty learn about the market for their graduates, emerging career opportunities, and current economic issues facing business and industry. In turn, recruiters and managers gain insight about changes in today's college students and issues facing higher education.

An established on-campus recruiting program also influences other areas of the university. "Placement statistics influence student admissions as well as companies' participation in campus research and their level of charitable giving" (Weatherall, 1989, p. 29). Frequently, a company's past success in hiring a university's graduates is used as justification for corporate gifts and grants to the institution. Prospective students and their parents often request lists of recruiters and placement statistics from admission's officials when choosing a college or university.

On-campus recruitment is not without its critics. Wilson (1990) contended that campus recruiting does not teach students how to assess their skills and interests and apply them to the world of work, and thus, it "is in direct conflict with the stated educational mission of our institutions and of our career offices" (p. 61). Hauser (1990) argued that on-campus recruiting promotes student passivity, increases dependence on Career Services, and teaches students an unrealistic lesson about the methodology of finding employment. While some students are wooed by campus recruiters, others from liberal arts disciplines not actively sought through campus recruitment, must fend for jobs on their own. Others argue that funds spent on campus recruiting programs could be used more effectively on other career education programs and services. Historically, on-campus recruitment programs have been dominated by Fortune 500 companies which routinely hired large numbers of recent graduates for entry-level positions and training programs. Always susceptible to economic ups and downs, in recent years, on-campus recruiting has decreased on many college campuses due, in part, to the recession of the early 1990s, major restructuring occurring in business and industry, and the downsizing of the military. In today's economy, in which small businesses predominate, Pritchard and Fidler (1993) cited fewer than a quarter of the recruiters travelling to campus to represent small organizations. Identifying ways to involve these small employers in campus recruitment programs has been the subject of several studies (The Small Business Committee of the Midwest College Placement Council, 1989; Gaines, 1992; Pritchard & Fidler, 1993).

Despite the discussion in recent years about the decline in on-campus recruiting and the need for alternative methods of recruiting, employer respondents to the *1994 College Relations & Recruitment Survey* continued to rate on-campus recruitment as the most effective method of attracting recent college graduates (College Placement Council, 1995). When recruiters select campuses to visit, they are influenced by a wide range of factors. In rank order of importance, these are: academic offerings, past success recruiting on campus, quality of academic programs, extent the curriculum is responsive to employers' needs, interest of graduates in the organization, graduates' willingness to relocate, helpfulness/interest/competence of Career Services staff, student work ethic, location of campus, number of minority graduates, provision for prescreening/preselection, success of alumni in their organization, accreditation of engineering or business school, faculty contacts, grade point average (GPA), quality of laboratories/research facilities, availability of internship opportunities, number of graduates, availability of co-op programs, prestige of faculty, management pressures, and potential for summer hires (College Placement Council, 1995). While Career Services professionals have little control over many of these variables, they can attract and retain recruiters by providing efficient and responsive services, training their students well for interviews, monitoring interview schedules for compliance with employer requirements, helping recruiters develop relationships with faculty and student leaders, and assisting employers with diversity recruitment efforts.

Career Days/Job Fairs

A central mission of Career Services is to facilitate student and employer contacts. Career days and job fairs enable students to gain valuable career information in an informal setting, make initial contact with employers, and in some cases, interview directly with many employers in a single location. Filer and Brainard (1992) attempt to describe the difference between the two programs. "Job fairs emphasize recruiting with some career information, whereas career days emphasize career information with some limited recruiting" (p. 65). Respondents to the *1994 College Relations & Recruitment Survey* rated career days/fairs as the second most effective strategy in attracting new college hires (College Placement Council, 1995). Bowling Green State University's Teacher Job Fair is an example of a specialized fair where education candidates and alumni interview for available or anticipated teaching openings with school systems from across the country. An example of a consortium effort is the Toledo Collegiate Employ-Net Job Fair, offered by nineteen colleges and universities in Northwestern Ohio and Southeastern Michigan to help their students find internship, part-time, summer, and full-time employment in the region. Often, Career Services offices design career days which focus on academic programs or colleges not usually served by on-campus recruitment. Involvement of alumni and parents as speakers in career information programs is recommended.

Computerized Services and Resume Referrals

The use of technology within Career Services has been developing at an accelerated pace since the mid-1980s. In 1984, fewer than 60 percent of Career Services Directors responding to the College Placement Council *Computer Usage Survey* reported using computers, while nearly 90 percent reported computer use in 1988 (Stewart, 1989). By the *1993 Career Services Survey,* 94 percent of directors used computers in their departments. The largest increase noted since the 1987 survey was in computerized student resume production, up 19.4 percentage points. Other uses of computers focusing primarily on students were career guidance/counseling (58.9 percent), candidate data bases (44.6 percent), career planning (42.1 percent), and interview sign-up systems (23.3 percent). In addition, Directors reported using computers for many clerical and administrative tasks (College Placement Council, 1994). Several authors report success in automating various operational functions such as interview sign-up scheduling, vacancy notification, and electronic registration (Miller, 1994; Roth & Jones, 1991; Van De Weert & Baumgartner, 1992).

It has become increasingly important for Career Services professionals to embrace emerging technologies and teach students how to use them as job hunting tools. Kennedy (1994) examined ten significant new developments in technology which are changing the way job seekers and recruiters access one another's employment information. Among the most promising are federal and state government data bases which permit public access to job openings via the Internet or electronic kiosks in public facilities, telephone dial-up job opportunities systems which enable employers to record job openings for applicants to access using touch-tone telephones, independent resume data base services which are offered as a benefit to members of professional associations, and on-line data banks of help-wanted advertisements available worldwide via the Internet or commercial on-line services. *JOBPLACE,* an interactive discussion group on the Internet, enables Career Services professionals to exchange ideas and share resources with colleagues around the world.

Resume referral is a popular method by which employers identify candidates for immediate openings. In this process, Career Services practitioners nominate qualified candidates by sending resumes to employers for review and consideration. Many centers employ student programmers or university computer services personnel to develop their own in-house databases designed for mainframe or personal computers. Thus support staff or students working at computer workstations are able to enter the information. At the same time, several commercial software packages became available (e.g., Resume Expert) allowing students to enter resume and candidate registration information (coded database information) into preprogrammed disks. The coded information could be uploaded into the Career Services database and a print image of the resume text captured. Once in an electronic format, candidate resumes could be sent to employers by electronic transfer, fax, computer disks, or printed for mailing. In recent years, a few Career Centers have experimented with scanning technology to capture student resumes for electronic transfer. Once loaded into an employer's computer, the text of the electronic resumes can be screened quickly using keywords or phrases.

Credential Files

More than three-fourths of Career Center Directors surveyed in 1993 still maintain credential files on individual students (College Placement Council, 1994). Credential files usually contain faculty evaluations, a student's resume, previous employer evaluations, student teaching evaluations, and completed grade transcripts. Prior to the Family Rights and Privacy Act (1975), all student records were considered confidential. Since that time, students may exercise the right to review contents of all institutional records. Students waiving these rights are unable to read letters of recommendation from faculty and employers. Generally, a Career Services staff member reviews letters and advises the student about retaining or deleting them from the credential file.

Occupational and Employer Information Libraries

A comprehensive career library is one of the essential services of a Career Services office. The collection should contain print, video, and computer resources supporting the career information needs of the students served. Types of print materials typically available include (1) career information books and pamphlets which describe trends, job duties, working conditions, educational preparation, training, methods of entering the occupation, advancement opportunities, salaries, related occupations, professional associations, and employment outlook; (2) career planning books which contain self-assessment, decision-making, and goal setting exercises; (3) educational information resources which cover admission guidelines for colleges and graduate schools, test preparation, and information on how to succeed in school; (4) job search, resume, and interview books which describe how to research and contact employers by writing resumes and cover letters or using the telephone, and how to interview and negotiate salaries; (5) business information sources such as national business directories which contain company product or service, names of key contacts, addresses and telephone numbers; (6) salary information sources which include lists of salaries for occupations, types of companies or industry and geographical location; (7) and relocation information sources which cover cost of living indexes, moving costs, and other relocation issues (Durrance, Savage, Ryan, & Mallinger, 1993). The National Career Development Association, formerly the National Vocational Guidance Association, established *Guidelines for the Preparation and Evaluation of Career Information Literature* recommending criteria for selecting materials for career libraries (NVGA, 1980). Planners should carefully examine materials for accuracy, currency, comprehensiveness, reader appeal, and usability. Three annotated bibliographies that assist staff in selecting appropriate materials for their library are the *Vocational Careers Sourcebook* (Savage & Hill, 1992), *Job Hunter's Sourcebook* (LeCompte, 1993), and *Library Services for Career Planning, Searching and Employment Opportunities* (Anderson, 1992).

Although a universal library classification system for career related material has not been developed, most staff members organize their materials by using one of the following schemes: (1) stages of the career development process (self assessment, career exploration and placement); (2) the numerical system of the *Dictionary of Occupational Titles;* and (3) the general themes of the Strong Interest Inventory. Watson's (1994) classification number scheme uses 20 broad subject categories, and two- and four-letter mnemonic symbols with accession numbers. The bibliographic database allows users to search by keyword, subject, title, or author.

Many companies and government agencies have developed videotapes describing the organization's history, products or services, career opportunities, and training programs. Increasingly, professional associations are producing videotapes which promote specific career fields. An excellent example is *Accounting: The One Degree with 360°s of Possibilities* developed by the American Institute of Certified Public Accountants (1993). Commercially-developed videotapes covering job hunting strategies, interviewing techniques, and resume and cover letter preparation are also widely available in college career libraries.

Career libraries are adding electronic media and storing business directories and college catalogs on CD–ROM. Interactive computer software is also popular. The two most widely used computer-aided career guidance systems are the Educational Testing Service's SIGI PLUS and American College Testing's Discover. In 1995, the Adams Media Corporation, a leading career publisher, released three new software packages using an interactive learning approach. Their base contains more than 1200 sample resumes and cover letters enabling users to customize their documents in minutes by pointing to and clicking on suggested phrases and sentences. With *Adams Job Interview Pro,* job hunters obtain expert advice on how to answer interview questions by watching multimedia tutorials and sample interview segments. *Adams JobBank* is a software package allowing users to access 7,500 employer profiles, listings of employment agencies and search firms, and job outlook by industry, region, or career field. In addition most states have made state-specific career information software available at reasonable prices to career center libraries. Career libraries often offer students access to databases such as the Federal Occupational and Career Information System (FOCUS) as an aid to identifying government career opportunities matching individual abilities, interests, and preferences.

Computer-Assisted Guidance Systems

In a national survey investigating the incidence and use of computer-assisted career guidance systems in four-year institutions, Helwig and

Snodgres (1990) found that 69 percent of public institutions had one or more systems while only 31 percent of private institutions had a system. SIGI PLUS and DISCOVER, two of the more popular guidance systems used on college campuses, contain interactive modules permitting users to: (1) become aware of their interests, values, and abilities through on-line assessment instruments; (2) conduct searches of occupational files based on self-information and/or important job characteristics; (3) learn about a planful decision-making process applicable to career or other life choices; and (4) gather information about vocational-technical, two-year, four-year, and graduate institutions in the United States (Harris-Bowlsbey, 1992). Clients using computer-assisted career guidance systems are more likely to seek individual career counseling and consult information resources in career libraries, thus becoming more involved in the career decision process (Garis & Bowlsbey, 1984). Niles and Garis (1990) studying the separate and combined effects of a computer-assisted guidance program with a career planning course, found that students who were in the course requiring use of SIGI PLUS obtained significantly lower scores on a measure of career indecision than students in the control group and those assigned to SIGI PLUS as a stand-alone intervention.

The National Career Development Association, National Board of Certified Counselors and the American Association for Counseling and Development developed standards calling for computer applications

> to be appropriate to the client, and prescribe that the client understand the purpose and operation of the computer application and that there be follow-up, both to correct possible problems, such as misconceptions and inappropriate uses, and to assess subsequent needs. (Howland & Palmer, 1992)

The standards also mandate evaluation of client use. To improve the orientation that clients received about SIGI PLUS, Posluszny (1992) designed a poster, handout and videotape to be utilized with first time users.

EDUCATIONAL PROGRAMS

"Career planning and placement today enhances student career development through a balance of structure (self-help, resources, programs) and personal support (counseling, workshops, classroom interventions)" (Bachhuber, 1988, p. 87). Yerian (1993) described more than 100 programming ideas collected nationally from Career Centers to illustrate the range and scope of programming activities offered. St. Cloud State University's Mock Interview Day, coordinated by students on its Career Development Council, provides an opportunity for students to practice a job interview and receive suggestions for improving interviewing skills from experienced recruiters (Ditlevson, 1995); the University of Virginia's EXTERN program enables students to shadow a professional in the student's career interest area (Mahanes, 1989); Keresztesi (1993) describes a successful community job support group program sponsored by Kellogg Community College in collaboration with outside agencies. Lake Forest College joined forces with its Office of Alumni Relations to develop a structured Mentor Program pairing juniors and seniors with alumni in the students' career interest area (Ewing, 1992); and Rea (1987) reports on the success of an assessment center which used simulations, group exercises, and various written assessments to give students feedback on their personal qualities and skills. Increasingly, Career Center staff are developing programs for special populations, such as gay, lesbian, or bisexual students (Sailer, Korschgen, & Lokken, 1994); international students (Goodman, Hartt, Pennington, & Terrell, 1988); racial and ethnic minority students (Barnard, Burney, & Hurley, 1990; McDonald, Dipeolu, Johnson, & Reardon, 1993); nontraditionally aged women students (Allen, 1995); disabled students (McCann, 1993; McCarty, 1990); and dual career couples (Preissler, 1989).

McBride & Muffo (1994, 1991) stressed the importance of using needs assessment in program planning to help practitioners identify students' perceptions of their programming needs and to examine current service delivery methods. Schmitz (1990) concluded that a properly focused and implemented needs assessment "can add structure and reason to the creation and adjustment of programs to meet recognized needs . . . [and] can provide accountability to administrators as well as justification for new and revised services" (p. 51). Schmitz (1990) described how the Arts & Sciences Career Planning and Placement Center at Indiana University developed a formalized needs assessment which provided accountability and justification to administrators for new and revised services. Others have found focus group interviews, a tool used in marketing research, especially useful for determining student needs and expectations (Hartman & Arora, 1988).

Virtually every Career Center offers placement-related workshops to teach students job search strategies, resume and cover letter writing, and interviewing techniques. Frequently, alumni and employers are invited to campus to present information about trends in the employment market, career options, and career transition and management issues. Specialized workshops are often tailored to the student group, by academic major, college, or degree level. An example of a targeted program is Bowling Green State University's Career Services Seminar, "Finding a Job in Academia," which acquaints doctoral and master's degree level students with the search process for faculty and administrative positions.

Nationally, it is estimated that 77 percent of college freshmen and sophomores are in the process of deciding on an academic major (Rayman, 1993). Career exploration programs directed primarily at these audiences are common. Multiple-session, structured career decision-making groups are also offered which introduce basic concepts of the career planning process; help students assess their occupational interests, values, aptitudes, skills, personality and work/lifestyle preferences; identify and explore college majors; orient them to career information resources; and instruct them in decision-making skills. Often, informal career counseling groups are used to discuss these same topics.

Career and life planning courses for credit were offered by 62 percent of the 100 Career centers surveyed to assist undecided students in selecting a major or career path (Korschgen, 1994). Areas typically addressed are: "Self-exploration exercises, assessment, supporting career counseling, educational and career information, review of career development theory . . . and career choice issues for special populations. . . ." (Herr, Rayman, & Garis, 1993, p. 184).

APPLICATION OF STUDENT DEVELOPMENT THEORY

The work of Career Services professionals, when practiced well, is influenced extensively by developmental theory. Forney (1991) indicated that knowledge of student development theory helps career development professionals "gain insights related to matching interventions to developmental issues for different groups" (p. 30). Yet many Career Services practitioners lack a background in college student personnel or counseling to draw upon in planning and delivering services. Career practitioners are typically so busy responding to the multiple demands of daily activity that little time is spent keeping current on theory and research in the field. Often the only basis for deciding what career development programs are needed is staff intuition or experience. Given the diverse populations served by these professionals, a deliberate and systematic approach is not only appropriate, but also a prerequisite for effective practice.

Since the late 1960s, numerous formal theories of student development have been advanced. Rodgers (1989), in a brief review of student development literature, cited at least 16 major theories. These can be clustered into four families: psychosocial, cognitive-development, typology, and person-environment theories.

Among the basic principles that can be derived from developmental theories which help professionals facilitate development in students are: (1) Human development is both continuous and cumulative in nature; (2) Development is a matter of movement from the simpler to the more complex; and (3) Human development tends to be orderly and stage related (Miller, Winston, & Mendenhall, 1983, pp. 13–14). In addition, these four principles common to developmental theories describing student growth were cited by Pascarella & Terenzini: (1) cognitive readiness is a necessary, but not sufficient, condition for development; (2) recognition of complexity precedes higher-level developmental change; (3) developmental movement originates in a challenge to the current state of development; and (4) the capacity for detachment from self and for empathy controls access to higher developmental tasks (pp. 45–46).

Many authors have attempted to demonstrate the application of formal theory to a given practice situation through the use of translation or process models (Blocher, 1987). An example is presented here to demonstrate a process model which provides a conceptual approach to theory application.

Sampson, Peterson, Lenz & Reardon (1992) described a process model utilizing a cognitive approach to deliver career services at Florida State University. This approach included a pyramid of information processing domains and a cycle of generic career-solving and decision-making skills referred to as the CASVE (Communication, Analysis, Synthesis, Valuing and Execution) Cycle. The important domains of cognition involved in career choice included

> self-knowledge (such as knowing one's own values, interests, and skills), occupational knowledge (knowledge of individual occupations and knowledge of a schema for organizing occupations, such as the Holland hexagon [Holland, 1985] or the World-of-Work Map [Prediger, 1976, 1981]), decision-making skills (understanding and mastering the decision-making process), and metacognitions (self-talk, self-awareness, and the monitoring and control of cognitions). (p. 67)

In the processes involved in the CASVE Cycle, students learn to understand external demands and internal stages that signal the need for problem solving; obtain and clarify knowledge about self, occupation, decision making, or metacognitions; generate alternatives; assign priority to various alternatives; and formulate a plan to implement a tentative choice which includes reality testing and employment seeking (Sampson, Peterson, Lenz & Reardon, 1992). An array of materials have been developed for counselor and student use in individual counseling, career courses and workshops to help clients better understand these components of career choice and processes of career decision making.

ADMINISTRATIVE AND ORGANIZATIONAL MODELS

Reporting Structure

Since the 1950s, administrative reporting relationships involving Career Services offices have changed significantly. In the late 1960s, 30 percent of Career Planning and Placement Directors reported directly to the president of their institution, 30 percent to the Dean of Students, and 27 percent to the Chief Academic Officer (Herrick, 1976). By 1981, most directors reported to the Chief Student Affairs Officer (Weber, 1981). This trend continues as the American College Personnel Association's *Career Center Directors' National Data Bank* revealed that 79 percent of respondents from public institutions reported to the Chief Student Affairs Officer or an immediate subordinate (Gast, 1991). Similar findings were reported in the *1993 Career Services Survey* (College Placement Council, 1994) with 74.1 percent of career services offices organizationally positioned within student services/student affairs. Advantages of this reporting structure include stronger communication, and thus an increased likelihood of referral between Career Services and other related student services areas; the ability of Career Services to compete successfully with other student services units for resources; support from the vice president for the service nature and for a student development point of view; and support for the costly career counseling and programming activities which are critical to a comprehensive approach to service delivery (Herr, Rayman, & Garis, 1993).

While today most Career Services offices are part of student affairs, on some campuses the reporting path may be to academic affairs, university relations, enrollment management, or directly to the president. The *CAS Standards and Guidelines for Career Planning and Placement* recommended that "career planning and placement should be organized as part of or closely related to the academic structure to increase faculty/staff awareness of the career development process and the current employment trends" (Council for the Advancement of Standards, 1986, p. 16). According to the *1993 Career Services Survey,* only 12 percent of directors reported directly through an academic channel. Where career services are decentralized, the most common reporting line is to an academic dean. In a centralized service, the reporting path typically leads to a vice president, vice provost, or vice chancellor. Being allied with academic affairs often enhances the quality of communication between career services and faculty, leads to greater credibility with and stronger support from faculty, and helps career services maintain its resource base (Herr, Rayman, & Garis, 1993).

Typically, the decision of where to locate career services was based on the historical development or unique character of the individual institution. Regardless of which reporting line is selected, the following guidelines are useful: (1) Faculty support, acceptance, and understanding of, and respect for, the career center and staff are essential; (2) Career Services professionals need to work collaboratively with student affairs professionals and with other staff who understand and value a student development approach; (3) Support for a comprehensive operation must come from the highest level of administration; (4) The Career Center should be funded in accordance with expectations of outcomes; (5) It is critical that there be a philosophical understanding between the comprehensive Career Center, and the Academic Counseling and Student Development Centers (Shea, 1995).

Organizational Models

The advantages and disadvantages of various organizational models for career services have been the subject of numerous publications (Babbush, Hawley, & Zeran, 1986; Boynton, 1949; Casella, 1990; Chervenik, Nord, & Aldridge, 1982; Herr, Rayman, & Garis, 1993; Herrick, 1976; Lentz, 1984; Robb, 1979; Shea, 1995; Shingleton, 1978; Swaim, 1968; Wrenn, 1951). To determine the appropriate structure, organizational planners must analyze the institution's physical layout, its academic offerings, a demographic profile of the student body, and the types of employment solicited by recruiters visiting the campus (Babbush, Hawley, & Zeran, 1986). The three organizational models implemented most frequently are (1) a centralized program for the entire institution, (2) a decentralized program within colleges or schools within the institution, and (3) a combination program using centralized and decentralized approaches within a single institution (Herr, Raymond, & Garis, 1993).

Results of the *1993 Career Services Survey* continue to support the trend toward centralized and away from decentralized services. Of 1,068 directors, 87.4 percent indicate that coordination of services, programs, operations, budgets, staff, and records was physically and administratively centralized on their campus. Decentralized models were used by only 11.5 percent of the directors surveyed. The remaining 1.1 percent of respondents described themselves as having satellite offices (College Placement Council, 1994).

Frequently cited advantages of the centralized model include more efficient use of staff, office space, and equipment; lower administrative overhead; convenience for students and employers; greater emphasis on career planning; and better coordination of student employment, volunteer programs, internships, and co-op programs. A centralized service can offer students one-stop shopping for all career needs. "Student employment, co-ops, and internship programs attract students to the center in the earlier stages of their academic careers, to their obvious benefit" (Shea, 1995, p. 31). Career counselors in a centralized model are more likely to have continuous exposure to employers and can lend their counseling expertise to employment realities.

> When career counseling is combined with the placement function, it is more likely to be perceived by students and faculty as an integral part of the educational mission of the institution rather than a remedial one, as is often the case when career counseling is combined with psychological counseling. (Herr, Raymond & Garis, 1993, p. 58)

Employers prefer a centralized service because it helps them through the *academic maze* and facilitates their interests in full college relations—recruiting through co-ops, internships, and academic contacts (Shea, 1995). They can interview all majors at one location on campus reducing recruitment costs and expediting the process. Certain disadvantages of the model also have been noted: staff members experience a tendency to become isolated from academic departments, faculty, and students and students may view a centralized office as too impersonal and there is a greater likelihood that students from academic disciplines not typically sought through campus recruiting could get lost in the crowd.

Advocates of the decentralized model base their opinion on the value derived by each specialty area on campus having their own career services and staff readily accessible. Negative outcomes are usually related to duplication of efforts, facilities, and staff; increased recruiting costs; and the fact that compartmentalization tends to deter students from pursuing a broad-based exploration of choices across academic disciplines.

HUMAN RESOURCES

The profile of the Career Services Director has changed since 1975 when the typical director was a white male in his mid-forties (Crouch & Tolle, 1982; Herrick, 1976). The *1993 Career Services Survey* revealed that women held 57.8 percent of office directorships (College Placement Council, 1994). More than half of the directors were between 35 and 49 years of age and the vast majority (89.1 percent) were Caucasian. Slightly more than 85 percent possessed at least a master's degree and 13.3 percent possessed a doctorate. The most frequently reported degrees were in guidance and counseling (27.9 percent), followed by education (21.3 percent). Only 12.9 percent named student personnel, a 1 percent increase since 1981. The directors have 11 years of experience in the field and 6.4 years in their current positions. Nearly half (46.7 percent) had an average of 6.9 years of prior work experience in college relations and recruitment field.

The director's role has become increasingly complex as demands for service from various constituent groups have expanded. Casella (1990) suggested that the director needs to be a flexible generalist who can "coordinate and mobilize the efforts of dozens of partners seeking similar service goals—academic departments, external agencies, student clubs, campus unions, local businesses, other student affairs departments, government offices, plus others" (p. 36). As Career Centers, especially on large campuses, have become increasingly sophisticated in the use of computer technology, directors face complex decisions about which database management systems, hardware, local area networks, and software to purchase. To supplement shrinking budgets, many directors solicit donations from corporations and foundations, and funding from other outside agencies. The scope of management responsibilities continues to expand as career planning, student employment, cooperative education and experiential education programs have been merged into the comprehensive Career Center. Herr, Raymond, and Garis (1993) recommended that

> in addition to having excellent management and organizational skills, it is necessary for a director to have a strong background in career and counseling psychology in order to provide the necessary leadership and supervision to assure that the core of the career center is solidly based in counseling theory and technique. (p. 103)

Other staff members in career services are usually categorized by functional area. An associate or assistant director and placement advisors have primary responsibilities to manage placement-related services including on-campus recruitment, referrals, workshops, seminars, career days and job fairs, placement advising, and to serve as liaisons with assigned faculty or departments. Job developers and co-op/internship coordinators advise students on experiential education opportunities, develop new sites, and maintain relationships with faculty and employers. Associate or assistant directors and career counselors often conduct individual and group counseling sessions, administer and interpret vocational assessments, teach career and life planning courses for credit, supervise graduate interns and instructors, and deliver a wide range of career decision-making programs. Increasingly, Career Services offices are hiring information specialists/systems analysts to design customized programs, evaluate commercially available software, and integrate information systems as well as train staff members and users of the services in new applications and emerging technologies.

Skills used by staff include project management, marketing, counseling, public speaking, writing, program evaluation, research, teaching, and information management. Several authors, including Parker (1994), and Wilson, and Greenberg (1990), stressed the importance of a planned program for professional development to update staff skills and understanding of student needs, promote continuous learning, and foster professional renewal.

The *1993 Career Services Survey* data revealed that 46 percent of professional staff members, other than the director, were between 35 and 49 years old, and 31 percent were between 25 and 34 years old (College Placement Council, 1994). Three-fourths were female and 82 percent were Caucasian. Clearly, improving the ethnic diversity, gender balance, and diversity of academic backgrounds of career services professionals needs to be addressed by the profession. Freeman (1994) suggested that staff members should be as multidisciplinary as the campus they serve. Individuals from science disciplines should be especially sought to enrich the mix of professionals with counseling, student affairs, education, and business backgrounds. As enrollment projections indicate that the largest new student markets for universities are ethnic minorities and older, returning adults, it is desirable for staff composition to reflect this diversity.

McKenzie and Monoogian-O'Dell (1988) reported the use of paraprofessionals in Career Centers as common in approximately 50 percent of private four-year institutions and 20 percent of institutions with graduate-level programs. The increased use of student paraprofessionals is in direct response to cuts in staff and budget (Klein & Step, 1992). Paraprofessionals complete a wide variety of assignments including outreach, public relations, career-fair work, resume and cover letter critiques, survey and research activities, and serve as library guides and recruiter hosts.

Entry-Level Qualifications for Employment

The minimum educational requirement for an entry-level Career Services position is usually a master's degree in guidance and counseling, clinical or counseling psychology, student affairs, education, or related discipline. Prior experience in career counseling and placement advising, teaching, and/or educational administration is preferred. New professionals responsible for career counseling, vocational assessment, and teaching career decision-making courses, are advised to obtain counselor certification and licensure. Knowledge of occupational and employment trends, career information resources and systems, program design and evaluation, and process consultation are also helpful.

PROFESSIONAL ASSOCIATIONS

The first professional association devoted to placement in the United States was established in 1924 as the National Association of Appointment Secretaries, an application of the British concept of appointment secretary to the American function of Placement Director (Herr, Rayman, & Garis, 1993). In 1940, President Gates of the University of Pennsylvania and chair of the Committee on Educational Cooperation of the Governor's Job Mobilization Program established the Pennsylvania Association of School and College Placement (Sinnott, Beebe, & Collins, 1990). Within a year, the state's name was dropped and the journal *School and College Placement* was published. In 1952, it became the *Journal of College Placement* and today is the *Journal of Career Planning and Employment.* The earlier national College Placement Council in 1995 became the National Association of Colleges and Employers (NACE). A report entitled the *New Organizational Structure for the Profession* (NACE, Special Report from the Presidents, April, 1994) outlined the principle roles and responsibilities for the national organization, whose primary role was to advocate for the profession and provide a national and international voice. Strategies which could be used include:

> establishing a process to ensure timely two-way communication between the national organization and the membership as it pertains to the media; training regional representatives in public relations techniques; identifying key issues annually for development in the media; producing publications, . . . identifying national and major regional media targets for new releases about the profession. (NACE, Special Report: From of the Presidents, April 1994, p. 2)

In collaboration with a network of seven regional associations, NACE seeks to provide national conferences, institutes, workshops, and seminars to the membership; symposia for special interest and network groups; a statement of ethical and professional conduct; national standards for career services offices and professionals; and promotion of the profession as a career (Special Report: From the Presidents, April, 1994).

The creation of regional associations can be traced through the expansion of placement services throughout the United States and by efforts of professionals to improve the coordination of placement activities and planning. In 1926, five charter members of the Eastern College Placement Officers (ECPO) sought to facilitate "professional improvements for the members through an interchange of information on common problems" (Powell & Kirts, 1980; Stephens, 1970). The other regional associations and their dates of establishment are: the Rocky Mountain and Southern College Placement Associations in 1946, the Middle Atlantic Placement Association in 1948, and the Southeast and the Midwest College Placement Associations in 1950. The last regional association to be formed was the Western College Placement Association, chartered in 1951. Reflecting the name change of the national association, most of the regional associations began modifying their names in 1995 to include Association of Colleges and Employers in the titles. Today, the principle role of the regional associations is to provide professional development services to their members, which enables them to: access high quality workshops and seminars, attend regional conferences, obtain leadership training for association volunteers, and participate in regional networking events (NACE, Special Report: From the Presidents, April, 1994).

Responding to the need for expanded member services, NACE launched JobWeb, a homepage on the World Wide Web. Through JobWeb, members can access employer information and literature, search bibliographic data bases, consult a calendar of professional events, participate in discussion groups, read professional journals, and order materials on-line (Allen, 1995). As JobWeb expands, it will also connect members to other home page sites on the Internet, enable them to place or read current job listings, tap into a virtual library of career information and job search resources, and access video conferencing, multi-media conferencing, and interactive training modules. Regional organizations are also developing home page sites.

CHALLENGES FACING PROFESSIONALS

The work of Career Services professionals has become increasingly complex. Much has been written about the current and future challenges facing career services (for in-depth discussion see Bechtel, 1993; Heppner & Johnston, 1994; Herr, Rayman & Garis, 1993; Rayman, 1993; Stewart, 1993; and Yerian, 1993). Among the most pressing issues are: (1) meeting the career development needs of diverse groups of students in a time of diminishing resources; (2) responding to increasing demands from alumni for counseling services for midlife career and job changes; (3) integrating new service imperatives such as student employment, internships, cooperative education, and other forms of experiential education in the design of a comprehensive career services delivery model; (4) employing emerging technologies to achieve greater efficiency and effectiveness in operations, by creating new learning systems and computerized assessment instruments, communicating the availability of job opportunities to graduates, and nominating candidates to employers; (5) developing new methods to evaluate services and measure their impact; (6) communicating more effectively the role of Career Services within the overall mission of the college or university; and (7) developing cooperative efforts with other internal and external groups (i.e., faculty, academic advisors, other functional areas within student affairs and employers).

REFERENCES

Allen, A.Z. (1995). Study of women over 40 studying again. *Journal of Career Planning and Employment, 55*(2), 58–60.

Allen, C. (1995). JobWeb: Welcome to our virtual office. *Journal of Career Planning and Employment, 55*(3), 6–8, 58.

American Institute of Certified Public Accountants (1993). *Accounting: The one degree with 360°s of possibilities.* [Video tape]. New York: Author.

Anderson, B. (Ed.). (1992). *Library services for career planning, job searching, and employment opportunities.* New York: Haworth Press.

Babbush, H.E., Hawley, W.W., & Zeran, J. (1986). The best of both worlds. *Journal of Career Planning and Employment, 46*(3), 48–53.

Bachhuber, T. (1988). Translating career information to student intelligence. *Journal of Career Planning and Employment, 49*(1), 82–88.

Barnard, C., Burney, D.A., & Hurley, J. (1990). Involving minority students in career services. *Journal of Career Planning and Employment, 50*(3), 43–47.

Bechtel, D.S. (1993). The organization and impact of career programs and services within higher education. In J.R. Rayman (Ed.), *The changing role of career services* (pp. 23–36). San Francisco: Jossey-Bass.

Bishop, J.F. (1966). Portents in college placement. In G.J. Klopf (Ed.), *College student personnel work in years ahead.* Student personnel monograph series, no. 7. Washington, DC: American Personnel and Guidance Association.

Blaska, B., & Schmidt, M.R. (1977). Placement. In W.T. Packwood (Ed.), *College student personnel services* (pp. 368–421). Springfield, IL: Charles C Thomas.

Blocher, D.H. (1987). On the uses and misuses of the term theory. *Journal of Counseling and Development, 66,* 67–68.

Boynton, P.W. (1949). *Selecting the new employee.* New York: Harper.

Brewer, J. (1942). *History of vocational guidance.* (p. 61). New York: Harper.

Cannon, D. (1991). Generation X: The way they do the things they do. *Journal of Career Planning and Employment, 51*(2), 34–38.

Casella, D.A. (1990). Career networking: The newest career center paradigm. *Journal of Career Planning and Employment, 50*(3), 33–39.

Chervenik, E., Nord, D., & Aldridge, M. (1982). Putting career planning and placement together. *Journal of College Placement, 42,* 48–51.

Chesler, H.A. (1995). Proof of worth: Career services help leads to better jobs faster. *Journal of Career Planning and Employment, 55*(2), 47–50.

College Placement Council (1994). *1993 Career services survey.* Bethlehem, PA.

College Placement Council (1995). 1994 College relations & recruitment survey. *Journal of Career Planning and Employment, 55*(3), 37–48.

College Placement Council (1984). Computer usage survey. Bethlehem, PA.

Council for the Advancement of Standards for Student Services/Development Programs.

(1986). *CAS standards and guidelines for student services/development programs.* Iowa City, IA: American College Testing Program.

Crites, J.O. (1981). *Career counseling models, methods, and materials.* New York: McGraw-Hill.

Crouch, L.R., & Tolle, D.J. (1982). The placement director of the '80's: A profile. *Journal of College Placement, 42,* 43–46.

Ditlevson, A.P. (1995). Real applause for an expanded 'mock interview day'. *Journal of Career Planning and Employment, 55*(2), 54–57.

Durrance, J.C., Savage, K.M., Ryan, M.J., & Mallinger, S.M. (1993). *Job seekers and career changers: A planning manual for public libraries.* Chicago: American Library Association.

Ebel, R.L., Noll, V.H., & Bauer, R. (1969). Encyclopedia of educational research. London: Macmillan.

Ewing, N.T. (1992). A mentoring match. Lake Forest alumni and students. *Journal of Career Planning and Employment, 52*(3), 22–24.

Filer, B., & Brainard, T. (1992). Step-by-step planning for a successful fair. *Journal of Career Planning and Employment, 52*(2), 65–68.

Forney, D.S. (1991). How career centers can maintain and gain momentum through the decade. *Journal of Career Planning and Employment, 51*(4), 28–31, 41–44.

Freeman, J. (1994). *A vision for the college placement center systems, paradigms, processes, people.* Westport, CT: Praeger.

Gaines, J.I. (1992). How small colleges approach employer development. *Journal of Career Planning and Employment, 52*(3), 75–83.

Garis, J.W., & Bowlsbey, J.H. (1984). DISCOVER and the counselor: Their effects upon college student career planning progress. *ACT Research Report, 85.*2(Ed.), *Student development on the small campus* (pp. 92–126). National Association of Personnel Workers.

McBride, J.L., & Muffo, J.A. (1991). Student needs assessment raises implications for career services. *Journal of Career Planning and Employment, 51*(2), 63–67.

McBride, J.L., & Muffo, J.A. (1994). Students assess their own career goals and services needs. *Journal of Career Planning and Employment, 54*(3), 26–31.

McCann, J. (1993). Listening to the community of the hearing-impaired. *Journal of Career Planning and Employment, 53*(4), 43–49.

McCarty, A. (1990). SUCCESS—Stanford University career counseling and experience for Stanford students with disabilities. *Journal of Career Planning and Employment, 51*(1), 64.

McDonald, J., Dipeolu, A., Johnson, T., & Reardon, R. (1993). Sigma Chi Iota means minority career development at Florida State. *Journal of Career Planning and Employment, 53*(2), 57–60.

McKenzie, I.L., & Monoogian-O'Dell, M. (1988). *Expanding the use of students in career services: Current programs and resources.* Alexandria, VA: American College Personnel Association Media Publication, No. 45.

McLoughlin, W.L. (1973). Placement's emerging role. *Journal of College Placement, 33,* 79–82.

Mahanes, J.R. (1989). Coming of age: Automation of an experiential learning program. *Journal of Career Planning and Employment, 50*(1), 47–49.

Mead, S., & Korschgen, A.J. (1994). A quick look at career development courses: Across the country. *Journal of Career Planning and Employment, 54*(3), 24–25.

Miller, S.J. (1994). Career planning and placement programs. In J.L. Baier, & T.S. Strong, (Eds.), *Technology in student affairs: Issues, applications and trends,* (pp. 135–145). Lanham, MD: American College Personnel Association.

Miller, T.K., Winston, R.B., Jr., & Mendenhall, W.R. (1983). Human development and higher education. In T.K. Miller, R.B. Winston, Jr., & W.R. Mendenhall (Eds.), *Administration and leadership in student affairs: Actualizing student development in higher education* (pp. 3–30). Muncie, IN: Accelerated Development, Inc.

Murray, N. (1993). Bridge for the Xs: A new career services model. *Journal of Career Planning & Employment, 53*(3), 28–35.

National Association of Colleges and Employers (1994). *Special report: From the presidents.* Bethlehem, PA: Author.

National Vocational Guidance Association (1980). Guidelines for the preparation and evaluation of career information literature. *Vocational Guidance Quarterly, 28,* 291–296.

Niles, S., & Garis, J.W. (1990). The effects of a career planning course and a computer-assisted career guidance program (SIGI PLUS) on undecided university students. *Journal of Career Development, 17*(4), 237–247.

Parker, L.B. (1994). A program for planned professional development. *Journal of Career Planning & Employment, 54*(4), 63–66.

Parsons, F. (1909). *Choosing a vocation.* Boston: Houghton-Mifflin.

Pascarella, E.T., & Terenzini, P.T. (1991). *How college affects students: Findings and insights from twenty years of research.* San Francisco: Jossey-Bass.

Posluszny, S.B. (1992). Career-counseling them all—and on a limited budget. *Journal of Career Planning & Employment, 52*(4), 51–53.

Powell, C.R., & Kirts, D.K. (1980). *Career services today.* Bethlehem, PA: College Placement Council.

Prediger, D.J. (1976). A world of work map for career exploration. *The Vocational Guidance Quarterly, 24,* 198–208.

Prediger, D.J. (1981). Mapping occupations and interests: A graphic aid for vocational guidance and research. *The Vocational Guidance Quarterly, 30,* 21–36.

Preissler, S. (1989). Job-search help for the 'trailing spouse'. *Journal of Career Planning and Employment, 50*(1), 83–84.

Pritchard, C.J., & Fidler, P.P. (1993). Firming up the small-firm connection. *Journal of Career Planning and Employment, 52*(4), 51–54.

Rayman, J.R. (Ed.). (1993). *The changing role of career services.* San Francisco: Jossey-Bass.

Rea, P.J. (1987). The assessment center as a career planning tool. *Journal of Career Planning and Employment, 47*(3), 21–22.

Robb, F.C. (1971). The three P's: Preparation, placement performance. *Journal of College Placement, 31,* 31.

Robb, W.D. (1979). Counseling—placement, must they be separate entities? *Journal of College Placement, 39,* 67–71.

Rodgers, R. (1989). Student development. In U. Delworth, G. Hanson, & Associates

(Eds.), *Student services: A handbook for the profession* (2nd ed.), (pp. 117–164). San Francisco: Jossey-Bass.

Roth, S.E. (1994). The role of career services within student affairs. *NASPA Journal, 31*(3), 169–175.

Roth, M.J., & Jones, D.A. (1991). Expanding career services via the campus-wide computer network. *Journal of Career Planning and Employment, 51*(4), 32–45.

Sailer, D.D., Korschgen, A.J., & Lokken, J.M. (1994). Responding to the career needs of gays, lesbians, and bisexuals. *Journal of Career Planning and Employment, 54*(3), 39–42.

Sampson, J.P., Jr., Peterson, G.W., Lenz, J.G., & Reardon, R.C. (1992). A cognitive approach to career services: Translating concepts into practice. *The Career Development Quarterly, 41,* 67–74.

Savage, K.M., & Hill, K. (Eds.). (1992). *Vocational careers sourcebook: Where to find help planning careers in skilled, trade, and nontechnical vocations.* Detroit, MI: Gale Research, Inc.

Schmitz, T. (1990). How to make a needs assessment program successful. *Journal of Career Planning and Employment, 50*(4), 28–30.

Scott, G.J. (1983). *Career planning and placement office: Implications for the future.* Bethlehem, PA: College Placement Council Foundation.

Shea, D.D. (1995). Merging career and ex ed centers: A perspective. *Journal of Career Planning and Employment, 55*(2), 29–35.

Shingleton, J.D. (1978). The three R's of placement. *Journal of College Placement, 38,* 33–38.

Shingleton, J.D., & Fitzpatrick, E.B. (1985). *Dynamics of placement . . . How to develop a successful planning and placement program.* Bethlehem, PA: CPC Foundation.

Sinnott, P.A., Beebe, W.B., & Collins, M. (1990). You're reading Vol. LI, No. 1 of a good, 50-year-old idea. *Journal of Career Planning and Employment, 51*(1), 26–31.

Sproul, J., & Sullivan, J. (1988). What to be or not to be: A career day for liberal arts and science students. *Journal of Career Planning and Employment, 48*(3), 21–24.

Stephens, E.W. (1970). *Career counseling and placement in higher education: A student personnel function.* Bethlehem, PA: College Placement Council.

Stewart, R.A. (1989). The use of computers in career planning, placement, and recruitment. *Journal of Career Planning and Employment, 49*(3), 51–53.

Stewart, R.A. (1993). Placement services. In J.R. Rayman (Ed.), *The changing role of career services* (pp. 37–54). San Francisco: Jossey-Bass.

Swaim, R. (1968). Centralization or decentralization: Two approaches to placement receive an up-to-date review. *Journal of College Placement, 28*(3), 117–128.

Teal, E.A., & Herrick, R.F. (Eds.) (1962). *The fundamentals of college placement.* Bethlehem, PA: College Placement Council.

The Small Business Committee of the Midwest College Placement Association. (1989). *Helping small business employers: A placement office perspective.* Bethlehem, PA: CPC Foundation.

Van De Weert, P.K., & Baumgartner, D. (1992). Computerizing the career services office for total management. *Journal of Career Planning and Employment, 52*(3), 25–27.

Watson, A. (1994). Setting up a career resource center library. *Journal of Career Planning and Employment, 54*(2), 65–67.

Weatherall, R.K. (1989). Campus recruiting in changing times. *Journal of Career Planning and Employment, 49*(2), 29–33.

Weatherall, R.K. (1990). A Journal pro-con forum: Is on-campus recruiting really working? *Journal of Career Planning and Employment, 50*(3), 40–41, 60–67.

Weber, D.W. (1982). *The status of career planning and placement.* Bethlehem, PA: College Placement Council.

Wilson, B.J. (1990). Without on-campus recruiting . . . what would we do in February, anyway? *Journal of Career Planning and Employment, 50*(3), 40–41, 60–67.

Wilson, E.P., & Greenberg, R.M. (1990). Creating a low-cost, high-impact staff development program. *Journal of Career Planning and Employment, 50*(2), 23–24.

Wrenn, C.G. (1951). *Student personnel work in college.* New York: Ronald.

Yerian, J.M. (1993). Career programming in a contemporary context. In J.R. Rayman (Ed.), *The changing role of career services* (pp. 79–100). San Francisco: Jossey-Bass.

Chapter 6

COUNSELING

ELIZABETH YARRIS

HISTORY

As far back as we have knowledge of the American college there is indication that, among faculty members, there were certain individuals who thoroughly enjoyed personal contact with their students. These were the men also to whom the students went for counsel and advice. (Hopkins, 1926, p. 27, as cited in Williamson, 1961)

Counseling has been identified as the generic service of student personnel work (Williamson, 1961), the earliest college counselors being college faculty and presidents (Gibson, Mitchell, & Higgins, 1983). A variety of influences led to the need for more specialized "counselors"—the student personnel workers of the late 19th and early 20th century. Colleges and universities had expanded both in number and in type of institution with the development of land-grant colleges, electives, and a renewed emphasis on technological and scientific education. An influx of American Ph.D.'s trained in Germany had a more impersonal and intellectualized approach to education that reduced the amount of student-faculty interaction. The first formal recognition that institutions of higher education had the obligation to provide a specifically designated "counseling service" for students may have been the appointments of a "Chief of Advisors" at Johns Hopkins University in 1889 and a "Dean of Student Relations" at Harvard in 1870 (Gibson et al., 1983).

Professionally trained counselors began to appear on a few college campuses after World War I as a result of the development of assessment techniques and other psychological advances (Schneider, 1977). In addition to the development of psychometrics, two other major influences led to the rise of the counseling profession and to a counseling center specialty within student personnel work (Berk, 1983; Hedahl, 1978; Tyler, 1969). First, the 1909 publication of Clifford Beers, *A Mind that Found Itself,* is cited as the beginning of the Mental Hygiene movement with attention to both the prevention and cure of less serious as well as more serious emotional difficulties (Tyler, 1969). The second influence was Frank Parsons' work in the Boston YMCA after World War I which began counseling as an organized service in public schools (Williamson, 1961). Parsons' *Choosing a Vocation* (1906) proposed a model of counseling which focused on the need for helping young people find suitable places in the world of work (Tyler, 1969). The vocational guidance model and the Mental Hygiene movement, along with the use of psychometrics, were the historical antecedents of two essential functions of counseling: to facilitate wise choices and decisions and to promote adjustment or mental health (Tyler, 1969).

The University Testing Bureau, established in 1932 at the University of Minnesota, appears to be the earliest separate unit organized to offer professional educational and vocational guidance (Hedahl, 1978). Most colleges, however, had no professional counselors on campus until after World War II when the Veterans Administration funded guidance bureaus to monitor the large numbers of veterans attending college with government subsidies. As the veteran population on campus declined, many colleges and universities assumed budgetary and administrative support of what became the forerunners of the modern counseling center.

1945 to 1955 were years of "transition and professionalism" (Heppner & Neal, 1983). In the early 1950s, counseling center directors began to meet annually to discuss mutual problems and concerns. Some of the growth and development during this period and into the 1960s paralleled changes within the field of counseling psychology (Whitely, 1984)—a trend that has continued into the 1990s (Cameron, Galassi, Birk, & Waggener, 1989; Sprinthall, 1990; Tyler, 1992). The phasing out of Veterans Administration support of counseling centers coincided with the development of counseling psychology as a specialty area within the American Psychological Association. If a counseling psychology faculty existed on campus, typically they were involved in the further growth of the counseling center (McKinley, 1980). Both counseling psychology and counseling centers followed a trend away from exclusively vocational guidance to a broad developmental form of "personal" counseling (Berk, 1983, p. 59).

The 1960s was a time of social unrest, "encounter groups," and draft counseling. For college and university counseling centers, it was a time of both expansion and consolidation (Heppner & Neal, 1983; Lamb, Garni, & Gelwick, 1983). However, the call for institutions to be more relevant to social concerns led administrators to ask counseling services to be more relevant to the goals of higher education and to do so on reduced budgets (Forman, 1977). From within the profession, Warnath (1971, 1973) called counseling centers to task for practicing within a medical model, viewing the student as "sick" and "in need of treatment," while serving only a small select group of students. As a result, the 1970s was a period of reassessment of the counseling center role (Lamb et al., 1983). However, groundwork had already begun for constructive change. In 1968 Morrill, Ivey, and Oetting (cited in McKinley, 1980) provided a major stimulus for change in function by proposing that counseling centers become centers for student development that would (1) move out into the campus to create programs to prevent problems; (2) mobilize community resources for mental health; and (3) redefine the counseling center role within a developmental framework (McKinley, 1980). A task force of counseling center directors developed guidelines (Kirk et al., 1971) distinguishing between "remedial" and "developmental/preventive" services. This separation of services and the concept of a human development center was given direction by the "cube" (Morrill, Oetting, & Hurst, 1974). This conceptual scheme for organizing the expanding role of counselors specified targets (individual, primary group, associational group, and institution or community), purposes (remedial, preventive, or developmental), and methods (direct, consultation and training, or media) for intervention on a college campus (McKinley, 1980). A related concept emerged during the 1970s, "campus ecology" emphasized the interrelationship between students and their environment. College and university counselors were encouraged to see the campus environment as client and to assist in creating campus environmental change (e.g., Aulepp & Delworth, 1976; Conyne et al., 1979).

Additional influences redesigning the role of counseling services during the 1970s were counseling center directors themselves, external accrediting bodies, and professional organizations (Lamb et al., 1983). Finally, legal requirements for licensure or certification of psychologists and counselors also affected the changing role of counseling centers. By the 1980s, counseling centers were functioning in broader and more comprehensive roles (Heppner & Neal, 1983).

MISSION/GOALS/PURPOSE

Most four-year postsecondary institutions (93%) reported having a counseling center on campus (Whiteley, Mahaffey, & Geer, 1987). Since the results of this survey overrepresented larger, public institutions, it is possible that smaller, private institutions are less likely to have such a resource. Earlier surveys indicated that 73 percent of institutions under 1,000 students, 94 percent of colleges with enrollments of 2,000 to 5,000, and more than 85 percent of community colleges had organized counseling services (Goodman & Beard, 1976; Richardson, Seim, Eddy, & Brindley, 1985).

The fundamental mission of counseling center work is to serve students (Corazzini, 1995). According to the Accreditation Standards of the International Association of Counseling Services, Inc. (IACS), counseling services are an integral part of the educational mission of the institution and support it by providing clinical and counseling services to students experiencing stress due to personal problems, decision making, or conflicts within the campus community (Kiracofe et al., 1994). Counseling center staff are advocates for student needs and are involved in program development, teaching, and consultation activities supporting the efforts of faculty and staff in improving the university environment. In addition, counseling service professionals work with faculty and administrators in promoting the goal of psychological and emotional development in many aspects of campus life (Kiracofe et al., 1994).

As described in the section on History, three purposes of a counseling center as conceptualized by the "cube" model (Morrill et al., 1974) are (1) remedial—to solve a problem that already exists, such as managing test anxiety, (2) preventive—to prevent a problem from occurring, such as providing study and anxiety management skills, and (3) developmental—such as enhancing interpersonal relationships by promoting communication between roommates.

The proportion of attention that should be given to each of these purposes has been debated. Selected sections of two sets of "general principles for university counseling centers" illustrate the 1980s version of the debate. Leventhal and Magoon (1979) stated that "counseling or psychotherapy in the counseling center is based upon an educational model of behavior rather than a model of disease" (p. 359), "consultation services are of equal importance to counseling/psychotherapeutic services" (p. 360), and "the counseling center implements alternatives to its traditional individual and group services" (p. 362). In a modification of these principles, Demos and Mead (1983) wrote "Personal counseling and therapy should be based on a developmental and clinical foundation — that is, counselsors should be well-versed in both developmental psychology and diagnosis and assessment procedures. Since a focus on any single theoretical background is too narrow, professional staff should be diverse in their training and background. Consultation services are important, but they are supplementary to counseling services, which are the primary function of the center" (p. 6). Demos and Mead clearly state that "a direct contact of students and counselors in counseling interactions, individual or group, is the major function of the psychological counseling center" (1983, p. 7).

Many current issues, including the possible impact of health care reform, have added to the long-standing debate over the ratio of direct service to the preventive and developmental functions of outreach and consultation (Drum, 1993). Although in practice it is difficult to avoid a large proportion of direct and remedial services, current recommendations for counseling center roles and functions are more similar to those of Leventhal and Magoon (1979). In major statements concerning counseling services of the 1990s, Bishop (1990) and Stone and Archer (1990) recommend increased attention to the use of consultation with a renewed emphasis on the goal of prevention of problems. The limitations of a counseling center's ability to enhance the development of individuals and to have an impact on environmental systems has been questioned (Stone & Archer, 1990).

ADMINISTRATION AND ORGANIZATION

Administration

All it takes is one letter from a grateful parent to enlighten a president regarding the role of counseling services on campus today: one suicide averted or one addiction recognized in time for recovery. The opposite outcomes can also bring the work of counseling services into the president's field of view (Likins, 1993, p. 90).

Counseling services are unique in that much of the work is confidential in nature and therefore less obvious to both the public and to administrators (Likins, 1993). Counseling services do not fit easily into the administrative bureaucracy (Schoenberg, 1992) and may have an ambiguous and insecure place in the organizational structure, with conflicts of interest arising because of simultaneous responsibilities to institution, client, and profession (Gilbert, 1989). Although the relationship to other units within the institution will vary according to the organizational structure and individual campus needs, the counseling service should be administratively neutral to preserve students' perceptions that information disclosed in counseling sessions will not affect academic, disciplinary, or other administrative decisions (Kiracofe, et al., 1994).

Counseling services are typically housed within student affairs and staff work closely with academic units, other student service offices, campus and community medical services, community mental health services, as well as with faculty and administrators (Kirakofe et al., 1994). Some college and universities have both an independent Counseling Center and a Mental Health Unit as a part of Student Health Services. Gallagher et al. (1993) found 16 percent of 355 counseling centers surveyed to be administratively linked to a student health service. Of those centers, 42 percent of the counseling center directors reported to the student health service director and 58 percent reported to the counseling center director (Gallagher et al., 1993). While both the counseling center and student health service might both report to student affairs, another organizational arrangement is illustrated at the University of Iowa where the counseling service is one of the services in the office of the Associate Provost for Student Services, while the student health service reports to the university hospital (Stone, 1995). In some institutions, a coordinator of sexual assault services reports to the counseling center (Gallagher et al., 1994). This is especially true for smaller institutions. Of the 264 (74% of 355 surveyed) institutions reporting having an alcohol abuse program (Gallagher et al., 1993), 39 percent of those programs were administratively housed in the counseling center.

Staffing

The personnel necessary for the effective operation of a counseling service depends upon the size and nature of the institution and the extent of other resources available on or off campus (Kiracofe et al., 1994). IACS guidelines recommend minimum staffing ratios of 1 FTE professional staff member to every 1,000 to 1,500 students and require hiring practices that are consistent with the goals of equal opportunity and affirmative action (Kiracofe et al., 1994). Magoon (1995) reported median ratios of professional staff to students of 1:1855 for large institutions and 1:932 for small schools.

Staff may include a range of specialties and levels of training, including paraprofessionals, practicum students, and interns. Credentials for entry-level professional staff are reviewed in the final section of this chapter.

The majority of counseling center directors possess the doctorate, most frequently in counseling psychology (39.7%), followed by clinical psychology (24.8%), and counseling, counselor education, or mental health (16.1%) (Gallagher et al., 1994). Doctoral degrees are more likely for directors with large staffs in public institutions and in centers accredited by IACS (Whiteley et al., 1987). IACS standards for accreditation recommend that the director should have an earned doctorate and equivalency criteria are recommended for nondoctorate directors (Kiracofe et al., 1994). Although approximately half of the directors held academic rank in 1994 (Gallagher et al.), since 1980, there has been a decline in the number of directors having academic rank in large institutions (Magoon, 1994). IACS standards expect "that professional staff members holding equivalent terminal degrees be accorded rights and privileges consistent with university and college faculty" (Kiracofe et al., 1994, p. 41).

Those centers with a predoctoral internship training program must have a Training Director and many larger centers delegate responsibilities to Directors of Clinical Services, Evaluation and Research, Career Services, and Consultation or Programming. Counseling centers with testing services might employ a psychometrist. There is an increasing trend, regardless of size of institution, to have a psychiatrist on staff, an arrangement that 75 percent of director's surveyed found very satisfactory (Gallagher, 1991). In 1988, 19 percent reported a psychiatrist, while the percentages increased to 23 percent in 1991 and 39 percent in 1992 (Gallagher, 1991, 1992). Since support staff plays an important role in students' impressions of the counseling service and often must make some preliminary decisions about student needs, they should be selected carefully and receive training not only in the operation of the service but also in issues regarding confidentiality and the limits of their functioning (Kiracofe et al., 1994).

Models

The model of a counseling center is related not only to the types of programs and services offered, but to the philosophy of the director and other administrators. Issues include: (1) size of staff and accreditation status of the center (Whiteley et al., 1987); (2) whether or not there are other counseling, psychological, and psychiatric services on campus or in the community; professional training programs on campus and their relationship to the Counseling Center; (3) the relationship between the Health Center and the Counseling Center; (4) the existence of a Placement Center or Career Planning Center and its relationship to the Counseling Center; (5) whether a campus has centralized or decentralized counseling and advising specialists; and (6) the location and extent of services available for sexual assault prevention, response, and the prevention and treatment of alcohol and other drug abuse.

The "original counseling center" followed a *vocational guidance model* (Oetting, Ivey, & Weigel, 1970), where testing and vocational choice counseling were the primary functions. Vocational guidance was the most prevalent model in the 1960s. Currently this type of counseling is more often referred to as career counseling and is more likely to be one of many types of counseling offered in a center, as well as available in other settings on campus. Of historical interest are the additional types of counseling centers found by a 1960s' survey: *personnel services model, academic affairs model, psychotherapy model, training model, research model, and traditional counseling model* (Oetting et al., 1970). The "traditional" model was found among those centers whose directors had formed the original counseling center directors' association and functioned as a separate campus agency, providing vocational counseling, short-term treatment of emotional problems, and some longer-term counseling. Service to clients was the primary orientation, although some intern and practica experiences existed (Oetting et al., 1970).

Following the work of Oetting et al. (1970), the next major effort to characterize types of counseling centers was a survey conducted in the 1980s (Whiteley et al., 1987). Five primary types of centers were identified from a sample that somewhat overrepresented responses from larger public institutions. The *macrocenter* (21% of the sample) provided the broadest range of services with an extensive number of both counseling and career-related services, testing, and special functions such as outreach and training. The *career-oriented center* (16%) offered minimal counseling and related services and focused on career planning and placement assistance. The *counseling-oriented center* (29%) was similar to the macrocenter but focused more on personal counseling functions and less on career services. The *general purpose center* (20%), more likely to be found at private schools, provided a more general level of services, with more responsibilities similar to those of a dean of students (e.g., responsibilities and services related to student organizations, fraternity and sorority advising). The *microcenter* (15%) offered some counseling services and a minimal level of other services. Models of counseling services in community colleges are discussed by Coll (1993a).

In a rapidly changing social environment, with limited resources and increasing demands, there has been a tendency to focus on counseling center issues and functions or upon models that highlight economic concerns (e.g., Bishop, 1990; Steenbarger, 1995; Stone & Archer, 1990). Crego (1990) admonished counseling center leaders to move beyond "simply adding programs, balancing programs, and . . . prioritizing programs" (p. 609), and noted that counseling centers continue with a model designed for the white, middle-class, full-time, traditional-aged, self-directed student. One attempt to reconceptualize models of counseling center functioning suggests "rounding out the cube" (Pace, Stamler, Yarris, & June, in press). According to Pace et al. (in press), the original cube: illustrated the counseling center as an independent and fixed structure with a closed uni-directional system and decision-making that was primarily internal; did not address resource allocation; and implied a noncollaborative style (e.g., the counseling center chooses targets and makes interventions). A "global" model for counseling centers has an "interactive" cube which: focuses on the institution as a system; is interdependent with the system; is a living system rather than a fixed structure; is multidirectional; makes decisions in consultation with the campus community; strives for a homeostatic balance of resources and services; and collaborates with the university community as equals.

Technology

The use of new technology to enhance the delivery and management of services and programs is quite recent for the counseling center (Baier, 1993). By 1990, 97 percent of counseling centers from large institutions and 92 percent from small institutions were using computers for purposes such as monthly reports and anonymous client demographic data, scheduling, billing and attendance records, and various assessment instruments (Gallagher, 1990). However, only 34 percent of counseling centers surveyed reported keeping client information on a computer (Gallagher, Bruner, & Lingenfelter, 1993).

Financial Support

Although most counseling centers are funded mainly by the institution, 19 percent of 310 counseling center directors surveyed reported pressure from their institutions to be more self-supporting (Gallagher, Bruner, & Weaver-Graham, 1994). A small percentage of centers collect third-party payments (5%) and while there are increasing trends to charge for services (11.6%) or for centers to be supported by mandatory student fees (28.7%) (Gallagher et al., 1994). A small number of centers generate income by assessing fees for: career testing, on- or off-campus consulting, psychological assessment for external groups, various national testing programs (e.g., CLEP, GED, professional school admissions), and rent charged for private practice hours (Gallagher et al., 1993).

Physical Facilities

Counseling services should be centrally located, physically separate from administrative offices, campus police, and judicial offices, and readily accessible to all students, including those who are physically challenged (Kiracofe et al., 1994). Additional recommendations by IACS include: Individual sound-proofed offices with a telephone, an interoffice communications system, audio- or video-recording equipment, and furnishings that create a relaxing environment for students; access to computers and other appropriate equipment to support record keeping, research, and publication activities; technical resources for media presentations and other adjuncts to treatment; a reception area that provides a comfortable and private waiting area; a central clerical area where all client records are kept secure; library resources; areas suitable for individual and group testing, for group counseling, and staff meetings; and for services with a training program, audio and visual recording facilities as well as facilities for direct observation (Kiracofe et al., 1994).

PROGRAMS AND SERVICES

Patterns of Use

In the 1970s and 1980s, research indicated that between 10 percent and 25 percent of students used the Counseling Center (Heppner & Neal, 1983). Earlier reports indicated that students were more likely to come to the center for career planning, negotiating the system, and coping with financial and academic concerns (Carney, Savitz, & Weiskott, 1979) but later came to view the center as an appropriate place to discuss personal and interpersonal concerns (Altmaier & Rapaport, 1984; Heppner & Neal, 1983). In the 1990s, numerous reports reflect increased requests for counseling services. A growing demand for services was documented by 67 percent of directors surveyed (Gallagher et al., 1994). In a needs assessment conducted at Columbia University, 16 percent of student respondents had made use of the university's mental health or counseling services and 39 percent reported a previous contact with a mental health practitioner (Bertocci, Hirsch, Sommer, & Williams, 1992). In a wider survey, it was found that over 40 percent of current students seeking help indicated previous counseling (Heitzman, Gilbert, Rabin, & Drum, 1991). More popular media have also addressed increasing requests for campus counseling services, with headlines such as "For More at College, Therapy is an Elective" in the *Philadelphia Enquirer* (Vigoda, 1995) and "Demand for Therapy on Campus is Growing Even Faster than Tuition" in *U.S. News and World Report* (Elfin, 1994). The above "patterns of use" refer to students who come to a Counseling Center requesting counseling. Other "patterns of use" have not been so well described in the literature but include such activities as counseling center staff going to a residence hall to discuss with students and staff the impact of a homicide in the hall (Waldo, Harman, O'Malley, 1993).

Types of Problems

Williamson (1939) discussed students' concerns with social maladjustments, speech adjustment, family conflicts, student discipline, educational orientation and achievement, occupational orientation, and finances. Many of the concerns voiced in today's counseling centers are related to the expected developmental tasks of college students: (1) adjusting to a new environment; (2) choosing a major and planning for a future career;

(3) establishing an identity separate from parents; (4) learning time management and study skills appropriate to higher education; (5) establishing intimate relationships; (6) exploring sexual identity; and (7) clarifying values. In the early 1990s developmental problems accounted for 13.5 percent of counseling center clientele, while a combination of developmental problems and emotional disorders accounted for another 53 percent (Gallagher et al., 1993).

Unexpected crisis events occur in college students' lives. Examples include: (1) death or suicide of a friend or family member; (2) chronic illness in a family member, friend, or self; (3) parents' divorce and remarriage; (4) sexual assault; (5) legal problems and pending jail terms; (6) disability from a car accident; (7) various types of harassment, including being stalked.

The types of problems students experience and bring to a counseling center may vary with year in school, age, gender, academic major, ethnicity, and previous history. The fact that the college years are stressful is well documented and it appears that stress among college students increased during the 1980s (Dunkel-Schetter & Lobel, 1990). Among the most frequently reported sources of problems are academic, career planning, social (including romantic relationships), family concerns (including a family history of alcohol abuse), and financial (e.g., Bertocci et al., 1992; Carney, Peterson, & Moberg, 1990; Dunkel-Schetter & Lobel, 1990; Heppner et al., 1994). Recent surveys also support an increase among general student concerns with drug and alcohol use, eating and weight problems, experiences of sexual assault and harassment, various forms of violence, and AIDS (Bertocci et al., 1992; Delene & Brogowicz, 1990; Roark, 1993). Hotelling (1995) cites the number of ways in which today's students feel vulnerable: (1) exposure to increased violence; (2) uncertainty over functioning in a more diverse environment; (3) fearing the loss of affirmative action; and (4) economic pressure to choose a major or a four-year degree program that is not wanted. Surveys of graduate students demonstrate some similar concerns (e.g., Baker, 1993; Bertocci et al., 1992; Hodgson & Simoni, 1995).

In addition to developmental issues, crisis situations, and environmental stressors, some students bring more chronic problems with them to college. Examples include: learning disabilities; inherited biochemical imbalances that might result in major depression, compulsive behaviors, or hallucinations if not treated with the proper medications; eating disorders which result in either self-starvation or a habitual pattern of overeating followed by self-induced vomiting or laxative abuse. An increase in the number of students presenting at counseling centers with serious psychological symptoms and emotional disorders has been well documented (e.g., Gallagher, 1990, 1991, 1992; Gallagher et al., 1993; Gallagher et al., 1994; Stone & Archer, 1990). In the 1980s, students increasingly turned to counseling centers for help with eating disorders while in the 1990s there has been an increase in problems caused by childhood physical or sexual abuse (Gallagher, 1990, 1991, 1992; Gallagher et al., 1993; Gallagher et al., 1994; Stone & Archer, 1990). Long-standing concerns, as well as the expected stresses of college life, can result in feelings of depression and anxiety, thoughts of suicide, substance abuse, somatic problems, interpersonal difficulties, as well as difficulty in concentrating on academic work (Heppner et al., 1994; Johnson, Ellison, & Heikkinen, 1989; Miller & Rice, 1993). Meilman, Pattis, and Kraus-Zeilmann (1994) found that at the College of William and Mary the most prevalent risk factor found in suicide attempters was work or school failure, while in those who threatened suicide it was difficulty in a relationship.

Programs and Services

The programs and services offered by a counseling center will depend upon the size and type of institution, the model of the center, the orientation of the director, and services offered elsewhere on campus. Some counseling centers will provide services to faculty, staff, and members of the community (Gallagher et al., 1994).

IACS standards require the following program functions: (1) individual and group counseling and therapy services that are responsive to student needs; (2) crisis intervention and emergency coverage either directly or through arrangements with other resources; (3) programming which focuses on the developmental needs of students; (4) consultative services to members of the university community; (5) research and evaluation of services; (6) training and professional development experiences for staff, interns, practicum students, and others in the university community (Kiracofe et al., 1994).

Most counseling centers offer individual counseling, with the wide range of functions required by IACS more likely to be found in state supported institutions with larger staffs (Whiteley et al., 1987). A student might approach the counseling center to speak individually with a counselor for any of the concerns mentioned above. Most centers (67%) provide career counseling, which helps a student identify interests and abilities to aid in the selection of a college major as well as in more general life planning (Gallagher et al., 1994). Due to increased requests for individual service, many centers are limiting the number of individual sessions that are available (Gallagher et al., 1994; Magoon, 1994; Stone & Archer, 1990). A student requesting counseling services might be referred to an appropriate group program either immediately or upon completion of a prescribed number of individual counseling sessions. Group goals might be remedial (most often called therapy groups) or preventive and developmental (most often called psychoeducational). Although counseling center directors report difficulty in filling them, most centers offer counseling groups (Gallagher, 1990, 1992; Gallagher et al., 1993; Gallagher et al., 1994). Some of the more successful groups focus on: survivors of events such as rape, incest, alcoholic families; eating disorders; relationships; career development; assertiveness; women's issues; men's issues, gay, lesbian, and bisexual issues; loss and grief; and social skills. Workshops held in a variety of locations on campus are referred to as "outreach." Outreach programming can be used to reach students who are less likely to make use of traditional counseling services (Kiracofe et al., 1994). Outreach programs frequently have a goal of prevention of problems and focus on issues such as: study skills, assertive communication, responsible decisions about the use of alcohol, and the prevention of sexual offenses. The target population of prevention programs might also be parents of students. For example, at Bowling Green State University, the counseling center is involved in a program for the parents and support givers of entering students. "Changing Relationships" helps parents anticipate changes in their relationships with their students and promotes discussion between parents and students with a goal of preventing problems such as acquaintance rape, dropping out of school, racism, and roommate conflicts. "Direct service" to students (individual and group counseling, psychoeducational groups, and workshops) accounts for an average of 25 hours of a 40-hour work week for counseling center staff, but in smaller centers direct service might fill all available time (Gallagher et al., 1994). In addition, most centers (67%) provide some type of self-help materials such as books or audio tapes (Gallagher et al., 1994).

Crisis intervention usually refers to a situation requiring immediate attention for students who are experiencing acute emotional distress, dangerous to self or others, or in need of immediate hospitalization (Kiracofe et al., 1994). After hours emergency work is considered part of a counselor's job in most (74%) centers and 58 percent of centers participate in a campus crisis team (Gallagher et al., 1994).

Consultation refers to activities in which the counseling service interprets and advocates for the needs of students to administrators, faculty, and staff of the institution (Kiracofe et al., 1994). Frequently, consultation refers to helping others respond to a student problem, such as suggesting to the gymnastics coach ways in which an athlete with a potential eating disorder might be referred for help. However, consultation might also focus on organizational dynamics such as a formalized consultation relationship between the Counseling Center and Residence Life at the University of Maryland (Westbrook et al., 1993).

An additional program, especially among larger counseling centers, is that of training. In addition to training paraprofessionals (e.g., Resident Advisors), many centers are involved in preprofessional training programs. These may include practicum placement for master's and doctoral level graduate students in Counseling Psychology, Clinical Psychology, Counseling and Guidance, and College Student Personnel. A more formal and structured training program exists in centers providing a predoctoral internship in professional psychology, especially if the training program is approved by the American Psychological Association. Counseling center staff can also be involved in a variety of training programs within the campus community. One example from Boise State University is a workshop on Dealing with Difficult People for student affairs personnel, followed by a stress management and communication skills training workshop for the staff in Financial Aid (Nicholson, Shelley, & Townsend, 1991).

Most counseling centers also make some types of testing services available. These might include use of instruments such as interest inventories or personality assessment or the administration of national testing programs such as the SAT, ACT, and GRE. As discussed in the section above on Models, some centers sponsor a variety of advising activities. Example of academic support services are The Learning Center, Supplemental Instruction, and the Tutoring Center that are a part of the Counseling Center at the University of Utah, and include services such as classes in Learning Skills (Boggs, 1992).

Finally, ongoing evaluation and accountability research, as well as contributions to the profession should be a part of all counseling center programs (Kiracofe et al., 1994).

APPLICATION OF STUDENT DEVELOPMENT THEORY

The history of counseling centers has parallelled that of the field of counseling psychology (Cameron et al., 1989; Sprinthall, 1990; Tyler, 1992; Whitely, 1984). Given the distinguishing feature of counseling psychology, its emphasis on development and life planning (Tyler, 1992), counseling centers began with an inherent focus on student development. In contrast to therapy, which is essentially for people who have something wrong with them, "Counseling, as it began, was a service for everybody" as "We are all faced with the necessity of choosing how we will live our lives" (Tyler, 1992, p. 343). In addition to the emphasis on choices throughout the lifespan, counseling psychology was also an outgrowth of the psychological study of individual differences (Tyler, 1992). Thus, counseling center staff are prepared to work with not only the traditionally aged college student, but also students from diverse backgrounds and adult learners. Counseling centers of the 1970s and 1980s were encouraged to become "student development centers" and to focus on student development as one of their major purposes (McKinley, 1980). Many individuals active in counseling center work were committed to student development and campus ecology (e.g., Aulepp & Delworth, 1976; Conyne et al., 1979; Drum, 1980; Hurst, 1978). Research demonstrated that counseling needs of students vary by class level, age, sex, and race (Carney et al., 1990) and attention to these developmental struggles and needs is a prerequisite to good counseling with college students (Grayson, 1989; Whitaker, 1992).

However, some are questioning the current meaning of "normal" developmental issues, given the evidence of problems related to pathological families and experiences. Stone and Archer (1990) asked:

> If 27% of the women in college have been raped since they were 14, is this becoming more of a "normal" developmental experience? With the large number of alcoholic, dysfunctional, and broken families, is it "normal" to have to deal with problems related to these experiences? (p. 546).

They concluded that "the developmental issues for many of our students include learning to overcome serious psychological problems" (p. 546). Early life experiences can complicate the resolution of expected developmental tasks of the college student. For example, White and Strange (1993) found that an unwanted childhood sexual experience had significant effects on subsequent psychosocial tasks of intimacy and career planning in a sample of college women. Similarly, typical college students' experimentation with new behaviors associated with physical, sexual, psychological, identity, and moral development, can increase risks of serious problems with substance abuse, violence, and exposure to HIV infection (Rivinus & Larimer, 1993; Triggs & McDermott, 1991). In a study of Georgetown University undergraduates hospitalized for psychiatric reasons, first- and second-year students were identified as being more likely to be admitted in the first two months of a term—a pattern that was not documented in the upperclass years. Since 90 percent of the total of hospitalized students lived more than 100 miles from home, the authors suggested that first- and second-year students may be more vulnerable to the psychological aspects of separating from home (Rosecan, Goldberg & Wise, 1992).

ISSUES OF THE 1980S AND 1990S

The major issues confronting the counseling center practitioner during the 1980s and 1990s have parallelled those within student affairs, higher education, and society at large and are related to increased diversity in our communities and a changing job market (Geer, 1995; Hotelling, 1995).

> The face of higher education is changing. More than half of college students are women, over 20 percent are members of underrepresented groups, nearly one-half of students attend part time, an increasing number have identified themselves as having a disability, and the median age of students is 28 (Garland & Grace, 1993).

Higher education is being affected by the "corporatizing of the academy" (Baron, 1995) and as illustrated by issues of *New Directions for Student Services*, student affairs professionals are concerned with *Responding to Violence on Campus* (Sherrill & Siegel, 1989), *Dealing with the Behavioral and Psychological Problems of Students* (Delworth, 1989), *Crisis Intervention and Prevention* (Pruett & Brown, 1990), and *Dealing with Students from Dysfunctional Families* (Witchel, 1991). Another issue that has recently arrived on campus is that of "internet addiction"—students who spend inordinate amounts of time "MUDDing, telnetting, and chatting live" (Robinson, personal communication, June 13, 1995).

Counseling center roles and functions have changed over time in response to social needs, such as moving away from a major focus on vocational counseling when it was no longer needed to serve returning veterans. By the 1980s, counseling centers had assumed multiple roles and functions and progressed toward a model of a student development center using the "cube" to direct counseling center functions (refer to section on History). There was an increased emphasis on personal counseling and continuation of career counseling. Prevention, outreach, training, and environmental design programs continued to increase, with a wide variety of programs offered, but the most frequent intervention involved direct, remedial, and individual approaches (Heppner & Neal, 1983). Due to the increase in more serious problems among students requesting help there is great concern and debate over managing these demands (e.g., Stone & Archer, 1990). Among the major concerns expressed by counseling center directors are: increased demand for services with no increase in resources; increased severity in problems presented by students; increase in waiting lists for counseling services; increased need to make outside referrals for long-term counseling and psychotherapy; and increased anxiety over legal issues (Gallagher, 1990, 1991, 1992; Gallagher et al., 1993; Gallagher et al., 1994). Attempts to cope with increased service demands have been made by using the short-term counseling model and group modalities. Other possibilities include some form of on-line counseling (Rosser, personal communication, July 3, 1995) or Counseling Center Home Page (Austin, personal communication, July 25, 1995).

Both legal and ethical issues continue to be a high priority for counseling centers. Guidelines of professional organizations and state laws suggest or require standards for professional practice (e.g., American College Personnel Association, 1990; American Psychological Association, 1992). The legal and ethical issue most frequently discussed is confidentiality (e.g., Sharkin, 1995; Stone & Lucas, 1990). In many states, there is legal privileged communication between client and psychologist and there is always an ethical obligation to keep confidential client information, including records. The rare exceptions to this caveat are situations where someone is potentially harmful to self or others and when there is a legal requirement to report child or elder abuse. How a counseling center handles issues of confidentiality can greatly affect its reputation and relationships on campus. On the one hand, students must be able to trust that, for example, parents will not be informed of declining grades or an acquaintance rape. On the other hand, parents' phone calls must be handled diplomatically and appropriate permission obtained from the client to consult with cooperating services such as the Health Service or Campus Police.

Issues of confidentiality and other legal and ethical issues have become even more complex since the 1970s due to modern technology (e.g., computer data bases and voice mail). In the early to mid-1990s, many counseling centers experienced budget cuts (Gallagher et al., 1994). Economic considerations and national health care reform may change funding patterns, or even eliminate some college and university counseling services. Reimbursement by insurance or managed health care programs requires the use of psychiatric diagnoses and possible review of records by third party payers. This presents many challenges to confidentiality as well as to adherence to a student development model (Crego, 1995; Gilbert, 1994). The need by many centers to limit the number of counseling sessions raises the question of whether it is ethical to provide any services for students who might require a consistent long-term therapy relationship, such as survivors of sexual abuse (Lilly-Weber, 1993). Just as the percentage of women enrolled in higher education increased steadily in the 1980s, women students constitute the majority of clients in most college counseling services and frequently request to talk with a female counselor (Pace, Stamler, & Yarris, 1992). Such requests could present ethical dilemmas such as a longer wait for services for female students and greater burn-out among female staff. As the number of students with serious emotional problems increases, so too does the risk of behavioral disturbances (Dannells & Stuber, 1992). Delworth (1989) distinguished among students who are disturbed, disturbing, or both. Students whose behavior is problematic to the community may warrant assessment, possible treatment, or mandatory psychiatric withdrawal (Dannells & Stuber, 1992). Counseling centers are being asked to intervene and make decisions about students who come to the attention of others on campus. Conflicting loyalties and confidentiality dilemmas might arise (Amanda, 1993; Gilbert, 1989). With increased requests for counseling centers to provide mandated disciplinary counseling, directors report ambivalence about the provision of such services (Stone & Lucas, 1994). Other challenges to confidentiality are the increased need to notify others of potential suicidal or homicidal behavior, the need to report child abuse, and questions about whether the unprotected sexual activity of a person living with

HIV constitutes reportable harm to others (Gallagher, 1990, 1991, 1992; Gallagher et al., 1993; Gallagher, 1994). Additionally, greater use of electronic communication has resulted in the need to develop policy statements such as that at Carnegie Mellon which indicate to students that counseling center staff will not respond to personal problems by E mail (Gallagher, personal communication, July 5, 1995).

In contrast to coping with increased service demands is the challenge of meeting the needs of those who are less likely to request services, such as some international students, ethnic minority students, and most students who kill themselves (e.g., Atkinson, Jennings, & Liongson, 1990; Oropeza, Fitzgibbon, & Baron, 1991; Shea, 1995). A major challenge to the counseling center practitioner has been response to acts of violence. There has been an increase in reported incidents of stalking (Gallagher et al., 1993; Gallagher et al., 1994), including those involving injuries and deaths. Federal legislation, such as the Campus Security Act, requires institutions to publish crime statistics and to actively respond to the needs of campus violence victims (Garland & Grace, 1993). Although the numbers of homicides on and around campuses are small, the impact of such disasters on the campus community is far-reaching and requires immediate and expert intervention (Allen, 1992). The University of Florida has had to deal with the fear and panic related to serial murders (Archer, 1992). At the University of Iowa, a graduate student who did not receive the recognition he had hoped for shot and killed three faculty members, a recent graduate from the Physics Department, the Associate Vice President for Academic Affairs, and then took his own life. A former student employee was permanently paralyzed (Stone, 1993). The difficulty in predicting and preventing violence to self and others was brought into question by an incident at Harvard University where a student stabbed her roommate to death and then hanged herself. Although the suicide rate among college students is less than among Americans aged 15 to 24 who are not in college, suicide remains the second leading cause of death (after accidents) of college students (Shea, 1995).

Lastly, more counseling centers are evaluating their services (Magoon, 1995). Accountability, along with strategic planning, is recommended in times of competition for resources (Stone and Archer, 1990). Other administrative issues of concern have been the slight trend toward merging of counseling centers with student health services and either charging a fee for services, or depending upon mandatory student fees.

For example, one survey found that 9.5 percent of previously independent counseling centers became administratively part of student health, while 6.4 percent became independent of student health (Gallagher et al., 1993). Another administrative change occurring at a small number of institutions is the movement of career counseling out of the counseling center (Gallagher et al., 1994). About 13 percent of 310 centers surveyed reported such a move between 1988 and 1993. However, the wisdom of such changes in counseling services delivery systems has been seriously questioned (e.g., Stone and Archer, 1990; Gillespie, Tentoni, Graham, Browne, & Morgan, 1995).

MAJOR PROFESSIONAL ASSOCIATIONS

Professional organizations provide opportunities for colleague interaction, professional development, collection and dissemination of information, contributions to the field through publications, presentations, and committees, as well as the establishment and maintenance of standards.

The Association for University and College Counseling Center Directors (AUCCCD) is the professional affiliation for directors of centers with three or more full-time equivalency staff (Gallagher et al., 1994). This organization is primarily concerned with the functioning of counseling centers as integral parts of collegiate institutions (Archer & Bingham, 1990). Annual Director's Conferences have been used to establish guidelines, review accountability issues, develop clearinghouses for the dissemination of innovative counseling programs, and to formulate constructive responses to the challenges facing counseling centers. AUCCCD established a Task Force to pursue methods to support and collaborate with directors of small counseling centers ("AUCCCD Establishes," 1994).

The major professional affiliations for counseling center staff members are the American Psychological Association (APA), with possible involvement in Division 17 (Counseling Psychology) and the American College Personnel Association (ACPA) (Magoon, 1994). Commission VII (Counseling and Psychological Services) of ACPA is a very active organization of a wide range of professionals interested in counseling and psychological services in community colleges, colleges, and universities. Affiliation with the American Counseling Association (formerly the American Personnel and Guidance Association) has declined, especially among staff of larger institutions (Magoon, 1994); however, this organization is reported to be the most popular national association for community college counselors (Coll, 1993a). Some counseling center staff also are active in their state psychological or college personnel associations and 3 percent are affiliated with the American College Health Association (Gallagher et al., 1994).

Those centers providing predoctoral internship training maintain memberships in the Association of Counseling Center Training Agents and the Association of Psychology Internship Centers. In addition to their own meeting schedule, these organizations as well as AUCCCD frequently meet at the annual conventions of APA and ACPA. It is important to note that in these rapidly changing times, traditional methods of professional communication—publications and meetings—have been greatly augmented by use of electronic communication.

The International Association of Counseling Services, Inc. developed standards that are used for the formal accreditation of college and university counseling programs (Kiracofe et al., 1994). Approximately half of the centers from institutions of over 15,000 are accredited by IACS (Gallagher et al., 1994).

Relevant periodicals for counseling center staff include: *The Counseling Psychologist, The Journal of Counseling Psychology,* and *Professional Psychology: Research and Practice,* all journals of the American Psychological Association. Also relevant are the *Journal of College Student Development* (ACPA), the *Journal of Counseling and Development* (ACA), the *Journal of Multicultural Counseling and Development* (ACA), *The Journal of College Student Psychotherapy,* and the newsletters of professional organizations (Hood & Arceneaux, 1990; Stone & Lucas, 1991).

In addition, various databanks are available such as the AUCCCD Data Bank collected by Dr. Thomas Magoon at the University of Maryland and the National Survey of Counseling Center Directors collected by Dr. Robert Gallagher at the University of Pittsburgh. The Research Consortium of Counseling and Psychological Services in Higher Education, organized by David Drum at the University of Texas at Austin currently includes forty institutions (Drum, 1995).

Finally, all professionals in counseling and higher education administration share a responsibility to continue the development of their professional skills and understanding, especially since student culture and needs change (Bishop, 1992). In some states, it is a legal requirement to demonstrate continuing education to maintain one's license in a professional field. Such continuing education credits might be earned from attendance at workshops aimed at a specific issue (such as a conference on counseling persons living with HIV and AIDS) and from relevant presentations at conventions such as those of ACPA and APA.

QUALIFICATIONS FOR ENTRY-LEVEL EMPLOYMENT

Counselors were the first of the student services staff to become professionals in terms of their training, and remain so because of the specific specialized training necessary, their professional organizations with codes of ethics, and the movement toward accreditation and licensure (Hood & Arceneaux, 1990).

A survey (Gallagher et al., 1994) of 310 counseling center directors found that about 85 percent of the centers have a licensed psychologist on staff, 32 percent reported staff as licensed M.S.W.s and 51 percent have a certified or licensed professional counselor. For institutions with enrollments over 15,000, almost 97 percent report having licensed psychologists on staff. A doctoral degree in clinical or counseling psychology has been the most typical educational requirement, especially for staff of centers at larger four-year colleges and universities. However, in community colleges, the staff is more likely to have master's degrees (Coll, 1993b). In many centers an entry-level staff member is expected to be licensed or license-eligible which means having completed a doctoral program that is either accredited by the American Psychological Association or otherwise fulfilling state requirements to be admitted to the licensing examination. This will include a year-long predoctoral internship and at least one year of supervised postdoctoral experience. Larger centers may require (20%) or prefer (35%) a psychologist with an APA approved internship (Gallagher, 1991). A similar process is required to become a licensed Social Worker or a Certified or Licensed Professional Counselor.

Accreditation Standards for University and College Counseling Centers (Kiracofe et al., 1994) require that professional staff should have at least a master's degree from disciplines such as counselor education, counseling psychology, clinical psychology, psychiatry, or social work. Doctoral-level staff are expected to be licensed and certified to practice within their specialty and nondoctoral staff are encouraged to seek a similar credential. Appropriate course work and supervised experience in the counseling of college-aged students are required. Those who have administrative responsibilities or who supervise the clinical work of others must hold a doctorate or have an appropriate master's degree and experience in the training of other professionals. A psychiatrist holds a medical degree and has completed a residency in psychiatry.

Finally, standards of practice require competence in working with human differences (American Psychological Association, 1992) and freedom from prejudice with respect to race, religion, age, sex, sexual orientation, or physical challenge (Kiracofe et al., 1994).

Although employment in a university or college counseling center setting has tended to increase identification with counseling psychology (Phelps, 1992), it is predicted that proportionately more master's level counselors and social workers will be employed (Baron, 1995; Hotelling, 1995; Toth, 1995). Some counseling centers such as at Duke, Portland State, and the University of Texas at Austin are already moving toward more multidisciplinary staffs (Prieto, Sieber, Gabbard, & Micon, 1995).

FUTURE TRENDS

Describing the challenges for counseling centers in the 1990s, Stone and Archer (1990) concluded: we have a much clearer understanding of how difficult it is to predict the future" (p. 599). Current debates focus on what is necessary to survive in a rapidly changing world and uncertain economic times, while retaining a commitment to the counseling center mission of serving students. Deliberation over what proportion of counseling center activity should be focused on which goal continues. Some predict a change in the percentage of time and type of direct service activity. For example, Baron (1995) predicts that 25 percent will be spent on individual counseling, 25 percent on group counseling, and 50 percent on psychoeducational modalities for prevention, health promotion, and treatment compliance. Hotelling (1995) addresses the need for increased time spent in case management; the record-keeping and consultation needed to serve a student with complex problems, and in responding to calls about potentially violent students, a trend she observed following the killings at the University of Iowa. Many universities are discussing downsizing (32%) or reorganizing (48%) student affairs, or downsizing (14%), reorganizing (22%), or privatizing (10%) counseling services (Gallagher et al., 1994). It is expected that counseling centers will continue with the trends of hiring both a multidisciplinary staff and more part-time staff members. Today, there are slight trends for counseling centers to merge with student health or to lose the career counseling function. Stone and Archer (1990) and Bishop (1990) made a number of recommendations that included: the need to balance demands and resources; to continue involvement in career counseling and consultation activities; to focus on the needs of special student populations such as racial and cultural minorities, international students, adult learners, and student athletes; and to increase accountability with more active administrative styles.

Trends in counseling centers over time have parallelled those of counseling psychology. Due to changes noted above and to the increase of more serious concerns among some students who request services, counseling psychology has become more like clinical psychology with its link to mental health, medicine, and abnormal psychology (Tyler, 1992). Tyler emphasized that "whatever happens to counseling psychology as a profession, counseling psychology as a skill must not be lost" (p. 344). It has been strongly recommended that counseling centers reverse the 1990s trend toward a medical model and return to a more comprehensive developmental approach (e.g., Crego, 1990; 1995). Since most student problems are not diagnosable and will not be reimbursed by third party payers, Crego cautions that counseling centers are in danger of inventing a model that does not fit students' needs (personal communication, November 28, 1994).

Although many counseling center directors (60%) are concerned about the impact of national health care reform, most (75%) are uncertain about its potential impact (Gallagher et al., 1994). Another concern, "outsourcing" or "privatizing," of college counseling is highly speculative at this time due to the number of services provided by counseling centers (e.g., faculty consultations, outreach, developmental counseling) which cannot be provided by those outside the university community (Gallagher et al., 1994). Both AUCCCD and Division 17 of the American Psychological Association have task forces studying these issues. Stone notes that there are regional and institutional differences and cautions counseling centers to "not buy a pig in a poke" and not to panic "until the dust settles on health care reform and you (collective institution you) decide what fits with your situation" (1995, p. 6).

Dr. Thomas Magoon, a former counseling center director with a long history of professional involvement, recommends that counseling centers need to be seen as part of the university academy and that research is the key to building that bridge (Dressel, 1995). Magoon also recommends that counseling center staff be active in professional organizations, especially at the state level where laws governing psychology are being made.

REFERENCES

Allen, R. D. (1992, November). The counseling center director's role in managing disaster response. *Commission VII Counseling & Psychological Services Newsletter, 19*(2), 4–5.

Altmaier, E. M., & Rapaport, R. J. (1984). An examination of student use of a counseling service. *Journal of College Student Personnel, 25,* 453–458.

Amanda, G. (1993). The role of the mental health consultant in dealing with disruptive college students. *Journal of College Student Psychotherapy, 8,* 121–137.

American College Personnel Association. (1990). Statement of ethical principles and standards. *Journal of College Student Development, 31,* 11–16.

American Psychological Association. (1992). Ethical principles of psychologists and code of conduct. *American Psychologist, 47,* 1597–1611.

Archer, J. (1992). Campus in crisis: Coping with fear and panic related to serial murders. *Journal of Counseling and Development, 71,* 96–100.

Archer, J., & Bingham, R. (1990). Task force on organizational structure. *Proceedings of the 39th Annual Conference of the Association of University and College Counseling Center Directors,* p. 119.

Atkinson, D. R., Jennings, R. G., & Liongson, L. (1990). Minority students' reasons for not seeking counseling and suggestions for improving services. *Journal of College Student Development, 31,* 342–350.

AUCCCD establishes task force on centers with less than 3 FTE staff. (1994, March). *Commission VII Counseling & Psychological Services Newsletter, 20*(3), p. 7.

Aulepp, L., & Delworth, U. (1976). *Training manual for an ecosystem model: Assessing and designing campus environments.* Boulder, CO: Western Interstate Commission for Higher Education.

Baier, J. L. (1993). Technological changes in student affairs administration. In M. J. Barr and Associates. *The handbook of student affairs administration.* San Francisco: Jossey-Bass.

Baker, H. K. (1993). Counseling needs and graduate student characteristics. *Journal of College Student Development, 34,* 74–75.

Baron, A. (1995, March). *Transforming the academy: A counseling center perspective.* Paper presented at the meeting of the American College Personnel Association, Boston.

Berk, S. E. (1983). Origins and historical development of university and college counseling. In P. J. Gallagher & G. D. Demos (Eds.), *Handbook of counseling in higher education* (pp. 50–71). New York: Praeger.

Bertocci, D., Hirsch, E., Sommer, W., & Williams, A. (1992). Student mental health needs: Survey results and implications for service. *Journal of American College Health, 41,* 3–10.

Bishop, J. B. (1990). The university counseling center: An agenda for the 1990s. *Journal of Counseling and Development, 68,* 408–413.

Bishop, J. B. (1992). The changing student culture: Implications for counselors and administrators. *Journal of College Student Psychotherapy, 3/4,* 37–57.

Boggs, K. R. (1992). University Counseling Center, University of Utah. In B. M. Schoenberg (Ed.), *Conceptualizations: Counseling center models* (Series No. 9) (pp. 50–59). Alexandria, VA: International Association of Counseling Services, Inc.

Cameron, A. S., Galassi, J. P., Birk, J. M., & Waggener, N. M. (1989). Trends in counseling psychology training programs: The council of counseling psychology training programs survey, 1975–1987. *The Counseling Psychologist, 17,* 301–313.

Carney, C. G., Peterson, K., & Moberg, T. F. (1990). How stable are student and faculty perceptions of student concerns and of a university counseling center? *Journal of College Student Development, 31,* 423–428.

Carney, C. G., Savitz, C. J., & Weiskott, G. N. (1979). Students' evaluations of a university counseling center and their intentions to use its programs. *Journal of Counseling Psychology, 26,* 242–249.

Coll, K. M. (1993a). *Community college counseling: Current status and needs.* (Series No. 10). Alexandria, VA: International Association of Counseling Services, Inc.

Coll, K. M. (1993b). Role conflict differences between community college counselors from accredited centers and nonaccredited centers. *Journal of College Student Development, 34,* 341–345.

Conyne, R. K., Banning, J. H., Clack, R. J., Corazzini, J. G., Huebner, L. A., Keating, L. A., & Wrenn, R. L. (1979). The campus environment as client: A new direction for college counselors. *Journal of College Student Personnel, 20,* 437–442.

Corazzini, J. G. (1995, March). Counseling centers have a future. *Commission VII Counseling & Psychological Services Newsletter, 21*(3), p. 8.

Crego, C. A. (1990). Challenges and limits in search of a model. *The Counseling Psychologist, 18,* 608–613.

Crego, C. A. (1995, March). The medicalization of Counseling Psychology: Managed care v.s. developmental models in university and college counseling centers. *Commission VII Counseling & Psychological Services Newsletter, 21*(3), 9.

Dannells, M., & Stuber, D. (1992). Mandatory psychiatric withdrawal of severely disturbed students: A study and policy recommendations. *NASPA Journal, 29,* 163–168.

Delene, L. M., & Brogowicz, A. A. (1990). Student healthcare needs, attitudes, and behavior: Marketing implications for college health centers. *Journal of American College Health, 38,* 157–164.

Delworth, U. (Ed.). (1989). *Dealing with the behavioral and psychological problems of students (New Directions for Student Services,* No. 45). San Francisco: Jossey-Bass.

Demos, G. D., & Mead, T. M. (1983). The psychological counseling center: Models and functions. In P. J. Gallagher & G. D. Demos (Eds.), *Handbook of counseling in higher education* (pp. 1–22). New York: Praeger.

Dressel, J. L. (1995, July). Commission VII: A historical perspective. *Commission VII Counseling & Psychological Services, 22*(1), 3–4.

Drum, D. J. (1980). Understanding student development. In W. H. Morrill, J. C. Hurst, and E. R. Oetting (Eds.), *Dimensions of interventions for student development.* New York: John Wiley & Sons.

Drum, D. J. (1993, January). *Health care reform for counseling centers.* Paper presented at a meeting sponsored by Indiana Counseling Center Directors, Indianapolis.

Drum, D. J. (1995, March). Paper presented at the meeting of the American College Personnel Association, Boston.

Dunkel-Schetter, C., & Lobel, M. (1990). Stress among students. In H. L. Pruett & V. B. Brown (Eds.), *Crisis intervention and prevention (New Directions for Student Services,* No. 49), pp. 17–34.

Elfin, M. (1994, September 26). America's best colleges. *U. S. News & World Report,* 86–88.

Forman, M. E. (1977). The changing scene in higher education and the identity of counseling psychology. *The Counseling Psychologist, 7,* 45–48.

Gallagher, R. P. (1990). *National survey of counseling center directors.* Pittsburgh, PA: University of Pittsburgh, University Counseling and Student Development Center.

Gallagher, R. P. (1991). *National survey of counseling center directors.* Pittsburgh, PA: University of Pittsburgh, University Counseling and Student Development Center.

Gallagher, R. P. (1992). *National survey of counseling center directors.* (Series No. 8b). Alexandria, VA: International Association of Counseling Services, Inc.

Gallagher, R. P., Bruner, L. A., & Lingenfelter, C. O. (1993). *National survey of counseling center directors* (Series No. 8C). Alexandria, VA: International Association of Counseling Services, Inc.

Gallagher, R. P., Bruner, L. A., & Weaver-Graham, W. (1994). *National survey of counseling center directors* (Series No. 8D). Alexandria, VA: International Association of Counseling Services, Inc.

Garland, P. H., & Grace, T. W. (1993). *New perspectives for student affairs professionals: Evolving realities, responsibilities and roles.* ASHE–ERIC Higher Education Report No. 7. Washington, DC: The George Washington University, School of Education and Human Development.

Geer, C. (1995, March). *Transforming the academy: A counseling center perspective.* Paper presented at the meeting of the American College Personnel Association, Boston.

Gelso, C. J., Birk, J. M., Utz, P. W., & Silver, A. E. (1977). A multigroup evaluation of the models and functions of university counseling centers. *Journal of Counseling Psychology, 24,* 338–348.

Gibson, R. L., Mitchell, M. H., & Higgins, R. E. (1983). *Development and management of counseling programs and guidance services.* New York: MacMillan.

Gilbert, S. P. (1989). The juggling act of the college counseling center: A point of view. *The Counseling Psychologist, 17,* 477–489.

Gilbert, S. P. (1994, August). Practicing ethically in managed care treatment settings. *Commission VII Counseling & Psychological Services Newsletter, 21*(1), 2–4.

Gillespie, J. F., Tentoni, S. C., Graham, J., Browne, D. S. J., & Morgan, T. A. (1994, August). *Student funded university counseling centers: Operational challenges for year 2000.* Paper presented at the meeting of the American Psychological Association, Los Angeles.

Goodman, L. H., & Beard, R. L. (1976). An analysis of reported counseling services in selected public community colleges in the Southeastern United States. *Community/ Junior College Research Quarterly, 1,* 81–90.

Grayson, P. A. (1989). The college psychotherapy client: An overview. In P. A. Grayson & K. Cauley (Eds.), *College psychotherapy* (pp. 8–28). New York: Gulford Press.

Hedahl, B. M. (1978). The professionalization of change agents: Growth and development of counseling centers as institutions. In B. M. Schoenberg (Ed.), *A handbook and guide for the college and university counseling center* (pp. 24–39). Westport, CT: Greenwood.

Heitzman, D., Gilbert, S., Rabin, L., & Drum, D. (1991). Increasing severity of client disturbance: Realities and responses. *Proceedings of the 40th Annual Conference of AUCCCD*, 42–44.

Heppner, P. P., Kivlighan, D. M., Good, G. E., Roehlke, H. J., Hills, H. I., & Ashby, J. S. (1994). Presenting problems of university counseling center clients: A snapshot and multivariate classification scheme. *Journal of Counseling Psychology, 41,* 315–324.

Heppner, P. P., & Neal, G. W. (1983). Holding up the mirror: Research on the roles and functions of counseling centers in higher education. *The Counseling Psychologist, 11,* 81–98.

Hodgson, C. S., & Simoni, J. M. (1995). Graduate student academic and psychological functioning. *Journal of College Student Development, 36,* 244–253.

Hood, A. B., & Arceneaux, C. (1990). *Key resources on student services: A guide to the field and its literature.* San Francisco: Jossey-Bass.

Hotelling, K. (1995, March). *Environmental change and students at risk: Implications for counseling centers.* Paper presented at the meeting of the American College Personnel Association, Boston.

Hurst, J. C. (1978). Chickering's vectors of development and student affairs programming. In C. A. Parker (Ed.), *Encouraging development in college students.* Minneapolis: University of Minnesota Press.

Johnson, R. W., Ellison, R. A., & Heikkinen, C. A. (1989). Psychological symptoms of counseling center clients. *Journal of Counseling Psychology, 36,* 110–114.

Kiracofe, N. M., Donn, P. A., Grant, C. O., Podolnick, E. E., Bingham, R. P., Bolland, H. R., Carney, C. G., Clementson, J., Gallagher, R. P., Grosz, R. D., Handy, L., Hansche, J. H., Mack, J. K., Sanz, D., Walker, L. J., & Yamada, K. T. (1994). Accreditation standards for university and college counseling centers. *Journal of Counseling and Development, 73,* 38–43.

Kirk, B. A., Johnson, A. P., Redfield, J. E., Free, J. E., Michel, J., Roston, R. A., & Warman, R. E. (1971). Guidelines for university and college counseling services. *American Psychologist, 26,* 585–589.

Lamb, D. H., Garni, K. F., & Gelwick, B. P. (1983). *A historical overview of university counseling centers: Changing functions and emerging trends.* Unpublished manuscript.

Leventhal, A. M., & Magoon, T. M. (1979). Some general principles for university counseling centers. *Professional Psychology, 10,* 357–364.

Likins, P. (1993). The president: Your master or your servant? In M. J. Barr & Associates, *The handbook of student affairs administration.* San Francisco: Jossey-Bass.

Lilly-Weber, J. (1993, November). Should survivors of sexual abuse be treated for this issue at college and university counseling centers? *Commission VII Counseling & Psychological Services Newsletter, 20*(2), pp. 3, 5.

Magoon, T. M. (1994). *College and university counseling center directors' data bank.* Unpublished manuscript, University of Maryland, College Park.

Magoon, T. M. (1995). *College and university counseling center directors' data bank.* Unpublished manuscript, University of Maryland, College Park.

McKinley, D. (1980). Counseling. In W. H. Morrill, J. C. Hurst, with E. R. Oetting and Others. *Dimensions of intervention for student development.* New York: Wiley.

Meilman, P. W., Pattis, J. A., & Kraus-Zeilmann, D. (1994). *Journal of American College Health, 42,* 147–154.

Miller, G. A., & Rice, K. G. (1993). A factor analysis of a university counseling center problem checklist. *Journal of College Student Development, 34,* 98–102.

Morrill, W. H., Oetting, E. R., & Hurst, J. C. (1974). Dimensions of counselor functioning. *Personnel and Guidance Journal, 52,* 354–359.

Nicholson, J. A., Shelley, R. F., & Townsend, D. (1991). The counseling center connection: A staff development program for student services personnel. *NASPA Journal, 28,* 278–284.

Oetting, E. R., Ivey, A. E., & Weigel, R. G. (1970). The college and university counseling center. *Student Personnel Series No. 11.* Washington, DC: American College Personnel Association.

Oropeza, B. A. C., Fitzgibbon, M., & Baron, A. (1991). Managing mental health crises of foreign college students. *Journal of Counseling and Development, 69,* 280–284.

Pace, D., Stamler, V. L., & Yarris, E. (1992). A challenge to the challenges: Counseling centers of the 1990s. *The Counseling Psychologist, 20,* 183–188.

Pace, D., Stamler, V. L., Yarris, E., & June, L. (in press). Rounding out the cube: Evolution to a global model for counseling centers. *Journal of Counseling and Development.*

Phelps, R. E. (1992). University and college counseling centers: One option for new professionals in counseling psychology. *The Counseling Psychologist, 20,* 24–31.

Prieto, S. L., Sieber, C., Gabbard, C. E., & Micon, J. (1995, March). *Organizational issues in merging mental health clinics and counseling centers.* Paper presented at the meeting of the American College Personnel Association, Boston.

Pruett, H. L., & Brown, V. B. (Eds.). (1990). *Crisis intervention and prevention (New Directions for Student Services,* No. 49). San Francisco: Jossey-Bass.

Richardson, B. K., Seim, D., Eddy, J. P., & Brindley, M. (1985). Delivery of counseling and psychological services in small colleges: A national study. *Journal of College Student Personnel, 26,* 508–512.

Rivinus, T. M., & Larimer, M. E. (1993). Violence, alcohol, other drugs and the college student. *Journal of College Student Psychotherapy, 8,* 71–119.

Roark, M. L. (1993). Conceptualizing campus violence: Definitions, underlying factors, and effects. *Journal of College Student Psychotherapy, 8,* 1–27.

Rosecan, A. S., Goldberg, R. L., & Wise, T. N. (1992). Psychiatrically hospitalized college students: A pilot study. *Journal of American College Health, 41,* 11–15.

Schneider, L. D. (1977). Counseling. In W. T. Packwood (Ed.), *College student personnel services* (pp. 340–367). Springfield, IL: Charles C Thomas.

Schoenberg, B. M..(Ed.). (1992). *Conceptualizations: Counseling center models* (Series No. 9). Alexandria, VA: International Association of Counseling Services, Inc.

Sharkin, B. S. (1995). Strains on confidentiality in college-student psychotherapy: Entangled therapeutic relationships, incidental encounters, and third-party inquiries. *Professional Psychology: Research and Practice, 26,* 184–189.

Shea, C. (1995, June 11). Suicide signals. *The Chronicle of Higher Education,* pp. A35–A36.

Sherrill, J. M., & Siegel, D. G. (Eds.). (1989). *Responding to violence on campus* (*New Directions for Student Services,* No. 47). San Francisco: Jossey-Bass.

Sprinthall, N. A. (1990). Counseling psychology from Greyston to Atlanta: On the road to Armageddon? *The Counseling Psychologist, 18,* 455–463.

Steenbarger, B. (1995, March). Managed care and the future of university counseling centers. *Commission VII Counseling & Psychological Services Newsletter, 21*(3), 2–4.

Stone, G. L. (1993). Psychological challenges and responses to a campus tragedy: The Iowa experience. *Journal of College Student Psychotherapy, 8,* 259–271.

Stone, G. L. (1995, March). Implications of managed care for counseling centers: A pig in a poke? *Commission VII Counseling & Psychological Services Newsletter, 21*(3), p. 6.

Stone, G. L., & Archer, J. (1990). College and university counseling centers in the 1990s: Challenges and limits. *The Counseling Psychologist, 18,* 539–607.

Stone, G. L., & Lucas, J. (1990). Knowledge and beliefs about confidentiality on a university campus. *Journal of College Student Development, 31,* 437–444.

Stone, G. L., & Lucas, J. (1991). Research and counseling centers: Assumptions and facts. *Journal of College Student Development, 32,* 497–501.

Stone, G. L., & Lucas, J. (1994). Disciplinary counseling in higher education: A neglected challenge. *Journal of Counseling and Development, 72,* 234–238.

Toth, M. (1995, March). *Transforming the academy: A counseling center perspective.* Paper presented at the meeting of the American College Personnel Association, Boston.

Triggs, J., & McDermott, D. (1991). Short-term counseling strategies for university students who test HIV-positive: The case of John Doe. *Journal of College Student Development, 32,* 17–23.

Tyler, L. E. (1992). Counseling psychology—why? *Professional Psychology: Research and Practice, 23,* 342–344.

Tyler, L. E. (1969). *The work of the counselor* (3rd ed.). Englewood Cliffs, NJ: Prentice-Hall.

Vigoda, R. (1995, June 19). For more at college, therapy is an elective. *The Philadelphia Enquirer,* A1, A6.

Waldo, M., Harman, M. J., & O'Malley (1993). Homicide in the university residence halls: One counseling center's response. *Journal of College Student Psychotherapy, 8,* 273–284.

Warnath, C. F. (1971). *New myths and old realities: College counseling in transition.* London: Jossey-Bass.

Warnath, C. F. (1973). *New directions for college counselors: A handbook for redesigning professional roles.* San Francisco: Jossey-Bass.

Westbrook, F. D., Kandell, J. J., Kirkland, S. E., Phillips, P. E., Regan, A. M., Medvene, A., & Oslin, Y. D. (1993). University campus consultation: Opportunities and limitations. *Journal of Counseling and Development, 71,* 684–688.

White, K., & Strange, C. (1993). Effects of unwanted childhood sexual experiences on psychosocial development of college women. *Journal of College Student Development, 34,* 289–294.

Whitaker, L. C. (1992). Psychotherapy as a developmental process. *Journal of College Student Psychotherapy, 6,* 1–23.

Whiteley, J. M. (Ed.). (1984). Counseling psychology: A historical perspective (Special issue). *The Counseling Psychologist, 12.*

Whiteley, S. M., Mahaffey, P. J., & Greer, C. A. (1987). The campus counseling center: A profile of staffing patterns and services. *Journal of College Student Personnel, 28,* 71–81.

Williamson, E. G. (1939). *How to counsel students.* New York: McGraw-Hill.

Williamson, E. G. (1961). *Student personnel services in colleges and universities.* New York: McGraw-Hill.

Witchel, R. L. (Ed.). (1991). *Dealing with students from dysfunctional families (New Directions for Student Services,* No. 54). San Francisco: Jossey-Bass.

Chapter 7

DISCIPLINE AND JUDICIAL AFFAIRS

MICHAEL DANNELLS

INTRODUCTION

A college or university is a *disciplined* community, a place where individuals accept their obligations to the group and where well-defined governance procedures guide behavior for the common good. (Carnegie Foundation for the Advancement of Teaching, 1990, p. 37)

Student discipline is a timely, complex, and controversial subject. It is timely because now, perhaps more than at any other time in the history of American higher education, campuses are in search of civility based on shared values while they are concerned about violence and disregard for others' rights (Carnegie Foundation, 1990). It is complex because it has many different and seemingly competing dimensions, including philosophical, legal, educational, and organizational issues. And it is controversial because it resides at the interface of community needs and individual liberties.

HISTORY

The history and evolution of college student discipline in America is very much reflective of the development of the institutions of higher education themselves (Smith, 1994). In colonial colleges, the president and faculty exerted total behavior control over students as part of the strict moral, ethical, and religious training that, along with the classical curriculum, was the accepted role and mission of the institution. "Discipline was *the* student affairs approach of this period ... " (Garland & Grace, 1993, p. 3). To control and mold the character of young colonial students, most of whom were in their early to mid-teens, extensively detailed codes of behavior and harsh penalties including public confessions and ridicule, fines, and corporal punishment, were commonly and liberally employed (Smith, 1994). The handling of more serious disciplinary matters was shared with the trustees, while the president often delegated less serious offenses to faculty (Leonard, 1956; Schetlin, 1967; Smith & Kirk, 1971).

Discipline became less paternalistic during the late 1700s and into the 1800s with the rise of the public university, the broadening of the university's mission, the increasing secularization and pluralism of higher education in general, and increasing enrollments. Punishments became milder, with corporal punishment almost disappearing; trustee participation in conduct matters declined; and counseling of student offenders emerged. As the president became increasingly occupied with an expanding curriculum, fiscal and administrative matters, and external relations, specialists were chosen from the faculty to deal with non-academic conduct of the students (Leonard, 1956; Schetlin, 1967).

During the 1800s, the introduction of the German university model, with its disregard for all but the intellectual growth of students and the demands of the Industrial Revolution on faculty for development of their academic disciplines, resulted in a major shift away from rigid behavior control to greater emphasis on self-discipline and self-governance (Brubacher & Rudy, 1968; Durst, 1969; Schetlin, 1967). More humanitarian and individualized methods of discipline were used, and more democratic systems involving student participation developed concurrent with student governments and honor systems (Smith, 1994). Student discipline encountered new challenges with the increasing attendance of women at colleges and universities; "supervising such daring activities as unmarried young men and women dining together in a campus dining hall" (Fenske, 1989, p. 30) complicated the administration of student discipline of the time.

By the turn of the century, the first deans of men and women had been appointed "to relieve administrators and faculties of problems of discipline" (ACE, 1937, p. 2); and during the early 1900s, these positions were established on most campuses. These early deans expanded both the philosophy and the programs of discipline in higher education. Idealistic and optimistic about the kinds of students they could develop, they approached discipline with the ultimate goal of self-control or self-discipline, and used more individualized, humanistic, and preventative methods. The concept of the student as a whole began to develop (Durst, 1969), and counseling as a form of corrective action became popular (Fley, 1964).

Discipline became an unfortunate point of separation between the early deans and the emerging student personnel specialists (Appleton, Briggs, & Rhatigan, 1978; Knock, 1985). While they had many purposes and approaches in common, the "personnel workers tended to view the deans' disciplining of students as antithetical to their developmental efforts" because they regarded the "dean's role as a disciplinarian only in the sense of punishment. This view, of course, separated the 'punishing' dean from the 'promoting' personnel worker" (Knock, 1985, pp. 32–33). As higher education expanded under the philosophies of meritocracy and egalitarianism, the campus student body became larger and more heterogeneous, resulting in increased disciplinary work for the dean, while the personnel worker "became the specialist in human development" (Knock, p. 33). Thus, the unfortunate schism widened as the dean was perceived as the "bad guy," interested more in control and punishment, while the student development specialist was viewed more positively as the true promoter of student interests and growth (Appleton et al., 1978).

After World War II and the influx of veterans into colleges and universities, campus facilities and regulations were tested by the large number of older and more worldly students who "could not digest the traditional palliatives served up by the dean to justify student conduct regulation and discipline" (Smith & Kirk, 1971, p. 277). But a crisis was avoided because veterans' overriding vocational orientation kept them preoccupied with academics. While they may have had little time for the dean's discipline, they also had little time or interest in revolting against it.

Throughout the 1950s and '60s, disciplinary affairs became less punishment and control-oriented, more democratic, and more focused on education and rehabilitation. Professionally trained counselors were delegated more responsibility and disciplinary hearing boards composed of both staff and students were established (Sims, 1971). The 1960s and '70s were characterized by increased student input into disciplinary codes and processes, broadened legal and educational conceptions of students' rights and responsibilities, and the introduction of due process safeguards in the hearing of misconduct cases. These developments may be attributed to several factors: more older students, the lowered age of majority, an increasingly permissive society, the civil rights movement, the realization of the power of student activism and disruption on many campuses, and court intervention in the disciplinary process (Gibbs, 1992; Smith, 1994).

This court intervention, coupled with genuine concern for students' constitutional rights, led many colleges and universities in the 1960s to establish formal, legalistic "judicial systems" for the adjudication of misconduct and the determination of sanctions. This movement caused concern that such adversarial systems, borrowed from our system of criminal justice, focused primarily on the mechanism of the disciplinary process to the detriment of the educative purpose (Dannells, 1978). The literature of the last two decades and contemporary practice of disciplinary affairs suggest a renewed and continuing interest in the reintegration of the concept and goals of student development within the framework of campus judicial systems designed to protect the legal rights of students and to educate all students involved in the process (Ardaiolo, 1983; Caruso & Travelstead, 1987; Greenleaf, 1978). The overzealous adoption of criminal-like proceedings seems to have faded (Dannells, 1990), in favor of a balanced approach designed to insure fairness, protection of the educational environment, *and* learning (Bracewell, 1988). But the court intervention of the '60s

> marked the beginning of a continuing struggle between two forces; the student development position that contends that discipline is an educational function and the legalistic position that views college discipline as an area of administration that should have identical or similar practices to those found in a public court of law. (Smith, 1994, p. 83)

DEFINITION, PURPOSE, AND SCOPE OF STUDENT DISCIPLINE

Probably no other specialty area has engendered so much debate, disagreement, and dissension in student affairs (Fley, 1964). As Appleton et al. (1978) put it, "the subject of discipline has been one of the most pervasive and painful topics in the history of student personnel administration" (p. 21). It raises fundamental questions about the goals of higher education, the role of student personnel work within it, and our view of students.

Much of the controversy and disagreement about discipline relates to its several meanings and purposes. Within the context of college student personnel work, discipline may be variously defined as: (1) *self-discipline,* or that virtue which may be regarded as the essence of education (Appleton et al., 1978; Hawkes, 1930; Mueller, 1961; Seward, 1961; Wrenn, 1949); (2) *the process of re-education* or rehabilitation (Appleton et al., 1978); or (3) *punishment* as a means of external control of behavior (Appleton et al., 1978; Seward, 1961; Wrenn, 1949).

Discipline defined as self-discipline has a firm grounding in educational philosophy and has received wide acceptance in the literature of the field. Discipline defined as re-education may be thought of as having self-discipline as its intended outcome, and it, too, has been generally accepted in the field. The first iteration of the Student Personnel Point of View (ACE, 1937) includes in its list of the components of an effective educational program, "[a]dministering student discipline to the end that the individual will be strengthened, and the welfare of the group preserved" (p. 4).

It is the third definition—discipline as punishment—which, while being generally rejected by today's student affairs professionals, tends to conjure up images of their predecessors, and perhaps some of their colleagues, as "snooping, petty battle-axes who made it their business to ferret out wickedness and punish all offenders promptly" (Fley, 1963; as quoted in Appleton et al., 1978, p. 22). According to Fley, this image led to the denial of the disciplinary function in the field. It is interesting to note that in the position statement, *A Perspective on Student Affairs* (NASPA, 1989), "campus discipline" is mentioned only in past tense and only in the section "Historical Overview." However, in its list of programs and services, the statement includes "[s]student affairs staff can be expected to . . . [s]support and advance institutional values by developing and enforcing behavioral standards for students" (NASPA, 1989, p. 16). Judging from the growing body of literature and research on the moral/ethical development of college students and its relationship to student discipline, it would appear that the discipline-as-punishment model has been rejected in favor of discipline-as-student-development (Ardaiolo, 1983; Boots, 1987; Caruso, 1978; Greenleaf, 1978; Ostroth & Hill, 1978; Pavela, 1985). In fact, the 1949 reiteration of the Student Personnel Point of View (ACE, 1949) explicitly sets forth the goal of "development of self-responsibility for behavior rather than in the spirit of punishment for misbehavior" (p. 10).

Authority to Discipline

Closely related to the purpose of student discipline is the matter of the institution's authority to do so. Seven different theories defining the institution's source of power to discipline its students and describing to some degree the nature of the student-institutional relationship have been identified (Dannells, 1977), but only three—the doctrine of *in loco parentis,* the contract theory, and the educational purpose theory—merit description here.

In loco parentis, literally "in the place of a parent; instead of a parent" (Black, 1968, p. 896), is a common law doctrine which views the institution as taking the role of the parent with respect to all student conduct. In this view, the institution is presumed to know best the needs of students and is vested with great latitude in the disciplinary process (see *Gott v. Berea College,* 1913). As such, this doctrine was once used as the justification for paternalistic, informal, and sometimes arbitrary use of power to discipline (Ratliff, 1972), even though, according to Appleton et al. (1978) "its formalization into the law occurred long after the original relationship was abandoned in practice" (p. 25). Ever since its application to the college disciplinary situation, this doctrine has been problematic; it has been criticized as impractical, erroneous, and misleading as a viable educational concept (Penney, 1967; Ratliff, 1972; Strickland, 1965). Today, while vestiges of paternalism may still exist in the reaffirmation of concern for the whole student as reflected in student development theory and practice (Gregory & Ballou, 1986; Parr & Buchanan, 1979; Pitts, 1980), the doctrine of *in loco parentis* as a legal description of the student-institutional relationship is generally considered to be inappropriate, untenable, intolerable, or simply dead.

Contract theory defines the relationship of the student and institution as a contractual one, the terms of which are set forth in the institution's catalogue, other publications, and oral addenda. Students enter the contract by signing the registration document and paying fees, and thereby accepting the conduct rules and academic regulations. Violations of the rules may then be met with those measures enumerated as sanctions in the contract. This theory was once restricted largely to private institutions and to academic affairs; but now, with the lowered age of majority, older students, increasing consumerism, and the general litigiousness in our society, it is seeing increasing acceptance and application to all student-institutional relationships (Barr, 1988; Hammond, 1978; Shur, 1983, 1988).

Educational *purpose theory* views the student-institutional relationship as an educational one, thereby limiting disciplinary control to student behavior adversely affecting the institution's pursuit of its educational mission. Given that the institution's *raison d'etre* is education and that this is the reason for its relationship with students, this view is considered by many to be the only realistic and justifiable basis for student discipline (Callis, 1967, 1969; Carnegie Commission, 1971; National Education Association, 1971; Penney, 1967; Van Alstyne, 1966). It stems from the premise that the academy is a special place, with a special atmosphere in which educators attempt to fashion an environment "where dialogue, debate, and the exchange of ideas can proceed unfettered, . . . [and] in which there is concern about preserving the sanctity of the classroom and protecting academic freedom" (Gehring & Bracewell, 1992, p. 90). This theory allows the institution to discipline students for the purpose of maintenance of order or in furtherance of its educational objectives vis-a-vis an individual student or group of students. It protects the institution from unwanted court intrusion by recognizing that the courts have historically adopted a policy of non-intervention or judicial restraint in the matters which are legitimately part of the educational enterprise (Ardaiolo, 1983; Travelstead, 1987). Furthermore, the educational purpose theory serves to remind us of the inherent superiority of achieving student discipline through proactive means, especially in the face of a permissive society. In the words of Georgia (1989):

> The key to maintaining discipline among college students in a permissive society lies in recognizing the university as a space of relative autonomy—as a protected enclave for the actualization of high professional standards and as an accepted arena for the untrammeled pursuit and advancement of knowledge. Whatever paradox or irony is sensed in this juxtaposition of freedom and discipline derives from our received, and ultimately false, opinion that discipline can only be maintained through control and punishment. By making the most of the social and intellectual space vouchsafed for the performance of their educational duties, educators can help maintain discipline and at the same time communicate important values to their students, even in the face of the more debilitating aspects of society's permissiveness. (p. 93)

Student Misconduct: Sources and Responses

What constitutes misconduct is a function of the goal of student discipline and of the nature and number of rules and regulations which follow (Foley, 1947; Seward, 1961; Williamson, 1956, 1961; Williamson & Foley, 1949; Wrenn, 1949). Other institutional factors which influence the frequency and nature of student misconduct include the full array of campus environmental conditions. It is understandable why residential campuses with largely traditional-aged student populations have greater disciplinary case loads than commuter/nonresidential campuses.

Intrapersonal sources of student misconduct may be categorized as pathological or nonpathological. Nonpathological misbehavior may be viewed as stemming from lack of information or understanding or from inadequate or incomplete development, once referred to as immaturity or adolescent mischievousness and excess energy (Williamson, 1956). Pathological origins of student behavior have become of greater interest and concern as serious psychopathology among college students seems to be on the rise, at least insofar as it is manifest in such behaviors as sexual harassment, acquaintance rape, other forms of dating violence, alcohol abuse, and "stalking" (Gallagher, Harmon, & Lingenfelter, 1994). However, the increasing concern for behaviors which stems from pathological origins has not been accompanied by a significant increase in the frequency of the types of disciplinary cases one might expect (Dannells, 1991).

Institutional responses may be categorized as punitive (commonly called "sanctions"), rehabilitative (educational or developmental are more popular terms today), and environmental (actions aimed at external sources of misconduct). The extent to which a given sanction is best categorized as punitive, or developmental, is a matter of philosophy and purpose. While sanctions may be viewed as punitive in the immediate — particularly by the recipient — they are a proper and effective developmental or therapeutic tool for much of the problematic behavior of traditional-aged college students, many of whom are still learning to manage impulses (Frederickson, 1992).

Sanctions commonly employed include various forms of "informative" disciplinary communications, such as oral and written warnings or admonitions, often accompanied by a reference to more severe sanctions to follow if problems continue; disciplinary probation; denial of relevant privileges or liberties, such as restrictions on social hours or the use of facilities, often used as a condition of probation; restitution, or monetary compensation for damage or injury; fines; denial of financial assistance (now thought to be rare); and actions which affect the student's status, such as suspension (the temporary dismissal of the student for either a finite period or indefinitely) and expulsion (permanent dismissal). In recent years many campuses have added to the range of disciplinary sanctions, often by adding fines and required labor, but the actual use of disciplinary sanctions and rehabilitative actions appears to have changed little (Dannells, 1990, 1991).

Institutional responses involving rehabilitation or intentional human development include counseling, referral for medical or psychiatric care, and the assignment of a civic or public service project designed to enhance appreciation or awareness of personal responsibility. Disciplinary counseling may involve a professionally trained counselor; other professionals within the institution, such as an administrator or faculty member associated with the campus judicial system or with the residence hall program; or extra-institutional assistance from parents, clergy, social workers, or other helping professionals.

Actions aimed at sources of misbehavior external to the student include changing living arrangements and finding financial assistance or employment. Other possible responses are academic assistance, such as tutoring or learning skills development, and policy revision, where the "misconduct" is more a function of outmoded or unnecessarily restrictive rules.

The choice of institutional response in a disciplinary situation is affected by a number of considerations: one's views on changing human behavior; the institution's educational mission as reflected in the nature and extent of its behavioral standards; the degree of divergence between those standards and those of its students; the behavior itself; what kinds of information about the accused are judged to be important (Janosik, 1995); the array of responses established in policy; and the creativity of the decision-maker(s).

Extent of Institutional Jurisdiction

Two basic questions arise with respect to the extent of the institution's jurisdiction: (1) Should it apply internal sanctions, seek external (i.e., criminal) sanctions, or both where institutional rules and criminal law both apply (Stein, 1972)?; and (2) Should the institution concern itself with students' off-campus behavior? Concerning both questions, the recent trend and in keeping with the educational purpose theory of discipline is that internal actions are appropriate in all cases, whether on- or off-campus behavior is involved, where the institutional mission is affected. Dannells' (1990) research on changes in the practice of disciplinary affairs over the period 1978 to 1988 showed a significant increase in the number of institutions that concerned themselves with the off-campus behavior of their students. The question of the application of criminal law is essentially a separate matter, especially in dealing with students who are legal adults and when the criminal act is of a serious nature (Sims, 1971; Stein, 1972).

Double jeopardy is an issue related to jurisdiction. On occasion, students have argued that, for the same act, to be both disciplined by their institution and tried for a criminal offense constitutes double jeopardy. However, it is well established that double jeopardy applies only to criminal proceedings and not to college disciplinary actions (Fisher, 1970; Rhode & Math, 1988). Nonetheless, it is recommended that the institution avoid the mere duplication of criminal punishments by emphasizing the educational approach of its proceedings and subsequent response (Ardaiolo & Walker, 1987; Fisher, 1970).

Constitutional Limitations on Jurisdiction

Another general jurisdictional issue is the extent to which the institution can proscribe students' behavior. In the area of students' constitutional rights, four principles are well established: (1) The college cannot put a blanket restraint on students' First Amendment rights of freedom of assembly and expression, but it may restrain assembly and expression which will interfere with its educational and administrative duties (Gibbs, 1992; Mager, 1978; Pavela, 1985; Sherry, 1966; Young, 1970). (2) The institution cannot restrict, prohibit, or censor the content of speech, except for extraordinarily compelling reasons, such as someone's safety (Mager, 1978; Pavela, 1985; Sherry, 1966). (3) The college cannot apply its rules in a discriminatory manner (Sherry, 1966). (4) Students are protected by the Fourth Amendment from unreasonable searches and seizures. For example, the institution may not enter and examine a residence hall room unless it does so in furtherance of its educational aims which include protection of its facilities (Bracewell, 1978; Fisher, 1970; Young, 1970).

Due Process

Due process, while a flexible concept (Bracewell, 1988) related to time and circumstances (Ardaiolo, 1983), may be defined as "an appropriate protection of the rights of an individual while determining his [her] liability for wrongdoing and the applicability of punishment" (Fisher, 1970, p. 1). It is a constitutional right granted by the Fifth Amendment with respect to action by the federal government and by the Fourteenth

Amendment with respect to state action. The well-established standard used by the courts when questions of due process have arisen in the context of student discipline is that of *fundamental fairness* (Ardaiolo, 1983; Bakken, 1968; Buchanan, 1978; Fisher, 1970; Young, 1972).

Procedural due process refers to the individual's rights in the adjudication of an offense. That which is "due," or owing, to insure fairness in any given circumstance will vary with the seriousness of the alleged offense and with the severity of the possible sanction. Substantive due process relates to the nature, purpose, or application of a rule or law. Again, applying the standard of fairness, rules must be clear and not overly broad, they must have a fair and reasonable purpose, and they must be applied in fairness and good faith (Young, 1972).

Since 1960, there have been many court cases on due process in disciplinary proceedings, especially dismissal hearings. Prior to that time, under a combination of contract and *in loco parentis* theories, the courts generally assumed the college to be acting fairly and in the best educational interests of all concerned. But the civil rights movement, during which some students were summarily dismissed from college because of their participation in civil rights demonstrations, prompted significant legal and philosophical changes (Ardaiolo, 1983; Bakken, 1968; Dannells, 1977). In the landmark case *Dixon v. Alabama State Board of Education* (1961), the court, on the basis of an analogy of education as property—thus bringing dismissal from a state college under the due process clause of the 14th Amendment—ruled that a student has almost a constitutional right to notice and a hearing. The *Dixon* court went on to recommend several procedural safeguards to insure fairness in such cases: the notice should give specific charges; the hearing should consider both sides of the case; the accused should be informed about witnesses against them and the nature of their testimony; the student should have a chance to present a defense; the findings of the hearing should be reported to the student; and the "requirements of due process are met in dismissal hearings where the rudiments of fair play are followed" (Dannells, 1977, p. 249).

Numerous court decisions since *Dixon* established it as precedent and further specified the procedural due process safeguards for dismissal and other serious conduct hearings from public institutions. A detailed summary of relevant court cases is available in Pavela (1985). All of the procedural safeguards required in criminal proceedings are not required in student conduct hearings (Correnti, 1988; Gehring & Bracewell,

1992; Shur, 1983) and no one particular model of procedural due process is required (Bracewell, 1988; Buchanan, 1978; Travelstead, 1987).

In the area of substantive due process, several principles are well established (Arndt, 1971; Buchanan, 1978): (1) Colleges have the authority to make and enforce rules of student conduct to maintain discipline and order. (2) Behavioral standards, including rules applied to off-campus behavior, must be consistent with the institution's lawful purpose and function. (3) Rules must be constitutionally fair, reasonable, and not capricious or arbitrary. (4) The code of conduct should be written and available for all to see. (5) The constitutionally guaranteed rights of students can be limited to enable the institution to function, but blanket prohibitions are not permitted. (6) A rule must be specific enough to give adequate notice of expected behavior and to allow the student to prepare a defense against a charge under it. Vague or overly broad rules, such as general proscriptions against "misconduct" or "conduct unbecoming a Siwash College student," have not been upheld (Gehring & Bracewell, 1992).

The courts have not required private institutions to meet due process standards because they are not engaged in state action and so do not fall under the 14th Amendment (Buchanan, 1978; Shur, 1983, 1988). The analogy of education as a property right has not been extended to private schools, and their relationship with their students is still considered largely contractual. Thus, despite many projections in the 1970s that the courts would abolish the public-private distinction in disciplinary matters, the private institution still legally has more latitude in defining and adjudicating student misconduct (Correnti, 1988; Shur, 1983, 1988). But procedural reforms tend to become normative in higher education; many private colleges now contract with their students to provide the basic due process protections expected in public institutions and having done so, they are contractually required to follow their own rules and procedures (Pavela, 1985; Shur, 1983, 1988).

The courts have generally distinguished between academic dismissal and dismissal for misconduct (Rhode, 1983; Rhode & Math, 1988), although this dichotomy "may be very difficult to apply in fact" (Ardaiolo, 1983, pp. 17–18). In the landmark case of *Board of Curators of the University of Missouri v. Horowitz* (1978), the U.S. Supreme Court placed limitations on the due process procedures required in academic dismissal situations. Instead of a hearing, the student need only be informed of the particular academic deficiencies and of the consequences of those shortcomings, e.g., dismissal, should they not be remedied. Once this warning has occurred, the decision-making person or body must then make a "careful and deliberate" decision based on "expert evaluation of cumulative information" (p. 79). The court noted that this process is "not readily adapted to the procedural tools of judicial or administrative decision making" (p. 79) and declined to enter this academic domain. It should be emphasized that this case involved the academic evaluation of a student, and was not a matter of academic misconduct, such as cheating or plagiarism, where an allegation of wrong-doing is made and fact-finding is central to the disciplinary process. That distinction may be blurred and problematic in cases where it is difficult to distinguish misconduct, e.g., plagiarism, from poor scholarship (Travelstead, 1987) or where standards of dress, personal hygiene, or interpersonal conduct are the focus of evaluation in professional/clinical training.

ADMINISTRATION AND ORGANIZATION

The administration of student discipline, or campus judicial affairs/systems/programs, may be divided into three areas: (1) the roles and functions of student affairs professionals in discipline; (2) the nature and scope of campus judicial systems; and (3) the handling of disciplinary records. Research findings have been consistent in one important respect—from campus to campus there is substantial heterogeneity in approaches to student discipline (Dannells, 1978, 1990; Durst, 1969; Dutton, Smith, & Zarle, 1969; Lancaster, Cooper, & Harman, 1993; Ostroth & Hill, 1978; Steele, Johnson, & Rickard, 1984). Institutional factors influencing the nature of a campus' system include its educational philosophy/mission; its size, type of control (public or private), and residential character (Lancaster et al., 1993); the needs of the community; and the extent to which governance is shared with students (Ardaiolo & Walker, 1987).

Roles and Functions of Student Affairs
Professionals in Discipline

Student affairs professionals may be charged with a broad range of roles and functions related to the disciplinary process. At one end of the spectrum, they may function in the role of an ombudsman or mediator, independently and informally facilitating the resolution of conflicts and handling minor complaints. This approach has the advantage of brevity, keeping the problem at the lowest possible level of resolution; and it provides an educational, nonadversarial alternative for settling differences in certain situations (Hayes & Balogh, 1990; Serr & Taber, 1987; Sisson & Todd, 1995). At the other end of the spectrum there may be a specialist—often called a hearing officer or judicial affairs officer—charged with the responsibility of the total disciplinary system, including orchestrating the workings of one or more tribunals or boards, handling all disciplinary records, and investigating and preparing cases in more serious matters. The main advantages of this model are expertise and freeing other staff from the disciplinary function. Continuity, equity, and improved management of the process are also arguments for the specialist (Steele et al., 1984). Specialized judicial affairs officers are uncommon in smaller colleges; Steele et al. found that of the 18 schools (12% of their respondents) which reported judicial affairs officers, ten were large (10,000 + students) institutions. Lancaster et al. (1993) found that commuter, public, and large institutions are significantly more likely to have judicial specialists.

The most common model is that of a middle-level student affairs professional, most often associated with the dean of students office or the office of residence life, who informally handles relatively minor violations and presents serious cases to a hearing board for final disposition. For many years at smaller and private institutions, the dean of students had and continues to retain major responsibility for adjudicating student misconduct (Dannells, 1978, 1990; Lancaster et al., 1993; Ostroth, Armstrong, & Campbell, 1978; Steele et al., 1984).

Dutton, Smith, and Zarle (1969) identified four levels of involvement for those responsible for discipline: (1) noninvolvement, which frees the student personnel worker to concentrate on other matters; (2) involvement limited to case investigation and preparation; (3) involvement limited to case investigation, preparation, and adjudication in minor cases; and (4) full involvement, with action in all minor cases and referral of major cases to a judicial body on which the administrator sits as chairperson and final authority. In choosing a level of involvement, they suggested several considerations: What are the dean's most essential functions? What is the purpose of discipline? What role should students and faculty have in the process? Should student conduct be more of an administrative or community concern? What approach best protects the student and the institution?

Student affairs professionals involved in disciplinary programs may function as educators in several ways. As coordinators, advisors, and trainers of members of tribunals and policy boards, they have opportunities to encourage the development of students along moral, ethical, and legal lines (Boots, 1987; Cordner & Brooks, 1987). Working with students whose behavior is in question, they may, through a combination of teaching and counseling techniques, help students gain insight and understanding about their behavior and responsibilities. Furthermore, discipline officers can contribute to the intellectual climate of the institution not only by helping to preserve a safe and educationally conducive atmosphere (Boots, 1987), but also by leading the entire campus community in the process of defining and disseminating a behavioral code which represents a set of shared beliefs and values about the educational environment and the student's responsibilities within it (Pavela, 1985).

Caruso (1978) defined the important roles of the student discipline specialist in terms of the basic student personnel functions outlined by Miller and Prince (1976). *Goal setting* is important for keeping the discipline system in accord with the broader institutional goals, for working developmentally with the individuals, and for designing outcomes-oriented training programs for student judicial boards. *Assessing student growth* can provide important, yet frequently lacking, evaluative information about the efficacy of the disciplinary process for all of the students involved. *Instruction* may take the form of teaching credit or noncredit courses on the legal aspects of the profession, may involve student leadership training and judicial board member education, or may take the form of offering "mainstream" coursework in a collaborative or team-teaching approach with another academic unit in subjects like moral development, legal aspects of higher education, parliamentary procedure, or one of various life skills such as parent effectiveness. *Consultation* includes working with the campus disciplinary policy/rules committee, judicial boards, and paraprofessionals in the residence halls, and assisting academic units with the administration of academic misconduct cases. *Environmental management* involves any response to a behavior problem which is designed to reduce or eliminate conditions which contribute to that problem, such as the placement of residence hall fire protection equipment, campus lighting, and the sale and distribution of alcoholic beverages on the campus. Lastly is the important function of *program evaluation* through which the discipline program may study itself for purposes of improvement and justification of resources.

Disciplinary counseling is another function basic to the educational approach to discipline. Williamson (1963, p. 13) defined it as "sympathetic but firm counseling to aid the individual to gain insight and be willing to accept restrictions on his [or her] individual autonomy and behavior." Frequently cited objectives of disciplinary counseling include rehabilitation and behavior change, insight, maturation, emotional stability, moral judgment, self-reliance, self-control, and understanding and accepting responsibility for and consequences of personal behavior (Dannells, 1977). The counseling techniques of information-giving (teaching) and confrontation are central to the "helping encounter in discipline" and may be employed throughout the disciplinary process (Ostroth & Hill, 1978).

The Nature and Scope of Campus Judicial Systems

Like the roles and functions of the student affairs professional in discipline, campus judicial systems vary greatly depending on those key institutional factors (philosophy, size, etc.) cited previously. Smaller and private institutions tend to have more informal, centralized systems, while larger and public schools tend toward the more formal, legalistic, and decentralized/specialized model (Dannells, 1978, 1990; Lancaster et al., 1993; Steele et al., 1984). Campus judicial systems may differ on the extent of their authority and responsibility; the differentiation between criminal and campus codes and procedures and between academic and non-academic misconduct; how specifically behavior is defined and proscribed; the due process rights accorded the student at both the prehearing and the hearing phases of the adjudicatory process; the availability and application of sanctions, conditions, appeals, and rehabilitative actions; the nature and extent of student input into the code of conduct; the level of student involvement in the process of adjudication; and the availability of alternative adjudicative mechanisms (Ardaiolo & Walker, 1987).

Research conducted during the past 30 years revealed the following trends about the administration of student discipline: (1) In the 1960s there was a dramatic increase in student input into conduct rules and procedures and the adjudication of misconduct (judicial boards). This trend has abated and student involvement remains high on most campuses. (2) There has been a similar trend in the provision of both procedural and substantive due process mechanisms, starting with a major shift toward more legalistic processes and leveling in more recent years. Today, on almost all campuses, students can be expected to be afforded fair notice and application of conduct rules and fair procedures in the process of adjudicating an offense. More formal, legalistic procedures can be expected for cases which may result in dismissal, while more informal processes are used with minor cases. (3) Milder sanctions are more often employed than stiffer penalties. Warnings, both oral and written, and disciplinary probation have been and continue to be the most common responses to student misconduct. (4) Disciplinary counseling continues to be the most common rehabilitative action, but over the years it is increasingly more likely to take place in either a disciplinary specialist's office or in the counseling center, especially in larger institutions. At smaller colleges, the disciplinary function, including posthearing counseling, continues to be performed in the dean of students office. (5) While most institutions do not anticipate changes in their programs, those that do indicate a need for change suggest that it should be in the direction of streamlining and simplifying their processes and making their hearings less legalistic. (6) Diversity continues to characterize the administration of disciplinary affairs (Van Alstyne, 1963; Durst, 1969; Dutton et al., 1969; Leslie and Satryb, 1974; Ostroth et al., 1978; Dannells, 1978, 1990; and Steele et al., 1984).

Drawing upon the CAS Standards for Judicial Services, the Statement of Principles of the Association of Student Judicial Affairs, and the research base on the subject, Lancaster et al. (1993) offered the following model for organizing and administering the disciplinary function:

1. Assign, as a primary responsibility, all disciplinary administration to a single staff member, even where multiple hearing bodies exist.
2. Place this staff member in a direct reporting relationship to the president or chief student affairs officer.
3. Create a philosophy for this staff member's practice and for the disciplinary system that fosters a developmental approach to discipline.
4. Create a formal training and assessment procedure, supported by appropriate documentation, for judicial officers and other regular participants. (p. 118)

The Management of Disciplinary Records

Prior to the Family Educational Rights and Privacy Act of 1974 and the lowering of the age of majority, college students' parents were routinely notified of their sons' or daughters' disciplinary, and student records, including disciplinary files, were available to other agencies and prospective employers. But within a few years after "Buckley," Dannells (1978) found that the great majority of respondent institutions conformed to the law by keeping students' academic and disciplinary records confidential. Four-fifths of colleges kept their disciplinary records separate from other student records, and very few made them available to outside agencies or prospective employers without the student's consent. Only 8 percent reported releasing records to parents. Parents were notified of their student's involvement in the disciplinary process by 37 percent of the respondents if the student was a minor, but 30 percent indicated they did not notify parents regardless of the student's age. Little change in these practices was found in a follow-up ten years later (Dannells, 1990).

The widespread inclusion of students on disciplinary hearing boards raises an interesting question under the Buckley Amendment. It permits access to student records by faculty and staff for educational or administrative purposes, but it does not allow students (other than the student about whom the record exists) access. Is it a violation of the law for student members of judicial panels to review prior conduct records in the determination of sanctions or rehabilitative actions? What of their role in the creation of new disciplinary records? Pavela (1985) noted that students do not have a constitutional right to an open hearing, but the Buckley Amendment "would preclude holding an 'open' hearing without the consent of the accused student" (p. 43). Since it is arguable that the presence of other students on the hearing board constitutes an "open" hearing, it may be prudent to obtain a signed release from the accused. In recent years, student charges of unfairness in campus judicial proceedings have prompted interest, especially among journalists, in opening such hearings to the public. In January, 1995, the U.S. Department of Education issued final rules that amended FERPA to include disciplinary proceedings and subsequent actions as educational records, thus maintaining their confidentiality. But according to Gehring (1995a), the law is still ambiguous regarding records initiated by campus law enforcement officials, which might be interpreted as open under the Crime Awareness and Campus Security Act of 1990.

DISCIPLINE AND STUDENT DEVELOPMENT THEORY

Seemingly in reaction to the perceived excessive proceduralism following the *Dixon* case, the student affairs profession in the last two to three decades has shown renewed interest in the educational nature of discipline and the application of student development to the conduct of disciplinary affairs. Not only is there concern for protection of the individual's rights and of the institution itself, but there appears to be a growing realization of the primacy of the educational value in the disciplinary function. This is not to suggest that meeting students' legal rights and fostering their development are incompatible, which they are not (Greenleaf, 1978), but rather that the increasingly adversarial nature of the process became a significant drain on and distraction to those charged with administering campuses' disciplinary system. It became more difficult to find that proper balance necessary to the survival of the Student Personnel Point of View (Caruso, 1978). With the growing body of theory, research, and literature on cognitive, moral, and ethical development, there appears to be increasing interest in its application to the disciplinary setting (Saddlemire, 1980).

Student discipline is, and always has been, an excellent opportunity for developmental efforts. The traditional dean of students knew this but operated without the benefit of formal developmental theories, especially those emphasizing moral and ethical growth and so lend themselves to the disciplinary process. Much of discipline involves teaching (Ardaiolo, 1983; Ostroth & Hill, 1978; Travelstead, 1987) and counseling (Foley, 1947; Gometz & Parker, 1968; Ostroth & Hill, 1978; Stone & Lucas, 1994; Williamson, 1963; Williamson & Foley, 1949). By the application of developmental theory, the individual may be better understood and counseling/developmental interventions may be more scientifically and accurately fashioned (Boots, 1987).

Various developmental theories have been applied to the disciplinary process and its impact on the individual student (e.g., see Boots, 1987; Greenleaf, 1978; Ostroth & Hill, 1978; Smith, 1978), and certain common elements and objectives of the different views and approaches are noted in the literature. These include: (1) insight as a commonly stated objective and means to further growth in the individual "offender" (Dannells, 1977); (2) self-understanding or clarification of personal identity, attitudes, and values, especially in relation to authority, for both the student whose behavior is in question and also for students who sit on judicial boards (Boots, 1987; Greenleaf, 1978); (3) goals of self-control, responsibility, and accountability (Caruso, 1978; Pavela, 1985, 1992; Travelstead, 1987); (4) the use of ethical dialogue in both confronting the impact of the individual's behavior and its moral implications and examining the fairness of rules (McBee, 1982; Pavela, 1985; Smith, 1978); and (5) there appears to have been an extension of the scope and goals of student discipline to a broader objective of moral and ethical development as it relates to contemporary social issues, such as prejudice, health and wellness, sexism, racism, and human sexuality (Dalton & Healy, 1984).

In a recent survey of counseling center directors, Stone and Lucas (1994) found the following frequencies of goals for disciplinary counseling: assessment/evaluation, 28 percent; behavior change, 27 percent; student insight, 16 percent; education, 10 percent; establishment of appropriate goals, 5 percent; and "other," 14 percent. When asked to identify "reference material that the respondent would recommend for counseling center staff in working with disciplinary referrals" (p. 235), none of the counseling center directors offered developmental theory/theorists. This lack of reference to developmental theory may be taken as evidence of the oft-bemoaned theory-to-practice gap in student affairs, and may lend credence to the critiques of the usefulness of student development theory in our practice (e.g., see Bloland, Stamatakos, & Rogers, 1994).

Nonetheless, the weight of authority is clearly in keeping with Boots' (1987) assertion that developmental theory can be a "proactive part of the total educational process" (p. 67). Dannells (1991) provided an example of how that might be done:

> For example, in working with a student involved in disruptive behavior and underage drinking at a residence hall party, the student affairs professional may render an informal assessment (King, 1990) of the student's level of moral reasoning at Level 1 (preconventional morality), Stage 2 (relative hedonism) using Kohlberg's (1969) model. Concurrently, using Chickering's (1969) theory, the student may be viewed as struggling with developing interpersonal competence and managing emotions. This may be a common diagnosis that would lend itself to a group intervention focusing on the campus regulations about alcohol, the reasons for them, and the ways that students can be socially engaged without using alcohol. (p. 170)

Developmental theory is also useful for thinking about the relative maturity level of students (Thomas, 1987) and about the positive outcomes for all students. Chickering and Reisser (1993) explained:

Students may learn about community values and ethical principles when they either violate the conduct code or serve in judicial systems. The latter case represents an opportunity to develop integrity. In hearing cases, reviewing disciplinary procedures, and determining sanctions, students consider moral dilemmas in a concrete way.... By serving on hearing committees, students also benefit from watching faculty members, administrators, and staff members grapple with the arguments. The need for rules has not disappeared.... The challenge now is engaging students to take more responsibility for maintaining a safe and positive learning environment, becoming aware of the institution's code of conduct, and respecting the processes of enforcing and amending regulations. (p. 448)

CURRENT ISSUES IN STUDENT DISCIPLINE

Balancing Legal Rights and Educational Purposes

Following the *Dixon* decision in 1961, many institutions, private and public, rushed to establish disciplinary systems affording students their "due" protections. Some overreacted, went far beyond the court's requirements, and became "mired in legalistic disputes" (Lamont, 1979, p. 85). Critics of this "creeping legalism," or proceduralism, argued that it has undermined the informal and uniquely educational aspect of the disciplinary process in higher education; it has resulted in costly, complex, and time-consuming processes; and it places the student and the institution in an unnecessarily adversarial relationship (Dannells, 1977; Pavela, 1985; Travelstead, 1987). Ironically, "[m]uch of the complaining about excessive proceduralism and legalism is hollow. The excessive proceduralism, where it exists, has been largely caused by the institutions themselves" (Travelstead, 1987, p. 15). Judging from the frequency of the reminders in the literature, it would appear student affairs administrators need to be periodically reminded that "due process" is, in fact, a flexible concept which allows for the less formal/legalistic disposition of most disciplinary cases, especially when the penalty or outcome is less than dismissal (Ardaiolo, 1983; Bracewell, 1988; Pavela, 1985; Travelstead, 1987). As Bracewell (1988) pointed out, "[i]n less than two decades, colleges and universities have accommodated this legal concept [due process] in their regulations and disciplinary procedures" (p. 275), but "[a] strange amalgam of legalism and counseling was created" (p. 274). This "strange amalgam," and the struggle between the two opposing forces that created it, continues to plague many student affairs professionals engaged in disciplinary work (Smith, 1994).

Demands for More Supervision of Students

Some may find it ironic that not long after the celebration of the 25th anniversary of the "Joint Statement on Rights and Freedoms of Students" (see generally Bryan & Mullendore, 1992), and "[h]aving moved from strict control over student conduct to treating students as adults subject to much less control, institutions now are being pressed to take more responsibility for students' behavior" (Pavela, 1992, p. B1). According to Pavela (1992), the same consumer-protection movement that aided the progress for students' rights left students with concurrent liabilities, including taking more responsibility for themselves and making it more difficult for them to hold colleges responsible for injuries suffered at the hands of other students. He observed that student-consumer protection statutes, like the Crime Awareness and Campus Security Act,

> frequently go well beyond setting guidelines for reporting information to students; they often contain explicit or implicit requirements that specific disciplinary policies—like restrictions against underage drinking—be adopted, enforced, and monitored by colleges to protect students and members of the public." (pp. B1–2)

He pointed out that besides legislation, other social and economic forces have conspired to pressure colleges to take greater responsibility for their students' behavior, whether on or off-campus, "at the worst possible time" (p. B2). He called on deans and presidents to take the creative lead in setting and enforcing standards of student behavior which will result in more responsible and civil student conduct.

Pavela's charge comes at a time when concerns for campus crime and student safety may be at an all-time high. Sloan (1994) reviewed the findings of the 1990 U.S. Congressional Hearings on Campus Crime and reported that from 1985–1989, campus crime steadily increased, over 80 percent of campus crime involved students as both perpetrators and victims, and 95 percent of campus crime involved the use of alcohol or other drugs. Similarly, Ordovensky (as cited in Sloan, 1994), concluded that in the academic year 1989–90 on 481 campuses with 3000 or more students, of the 195,000 reported offenses, 64 percent of them were for burglary or theft, 19 percent were for vandalism, 11 percent were alcohol or other drug related, and less than 2 percent were for serious violent crime. He calculated the rate of reported crime for that period at 33 offenses was per 1000 students.

While "[m]ost studies of campus crime show that colleges are safer than the communities around them" (Lederman, 1995, p. A41), a recent

Chronicle of Higher Education report (Lederman, 1995) showed a "continuing increase in the number of violent crimes" on campuses with enrollments over 5000 (p. A41). With such reports, the pressure mounts for institutions to respond with preventative measures, criminal prosecution, and disciplinary action.

For more complete treatments of this subject, the reader is referred to Pezza (1995), Pezza and Bellotti (1995), and Sherrill and Siegel (1989).

Psychiatric Withdrawal Policies

Psychiatric withdrawal policies are troublesome because discrimination based on mental disorders is prohibited by the Americans with Disabilities Act and corresponding state statutes. Students may not be sanctioned, withdrawn, or treated in any other way solely on the basis of their perceived mental or medical state. However, if the student's behavior is disruptive to the educational environment or constitutes a danger to him/herself or others, the student may be involuntarily withdrawn pending a hearing wherein the usual due process safeguards are present (Pavela, 1985).

Since the behavioral manifestations of a "protected" mental/medical condition may be dealt with through regular disciplinary processes, it is reasonable to question the wisdom of psychiatric withdrawal policies. But as Brown and DeCoster (1989) noted, students in need of psychiatric care often do not see the relevance of such proceedings, peer paraprofessionals and/or volunteers often staff these systems, and the campus community may need immediate protection. In short, normal channels may not be sufficient, in which case psychiatric withdrawal may be necessary.

Many colleges either do not have a clear policy for such cases (Dannells & Stuber, 1992) or their policies give too much discretionary authority (Pavela, 1985; Steele, Johnson, & Rickard, 1984). According to Steele et al. (1984), after noting that 93 students were withdrawn from only 7 institutions in two years and one institution alone removed 21 during the same period, "some schools might be resorting to psychiatric withdrawals as an alternative to the traditional disciplinary process, by employing them to remove students who are simply perceived as troublesome or eccentric" (pp. 340–341).

Campuses approaching policy formation in this area might do well to consider the Assessment-Intervention of Student Problems (AISP) model articulated in Delworth (1989). The AISP model makes useful distinctions between a disturbing student, a disturbed student, and those who are both disturbing and disturbed. It also provides guidance about policy and procedure formulation for responding to behavioral and psychological problems of students.

Increasing Concerns about Academic Misconduct

In addressing this issue, it is important to distinguish between academic *evaluation* and academic *misconduct*. Academic evaluation refers to evaluative judgments made, typically by faculty, about the student's performance in a course or in the course of a professional training program. The courts have been reluctant to hear cases involving such professional judgments. In the determination of such decisions, including a decision to dismiss on the basis of academic deficiencies, students need not be afforded the same due process safeguards required in disciplinary cases. The landmark case in this area is *Board of Curators of the University of Missouri v. Horowitz* (1978).

Academic misconduct refers to violations of rules of academic honesty or integrity, such as cheating on tests or plagiarism "that involve students giving or receiving unauthorized assistance in an academic exercise or receiving credit for work that is not their own" (Kibler, 1993a, p. 253). The standards of due process in cases of academic misconduct are generally the same as those in nonacademic, or social, misconduct.

Academic misconduct, as it represents deviance from and erosion of the core value of academic integrity, has always been of concern in higher education; but in recent years the concern has grown even though empirical evidence of the increasing incidence of cheating is lacking (McCabe & Bowers, 1994). Estimates of the extent of cheating by college students vary widely. May and Loyd's review of research done in the 1980s found that "between 40% and 90% of all college students cheat" (1993, p. 125). Kibler (1993b) observed that cheating occurs on most, if not all, campuses; and that although it is difficult to prove it is actually increasing, "it is generally agreed that academic dishonesty is a serious issue for all segments of higher education" (p. 9).

The causes of academic misconduct and the many possible solutions to it are complex and beyond the scope of this chapter. However, one general approach deserves mention. As Gehring (1995b) has pointed out,

[b]oth NASPA's "Reasonable Expectations" and ACPAs "Student Learning Imperative" call for greater cooperation between student affairs and faculty affairs to enhance student learning. One area in which this can take place is that of fostering academic integrity. There are many issues involved in breaches of academic integrity—institutional environments, expectations, rules and regulations, moral reasoning and legal rights and responsibilities. Student affairs practitioners have expertise in many of these issues and could use that knowledge to assist faculty in improving the campus climate relative to academic integrity. (p. 6)

For student affairs professionals to assert their expertise into what many faculty consider their exclusive domain will not be easy. Faculty tend to ignore formal academic dishonesty policies and procedures (Aaron & Georgia, 1994; Jendrek, 1989). Despite its unpleasantness, faculty have a strong sense of duty in this area and possess more expertise when poor scholarship confounds the problem. But as Gehring (1995b) noted, many faculty do not understand the differences between academic judgments and misconduct decisions requiring due process— "something student affairs practitioners have been instructed in for the past 35 years" (p. 6). As Bracewell (1988) observed, the processes and procedures normally managed by student affairs professionals are ideally suited to the adjudication of academic dishonesty.

The Issue of Disciplinary Counseling

As previously defined, disciplinary counseling is one possible rehabilitative or educational response to student misconduct. It has a long history in the literature on student discipline (see, for example, ACE, 1937, 1949; Gometz & Parker, 1968; Snoxell, 1960; Williamson, 1956, 1963; Williamson & Foley, 1949; Wrenn, 1949), and was a commonly accepted practice since 1900. But with the rise of professional mental health centers on campuses, administrators charged with the responsibility for discipline began sending students for counseling as a form of rehabilitation, often as a condition of continued enrollment, and often with the expectation that the counselor would make some report on the progress of the student's development of insight and perhaps forecast the student's future behavior. By definition, disciplinary counseling is mandatory, or nonvoluntary, unless one supports the argument that the student can always choose dismissal rather than accept counseling, in which case it is, at least, coercive.

Referrals for disciplinary counseling appear to be increasing and disciplinary counseling is widely practiced (Dannells, 1990, 1991; Stone & Lucas, 1994) despite being highly controversial on two main points: ethics and efficacy. Almost half (48%) of the counseling center directors surveyed by Stone and Lucas (1994) responded that counseling centers should not do disciplinary counseling citing primary reservations as ethics (involving issues of coercion, confidentiality, and role conflicts) and management and effectiveness issues. Stone and Lucas concluded there is considerable confusion, ambivalence, and ambiguity about disciplinary counseling in the minds of counseling center directors. They called for a distinction between disciplinary *therapy* and disciplinary *education,* while admitting that such "sharply drawn conceptual differences often disappear in practice" (p. 238).

Amada (1993) strenuously objected to mandatory disciplinary psychotherapy for college students on several counts, including that it "distorts and undermines the basis for corrective disciplinary action" (p. 128); is "often motivated by fanciful and naive notions about psychotherapy" (p. 129); is "unequivocally a coercive measure that serves to instill in the student resentment toward the therapist and therapy itself" (p. 129); it lacks confidentiality; it is probably in violation of the laws that protect persons with handicaps from discriminatory treatment; and it "tends to transfer the responsibility and authority for administering discipline from where it rightly belongs—the office of the designated administrator—to where it does not belong—the offices of counselors and therapists" (p. 130). He concluded that disciplinary therapy is definitely unethical.

If disciplinary counseling (or psychotherapy) should not be performed in counseling centers, should it be the duty of administrators who also have the authority to sanction? If so, who is the "client"? The student? The institution? Both? These, and the foregoing issues are complex and challenging questions which deserve serious attention from student affairs professionals engaged in the disciplinary process.

PROFESSIONAL ASSOCIATIONS

Professionals engaged in the disciplinary process on their campuses would likely find benefit in membership in at least three professional associations: (1) The American College Personnel Association has a commission structure which includes Commission XV, Judicial Affairs and Legal Issues; (2) The Association for Student Judicial Affairs exists exclusively to address issues faced by administrators of campus discipline/

judicial systems; and (3) The National Association of Student Personnel Administrators addresses leadership and professional growth opportunities for senior student affairs officers and others who are charged with disciplinary responsibilities.

ENTRY–LEVEL QUALIFICATIONS

The Council for the Advancement of Standards (CAS, 1988), in its Standards and Guidelines for Judicial Programs, requires that professional staff members in judicial programs and services "have a graduate degree in a field of study relevant to the particular job in question and must have an appropriate combination of education and experience" (p. 23). And a "qualified member of the campus community must be designated as the person responsible for judicial programs" (p. 24). Qualifications for this designated individual are also provided:

> The designee should have an educational background in the behavioral sciences (e.g., psychology, sociology, student services/development, including moral and ethical development, higher education administration, counseling, law, criminology, or criminal justice).

> The designee and any other professional staff member in the judicial programs should possess: a clear understanding of the legal requirements for substantive and procedural due process; legal knowledge sufficient to confer with attorneys involved in student disciplinary proceedings and other aspects of the judicial services system; a general interest in the welfare and development of students who participate on boards or who are involved in cases; demonstrated skills in working with decision-making processes and conflict resolution; teaching and consulting skills appropriate for the education, advising, and coordination of hearing bodies; ability to communicate and interact with students regardless of race, sex, physical disability, or other personal characteristics; understanding of the requirements relative to confidentiality and security of judicial programs files; and ability to create an atmosphere where students feel free to ask questions and obtain assistance. Preprofessional staff from graduate programs, particularly in areas such as counseling, student services/development, or higher education administration and criminology, may assist the judicial programs through practica, internships, and assistantships. (p. 25).

THE FUTURE OF DISCIPLINARY AFFAIRS

The future of the disciplinary function in student affairs is inextricably tied to the futures of student affairs and of higher education. Innumerable influences will come to bear on those institutions, rendering futurism a risky and perhaps foolish enterprise. But as Sandeen and Rhatigan (1990) said, the "difficulty of accurate forecasting has never deterred people from the effort" (p. 98).

It is tempting to refer the reader to the section on current issues in disciplinary affairs and forecast more of the same. In many instances that strategy might well prove accurate, but there are some new, some different, and some continuing trends and indicators to consider in thinking about the future of disciplinary work in higher education.

The Changing Legal Environment

With the growing recognition and acceptance that the academy is a part of the "real world" and a microcosm of the greater society, the student-institutional relationship has become increasingly viewed as a consumer-business one subject to many of the same contractual expectations and constraints as any other seller-buyer, or landlord-tenant, relationship. Society, students, and even some students' parents no longer expect institutions of higher education to act on a vague set of social or parental rules in disciplinary matters. In particular, older students have little tolerance for paternalistic policies and processes. Instead, they wish to know exactly what is expected of them as adults. This has undoubtedly influenced many institutions to review carefully catalogues and other official documents, including codes of conduct, which may be considered part of the enrollment contract. This trend will continue, and it will benefit those who administer their campus' disciplinary system to closely review their rules and methods to ensure they are treating students like the adults they legally are.

Related to this is the projection (Hodgkinson, 1985; Kuh, 1990) that in addition to the increasing average age of future students, more will be part-time and more will be attending commuter institutions in urban settings. Since most student misconduct involves traditional-aged students in residential settings, this would suggest that the relative incidence of student misconduct should decrease over time. Alternatively, increasing pressure to get good grades may lead to higher rates of academic dishonesty. Both hypotheses are ripe for future research.

Forecasting the future regulatory and legal issues for student affairs, Fenske and Johnson (1990) noted seven crucial issues, two of which are most directly relevant for disciplinary affairs. One is that "[s]tudent affairs professionals will be increasingly involved in balancing the constitutional rights of students with the elimination of prejudice and harassment and the promotion of tolerance" (p. 133). The second is that "[c]ourt rulings and state laws on liability will require closer monitoring of on-campus and off-campus social events where alcohol is served, as well as increased willingness to take action against illegal drug and alcohol abuse" (pp. 133–134). Both of these issues have implications for codes of conduct and their enforcement.

The Continuing Need for Program Evaluation

Like any other student affairs program, disciplinary programs should be periodically and systematically evaluated to ensure that they are effectively meeting their established objectives (CAS, 1988). Those objectives should be defined in terms of measurable outcomes statements and evaluated on the basis of pre-established criteria and processes. The various components of the program; such as its publications, training program for judicial board members, consistency of sanctions, and procedures and practices, as well as the personnel involved in the execution of the program; should be included in a comprehensive review. Methods of evaluation will vary according to the nature and needs of the individual program, but may include interviews, direct observation, written reports, surveys, community feedback, task force review, and questionnaires (Emmanuel & Miser, 1987). It must be acknowledged, however, that scientific research in the area of student discipline has been and will continue to be problematic because of difficulties in identifying and controlling variables, in gathering data from recalcitrant program participants, and in meeting legal and ethical requirements for confidentiality and informed consent.

The Search for Common Values

Many institutions have recently engaged in lengthy processes to clarify institutional values as they are reflected in such documents as mission statements, codes of conduct, and academic integrity policies. Many institutions have yet to approach this formidable set of tasks, but they must, and most will do so.

The increasing diversity of the many constituents on campuses makes more challenging the task of finding and implementing common values. Cultural differences can be expected to complicate the disciplinary function; consensus about what constitutes acceptable behavior may no longer be taken for granted. Thus, it is all the more important that colleges and universities that for some time have not reviewed their codes of conduct do so, and in so doing to involve students, faculty, and staff from diverse backgrounds to insure a set of behavioral principles as widely accepted as possible.

The apparent increase in, and the new or renewed concern about, student cheating may prove an important and useful ground for the collaboration of academic affairs and student affairs leaders. Codes of conduct should include clear policy statements on academic integrity which are acceptable to faculty, understandable to students, and enforceable for faculty and the administrators who are responsible for discipline/judicial systems.

Garland and Grace (1993) listed twelve "potential focal points for collaboration between academic affairs and student affairs" (p. 62). At least four of them fall directly within the area of student discipline or have direct implications for it. They are:

> Manage disciplinary problems from a unified rather than a unilateral approach for consistency in response.
>
> Respond to alcohol and drugs on campus to prevent personal and academic debilitation.
>
> Respond to increased violence on campus.
>
> Respond to increased psychopathology, balancing the needs of troubled students and the community. (Garland & Grace, 1993, p. 62)

The Profession and Discipline

Student discipline has been, and perhaps should continue to be, a topic of professional concern and debate because it is such a dramatic reflection of our attitudes and assumptions about the nature of our students, our relationship to them, and our role in their development. There was a period in our profession's history when the subject was all but ignored, a source of embarrassment to be apologetically dispatched and forgotten in favor of more glamorous and "positive" functions.

Not long ago, after a careful analysis of the undergraduate experience at American colleges and universities, Ernest Boyer, President of the Carnegie Foundation for the Advancement of Teaching, wrote:

> What we found particularly disturbing is the ambivalence college administrators feel about their overall responsibility for student behavior. Most of the college

leaders with whom we spoke had an unmistakable sense of unease—or was it anxiety? Many were not sure what standards to expect or require. Where does the responsibility of the college begin and end? Where is the balance to be struck between students' personal "rights" and institutional concerns. . . . Unclear about what standards to maintain and the principles by which student life should be judged, many administrators seek to ignore rather than confront the issues. (Boyer, 1987, p. 203)

Student affairs leaders, particularly those charged with the responsibility for discipline, must actively and positively embrace that responsibility and stimulate the dialogue on campus necessary to insure that it is not ignored or dispatched halfheartedly and, ultimately, poorly.

Student Discipline, the Core Curriculum, and Liberal Education

Those concerned with student behavior and disciplinary/judicial systems should find encouragement in the widespread efforts in higher education to develop an integrated core curriculum which reaffirms the traditional principles of a liberal education and which may help create a climate on campuses where the development of the whole person, including the moral aspect, is once again paramount. This movement suggests exciting possibilities for student affairs professionals to "return to the academy" (Brown, 1972).

Many institutions are considering team-taught, interdisciplinary subject matter which will challenge an increasingly materialistic, aphilosophic, and career-oriented student body. Might there not be a place for a course entitled "Student Rights and Responsibilities in the College and the Community"? Such a course could be approached from a myriad of combinations of the different disciplines of law, political science, sociology, psychology, education, and philosophy (ethics) and could include the campus' chief disciplinary/judicial officer. In this way the subject of student conduct and moral/ethical development could be considered within the broader context of civic responsibility and community involvement. Thus, the moral dialogue inherent in a developmental approach to discipline (Pavela, 1985) could be brought to the classroom with the student affairs professional as an integral part of the teaching/learning partnership and process.

REFERENCES

Aaron, R. M., & Georgia, R. T. (1994). Administrator perceptions of student academic dishonesty. *NASPA Journal, 31*, 83–91.

Amada, G. (1993). The role of the mental health consultant in dealing with disruptive college students. *Journal of College Student Psychotherapy, 8*, 121–137.

American Council on Education (ACE). (1937). *The student personnel point of view* (American Council on Education Studies, Series 1, Vol. 1, No. 3). Washington, DC: Author.

American Council on Education (ACE). (1949). *The student personnel point of view* (Rev. Ed.). American Council on Education Studies, Series 6, Vol. 13, No. 13. Washington, DC: Author.

Appleton, J. R., Briggs, C. M., & Rhatigan, J. J. (1978). *Pieces of Eight.* Portland, OR: National Association of Student Personnel Administrators.

Ardaiolo, F. P. (1983). What process is due? In M. J. Barr (Ed.), *New Directions for Student Services: No 22. Student affairs and the law* (pp. 13–25). San Francisco: Jossey-Bass.

Ardaiolo, F. P., & Walker, S. J. (1987). Models of practice. In R. Caruso & W. W. Travelstead (Eds.), *New Directions for Student Services: No. 39. Enhancing campus judicial systems* (pp. 43–61). San Francisco: Jossey-Bass.

Arndt, J. R. (1971). Substantive due process in public higher education: 1959–1969. *Journal of College Student Personnel, 12*, 83–94.

Bakken, C. J. (1968). *The legal basis of college student personnel work* (Student Personnel Monograph Series No. 2). Washington, DC: American Personnel and Guidance Association.

Barr, M. J. (1988). Conclusion: The evolving legal environment of student affairs administration. In M. J. Barr & Associates, *Student services and the law* (pp. 347–353). San Francisco: Jossey-Bass.

Black, H. C. (1968). *Black's law dictionary.* St. Paul, MN: West.

Bloland, P. A., Stamatakos, L. C., & Rogers, R. R. (1994). *Reform in student affairs: A critique of student development.* Greensboro, NC: ERIC Counseling and Student Services Clearinghouse, University of North Carolina.

Board of Curators of the University of Missouri v. Horowitz, 90 S. Ct. 948 (1978).

Boots, C. C. (1987). Human development theory applied to judicial affairs work. In R. Caruso & W. W. Travelstead (Eds.), *New Directions for Student Services: No. 39. Enhancing campus judicial systems* (pp. 63–72). San Francisco: Jossey-Bass.

Boyer, E. L. (1987). *College: The undergraduate experience in America.* New York: Harper & Row.

Bracewell, W. R. (1978). An application of the privacy concept to student life. In E. H. Hammond & R. H. Shaffer (Eds.), *The legal foundations of student personnel services in higher education* (pp. 24–33). Washington, DC: American College Personnel Association.

Bracewell, W. R. (1988). Student discipline. In M. J. Barr & Associates, *Student services and the law* (pp. 273–283). San Francisco: Jossey-Bass.

Brown, R. D. (1972). *Student development in tomorrow's higher education—a return to the academy.* Washington, DC: American College Personnel Association.

Brown, V. L., & DeCoster, D. A. (1989). The disturbed and disturbing student. In U. Delworth (Ed.), *New Directions for Student Services: No. 45. Dealing with the behavioral and psychological problems of student* (pp. 43–56). San Francisco: Jossey-Bass.

Brubacher, J. S., & Rudy, W. (1968). *Higher education in transition.* New York: Harper & Row.

Bryan, W. A., & Mullendore, R. H. (Eds.). (1992). *New Directions for Student Services: No. 59. Rights, freedoms, and responsibilities of students.* San Francisco: Jossey-Bass.

Buchanan, E. T., III. (1978). Student disciplinary proceedings in collegiate institutions— Substantive and procedural due process requirements. In E. H. Hammond & R. H. Shaffer (Eds.), *The legal foundation of student personnel services in higher education* (pp. 94–115). Washington, DC: American College Personnel Association.

Callis, R. (1967). Educational aspects of in loco parentis. *Journal of College Student Personnel, 8,* 231–233.

Callis, R. (1969). The courts and the colleges: 1968. *Journal of College Student Personnel, 10,* 75–86.

Carnegie Commission on Higher Education. (1971). *Dissent and disruption.* New York: McGraw-Hill.

Carnegie Foundation for the Advancement of Teaching. (1990). *Campus life: In search of community.* Princeton, NJ: Author.

Caruso, R. G. (1978). The professional approach to student discipline in the years ahead. In E. H. Hammond & R. H. Shaffer (Eds.) *The legal foundations of student personnel services in higher education* (pp. 116–127). Washington, DC: American College Personnel Association.

Caruso, R., & Travelstead, W. W. (Eds.). (1987). *New Directions for Student Services: No. 39. Enhancing campus judicial systems.* San Francisco: Jossey-Bass.

Chickering, A. W. (1969). *Education and identity.* San Francisco: Jossey-Bass.

Chickering, A. W., & Reisser, L. (1993). *Education and identity* (2nd ed.). San Francisco: Jossey-Bass.

Cordner, P., & Brooks, T. F. (1987). Training techniques for judicial systems. In R. Caruso & W. W. Travelstead (Eds.), *New Directions for Student Services: No. 39. Enhancing campus judicial systems* (pp. 31–42). San Francisco: Jossey-Bass.

Correnti, R. J. (1988). How public and private institutions differ under the law. In M. J. Barr & Associates, *Student services and the law* (pp. 25–43). San Francisco: Jossey-Bass.

Council for the Advancement of Standards for Student Services/Development Programs (CAS). (1988). *CAS standards and guidelines for student services/development programs: Judicial programs and services.* Washington, DC: Author.

Dalton, J. C., & Healy, M. A. (1984). Using values education activities to confront student conduct issues. *NASPA Journal, 22*(2), 19–25.

Dannells, M. (1977). Discipline. In W. T. Packwood (Ed.), *College student personnel services* (pp. 232–278). Springfield, IL: Charles C Thomas.

Dannells, M. (1978). *Disciplinary practices and procedures in baccalaureate-granting institu-*

tions of higher education in the United States. Unpublished doctoral dissertation, University of Iowa, Iowa City, IA.

Dannells, M. (1990). Changes in disciplinary policies and practices over 10 years. *Journal of College Student Development, 31,* 408–414.

Dannells, M. (1991). Changes in student misconduct and institutional response over 10 years. *Journal of College Student Development, 32,* 166–170.

Dannells, M., & Stuber, D. (1992). Mandatory psychiatric withdrawal of severely disturbed students: A study and policy recommendations. *NASPA Journal, 29,* 163–168.

Delworth, U. (Ed.). (1989). *New Directions for Student Services: No. 45. Dealing with the behavioral and psychological problems of students.* San Francisco: Jossey-Bass.

Dixon v. Alabama State Board of Education, 294 F. 2d 150 (1961).

Durst, R. H. (1969). *The impact of court decisions rendered in the Dixon and Knight cases on student disciplinary procedures in public institutions of higher education in the United States* (Doctoral dissertation, Purdue University, 1968). *Dissertation abstracts, 29,* 2473A–2474A. University Microfilms No. 69-2910.

Dutton, T. B., Smith, F. W., & Zarle, T. (1969). *Institutional approaches to the adjudication of student misconduct.* Washington, DC: National Association of Student Personnel Administrators.

Emmanuel, N. R., & Miser, K. M. (1987). Evaluating judicial program effectiveness. In R. Caruso, & W. W. Travelstead (Eds.), *New Directions for Student Services: No. 39. Enhancing campus judicial systems* (pp. 85–94). San Francisco: Jossey-Bass.

Fenske, R. H. (1989). Evolution of the student services profession. In U. Delworth, G. R. Hanson, & Associates, *Student services: A handbook for the profession* (2nd ed.) (pp. 25–56). San Francisco: Jossey-Bass.

Fenske, R. H., & Johnson, E. A. (1990). Changing regulatory and legal environments. In M. J. Barr, M. L. Upcraft, & Associates, *New futures for student affairs* (pp. 114–137). San Francisco: Jossey-Bass.

Fisher, T. C. (1970). *Due process in the student-institutional relationship.* Washington, DC: American Association of State Colleges and Universities.

Fley, J. (1963). *Discipline in student personnel work: The changing views of deans and personnel workers.* Unpublished doctoral dissertation, University of Illinois, Champaign, IL.

Fley, J. (1964). Changing approaches to discipline in student personnel work. *Journal of the National Association for Women Deans, Administrators, and Counselors, 27,* 105–113.

Foley, J. D. (1947). Discipline: A student counseling approach. *Educational and Psychological Measurement, 7,* 569–582.

Frederickson, J. (1992). Disciplinary sanctioning of impulsive university students. *NASPA Journal, 29,* 143–148.

Gallagher, R. P., Harmon, W. W., & Lingenfelter, C. O. (1994). CSAOs' perceptions of the changing incidence of problematic college student behavior. *NASPA Journal, 32,* 37–45.

Garland, P. H., & Grace, T. W. (1993). *New perspectives for student affairs professionals: Evolving realities, responsibilities and roles* (1993 ASHE–ERIC Higher Education

Report No. 7). Washington, DC: George Washington University, School of Education and Human Development.

Gehring, D. D. (1995a, March). Abreast of the law: Disciplinary records remain confidential under FERPA. *NASPA Forum, 6.*

Gehring, D. D. (1995b, April/May). Abreast of the law: Academic and disciplinary dismissals. *NASPA Forum, 6.*

Gehring, D. D., & Bracewell, W. R. (1992). Standards of behavior and disciplinary proceedings. In W. A. Bryan & R. H. Mullendore (Eds.), *New Directions for Student Services: No. 59. Rights, freedoms, and responsibilities of students* (pp. 89–99). San Francisco: Jossey-Bass.

Georgia, R. T. (1989). Permissiveness and discipline in the higher education setting: A prolegomenon. *NASPA Journal, 27,* 90–94.

Gibbs, A. (1992). *Reconciling the rights and responsibilities of colleges and students: Offensive speech, assembly, drug testing, and safety* (1992 ASHE–ERIC Higher Education Report No. 5). Washington, DC: George Washington University, School of Education and Human Development.

Gometz, L., & Parker, C. A. (1968). Disciplinary counseling: A contradiction? *Personnel and Guidance Journal, 46,* 437–43.

Gott v. Berea College, 156 Ky 376 (1913).

Greenleaf, E. A. (1978). The relationship of legal issues and procedures to student development. In E. H. Hammond & R. H. Shaffer (Eds.), *The legal foundations of student personnel services in higher education* (pp. 34–46). Washington, DC: American College Personnel Association.

Gregory, D. E., & Ballou, R. A. (1986). Point of view: In loco parentis reinventis: Is there still a parenting function in higher education? *NASPA Journal, 24*(2), 28–31.

Hammond, E. H. (1978). The consumer-institutional relationship. In E. H. Hammond & R. H. Shaffer (Eds.), *The legal foundations of student personnel services in higher education* (pp. 1–11). Washington, DC: American College Personnel Association.

Hawkes, H. E. (1930). College administration. *Journal of Higher Education, 1,* 245–253.

Hayes, J. A., & Balogh, C. P. (1990). Mediation: An emerging form of dispute resolution on college campuses. *NASPA Journal, 27,* 236–240.

Hodgkinson, H. L. (1985). *All one system: Demographics of education—Kindergarten through graduate school.* Washington, DC: Institute for Educational Leadership.

Janosik, S. M. (1995). Judicial decision-making and sanctioning: Agreement among students, faculty, and administrators. *NASPA Journal, 32,* 138–144.

Jendrek, M. P. (1989). Faculty reactions to academic dishonesty. *Journal of College Student Development, 30,* 401–406.

Kibler, W. L. (1993a). Academic dishonesty: A student development dilemma. *NASPA Journal, 30,* 252–267.

Kibler, W. L. (1993b). A framework for addressing academic dishonesty from a student development perspective. *NASPA, 31,* 8–18.

King, P. M. (1990). Assessing development from a cognitive-developmental perspective. In D. G. Creamer & Associates, *College student development: Theory and practice for the 1990s* (pp. 81–98). Alexandria, VA: American College Personnel Association.

Knock, G. H. (1985). Development of student services in higher education. In M. J.

Barr, L. A. Keating, & Associates, *Developing effective student services programs* (pp. 15–42). San Francisco: Jossey-Bass.

Kohlberg, L. (1969). Stage and sequence: The cognitive-developmental approach to socialization. In D. Goslin (Ed.), *Handbook of socialization theory and research* (pp. 347–380). Chicago: Rand McNally.

Kuh, G. D. (1990). The demographic juggernaut. In M. J. Barr, M. L. Upcraft & Associates, *New futures for student affairs* (pp. 71–97). San Francisco: Jossey-Bass.

Lamont, L. (1979). *Campus shock.* New York: Dutton.

Lancaster, J. M., Cooper, D. L., & Harman, A. E. (1993). Current practices in student disciplinary administration. *NASPA Journal, 30,* 108–119.

Lederman, D. (1995, February 3). Colleges report rise in violent crime. *Chronicle of Higher Education,* A31–42.

Leonard, E. A. (1956). *Origins of personnel services in American higher education.* Minneapolis: University of Minnesota Press.

Leslie, D. W., & Satryb, R. P. (1974). Due process on due process? Some observations. *Journal of College Student Personnel, 15,* 340–345.

Mager, T. R. (1978). A new perspective for the first amendment in higher education. In E. H. Hammond & R. H. Shaffer (Eds.), *The legal foundations of student personnel services in higher education* (pp. 12–23). Washington, DC: American College Personnel Association.

May, K. M., & Loyd, B. H. (1993). Academic dishonesty: The honor system and students' attitudes. *Journal of College Student Development, 34,* 125–129.

McBee, M. L. (1982). Moral development: From direction to dialog. *NASPA Journal, 20*(1), 30–35.

McCabe, D. L., & Bowers, W. J. (1994). Academic dishonesty among males in college: A thirty year perspective. *Journal of College Student Development, 35,* 5–10.

Miller, T. K., & Prince, J. S. (1976). *The future of student affairs.* San Francisco: Jossey-Bass.

Mueller, K. H. (1961). *Student personnel work in higher education.* Boston: Houghton Mifflin.

National Association of Student Personnel Administrators (NASPA). (1989). A perspective on student affairs (originally published in 1987). *Points of view.* Washington, DC: Author.

National Education Association Task Force on Student Involvement (1971). *Code of student rights and responsibilities.* Washington, DC: National Education Association.

Ostroth, D. D., Armstrong, M. R., & Campbell, T. J., III. (1978). A nationwide survey of judicial systems in large institutions of higher education. *Journal of College Student Personnel, 19,* 21–27.

Ostroth, D. D., & Hill, D. E. (1978). The helping relationship in student discipline. *NASPA Journal, 16*(2), 33–39.

Parr, P., & Buchanan, E. T. (1979). Responses to the law: A word of caution. *NASPA Journal, 17*(2), 12–15.

Pavela, G. (1985). *The dismissal of students with mental disorders.* Asheville, NC: College Administration Publications.

Pavela, G. (1992, July 29). Today's college students need both freedom and structure. *Chronicle of Higher Education,* B1–2.

Penney, J. F. (1967). Variations on a theme: In loco parentis. *Journal of College Student Personnel, 8,* 22–25.

Pezza, P. E. (1995). College campus violence: The nature of the problem and its frequency. *Educational Psychology Review, 7,* 93–103.

Pezza, P. E., & Bellotti, A. (1995). College campus violence: Origins, impacts, and responses. *Educational Psychology Review, 7,* 105–123.

Pitts, J. H. (1980). In loco parentis indulgentis? *NASPA Journal, 17*(4), 20–25.

Ratliff, R. C. (1972). *Constitutional rights of college students: A study in case law.* Metuchen, NJ: Scarecrow Press.

Rhode, S. (1983). Use of legal counsel: Avoiding problems. In M. J. Barr (Ed.), *New Directions for Student Services: No. 22. Student affairs and the law* (pp. 67–80). San Francisco: Jossey-Bass.

Rhode, S. R., & Math, M. G. (1988). Student conduct, discipline, and control: Understanding institutional options and limits. In M. J. Barr and Associates, *Student services and the law* (pp. 152–178). San Francisco: Jossey-Bass.

Saddlemire, G. L. (1980). Professional developments. In U. Delworth, G. R. Hanson, & Associates, *Student services: A handbook for the profession* (pp. 25–44). San Francisco: Jossey-Bass.

Sandeen, A., & Rhatigan, J. J. (1990). New pressures for social responsiveness and accountability. In M. J. Barr, M. L. Upcraft, & Associates, *New futures for student affairs.* San Francisco: Jossey-Bass.

Schetlin, E. M. (1967). Disorders, deans, and discipline: A record of change. *Journal of the National Association for Women Deans, Administrators, and Counselors, 30,* 169–173.

Serr, R. L., & Taber, R. S. (1987). Mediation: A judicial affairs alternative. In R. Caruso & W. W. Travelstead (Eds.), *New Directions for Student Services: No. 39. Enhancing campus judicial systems* (pp. 73–84). San Francisco: Jossey-Bass.

Seward, D. M. (1961). Educational discipline. *Journal of the National Association for Women Deans, Administrators, and Counselors, 24,* 192–197.

Sherrill, J. M., & Siegel, D. G. (Eds.). (1989). *New Directions for Student Services: No. 47. Responding to campus violence.* San Francisco: Jossey-Bass.

Sherry, A. H. (1966). Governance of the university: Rules, rights, and responsibilities. *California Law Review, 54,* 23–39.

Shur, G. M. (1983). Contractual relationships. In M. J. Barr (Ed.), *New Directions for Student Services: No. 22. Student affairs and the law* (pp. 27–38). San Francisco: Jossey-Bass.

Shur, G. M. (1988). Contractual agreements: Defining relationships between students and institutions. In M. J. Barr & Associates, *Student services and the law* (pp. 74–97). San Francisco: Jossey-Bass.

Sims, O. H. (1971). Student conduct and campus law enforcement: A proposal. In O. S. Sims (Ed.), *New directions in campus law enforcement.* Athens, GA: University of Georgia, Center for Continuing Education.

Sisson, V. S., & Todd, S. R. (1995). Using mediation in response to sexual assault on college and university campuses. *NASPA Journal, 32,* 262–269.

Sloan, J. J. (1994). The correlates of campus crime: An analysis of reported crimes on college and university campuses. *Journal of Criminal Justice, 22,* 51–61.

Smith, A. F. (1978). Lawrence Kohlberg's cognitive stage theory of the development of moral judgment. In L. Knefelkamp, C. Widick, & C. A. Parker (Eds.), *New Directions in Student Services. Applying new developmental findings.* (pp. 53–67). San Francisco: Jossey-Bass.

Smith, D. B. (1994, Winter). Student discipline in American colleges and universities: A historical overview. *Educational Horizons,* 78–85.

Smith, G. P., & Kirk, H. P. (1971). Student discipline in transition. *NASPA Journal, 8,* 276–282.

Snoxell, L. F. (1960). Counseling reluctant and recalcitrant students. *Journal of College Student Personnel, 2,* 16–20.

Snoxell, L. F. (1965). Due process and discipline. In T. A. Brady & L. F. Snoxell, *Student discipline in higher education* (Student Personnel Monograph Series No. 5, pp. 27–35). Washington, DC: American Personnel and Guidance Association.

Steele, B. H., Johnson, D. H., & Rickard, S. T. (1984). Managing the judicial function in student affairs. *Journal of College Student Personnel, 25,* 337–342.

Stein, R. H. (1972). Discipline: On campus, downtown, or both, a need for a standard. *NASPA Journal, 10,* 41–47.

Stone, G. L., & Lucas, J. (1994). Disciplinary counseling in higher education: A neglected challenge. *Journal of Counseling and Development, 72,* 234–238.

Strickland, D. A. (1965). In loco parentis—legal mots and student morals. *Journal of College Student Personnel, 6,* 335–340.

Thomas, R. (1987). Systems for guiding college student behavior: Growth or punishment. *NASPA Journal, 25,* 54–61.

Travelstead, W. W. (1987). Introduction and historical context. In R. Caruso & W. W. Travelstead (Eds.), *New Directions for Student Services: No. 39. Enhancing campus judicial systems* (pp. 3–16). San Francisco: Jossey-Bass.

Van Alstyne, W. W. (1963). Procedural due process and state university students. *UCLA Law Review, 10,* 368–389.

Van Alstyne, W. W. (1966). The prerogatives of students, the powers of universities, and the due process of law. *Journal of the National Association for Women Deans, Administrators, and Counselors, 30,* 11–16.

Williamson, E. G. (1956). Preventative aspects of disciplinary counseling. *Educational and Psychological Measurement, 16,* 68–81.

Williamson, E. G. (1961). *Student personnel services in colleges and universities.* New York: McGraw-Hill.

Williamson, E. G. (1963). A new look at discipline. *Journal of Secondary Education, 38,* 10–14.

Williamson, E. G., & Foley, J. D. (1949). *Counseling and discipline.* New York: McGraw-Hill.

Wrenn, C. G. (1949). Student discipline in college. *Educational and Psychological Measurement, 9,* 625–633.

Young, D. P. (1970). *The legal aspects of student dissent and discipline in higher education.* Athens, GA: University of Georgia, Institute of Higher Education.

Young, D. P. (1972). The colleges and the courts. In L. J. Peterson & L. O. Garber (Eds.), *The yearbook of school law 1972* (pp. 201–260). Topeka, KS: National Organization on Legal Problems of Education.

Chapter 8

MULTICULTURAL AFFAIRS

Carolyn J. Palmer and Bettina C. Shuford

CULTURE AND MULTICULTURALISM

[We] have been entrusted with the difficult task of speaking about culture. But there is nothing in the world more elusive... An attempt to encompass its meaning in words is like trying to seize the air in the hand when one finds that it is everywhere except within one's grasp. (Lowell, cited in Kuh & Whitt, 1988, p. 10)

There may indeed be as many different definitions of the term "culture" as there are people attempting to define it. However, there appears to be agreement regarding the various elements constituting culture. Generally, these include shared histories; languages; foods; dress; artifacts; symbols; traditions, customs, rites, rituals, ceremonies, and other practices or patterns of behavior; and belief systems, assumptions, philosophies or ideologies, values, norms, moral standards, ethical principles, and other common understandings (Kuh & Whitt, 1988). College students have many ties that bind them to their families, friends, home communities, religious institutions, and other aspects of their precollege lives. They arrive on campus with expectations, needs, and aspirations that have, to varying degrees, been shaped by their cultural experiences.

Many students seek out others whose cultural characteristics are similar to their own. Relationships with these others provide social support and foster a sense of identity with and commitment to groups or subgroups where students feel welcome and comfortable. Depending on the extent to which broader institutional cultures support truly inclusive campus communities, within which all members feel they genuinely "belong" or "matter," students may or may not develop similar identity with and commitment to their colleges or universities. Nevertheless, cultural experiences before and during college undoubtedly provide "a frame of reference within which to interpret the meaning of events and actions on and off campus" (Kuh & Whitt, 1988, p. 13).

Given this admittedly incomplete, but hopefully sufficient introduction to culture, what is multiculturalism and how are multicultural institutions to be defined? Multiculturalism is commonly described using a "salad bowl" vs. "melting pot" analogy. The major difference between the two is that the ingredients of a salad maintain their own integrity. People do not generally want the tomato to taste like a cucumber, expect the carrot to turn into lettuce, or have any desire to use a blender (or melting pot) to ensure that every part of the salad will be exactly the same. Rather, the salad is enriched when a number of ingredients, which remain distinct, come together. Similarly, multiculturalism is based on the premise that a group of people can be enriched when they come together, yet maintain their uniqueness as individuals.

The mere presence of members of various subgroups may make a student population diverse, but does not necessarily guarantee that an institution is providing a multicultural environment (Hill, 1991). Rather, a multicultural institution is one in which the cultures of diverse groups are not merely acknowledged or tolerated but accepted, respected, included, appreciated, and celebrated within the larger institutional culture. The cultures of many colleges and universities were historically based on rather homogeneous student, faculty, and staff populations. However, increasing diversity within these populations has inspired many campus leaders to reconcile some of the traditional elements of their institutional cultures with the more contemporary values of multiculturalism (McEwen & Roper, 1994a) in an attempt to create campus cultures that are inclusive of all subgroups within the college or university community.

THE BLESSINGS AND CHALLENGES OF DIVERSITY

Willer (1992) quoted an ancient Chinese saying: "May you be blessed with the opportunity to live in interesting times" (p. 161). Student affairs professionals have been blessed with opportunities to work with increasingly diverse student populations. Of course, this blessing is also a challenge. Simply stated, diversity often increases the potential for conflict. For example, when students of many races, religions, social backgrounds, life-styles, value systems, and sensibilities live together in "concentrated proximity" in residence halls, it becomes "inevitable that interpersonal tensions, misunderstandings, incivilities, and disharmonies will arise" (Amada, 1994, p. 39). Consequently, higher education needs professionals "who are capable of solving problems, managing diverse environments, delivering effective services to a diverse student body, and working as part of interracial work groups" (McEwen & Roper, 1994b, p. 86).

Although challenging, there is also great personal reward to be gained from helping to create a campus "laboratory for learning how to live and interrelate in a complex world" (Spees & Spees, 1986, p. 5) and to prepare students to make significant contributions to that world. Pickert (1992) emphasized the need for college graduates to be "familiar with other cultures and their histories, languages, and institutions . . . [and] willing to consider perspectives held by people whose cultures differ from their own" (p. 61). Thus, opportunities for student affairs professionals to increase awareness and sensitivity, foster cross-cultural communication skills that contribute to human understanding and human development, and in other ways help to make "the university experience the universal experience it should be" (Thielen & Limbird, 1992, p. 124) are perceived by many as "blessings."

Although many of the concepts addressed in this chapter apply to many diverse groups, page limitations clearly prohibit adequate discussion of issues pertaining to foreign-born immigrants to the United States (Otuya, 1994); international students (McIntire & Willer, 1992; Pikert, 1992; Pyle, 1986); women (Hall & Sandler, 1984; Sandler & Hall, 1986; Women's Issues Project, 1991); gay, lesbian, and bisexual students (Evans & Wall, 1991; Geller, 1991); adult learners (Kasworm, 1990; Nutter, Kroeger, & Kinnick, 1991; MacKinnon-Slaney, 1994); students with various disabilities (Kroger & Schuck, 1993; Ryan & McCarthy, 1994); Jewish students (Sirkis, 1991); commuter students (Likins, 1991); transfer students (Vaala, 1991); and the many other subgroups comprising today's college student population. Therefore, the remainder of the chapter focuses on American racial/ethnic minority students.

RACIAL/ETHNIC MINORITIES: DIVERSITY WITHIN MINORITY GROUPS

One-Third of a Nation, a report published by the American Council on Education and Education Commission of the States (1988) predicted that by the year 2000 approximately one-third of all school-age Americans will be racial/ethnic minorities. Changes in the composition of college student populations are based on continued immigration to the United States, as well as differential birth rates among American racial/ethnic groups. For example, there has been a "more than 10-fold growth since 1945 in the number of international students on U.S. campuses" (Thielen & Limbird, 1992, p. 121). Otuya (1994) reported that "the foreign-born population of the United States (nearly 20 million) is growing four times faster than the total U.S. population. Approximately two million foreign-born immigrants, many of them naturalized citizens of the United States, were enrolled in American higher education in 1990 (Otuya, 1994).

Although African Americans, Hispanic/Latino Americans, Native Americans, and Asian Americans comprise four broad racial/ethnic groups, there is considerable diversity within each of these groups. For example, Asian and Latino Americans have cultural heritages within many different countries, represent different ethnic or religious groups, speak different languages, wear different clothing, eat different foods, share different value systems, honor different traditions, and celebrate different holidays (Chan & Wang, 1991; Chew & Ogi, 1987; O'Brien, 1993; Quevedo-Garcia, 1987). Similarly, American Indian tribes have "language differences and custom variations" (LaCounte, 1987, p. 66), and African Americans do not comprise a monolithic group within which all members share the same backgrounds, belief systems, expectations, aspirations, behavioral norms, or other cultural characteristics.

Even though many members of a specific cultural group may share certain experiences or perspectives, there are often exceptions that differentiate individual members of the group. Discussion of commonalities within and among groups may foster understanding of many group members, but should never be used to stereotype all members or to prejudge or make unfounded assumptions about a particular individual.

THE HISTORY OF MINORITIES IN AMERICAN HIGHER EDUCATION

Cultural groups are, to varying degrees, affected by their histories. What have been the histories of racial/ethnic minority groups within American higher education?

Native Americans

Native American tribes undoubtedly socialized, acculturated, trained, and educated their own members throughout their history. The education of Indians by non-Indians began at least as early as 1568, when Spanish missionaries established schools to Christianize Indians in what is now Florida. For many years thereafter, European settlers made sporadic efforts to train or educate Indians (Ranbom & Lynch, 1987/1988). For example, special facilities for Indian students were provided at William and Mary in 1723, and "the Continental Congress approved $500 in 1775 for the education of Indians at Dartmouth College" (LaCounte, 1987, p. 65). Despite these early efforts, "only in very recent years have white institutions, with any fervor, sought Indian students" (Wright, 1987, p. 7).

Tribal colleges have played a significant role in the education of Indian students. Of the 25 tribal colleges provided today, 22 are two-year community colleges, and most are located in North Dakota, South Dakota, and Montana (Darden, Bagaka's, Armstrong, & Payne, 1994). Like many other two-year institutions, tribal colleges are attempting to increase their communication with four-year institutions in order to enable more of the students who begin college in familiar surroundings (e.g., on their own reservations) to continue their educations (LaCounte, 1987).

Native Americans continue to be underrepresented in higher education (Darden et al., 1994). Their low matriculation rates, particularly at off-reservation four-year institutions, are related to a high school dropout rate of approximately 45 percent, underpreparation for college, and limited awareness of career opportunities for college graduates. Many have limited financial resources and receive inadequate assistance when applying for financial aid. Strong ties to family and community, culture shock in moving away from primarily Indian environments, low participation in orientation programs, insufficient personal and academic support systems for Indian students on campus, and lack of Indian professionals serving as role models also affect their adjustment to the college environment (LaCounte, 1987).

African Americans

Although some African Americans were self-educated, served apprenticeships, and, to a limited extent, studied abroad (Thomas & Hill, 1987), only 28 African Americans received baccalaureates from American colleges prior to the Civil War (Bowles & DeCosta, 1971). Their pre-Civil War experiences with American higher education were limited to a few predominantly white institutions (PWIs) that would accept blacks, and a few historically black institutions (HBIs) in existence at the time. Additional HBIs were founded during the years between the Civil War and 1890 (Bowles & DeCosta, 1971), after the second Morrill Act of 1890 provided that "funds for black education be distributed on a 'just and equitable basis'" (Ranbom & Lynch, 1987/1988, p. 17), and after the United States Supreme Court, in the case of *Plessey v. Ferguson,* ruled on the constitutionality of the "separate but equal" doctrine in 1896.

It was not until 1954 that the Supreme Court ruled, in *Brown v. Board of Education* and other cases, that separate but equal (or racial segregation within public education) was unconstitutional (Bowles & DeCosta, 1971). Still, some states continued to operate dual educational systems for blacks and whites (Williams, 1991) until Title VI of the Civil Rights Act of 1964 indicated that "no person in the United States, on the grounds of race, color, or national origin, be excluded from participation in, or be denied the benefits of, or be subjected to discrimination under any program or activity receiving Federal financial assistance" (Malaney, 1987, p. 17). This legislation was largely responsible for opening the doors of PWIs to blacks, and HBIs to whites. By 1982, white students constituted approximately 10 percent of the undergraduate and 17 percent of the graduate populations of HBIs. Although HBIs represented only about 3 percent of all colleges and universities in the United States, they enrolled approximately 16 percent of all African American college students, and, during the 1980–81 academic year, awarded 35 percent of the bachelors degrees in engineering, 40 percent of the degrees in biology and in the physical sciences, and 51 percent of the degrees in mathematics that were awarded to African American students across the nation (Thomas & Hill, 1987).

Hispanic/Latino Americans

According to Wright (1987), "the collegiate history of Hispanics had scarcely begun before World War II. Even when they were admitted, Hispanics often had to deny or restrict their cultural identity in order to matriculate" (p. 7). Not until 1968, primarily as a result of the Civil Rights movement, particularly the "La Raza" movement, and the Civil Rights legislation described earlier in this chapter, did large numbers of

Latino students participate in American higher education, primarily at two-year colleges (Wright, 1987).

O'Brien (1993) reported that, in 1991, more than one-third of all Latinos dropped out of high school, and more than half (56%) of all Latino college students were enrolled at two-year institutions. These findings may be related to statistics showing that half of all Latinos had family incomes lower than $20,000 and thus had to work instead of attending school or while attending school part-time (O'Brien, 1993).

In 1991, Latinos received only 3 percent of all bachelor's, graduate, and professional degrees awarded in the United States, even though they constituted 10 percent of the nation's elementary and secondary school population (O'Brien, 1993). Census data showing that the Latino American population is growing at a rate more than five times the national average (O'Brien, 1993) have inspired higher education to address the specific needs of Latino students.

Many Latino students attend Hispanic-serving institutions (HSIs), which enroll at least 25 percent and up to 99.3 percent Latino students. For example, O'Brien (1993) noted that of the 758,000 Latinos enrolled in college in 1990, 240,000 were at 89 mainland HSIs, and 151,000 were at 34 institutions in Puerto Rico. HSIs, HBIs, and tribal colleges have been successful in recruiting, retaining, and graduating substantial numbers of minority students, many of them from lower socioeconomic backgrounds and with admissions credentials suggesting that they may be academically marginal college students. This success may be related to the extent to which these colleges and universities provide academic programs, student services, and psychosocial support systems that are congruent with the cultural identities of their students.

Asian Americans

Asian Americans are the most recent group to immigrate to the United States in formerly unprecedented numbers. As a result of many military, economic, and political events (Wright, 1987), between 1970 and 1980, the United States received "a steady stream of Asian immigrants and refugees" (Hsia & Hirano-Nakanishi, 1989, p. 22). During this one decade, the Asian American population more than doubled, or grew at a rate "more than ten times that of the U.S. population as a whole" (Chew & Ogi, 1987). Between 1976 and 1986 the number of Asian American undergraduates in American colleges and universities almost tripled, with the greatest increases at urban two-year and commuter institutions (Hsia & Hirano-Nakanishi, 1989).

Poverty, unemployment, underemployment, and undereducation are not uncommon in some Asian American communities (Chan & Wang, 1991). Like other minority group members, Asian Americans are strongly connected to their communities and particularly to their families. Many commute to college so they can continue to help their families and/or work while they are in college in order to provide financial assistance to their families. Like some Latinos and Native Americans, some Asian Americans have difficulties with English, in part because English is seldom or never spoken in their homes.

Although campus racial incidents are often described in terms of blacks and whites, "other students of color, including those of Hispanic and Asian origins, have likewise been affected by rising racial tensions in colleges and universities" (Chan & Wang, 1991, p. 43). Asian Americans are sometimes victimized or ostracized by their non-Asian peers. A given student may be the "only" Asian American (or one of very few) in the classroom, residence hall, or other campus environments.

As a result of many commonalities, Asian Americans have often joined with other minorities to request or demand campus programs and services for students of color. For example, Asian American Studies programs were developed following student protests in 1968–69 seeking "ethnic studies programs that would highlight the history and contemporary experiences of nonwhite groups in the United States, in order to counter the existing Eurocentric curriculum that either failed to include any information about people of color, or worse, badly distorted the latter's history" (Chan & Wang, 1991, p. 46).

One rather unique challenge faced by Asian American students is that they have been characterized as "the model minority" (Chan & Wang, 1991), in part because many Asian Americans do well in school. This stereotype, however, minimizes the fact that, like many other students, they must struggle with their academic endeavors. Further, it discounts the hard work many have done in order to succeed. Because many Asian Americans earn good grades and receive high scores on standardized tests, it has been alleged that some colleges and universities have used quotas or other means to restrict their admission (Chan & Wang, 1991; Hsia & Hirano-Nakanishi, 1989; Nakanishi, 1988). Nakanishi (1988) explained that in spite of great diversity within the Asian American population, "there is unmistakeable unanimity in the belief that higher education is the *sine qua non* for individual and group survival and advancement in American society" (p. 39). Thus, the admissions controversy "has placed Asian Americans on an unexpected collision course with their most prized vehicle for social mobility" (p. 39).

Summary

Although historically black institutions (HBIs) and a few almost all-white institutions have provided undergraduate education for relatively small numbers of students of color over the course of many years, it was not until the 1960s and later, well over 300 years after the founding of Harvard, that substantial numbers of students of color entered American higher education. Many are currently enrolled at HBIs, HSIs, and tribally-controlled institutions; urban commuter institutions; and two-year community colleges. For many reasons related to both historical and current realities, racial/ethnic minorities continue to be underrepresented in higher education, particularly at predominantly white, residential, four-year, and graduate/professional institutions.

MINORITY STUDENT SERVICES AND MULTICULTURAL AFFAIRS

Historical Overview

When large numbers of minority students, particularly African Americans, began to appear on predominantly white campuses during the 1960s, little was done to address their special needs (Pounds, 1987; Young, 1986). A laissez-faire attitude on the part of faculty and administrators may have been based on the naive assumption that minority students would simply assimilate into the institutional culture with no effort by the institution to meet the needs of these students (Gibbs, 1973). According to Quevedo-Garcia (1987), assimilation requires "relinquishing one's cultural identity" (p. 52) and developing a new identity that coincides with the new or dominant culture. Minority students, most of whom had no desire to sacrifice their cultural identities in order to "fit into" the campus culture, felt isolated, lonely, alienated, and disenfranchised (Gibbs, 1973; Fleming, 1984; Young, 1986). They realized they were "in these universities but not of these universities"

(Stennis-Williams, Terrell, & Haynes, 1988, p. 74). Many responded with apathy or anger (Young, 1986).

In response to student protests and community pressures, along with court orders enforcing new laws emanating from the Civil Rights movement, institutions developed offices of minority student services (Wright, 1987), which many students of color considered "safe havens in an alien environment" (Young, 1986, p. 18). At approximately the same time, in response to government mandates and with the help of government funds, "colleges witnessed the creation of such programs as the TRIO and Upward Bound programs" (Pounds, 1987, p. 33), designed to prepare students from low-income or disadvantaged families for college, recruit them to college, and assist them once they were in college. Many of the participants in these special services programs were first-generation minority students. Today some of these earlier programs, along with newer endeavors, continue to identify talented individuals; provide precollege enrichment programs, which may include day-long or summer-long experiences on college campuses; and offer valuable services to students once they are enrolled in higher education (J. A. Taylor, Jr., personal communication, November 28, 1995).

Although some professionals within offices of minority student services assisted with or were responsible for precollege enrichment and minority student recruitment programs, most were charged with responding to the needs of already-enrolled students of color. Many provided leadership development and advising for increasing numbers of minority student groups (e.g., Latino Student Unions, Native American Student Associations, Black Greek Letter Organizations) and offered academic and financial aid advising, tutoring services, personal counseling, career development and placement services, student activities, and cultural programs (J. A. Taylor, Jr., personal communication, November 28, 1995). In some ways, these offices served as mini-student affairs divisions for minority students.

Gradually, over the course of several years, many offices of minority student services evolved into offices focusing on multicultural affairs. Although most of these offices still provided many valuable services to minority students, their missions began to include a number of outreach projects within the broader institutional community. For example, many staff in minority student services began to help their colleagues in other student affairs units to recognize, be sensitive to, and respond appropriately to cultural issues so that, for example, those in the Academic Advising Center could be effective academic advisers for minority students.

Student affairs professionals who worked in offices of minority student services or multicultural affairs helped to develop major programs (e.g., those associated with Black History Month) and campus cultural centers (e.g., La Casa Latina Cultural Centers), which were designed to address the educational needs of both minority and majority students. In addition, they often assisted their faculty colleagues in developing individual courses (e.g., Asian American History), departments (e.g., Black Studies), and interdepartmental programs related to ethnic studies, which emerged on many campuses in the late-1960s and 1970s (Chan & Wang, 1991) and expanded during the 1980s and 1990s.

The Roles of Minority/Multicultural Affairs Offices Today

Although the titles and organizational placements of offices focusing on minority and/or multicultural affairs, the clientele served by these offices, and the breadth and depth of their programs vary by institution (Wright, 1987), professionals in these offices generally serve as educators and advisers for their colleagues across their campuses and coordinate multicultural endeavors for their institutions, while at the same time providing valuable services, programs, and role models for students of color.

Missions

The missions of a minority/multicultural affairs office should be threefold.

1. The office should provide support to underrepresented ethnic groups. This support should include assessment and other efforts designed to identify the psychosocial, academic, and other needs of minority students; communication of these needs, along with recommendations for meeting them, to other units on campus; programs and services that enhance students' personal, social, educational, and cultural development; and efforts to encourage students of color to participate in and contribute to the life of the campus.

2. The office should provide multicultural education for all students. Educational endeavors should assist majority and minority stu-

dents to identify their commonalities and recognize, understand, accept, respect, and value their differences. Students should learn to relate to members of diverse groups, communicate effectively across racial or cultural lines, and transfer these skills to a variety of settings (Hoopes, 1979).

3. The office should promote systemic change that fosters a multi-cultural perspective across the campus. As change agents, minority/culticultural affairs professionals should work with various allies to incorporate diverse perspectives into every facet of the institution, including its admissions and hiring practices, administrative policies and procedures, academic curriculum, and co-curricular activities. Only when every unit on campus and the institution as a whole address multicultural issues in an optimal manner will minority/multicultural affairs offices no longer be needed.

Professional Standards

The Council for the Advancement of Standards for Student Services/Development Programs (1986) emphasized that minority student programs and services must include the following elements:

1. Assessment of the educational goals, academic skills, personal development levels, and social, recreational, and cultural needs of minority students.
2. Educational programs to enhance the knowledge, understanding, and skills necessary for academic success.
3. Educational programs to enhance the knowledge, understanding, and skills necessary for personal development.
4. Educational programs to enhance the knowledge, understanding, and skills necessary for the exercise of leadership.
5. Supplemental orientation programming to enhance knowledge and understanding of the purposes of the institution, its values, and predictable ways of behaving.
6. Programming to enhance the knowledge and understanding of each student's own culture and heritage.
7. Human relations programming to explore awareness of cultural differences, self-assessment of possible prejudices, and the facilitation of desired behavioral changes.
8. Advocacy within the institution for minority student life experiences and organizations.
9. Advising of groups and individual students. (pp. 69–70)

Challenges Facing Minority/Multicultural Affairs in the Future

In response to a study conducted by Moyer (1992), senior minority affairs administrators identified the following issues most likely to affect minority affairs in the next decade: maximizing the institutional effectiveness of minority affairs offices, sustaining or increasing institutional commitment to addressing minority concerns and changing campus cultures, rectifying budgetary problems, increasing financial assistance to students, assisting underprepared students, developing curricula that are reflective of the diverse student population, developing retention programs for minority students, and merging racial and gender issues. This study also showed that respondent offices had expanded in recent years to include support for international students, gay/lesbian/bisexual students, and other subgroups on campus. Many respondents expressed concerns regarding insufficient resources to meet the needs of racial/ethic minority students and other subgroups within the next decade.

MINORITY/MULTICULTURAL CENTERS

A number of multicultural centers evolved from black houses, which had been requested by black student organizations in the 1960s (Stennis-Williams et al., 1988). The initial purposes of these centers included helping students of color with their transition to the university community, promoting cultural self-understanding, and serving as social centers for students (Young, 1986). However, their service missions changed over time to reflect an educational orientation (Young, 1986). Some center staff have had faculty status or have collaborated with faculty in offering credited courses and noncredit programs (e.g., guest lecture series) related to ethnicity and academic support services (Stennis-Williams et al., 1988). These educational efforts have helped to compensate for the omission of multicultural perspectives in the mainstream curriculum and have been instrumental in helping to retain students of color. However, in addition to meeting the needs of minority students, today's multicultural centers should "appeal to nonminority groups on the majority white campus" (Stennis-Williams et al., 1988, p. 92).

ADDRESSING MULTICULTURAL ISSUES THROUGHOUT STUDENT AFFAIRS

In reference to international students, Thielen and Limbird (1992) emphasized that "it is inappropriate to cast them as 'experts' in all matters pertaining to their home countries" (p. 127). Similarly, it is inappropriate to expect American minorities to perform the impossible task of articulating the views or describing the cultures of very diverse racial or ethnic groups, and it is both unfair and irresponsible to delegate responsibility for assisting minority students and fostering multiculturalism on campus to those in a single functional area. Consequently, the General Standards of the Council for the Advancement of Standards for Student Services/Development Programs (1986) stressed that such responsibility should be assumed throughout student affairs:

> Each functional area must adhere to the spirit and intent of equal opportunity laws in all activities ... Personnel policies shall not discriminate on the basis of race, sex, color, religion, age, national origin, and/or handicap. In hiring and promotion policies, student services professionals must take affirmative action that strives to remedy significant staffing imbalances, particularly when resulting from past discriminatory practices ... The institution must provide to members of its majority and minority cultures educational efforts that focus on awareness of cultural differences, self-assessment of possible prejudices, and desirable behavioral changes. The institution must also provide educational programs for minority students that identify their unique needs, prioritize those needs, and respond to the priorities to the degree that numbers of students, facilities, and resources permit. In addition, the institution must orient minority students to the culture of the institution and promote and deepen their understanding of their own culture and heritage. (pp. 6–7)

Jones (1987) emphasized the role of student affairs professionals, programs, and services in helping students develop not only appreciation for the contributions of minority groups but also "effective interpersonal and group interactions among campus ethnic groups; ... values, attitudes, and behaviors that accept ethnic pluralism; ... [and] ... decision-making, social, and political skills for entry into an ethnically diverse work world" (p. 87). In order to foster "positive multiethnic interactions among students, faculty, and professional and clerical support staff" (Jones, 1987, p. 86), "every faculty and staff member should have a sensitivity to and awareness of cultural diversity issues" (McIntire, 1992, p. xviii). The following sections address some of these issues.

Applying Student Development Theory to Minority Students

Many institutional values, including those inherent in some student affairs functions and student development theories, are Eurocentric in nature, and may conflict with the values of minority cultures (Wright, 1987). For example, the importance of individualism is often incompatible with belief systems that place the needs of the family, community, or group above the needs or the achievements of the individual (Wright, 1987; Armstrong-West & de la Teja, 1988). The dissonance created when students are assumed or expected to accept cultural perspectives that, in fact, differ from their own may cause misunderstanding, frustration, and alienation.

It is incumbent on student affairs professionals to examine "social environmental factors, such as economics (especially poverty), ethnic or cultural background, and racial and gender bias, and the interactive effects of American society on minority college students' growth" (Wright, 1987, p. 11) in creating models of student development that incorporate the unique needs and experiences of students of color. For example, McEwen, Roper, Bryant, and Langa (1990) examined the unique history and oppression of African Americans and their cultural perspectives regarding family life, oral traditions, time orientation, group consciousness, spirituality, and other issues, and they identified nine dimensions of African American student development that are inadequately addressed by traditional psychosocial theories. These include developing ethnic and racial identity, interacting with the dominant culture, developing cultural aesthetics and awareness, developing identity, developing interdependence, fulfilling affiliation needs, surviving intellectually, developing spirituality, and developing social responsibility (McEwen et al., 1990). Wright (1987) similarly identified a number of developmental issues of particular significance to students of color. These involved formulating an integrated philosophy of life; maintaining personal health and wellness; and developing healthy sex roles and sexual identity, interpersonal relationships, social responsibility, academic and intellectual competence, career/life-style plans, and cultural esthetics and awareness.

Student affairs practitioners can use their knowledge of developmental tasks faced by minority students to build programming models with goals and activities that are culturally sensitive to students of color (Manning, 1994). According to Stage and Manning (1992), typical programming models for students of color have included a number of activities generally offered in piecemeal fashion, whereas a more wholistic or systematic approach may be more effective in fostering the students' development.

Implementing a Cultural Environment Transitions Model

The Cultural Environment Transitions Model (Manning & Coleman-Boatwright, 1991) "assumes that organizational growth occurs as members of the community acquire knowledge about other cultures, gain experience with people different from themselves, and are challenged with structural and systemic change through these efforts" (p. 369). According to Manning (1994), multicultural organization models bring to light the value structures that support institutional policies and practices, and that often perpetuate a cultural hierarchy of privilege. This knowledge may inspire administrators to question or eradicate the values and actions that maintain this hierarchy. Organizations implementing the Cultural Environment Transitions Model progress from "monoculturalism, through a period in which some college members are aware but unable to effect change in the institution, into a time of openly expressed conflict, through organizational rebirth reflective of multicultural goals, and finally, into a state of multiculturalism that is systemic and institutional" (Manning & Coleman-Boatwright, 1991, p. 371).

Becoming a Cultural Broker

Stage and Manning (1992) prescribed the use of a cultural brokering approach to the creation of an educational system that empowers faculty, staff, and students to address the strengths and weaknesses of the various cultural systems on campus, with the desired outcome being a multicultural campus where there is a "seamless fabric of efforts" across the entire institution (p. 16). The components of the model include learning to think contextually, spanning boundaries, ensuring optimal performance, and taking action.

According to Stage and Manning (1992), "the task of learning to think contextually starts with an examination of one's underlying cultural assumptions . . . This awareness then builds a realization that administrative actions and educational practices are not objective but rather reflect cultural backgrounds and assumptions" (pp. 17–18). A very simple example might involve one's recognition of programmatic attention to Christian, but not other religious holidays. When student activities staff decorate a Christmas tree in their office, sponsor a Christmas concert, or identify the break between semesters as "Christmas vacation" in their calendar of events, they should try to use different cultural lenses to envision how non-Christians might respond. Further, they should span the boundaries of the dominant perspective by exploring various ways in which Hanukkah and other religious holidays or holy days might be celebrated or recognized on campus.

Removing barriers to cultural expression and changing various aspects of campus life in order to welcome and include students of color helps to ensure optimal performance (Stage & Manning, 1992). For example, orientation leaders who work in collaboration with their colleagues in minority/multicultural affairs, academic enhancement or advising, and other units to identify the unique needs of students of color and make plans to address those needs in orientation programs are examples of professionals who are attempting to remove barriers to the success of minority students.

The final step in the cultural brokering model involves taking action that includes a variety of cultural perspectives in making decisions, developing policies, and implementing programs (Stage & Manning, 1992). Actions that may be taken in residence life, for example, would include not only deliberate efforts to recruit staff who represent diverse groups, but effective inclusion of those staff in decisions regarding policies and procedures, physical facilities, food services, staffing patterns, student programs, and all other matters pertaining to residence life. Indeed, Hill (1991) warned that many subgroups of students, faculty, and staff will continue to be marginalized if all perspectives do not become central to the organization, and if all voices are not heard at the decision-making table.

THE ACADEMIC DOMAIN

Student affairs professionals are not alone in their attempts to assist racial/ethnic minority students and to foster multiculturalism on campus. "The cultural values of institutions affect what students are taught, how they are taught, and how student learning is evaluated" (McEwen et al., 1990, p. 429). Consequently, faculty contribute to or are affected by multiculturalism in several ways. First, consider changes to what is taught in college classrooms. "One need only look at a college curriculum of one hundred years ago to see that revising today's curriculum is part of a long and continuous process . . . Curricular changes have always been difficult and accompanied by anguished cries from both sides because they require a basic redefinition of what is worthy of study" (Lutzker, 1995, p. 1).

Democratic and academic values suggest that diversity of opinions should be welcomed and even cherished in higher education, yet some faculty [and perhaps some student affairs professionals] may feel uncomfortable hearing previously absent or marginalized voices that seek to express new and different viewpoints, raise questions having no "right" or "wrong" answers, confront unresolved conflicts, and explore the unknown (Hill, 1991). Nevertheless, Katz (1991) suggested that resisting exposure to diverse perspectives may be overcome by "the realization of people who take the first steps that they are growing as people; that they are less defensive in their imagination, thinking, and experience; and that they have a new warmth in their perception of others and—astonishingly—of themselves. The ultimate incentive is that the process enables one to become more fully human" (p. 195). Studies of minority students have shown that "close student/faculty contact can greatly increase student retention" (Rendon & Nora, 1987/1988, p. 82). Many faculty have come to realize that they too reap many rewards from their interactions with students.

Indeed, many faculty are redefining their disciplines and making efforts to incorporate multiculturalism in their teaching. Some fear that students and others may resent their attempts to teach about oppressed groups because they personally are not members of such groups (Lutzker, 1995). However, diversity issues can be understood to a great extent through study and through direct experiences, including interpersonal relationships with members of diverse groups, and what is understood can be taught (Lutzker, 1995). Border and Chism (1992) noted several compelling reasons for faculty, administrators, support staff, and others to address diversity issues in their classes and programs "even in the face of incomplete information and complicated arguments and counterarguments" (p. 2). To assist those who wish to embrace multiculturalism in their work with college students, Lutzker (1995) devoted 64 pages to annotations and descriptions of hundreds of resources (e.g., books, periodicals, online information, Internet listservs, films, videos, posters), many of which may be of considerable interest to student affairs professionals.

Multiculturalism is also affecting the content and process of scholarly inquiry, including research concerning race and ethnicity (Stanfield & Dennis, 1993) and research involving college students (Banta, Lund, Black, & Oblander, 1996). Just as higher education can no longer be content to develop programs "geared toward the mythical 'average college student'" (Stage, 1992, p. 140), assessments of student learning and other outcomes of such programs must take into account the many different frames of reference used by various subgroups of students in interpreting and responding to their college experiences (Attinasi & Nora, 1992). Whether tests used in the admissions process or more informal assessments of student interests in various activities are involved, all persons who collect or interpret assessment information must be well-informed of diversity issues that may affect the applicability of that information in the decision-making process (Rendon & Nora, 1987/1988).

CONCLUSION

Increasing numbers of racial/ethnic minority students and members of other cultural groups within higher education have not guaranteed their full involvement in the college or university experience. Student affairs professionals in multicultural affairs and all other functional areas must continue to identify the barriers that inhibit the inclusion of minority group members and eradicate the barriers by addressing the specific needs of diverse students and by creating conditions that encourage communication and collaboration among diverse groups. Opportunities to create multicultural campus communities that maximize social integration and cross-cultural understanding, while honoring and celebrating individual and group differences, represent both challenges and blessings to today's student affairs professionals. Their efforts to foster multicultural and global understanding will be rewarded each time students can send the following poem to college friends who are in various ways "different" from themselves:

> I would like to think of our friendship
> as being like that of two rivers, which
> one day, within the fleeting moments of time,
> met and suffused—two rivers that arose from
> different valleys to flow together to the sea.

As time would have it, our lives, like rivers,
stir and break to curve separate courses
toward destiny's distant, alas, uncharted waters.
No longer will the rivers together flow.
Time and space will be between them.
But as friends who together flowed
through the valley of knowledge,
each will retain a part of the other.
Sometimes rivers meet again, if only for a span,
so perhaps somewhere within the eternity of time
our lives again will converge. But . . .
if even for a moment, we can relive together
the friendship we have had, I will cherish until death
the mere fact that I have known you.
(Author unknown, cited in Thielen & Limbird, 1992, pp. 133–134)

REFERENCES

Amada, G. (1994). Coping with the disruptive college student: A practical model. Asheville, NC: College Administration Publications, Inc.

American Council on Education and Education Commission of the States. (1988). *One third of a nation* (A Report of The Commission on Minority Participation in Education and American Life). Washington, DC: Authors.

Armstrong-West, S., & de la Teja, M. H. (1988). Social and psychological factors affecting the retention of minority students. In M. C. Terrell & D. J. Wright (Eds.), *From survival to success: Promoting minority student retention* (pp. 25–53). Washington, DC: NASPA.

Attinasi, L. C., Jr., & Nora, A. (1992). Diverse students and complex issues: A case for multiple methods in college student research. In F. K. Stage (Ed.), *Diverse methods for research and assessment of college students* (pp. 13–27). Alexandria, VA: American College Personnel Association.

Banta, T. W., Lund, J. P., Black, K. E., & Oblander, F. W. (1996). *Assessment in practice: Putting principles to work on college campuses.* San Francisco: Jossey-Bass.

Border, L. L. B., & Chism, N. V. N. (Eds.). (1992). *Teaching for diversity (New Directions for Teaching and Learning, No. 49).* San Francisco: Jossey-Bass.

Bowles, F., & DeCosta, F. A. (1971). *Between two worlds: A profile of Negro education.* New York: McGraw-Hill.

Chan, S., & Wang, L. (1991). Racism and the model monority: Asian Americans in higher education. In P. G. Altbach & K. Lomotey (Eds.), *The racial crisis in American higher education* (pp. 43–67). Albany, NY: State University of New York Press.

Chew, C. A., & Ogi, A. Y. (1987). Asian American college student perspectives. In D. J. Wright (Ed.), *Responding to the needs of today's minority students* (*New Directions for Student Services, No. 38,* pp. 39–48). San Francisco: Jossey-Bass.

Council for the Advancement of Standards for Student Services/Development Programs. (1986). *CAS standards and guidelines for student services/development programs.* College Park, MD: Author.

Darden, J. T., Bagakas, J. G., Armstrong, T., & Payne, T. (1994). Segregation of American Indian undergraduate students in institutions of higher education. *Equity & Excellence in Education, 27*(3), 61–68.

Evans, N. J., & Wall, V. A. (Eds.). (1991). *Beyond tolerance: Gays, lesbians, and bisexuals on campus.* Alexandria, VA: American College Personnel Association.

Fleming, J. (1984). *Blacks in college.* San Francisco: Jossey-Bass.

Geller, W. W. (1991). Lesbian and gay topics: Awakening a campus. *Journal of College Student Development, 32*(1), 91–92.

Gibbs, J. T. (1973). Black students/white university: Different expectation. *Personnel and Guidance Journal, 51*(7), 465–469.

Hall, R. M., & Sandler, B. R. (1984). *Out of the classroom: A chilly campus climate for women?* Washington, DC: Association of American Colleges, Project on the Status and Education of Women.

Hill, P. J. (1991, July/August). Multi-culturalism: The crucial philosophical and organizational issues. *Change,* pp. 38–47.

Hoopes, D. S. (1979). Intercultural communication concepts and the psychology of intercultural experience. In M. D. Pusch (Ed.), *Multicultural education: A cross cultural training approach* (pp. 10–38). La Grange Park, IL: Intercultural Network.

Hsia, J., & Hirano-Nakanishi, M. (1989, November/December). The demographics of diversity: Asian Americans and higher education. *Change,* pp. 39–47.

Jones, W. T. (1987). Enhancing minority-white peer interactions. In D. J. Wright (Ed.), *Responding to the needs of today's minority students* (*New Directions for Student Services, No. 38,* pp. 81–94). San Francisco: Jossey-Bass.

Kasworm, C. E. (1990). Adult undergraduates in higher education: A review of past research perspectives. *Review of Educational Research, 60*(3), 345–372.

Katz, J. (1991). White faculty struggling with the effects of racism. In P. G. Altbach & K. Lomotey (Eds.), *The racial crisis in American higher education* (pp. 187–196). Albany, NY: State University of New York Press.

Kroeger, S., & Schuck, J. (Eds.). (1993). *Responding to disability issues in student affairs (New Directions for Student Services, No. 64).* San Francisco: Jossey-Bass.

Kuh, G. D., & Whitt, E. J. (1988). *The invisible tapestry: Culture in American colleges and universities (ASHE–ERIC Higher Education Report, No. 1).* Washington, DC: Association for the Study of Higher Education.

LaCounte, D. W. (1987). American Indian students in college. In D. J. Wright (Ed.), *Responding to the needs of today's minority students* (*New Directions for Student Services, No. 38,* pp. 65–79). San Francisco: Jossey-Bass.

Likins, J. M. (1991). Research refutes a myth: Commuter students do want to be involved. *NASPA Journal, 29*(1), 68–74.

Lutzker, M. (1995). *Multiculturalism in the college curriculum: A handbook of strategies and resources for faculty.* Westport, CT: Greenwood Press.

MacKinnon-Slaney, F. (1994, January/February). The adult persistence in learning model: A road map to counseling services for adult learners. *Journal of Counseling & Development, 72*, 268–275.

Malaney, G. D. (1987). A review of early decisions in Adams v. Richardson. In Pruitt, A. S. (Ed.), *In pursuit of equality in higher education* (pp. 17–22). Dix Hills, New York: General Hall.

Manning, K. (1994). Multicultural theories for multicultural practices. *NASPA Journal, 31*(3), 176–185.

Manning, K., & Coleman-Boatwright, F. (1991). Student affairs initiatives toward a multicultural university. *Journal of College Student Development, 32*(4), 367–374.

McEwen, M. K., & Roper, L. D. (1994a). Incorporating multiculturalism into student affairs preparation programs: Suggestions from the literature. *Journal of College Student Development, 35*(1), 46–53.

McEwen, M. K., & Roper, L. D. (1994b). Interracial experiences, knowledge, and skills of master's degree students in graduate programs in student affairs. *Journal of College Student Development, 35*(2), 81–87.

McEwen, M. K., Roper, L. D., Bryant, D. R., & Langa, M. J. (1990). Incorporating the development of African-American students into psychosocial theories of student development. *Journal of College Student Development, 31*, 429–436.

McIntire, D. (1992). Introduction. In D. McIntire & P. Willer (Eds.), *Working with international students and scholars on American campuses* (pp. xi–xx). Washington, DC: National Association of Student Personnel Administrators.

McIntire, D., & Willer, P. (Eds.). (1992). *Working with international students and scholars on American campuses.* Washington, DC: National Association of Student Personnel Administrators.

Moyer, R. A. (1992). *A conceptual analysis of the status, role and function of chief minority affairs administrators on state assisted universities in Ohio.* Unpublished doctoral dissertation, Kent State University.

Nakanishi, D. T. (1988, November/December). A quota on excellence? The Asian American admissions debate. *Change,* pp. 39–47.

Nutter, K. J., Kroeger, S. A., & Kinnick, B. C. (1991). Adult undergraduates: Involvement with the college environment. *NASPA Journal, 28*(4), 348–354.

O'Brien, E. M. (1993). *Latinos in higher education (Research Briefs, Vol. 4, No. 4).* Washington, DC: American Council on Education, Division of Policy Analysis and Research.

Otuya, E. (1994). *The foreign-born population of the 1990s: A summary profile (Research Briefs, Vol. 6, No. 5).* Washington, DC: American Council on Education, Division of Policy Analysis and Research.

Pickert, S. M. (1992). *Preparing for a global community: Achieving an international perspective in higher education (ASHE–ERIC Higher Education Report, No. 2).* Washington, DC: The George Washington University, School of Education and Human Development.

Pounds, A. W. (1987). Black students' needs on predominantly white campuses. In D. J. Wright (Ed.), *Responding to the needs of today's minority students (New Directions for Students Services, No. 38,* pp. 23–38). San Francisco: Jossey-Bass.

Pyle, K. R. (Ed.). (1986). *Guiding the development of foreign students (New Directions for Student Services, No. 36)*. San Francisco: Jossey-Bass.

Quevedo-Garcia, E. L. (1987). Facilitating the development of Hispanic college students. In D. J. Wright (Ed.), *Responding to the needs of today's minority students (New Directions for Students Services, No. 38*, pp. 49–63). San Francisco: Jossey-Bass.

Ranbom, S., & Lynch, J. (1987/1988). Timeline: The long hard road to educational equality. *Educational Record, 68*(4)/*69*(1), 16–22.

Rendon, L. I., & Nora, A. (1987/1988). Hispanic students: Stopping the leaks in the pipeline. *Educational Record, 68*(4)/*69*(1), 79–85.

Ryan, D., & McCarthy, M. (Eds.). (1994). *A student affairs guide to the ADA and disability issues*. Washington, DC: National Association of Student Personnel Administrators.

Sandler, B. R., & Hall, R. M. (1986). *The campus climate revisited: Chilly for women faculty, administrators, and graduate students*. Washington, DC: Association of American Colleges, Project on the Status and Education of Women.

Sirkis, T. (1991). *An introductory guide to Judaism and the college student*. Madison, WI: University of Wisconsin, Division of University Housing.

Spees, E. C., & Spees, E. R. (1986). Internationalizing the campus: Questions and concerns. In K. R. Pyle (Ed.), *Guiding the development of foreign students (New Directions for Student Services, No. 36*, pp. 5–18). San Francisco: Jossey-Bass.

Stage, F. K., & Manning, K. (1992). *Enhancing the multicultural campus environment: A cultural brokering approach (New Directions for Student Services, No. 60)*. San Francisco: Jossey-Bass.

Stanfield, J. H. II, & Dennis, R. M. (1993). *Race and ethnicity in research methods*. Newbury Park, CA: Sage.

Stennis-Williams, S., Terrell, M. C., & Haynes, A. W. (1988). The emergent role of multicultural education centers on predominantly white campuses. In M. C. Terrell & D. J. Wright (Eds.), *From survival to success: Promoting minority student retention, (NASPA Monograph Series No. 9)* (pp. 73–98). Washington, DC: NASPA.

Thielen, T., & Limbird, M. (1992). Integrating foreign students into the university community. In D. McIntire & P. Willer (Eds.). *Working with international students and scholars on American campuses* (pp. 119–135). Washington, DC: National Association of Student Personnel Administrators.

Thomas, G. E., & Hill, S. (1987). Black institutions in U.S. higher education: Present roles, contributions, future projections. *Journal of College Student Personnel, 28*(6), 496–503.

Vaala, L. D. (1991). Making the transition: Influences on transfer students. *NASPA Journal, 28*(4), 305–311.

Willer, P. (1992). Student affairs professionals as international educators: A challenge for the next century. In D. McIntire & P. Willer (Eds.). *Working with international students and scholars on American campuses* (pp. 161–167). Washington, DC: National Association of Student Personnel Administrators.

Williams, J. B. (1991). Systemwide Title VI regulation of higher education, 1968–88: *Implications for increased minority participation*. In C. V. Willie, A. M. Garibaldi, &

W. L. Reed (Eds.), *The Education of African-Americans* (pp. 110–118). New York: Auburn House.

Women's Issues Project. (1991). *About women on campus, 1*(1). Washington, DC: National Association for Women in Education.

Wright, D. J. (1987). Minority students: Developmental beginnings. In D. J. Wright (Ed.), *Responding to the needs of today's minority students (New Directions for Student Services, No. 38)* (pp. 5–21). San Francisco: Jossey-Bass.

Young, L. W. (1986). The role minority student centers play on predominantly white campuses. In C. A. Taylor (Ed.), *The handbook of minority student services* (pp. 15–22). Madison, WI: National Minority Campus Chronicle, Inc.

Gratitude is expressed to Dr. Jack A. Taylor, Jr., Assistant Vice President for Student Affairs/Director of Multicultural Affairs and Student Services at Bowling Green State University, for information cited as "personal communication."

Chapter 9

ORIENTATION

AUDREY L. RENTZ

The objectives of orientation are the objectives of the whole student personnel program in miniature... His (the student personnel worker) objective is to persuade the freshman to assume responsibility for himself as soon as possible; therefore his greatest problem is exactly how much help to give the freshman, neither too little nor too much. A second objective is to find out all he can about the student at the same time that the student is informing himself about the college. (1961, p. 223–224)

INTRODUCTION

For as long as new undergraduate students have experienced a period of transition to their new educational environment, orientation programs have been a part of American higher education. Whether formally or informally organized, their purpose has been to assist entering students during that initial adjustment period. Young men starting classes at Harvard in the 1640s were assisted by the shared efforts of dons and a graduate student or tutor whose job was "to counsel and befriend the young lads" (Morison, p. 1936, p. 253). While orientation's presence within the academic community has remained constant, its popularity has not. Periodically both faculty and students have criticized orientation programs because the needs they were designed to meet were needs perceived by institutions, rather than those identified by students. Since the 1980s, the previous value attached to orientation programs has once again reached a peak. Research has been able to demonstrate a positive relationship between assessed educational outcomes of participation in orientation programs with student satisfaction with the institutional environment and student persistence. Retention has become a major concern of most college and university administrators. Declining numbers of college applicants and the increasing diversity in today's student population have provided orientation professionals with opportunities and challenges never before encountered. Viewed as one of the most

238

significant campus forces capable of influencing student retention, as well as students' educational and personal development, many orientation directors are now members of their college's or university's enrollment management team. This innovative team concept has allowed orientation professionals to draw upon their rich and broad history of activities and program successes to help an institution foster a holistic and developmental view of the collegiate experience.

Student affairs specialists in orientation must be sensitive to the nature of their students being served. Programs are often modified as new information about the changing demographics of students is gathered. In the 1920s, undergraduate students were viewed as a homogeneous group. Today on most campuses, the undergraduate student body is recognized as being diverse. Individuals representing one or more of the following student groups compose today's class of new students: ethnic and racial minorities; cross-cultural; physically challenged; gay, lesbian and bisexual; transfers; and returning adult learners. To be effective, orientation professionals no longer can assume that a single, general broad-based program can meet the needs of all entering students.

To help the reader understand the dynamic nature of orientation, this chapter examines nine major themes of this specialty within student affairs. These themes are history; definition, purpose and goals; changing student needs; program models; staffing; effective programs; serving students; entry-level qualifications; and issues. In each section, whenever possible, the material is presented in chronological sequence to allow the reader to become familiar with the changes in the major themes in response to shifts in philosophy and societal events.

HISTORY

Two distinct programmatic emphases have been identified within orientation's history. The first emerged in 1888, at Boston University, when an orientation day for new students was offered. For the next 28 years, the professional literature described a variety of single day orientation programs. These one-day programs had as their focus students' personal adjustment to college rather than an introduction to specific academic disciplines or to the world of higher education (Bennett, 1966; Butts, 1966).

The second programmatic emphasis was developed at Reed College in 1911, with the introduction of a freshman course for credit entitled,

"The College Life Course" (Brubacher & Rudy, 1958). Within several months, both the University of Washington and the University of Michigan sponsored weekly meetings for entering students and rewarded attendance with academic credit (Butts, 1966). These early courses, usually scheduled in a series of 25 sessions, were designed to teach students "how to use the library, . . . how to study . . . the purposes and aims of college and . . . how to participate in campus activities" (Fitts & Swift, 1928). National acceptance of these structured for credit courses was quickly achieved. Interest in this program format grew dramatically, from six institutions in 1915–1916 to 82 sponsoring institutions only a decade later (Wharton, 1942).

In *Advice to Freshmen by Freshmen,* University of Michigan president M.L. Burton (1921) described expectations for this time of transition: "Remember that the change from high school to college is tremendous. You are no longer a high school boy or girl. You are a college man or woman. The University is a place of freedom. You are thrown upon your own resources. You are independent. But do not forget, I beg of you, that independence and freedom do not mean anarchy and license. Obedience to law is liberty" (Crocker, 1921, p. 1).

Student personnel professionals accepted the orientation function as a specialized responsibility within their administrative domain shortly after World War I. By 1930, nearly a third of all higher education institutions offered credit courses (Mueller, 1961). During the 1930s, under the direction of E. G. Williamson, the University of Minnesota sponsored an orientation program for entering students that addressed the following areas of perceived student concern: personal living, home life, vocational orientation, and socio-civic orientation (Bennett, 1946). By the beginning of the 1940s these courses were required for ninety percent of all new students (Wharton, 1942).

Although these two models played a crucial role in the development of contemporary orientation programs, they were not without their critics. Some argued about their proper length. For example, since the mid-1920s, the most effective length of an orientation program has been the subject of intense debate: " . . . some personnel workers have recommended that a really effective program will continue through the subsequent collegiate years to help students avoid difficulties—scholastic, health, social, economic, vocational and emotional" (Doermann, 1926). Thirty years later, Strang (1951), Wrenn (1951), and subsequently Mueller (1961) expressed their belief that an orientation program should not be a one- or two-day event, but rather should be a continuous and dynamic process beginning in high school and ending after college graduation. According to this belief, orientation is viewed as a developmental process assisting entering students with specific tasks associated with the transition to higher education and the subsequent goals of self-direction and interdependence. Still today, the debate over the most effective length of an orientation program continues.

As the number of orientation professionals on campuses increased, they sensed a need to come together to share ideas and to discuss common problems. Twenty-four orientation directors met in Columbus (OH) in 1948 and convened the "First Annual Conference" of the major association now known as the National Orientation Directors Association (NODA). However, official charter approval was not achieved until 1974 (Dannells, 1986).

Formal recognition and widespread support for orientation was achieved in 1943 when the Council of Guidance and Personnel Associations recommended that orientation programs be sponsored at the high school level as well as by higher education institutions. The Council recommended three major program goals: increasing the understanding of occupational and social problems; personal adjustment; and increasing the awareness of the importance of physical fitness, including social hygiene (Council of Guidance and Personnel Associations, 1943). Responses from all 123 institutional members of the North Central Association of Colleges and Secondary Schools, verified commitments to offer orientation programs that would include: general lectures, testing, social activities, campus tours, religious activities, counseling, details of registration, establishment of faculty-student relationships, and "enabling courses" (voice and reading improvement) (Bookman, 1948; Kamm & Wrenn, 1947). The relevance of these topics has not changed. Many continue to form the core of contemporary programs.

In the 1960s, in the midst of student activism and a new wave of accountability in higher education, orientation programs once again became the subject of scrutiny and criticism. Freshman Week was labeled "disorientation week" (Riesman, 1961). Orientation courses would no longer be included in the institution's curriculum unless documentation could be provided that these programs served a utilitarian and meaningful purpose on campus (Caple, 1964). Few research studies had been undertaken that could identify and assess the specific educational outcomes associated with participation in orientation activities. Involvement had not yet appeared in the professional literature let alone its relationship to student satisfaction and retention. Additionally, the lack of a theoretical foundation underpinning orientation programs led to the criticism that these activities were " . . . made of hopes, good will, educated guesses and what we fondly believe to be the needs of new students" (Grier, 1966). Nevertheless, orientation directors remained committed to the concept of orientation and continued to plan and provide programs that challenged students to learn to act on their own and to develop a sense of self-responsibility (Black, 1974).

From 1966 to 1976, modifications in programs included the creation of two- or three-day, overnight programs not only for new students, but their parents as well. Some small institutions developed mini-courses taught by freshman faculty advisors during the five- to ten-day period before classes providing a brief preview of academic life. Other campuses, used small group sessions to teach T-group and other human relations skills, and Friendship Days emerged with a focus on social needs (Cohen & Judy, 1978; Foxley, 1969; Hall, 1982; Klosterman & Merseal, 1978; Terenzini & Pascarella, 1980).

A projected decline in the number of college applicants provided additional value and significance to the efforts of orientation professionals in the 1960s and 1970s. Student satisfaction and retention became issues of major importance to many administrators in higher education. Consequently, orientation programs came to be viewed as contributing significantly to the economic stability of many colleges and universities. Support for the relationship between participation in orientation programs, student satisfaction and persistence appeared with greater and greater frequency in the research literature (Astin, 1976; Feldman & Newcomb et al., 1970; Beal & Noel, 1980; Lenning, Sauer, & Beal, 1980; Ramist, 1981). The need for congruence between student and institutional "fit" and the necessity of balancing competing forces of support and challenge were recognized. Previously hypothesized relationships were now no longer viewed as tentative, but confirmed. With the emergence of enrollment management within higher education, and an increase in the number of research studies tying orientation programs to retention, orientation professionals found themselves playing new and essential roles as members of institutional enrollment teams.

A number of traditions have been linked to freshmen and orientation activities. Mention the term orientation to most individuals, and depending on their age, one or more images appear in their mind's eye. Raccoon fur coats, yellow pompoms, football banners, and the swallowing of goldfish were prevalent in the 1920s and 1930s; freshman "beanies" were the symbols for a rite of passage during the 1950s; and college blazers, T-shirts, and buttons were mandatory in the 1960s. All of these helped entering students maintain a visible profile on campus. Such adornments differ dramatically from the distinguishing lengths of the black academic robes worn by faculty and students at Harvard to denote the levels of status within the academic community; ankle-length for faculty, knee-length for upperclassmen, and mid-thigh for freshmen. Throughout the years, specific wardrobe items, customs, and rituals helped identify entering students to others on campus and were required elements of a process of both adjustment and socialization. Regardless of such symbols, entering students must successfully complete the transition to their new educational surroundings. This socialization process has been and continues to be the domain of orientation professionals.

DEFINITION, PURPOSE AND GOALS

In its broadest sense, orientation has been described as "any effort on the part of the institution to help entering students make the transition from their previous environment to the college environment and to enhance success in college" (Upcraft & Farnsworth, 1984). Involving the entering student with resource persons, namely faculty, student organization members, and other forms of human support is viewed as one of the most important contributions of orientation programs (Anderson, 1985). Contemporary student affairs professionals, with practice guided by the theoretical approaches of Chickering (1972), Chickering & Reisser (1993), and others view the goal of human development as a series of sequential tasks toward which they seek to move students by involving them in structured intentional activities.

While orientation's purpose has remained constant, support for it and related activities, discussions of goal statements and the degree of institutional commitment afforded to it have varied greatly during the past century. At times it has been seen as an essential and required experience, while during other periods its activities were viewed as frivolous and extraneous.

As discussed earlier, orientation's programmatic emphases change in response to changes in higher education's mission and in student affairs professionals' perceptions of undergraduate students. Consider the following representative goal statements gathered from a review of thirty years of literature: (1) to gain perspective, a sense of purpose and balance between the demands and opportunities of college life (Strang, 1951); (2) to increase the student's receptivity to the total higher education experience (McCann, 1967); (3) to complete enrollment procedures in a humane manner (Butts, 1971); (4) to develop cognitive, behavioral and communication skills to facilitate assimilation into the campus environment and (5) to foster development of a peer group, creating an atmosphere of comfortableness and reduced anxiety (Krall, 1981).

Responding to a perceived exaggerated emphasis on students' social and personal needs in orientation programs of the 1950s, subsequent writers argued persuasively for a return to a focus on academic disciplines and the mission of higher education (Drake, 1966a). Orientation should be defined as "an induction into or at least consistent with, college intellectual life rather than" an attempt to "meet freshmen and institutional needs" (Drake, 1966). In 1960, the American Council of Education provided an authoritative definition of orientation viewing it as the process of inducting students into the community of learning (Brown, 1961). Sanford observed the power of campus forces opposing such a position when he suggested that "the major forces that oppose us when we try to initiate the freshman into the intellectual life are the student peer culture which makes relatively few or no intellectual demands, and an adult culture which accentuates grades and the practical aspects of the college experience" (Brown, 1962).

Four goals for orientation program planners were proposed in an attempt to respond to different institutional missions and the growing variety of programs offered during the mid-1980s. All programs should: (1) aid students in their academic adjustment; (2) provide assistance with personal adjustment; (3) help entering students' families understand the collegiate experience; and (4) assist the institution in gathering data about its entering students (Upcraft & Farnsworth, 1984). These goal statements appear to reflect the influence of earlier student personnel writers cited in previous sections of this chapter (e.g., Strang, 1951; Mueller, 1961).

As program emphases multiplied, Sagaria (1979) suggested a framework for classifying programs. Her three categories were: *interdisciplinary*, offered through liberal arts or general education departments and focusing on student as learner; *developmental*, affiliated with counseling services or general education areas and emphasizing the student as a person as well as his/her self-perceptions and relationships with others; and *utilitarian,* aligned with student affairs divisions emphasizing the mastery of a defined knowledge base and resources as basic skills.

Attempts were made to develop a generic mission or purpose statement as well as a set of common goals that might apply to all programs regardless of the institution. The most recent effort resulted in the Council for the Advancement of Standards in Student Services/ Development Programs' publication of *Guidelines for Student Services/ Development Programs* in 1986. In this document, the Council defined orientation as the provision of: " . . . continuing services and assistance that will: (1) aid new students in their transition to the institution; (2) expose new students to the broad educational opportunities of the institution; (3) integrate new students into the life of the institution" (Council for the Advancement of Standards, 1986, p. 97). All orientation programs should provide "an introduction to both the academic and student life aspects of the institution; and structured opportunities for the interaction of new students, faculty, staff and continuing student" (p. 97).

In addition, the Council recommended a list of 18 goals to help orientation professionals design programs and activities in a variety of institutional settings. The comprehensive list implies a broad institutional role for orientation. These goals are: "(1) to assist students in understanding the purposes of higher education; (2) assist students in understanding the mission of the specific institution; (3) assist students in determining their purpose in attending the institution, and developing relationships with faculty, staff, peers and other individuals within the community; (4) help students understand the institution's expectations of themselves; (5) provide information about and opportunities for self-assessment; (6) identify costs in attending the institution, both in terms of dollars and personal commitment; (7) improve the retention rate of new students; (8) provide an atmosphere and sufficient information to enable students to make reasoned and well-informed choices; (9) provide information concerning academic policies, procedures, requirements, and programs; (10) promote an awareness of nonclassroom opportunities; (11) provide referrals to qualified counselors and advisors; (13) explain the processes for class scheduling and registration and provide trained supportive assistance to accomplish these tasks; (13) develop familiarity with physical surroundings; (14) provide information and exposure to available institutional resources; (15) help students identify and evaluate housing and commuting options; (16) create an atmosphere that minimizes anxiety, promotes positive attitudes, and stimulates an excitement for learning; (17) provide appropriate information on personal safety and security; and (18) provide opportunities for new students to discuss expectations and perceptions of the campus with continuing students" (National Orientation Directors Association, 1986, p. 95).

Three years later, Twale (1989) reminded us of the complexity of the process of transition from one environment to another as she shared her view of freshman orientation while identifying the differing lenses used by others.

> Anthropologists see the campus as a strange new culture to which students must become acculturated. While freshmen orient to the social environment of a campus, they must channel their enthusiasm to the challenges of academic life as they explore and cope with the new culture. Sociologists view the campus as an interlocking configuration of social systems where success in mastering one subsystem may depend on careful adaptation to another. They believe that in order for freshmen to succeed academically, they must become integrated into the campus environment. Social psychologists see the campus as an arena of human interaction and encounter that affects the self-esteem and self-actualizing qualities of each developing human. In fact, while freshmen acclimate to subsystems within the total system, they form and modify their attitudes, self-concept, and their self-awareness within their new situation. Finally, the educator is concerned with the manner and method of communication by which these cultural and social messages are transmitted and retained. By establishing a system of information motivators and encouraging participation in various activities, orientation can arouse loyalties, inspire self-exploration, and bind a diverse group of students to a campus (1989, p. 161).

CHANGING STUDENT NEEDS

Program emphases change not only in relation to our understanding of the students to be served, but in response to societal and world events as well. Consider the following profile of the typical student of past decades compared to that of the typical student of today. From 1920 until the 1950s, entering students' needs were defined in terms describing the characteristics of the typical 18-year-old, middle-class, Caucasian undergraduate student. For most of these first generation college students, the move to their new collegiate environment was usually their first experience in living away from their family, friends, and hometown. Their needs were described most often in terms of perceived levels of their development.

Student personnel literature reflecting this student profile, provided four concerns believed to be common to all new students: breaking away from the family; choosing a vocation; establishing satisfactory relationships with members of the opposite sex; and integrating the personality. Later Mueller (1961) recast these concerns into three developmental tasks using a somewhat more psychosocial perspective: ego-integration (the process of achieving physical control, emotional development, and integration values); identification of different roles for the self (sex roles, dating, and new identities); and practice in future roles (social responsibilities, occupational roles, civic competence, and family life). Each of these bears a striking resemblance to the developmental tasks that would be found in the professional literature and attributed to Chickering and others more than ten years later.

Formal assessments of the needs of entering students' were undertaken by student affairs professionals during the 1950s as they responded to the need to provide data not only evaluating but supporting the continued existence of orientation programs. Entering students reported several fears they had about their entrance into a new educational community. Among them: their inability to do college work, to select the right major, to make friends, and to find a desirable roommate. The friendliness or anticipated lack of friendliness of college and university faculty was also frequently mentioned as an area of concern (Drake, 1955). Issues more directly related to the academic arena soon were replaced by concerns about social and personal adjustment among entering students as evidenced by Purdue's new students' rankings of their orientation needs: (1) inform them of academic responsibilities; (2) assist them with academic program planning; and (3) familiarize them with the campus (Tautfest, 1961). During the next ten years, the role of personal and social orientation to the academic community was viewed as less important to students than issues tied to their future academic achievement (Keil, 1966).

Many of the views expressed by student activists during the 1960s reflected criticisms directed toward social institutions such as the federal government and higher education. Students labeled these institutions "the Establishment" and believed that these bureaucratic organizations needed to be reorganized around a more humanistic philosophy. Among the changes demanded by student activists was a greater value to be assigned to the individual within complex bureaucracies. Related to this was their demand that the individual be allowed to assume a greater role within organizations promoting or creating change. Characteristic of their lack of acceptance of institutionalized authority, student activists argued that anyone over 30 years of age was not to be trusted. Their opposition to American involvement in the Vietnam war was expressed by the slogan, "Make love, not war!". They yelled "Do not fold, staple or mutilate" in response to the perceived impersonal environment of higher education created by the swelling number of students and the use of technology to assist in class registration. These attitudes significantly changed the roles performed by student affairs professionals and altered the nature of their interactions with students. The traditional student personnel role of surrogate parent was recast as that of advisor, advocate, facilitator, counselor and/or educator. Students were now viewed as responsible adults capable of assuming responsibility for their own development. No longer were they perceived as passive adolescents. The value previously linked to *in loco parentis* disappeared.

Increasingly, students questioned the relevance of their college courses and the extent to which their academic preparation would help them solve the problems they perceived outside the campus walls in American society. As a result, general education or core curriculum requirements were changed to permit students to pursue a wider range of interdisciplinary and individually designed topic-oriented seminars and degree programs.

Research on student satisfaction emerged during the 1960s and 1970s, a problematic period in American higher education. Several studies focused on measuring student satisfaction in purely academic terms by assessing when majors were chosen or by looking at students' years in school (Pervin, 1967; Schmidt & Sedlacek, 1972; Sturtz, 1971). During this same period, students' responses to orientation need assessments reflected yet another change. Students' newly expressed interest in vocational preparation now ranked equally with their previous concern for academic issues. A period of vocationalism, described by Astin (1972) and later by Levine (1979), had begun. These entering students perceived "orientation to the academic discipline, its purpose, and career-related goals as primary objectives" of an orientation program (Moore, Pappas, & Vinton, 1979).

A new significance was attached to the freshman year, particularly to the initial months. These early weeks were now viewed as the critical time during which new students' attitudes, values, and adjustment to higher education were influenced the most (Butts, 1971; Chickering & Havinghurst, 1981; Feldman & Newcomb, 1969; Knott & Daher, 1978;

Lange & Gentry, 1974; Lowe, 1980). This new knowledge and research base helped administrators increase their awareness of the significance of the freshman year and the value of the relationship between student satisfaction and student retention. Administrators, confronted by predicted declines in enrollment and the probable need to operate with reduced budgets and staff personnel, were quick to support research efforts that sought to identify and examine the many factors associated with student persistence.

Early retention research efforts included studies to identify factors contributing to student attrition. One such conclusion was that attrition was most severe during or at the end of the freshman year (Sagaria, 1979). At four-year institutions, factors related to attrition were gleaned from student questionnaires: coursework requiring study habits many students did not possess; large classes; an impersonal, uncomfortable campus environment; and academic and social regulations (Beal & Noel, 1980; Hall, 1982). This information and the new role orientation could assume in the transition process as an aid to student persistence resulted in additional institutional support for orientation professionals and programs. Retention became so strongly linked with orientation programs that it was almost viewed as the primary reason for their existence. However, Tinto (1985), a respected author of retention literature, suggested that the most important goal of freshman orientation experiences should be education and not simply retention.

High school students were the subjects of considerable research in attempts to identify personal characteristics thought to be associated with a successful transition to higher education. Entering students who later completed their transition more effectively were found to share a set of characteristics. In general, they possessed a competent self-image, they were motivated to pursue activities to stimulate growth and development, and they were willing to take risks (Knott & Daher, 1978). As a result programs were designed to develop or enhance these attitudes and behaviors among new students.

After studying retention and attrition, the American Testing Service cited several issues linked with high rates of student withdrawal. Most important were academic boredom; academic unpreparedness; uncertainty regarding academic major or career choice; transition and adjustment difficulties; dissonance or incompatibility; irrelevancy of education (Dannells, 1986). The significance of these issues has not changed and they continue to be the agenda items addressed by orientation professionals today.

PROGRAM MODELS

Three prototypes or models of programs serve as the foundation from which many of today's orientation programs evolved. They are: the Freshman Day or Week model (scheduled during the first semester of academic classes); the credit course model (scheduled during the first semester or the entire year); and the pre-orientation or pre-registration model (offered during the summer months) (Bergman, 1978; Harris, 1980; Herron, 1974; McCann, 1967; Strang, 1951).

In addition, two philosophical viewpoints emerged during the 1960s that influenced the content of orientation programs. The first was known as "microcosmic" and stressed testing, campus tours, informational meetings and pre-registration activities. The second, called "macrocosmic," emphasized issues associated with the intellectual challenges of academic life, cognitive development and the mission of higher education (Fitzgerald & Evans, 1963). Elements of these two viewpoints continue to dictate most orientation programs offered today.

Three other program models can be found in more recent literature reflecting additional changes in program emphases. These are the emerging leaders model, the institutional integration model, and the holistic model (Murray & Apilado, 1989; Striffolino & Saunders, 1989; Upcraft, Gardner & Associates, 1989, Wolfe, 1993). Since they have yet to achieve national stature they will not be reviewed here and readers are encouraged to pursue the references above.

The Freshman Day or Week Model

The University of Maine is credited with developing the first Freshman Week in 1923. Large meetings were the preferred format and the agendas emphasized sharing information, testing, counseling, registration, campus tours, recreational activities, and social events (Drake, 1966; Jones, 1927). As was true of other elements in the history of orientation, the popularity attached to this program model varied widely. By 1938, 83 percent of all higher education institutions offered programs based on this model. Support declined during the 1940s when this initial model was replaced by the structured, for academic credit, orientation course.

Twenty years later, however, in the mid-1960s, the Freshman Week model regained its earlier stature. On many campuses today, orientation professionals implement this model, generally as an extension of a summer preregistration or preorientation program.

The Pre-registration Model

The Pre-College Clinic, established in 1949 at Michigan State University, was a summer program scheduled from two to four days and included testing, counseling, information dissemination, and social events (Goodrich & Pierson, 1959). Its value as a public relations tool quickly became apparent as an aid to personalizing large university environments and a means of improving students' initial adjustment and grades. During the mid-1960s, both the Clinic and the Freshman Week prototypes became the two most frequently implemented program models (Dannells & Kuh, 1977; Forrest & Knapp, 1966; Wall & Ford, 1966).

The Freshman Course Model

The traditional Freshman Course model was developed to introduce new students to available fields of study and to assist them in coping with problems associated with their freshman status (Drake, 1966). These courses sprung from the counseling movement in higher education and were motivated by the perceived need to help entering students during their initial adjustment to a new educational setting. Slightly more than half of all institutions sponsored programs of this type with their emphasis on freshman adjustment issues during the decades before 1960 (Knode, 1930; Miller, 1930). However, by the mid-1960s and in the midst of student activism, this model was viewed as obsolete (Drake, 1966). Faculty voiced strong opposition to its perceived emphasis on "fun and games," social events, and personal adjustment. They argued strongly and persuasively for a return to an orientation program that focused on academic concerns and the mission of general education (Dannells & Kuh, 1977). A revival of interest in the academic course mode resulted, and orientation directors responded by designing programs to meet students' academic and personal/social needs (O'Banion, 1969; Snider, 1970).

Three forces seemed to merge during the 1960s and 1970s that caused administrators to seek new programs that would teach entering students about the institution's system and how to deal with it effectively. In the words of Upcraft et al. (1989): "First, new students, many of whom were the first members of their families to go beyond high school, arrived on campus without 'the skills of studenthood' (Cohen & Jody, 1978, p. 2). Second, because of revisions in curricula and changes in regulations on campus, the choices for freshmen became more complex. Finally, peer culture, with its great potential for assistance to freshmen, 'seemed to have lost much of its potency in helping students to adapt' " (Cohen & Jody, 1978, p. 2). It was less likely that an administrator would observe among freshmen, as Kingman Brewster had done at Yale in the 1960s, a single year's "progress from arrogance to self-doubt, to self-pity, to rediscovery, and finally to mature ambition" (Brewster, 1968, p. vii)" (p. 38–39). Out of this context, perhaps one of the most popular and influential programs ever developed was established by John Gardner at the University of South Carolina entitled, "The Freshman Seminar." This model meshes two major elements: sharing information to help students understand their initial transition period and establishing an environment that is socially supportive (Gordon & Grites, 1984). Most frequently, small classes are taught by a faculty member (on a pass/fail basis) teamed with an upperclass student paraprofessional allowing close student-faculty relationships to be developed. Thus, faculty can provide valuable feedback to students without the negative influence of a grading relationship (Upcraft et al., 1989).

The Freshman Seminar model is probably the most popular model in use on large and small campuses today. While several studies have been completed demonstrating the relationship between participation in a Freshman Seminar experience and student success and retention, few have turned their attention to identifying and evaluating the outcomes of the experience on early adjustment. Using the familiar Baker & Siryk's Student Adjustment to College Questionnaire and Tricket & Moos' Classroom Environment Scale (an assessment of the "psychosocial environment of classrooms" (Tricket & Moos, 1973), 1991 findings revealed that the freshmen seminar experience "seems to be a timely, effective program for mediating the normal decline in first-semester adjustment that leaves many students vulnerable to later attrition" (Schwitzer, McGovern, & Robbins, 1991, p. 488). More specifically, an increase in social adjustment was noted on a pre-post comparison basis and a high level of perceived social support was reported by students at the end of the experience. Lastly, all 113 volunteer participants returned to the institution for the second semester.

In a 1985 American Council on Education study, more than three-fourths of 2600 institutions reported offering either a for credit or noncredit course labelled, "Coping with College" (El-Khawas, 1985).

STAFFING

Staffing patterns also reflect changing times and perspectives. Traditionally, orientation activities have been the sole responsibility of student affairs professionals. During the years when the value ascribed to academic concerns was high, faculty members shared in planning and staffing programs. Others were added to the implementation team when in the mid-1960s, the student affairs community's perception of students changed and undergraduates assumed new roles as co-participants and collaborators in planning and as peer facilitators. This type of student involvement was studied in 1989 and student paraprofessionals reported significantly higher gain scores on the developmental tasks of interdependence and tolerance than their control group peers (Holland & Huba, 1989). In addition to the economic benefits of student paraprofessionals, these student leaders gained significantly from the experience themselves (Holland & Huba, 1989).

Generally, today's programs are the responsibility of a Director of Orientation or of New Students and their implementation is made possible by a largely volunteer student staff at both large and small institutions. Most often, the Director or the person responsible for orientation who may have other duties as well reports either to the Senior Student Affairs Officer or to an individual who reports to the SSAO.

EFFECTIVE PROGRAMS

Needing information to help plan, evaluate and substantiate orientation programs during the mid-1980s, professionals looked to research to guide them. Conclusions from a study of successful programs, proposed that all orientation programs should incorporate the following: (1) there should be a concern for the student as individual; (2) new students should be afforded the opportunity to establish relationships with faculty; (3) primary emphasis of the program should be academic; (4) small group meetings should be used to ease the adjustment of new students; and (5) there should be a recognition of the stressful transition experienced by entering students (Kramer & Washburn, 1983).

In a similar review, Upcraft and Farnsworth (1984) found seven traits characteristic of successful orientation programs. Such a program must "(1) be a sustained and coordinated effort . . . ; (2) have the support and involvement of the entire campus community . . . ; (3) be based on sound concepts of student development and on what is known about the influence of the collegiate environment . . . and "on all available information concerning entering students . . . " (p. 30). Other traits were that "(4) the program be subject to evaluation; (5) use a wide variety of interventions including media approaches, group programming, academic courses, and individual tutoring, advising and counseling . . . (6) be appropriately timed . . . ; and (7) must be coordinated by a central office or personnel . . . " (p. 30).

SERVING STUDENTS

As the diversity among entering students increases, orientation professionals must be able to design programs that meet specific needs requiring them to be familiar with particular characteristics of various student subgroups. Often referred to as minorities, members of a minority grouping are defined by the characteristics of a particular institutional environment. The term is derived from the identification of the majority student population within a given environment. As an example, entering minority students might be Baptists at a Catholic college or women students at a men's university. Other applications of the label may refer to physically challenged students; adult learners; gay, lesbian, or bisexual students; educationally disadvantaged students; transfer students; cross-cultural or international students. While a complete review of the literature describing each of these student groups is beyond the scope of this chapter, readers are encouraged to pursue selections focusing on the group or groups of their choice. As an illustration of the kind of expertise needed by orientation professionals, a profile of transfer students is provided following brief reviews of recent literature describing Hispanic and returning adult learners.

Hispanic Students

For the past several years, "minority student" has been applied to a wide range of ethnic and racial minorities, such as Hispanic, Japanese, Native Indians, and Alaskan Aleuts. While cultural and ethnic factors underscore differences among minority students, students in these groups tend to share a common background that includes a heritage of oppression, experiences as first generation college students, an emphasis on family life, and an appreciation of community membership.

Literature describing ethnic minority students continues to reinforce the need for the orientation professional to be aware of diversity and its implications for entering students. An ability to meet students' needs is closely related to the student development educator's familiarity and knowledge of the historical and societal context of the institutions previously attended by these students. Developing specific programs whose content differs significantly may not be as valuable as altering the format and the scheduling of a traditional orientation program (Wright, 1984).

Upcraft et al. (1989) identify barriers to Hispanic freshman achievement. "Hispanics are generally first-generation college students (without) . . . a thorough understanding and appreciation of the higher education system and the benefits of college" (p. 264). They are expected to work part-time while studying to help support the family. Hispanic daughters are less likely to be encouraged or allowed to enroll at an institution far from their parents' home. Language can be a major barrier to their academic success.

Orientation professionals are encouraged to develop mentorship programs between Hispanic students and faculty. Tutorial programs in basic skill areas such as reading and writing should be made available. Priority should be given to providing academic and support services for first and second year Hispanic students (Justiz & Rendon, 1989).

Returning Adult Learners

Returning adult learners numbered approximately six million in 1988 (Hirschorn, 1988) and are expected to be more than half of all students in higher education by the mid-1990s (College Entrance Examination Board, 1985). Factors motivating returning adult learners to pursue higher education reflect their particular needs. Some adult learners find themselves without employment because of downsizing. Others may be recently divorced or widowed and have a new need to gain financial independence. Some simply desire to make a mid-life career change. Obviously, these people are experiencing significant transitions in their own lives as well as in their new educational setting. Researchers have suggested that these students are generally characterized by low levels of self-esteem and a lack of self-confidence, not only about themselves, but also their ability to perform satisfactorily in an academic environment. By adopting the student role in addition to the other roles in their lives, they are subjected to increased stress (Greenfeig & Greenfeig, 1984).

Because of the adult learners' special needs, orientation programs for them should begin at admission, continue through the first few days on the new campus and progress the entire year (Greenfeig & Greenfeig, 1984). Program planners need to create environments in which adult learners sense they belong and matter. They need to attempt to remove "complex and rigid admissions procedures; . . . provide flexible scheduling so that degrees can be earned wholly by evening or weekend attendance; . . . provide print materials that are geared for the returning adult" (Copland, 1989, p. 315). Peer counseling, social activities, workshops, and individual advising may all be required. Additionally, information dissemination and the provision of support remain critical elements. To compensate for many adult learners' feelings of isolation, opportunities must be made available that permit them to meet and interact with their peers and other successful adult learners (Apps, 1982).

Transfer Students

Despite the tremendous growth of community colleges and two-year institutions during the 1960s, students transferring to four-year institutions were often left to their own resources during their transition period. A national survey of NASPA member institutions revealed that less than half of all campuses responding offered special programs for transfer students (Knoell & Medsker, 1965; Sandeen & Goodale, 1972).

Harrison and Varcoe (1983) surveyed 425 four-year institutions with minimum enrollments of 3,000 students to determine orientation practices developed for transfer students. With a 40 percent return rate, they were able to conclude that the percentage of institutions having special student need-based programs increased only slightly from previous studies:

68 percent now responded affirmatively. Most institutional programs were designed to include transfer students in mass meetings with other first-time entering students. Transcript evaluations, academic advising, and registration information were typical agenda items. Continuous orientation programs scheduled during the first semester appeared to hold the most potential for assisting transfer students; however, only 16 percent of responding institutions sponsored such programs. Of all the developmental tasks, only academic and intellectual development and interpersonal relationships were perceived to be appropriate goals of orientation programs. Similar dissatisfaction with this same narrow emphasis was expressed decades earlier by Wrenn (1951). Despite the changes in orientation program goals and formats, other student development tasks have not been integrated into programs for transfer students.

Sometimes referred to as "educational middlemen" (Kintzer, 1973), transfer students possess unique characteristics. Generally, their test scores and high school grades are lower than native four-year students; their grades decline during the first term and improve thereafter; and their retention rate is lower than first-time entering students. Other traits suggest that transfers require more time to complete baccalaureate degree programs since many of them are employed while attending classes. Additionally, fewer scholarships, grants, or fellowships are awarded to transfer students and their educational aspirations do not generally go beyond the baccalaureate degree (Harrison & Varcoe, 1984).

Reporting the results of a survey of 425 four-year institutions with enrollments of at least 3,000 students, Harrison & Varcoe (1984) recommended that all orientation programs for transfer students need to address the issues of academic articulation, academic transition, living or transportation arrangements, financial considerations, environmental adjustments, and developmental needs (Harrison & Varcoe, 1984).

Traditionally thought of as a rather homogeneous group of students, transfers have generally been thought of as individuals who transfer from one higher education institution to another. But not all transfer students are alike. Their pre- and post-transfer performance has been shown to vary by age, year of transfer, institution of origin, and previous GPA (Flum, 1989). For example, while greater rates of males transfer from community colleges to four year campuses (Velez & Javalgi, 1987), men and women tend to graduate at similar rates (Holohan, Gree, & Kelley, 1983).

From one of the more recent pieces of literature, differences were found between transfer students and freshmen: (1) fewer transfers identified themselves as being in the top 5 to 10 percent of their high school classes; (2) less than half of transfers reported working only during the summer; (3) more than 7 percent were employed full-time; (4) nearly two-thirds had college graduates as parents compared to 84 percent of the freshmen; and (5) more transfers than freshmen believed that earning satisfactory grades and studying efficiently would be among the easiest parts of their adjustment (Milville & Sedlacek, 1995, p. 148–149).

Based on the above findings, it appears that orientation professionals need to incorporate more than the usual array of events and traditional meetings when planning programs for these special students. Innovative techniques such as mail, telephone, or e-mail, should be considered as means of reaching this unique student subgroup. In addition, such accommodations as evening or weekend scheduling of events with attention paid to many transfer students' status as a single parent would seem to be in order (Miville & Sedlacek, 1995).

ENTRY–LEVEL QUALIFICATIONS

As with several other specialties within student affairs (i.e., residence halls and student activities), many professionals gained their initial experience as undergraduate student participants or leaders. Many graduate students hold assistantships that are comparable to entry-level positions while pursuing graduate work. Full-time Directors generally possess a master's degree. Some positions, particularly on smaller campuses, place responsibilities for orientation programs under a full-time professional staff member who may also supervise student activities or other areas within student affairs. Student affairs professionals specializing in orientation need to have a skill base that allows them to plan purposeful interventions in students' lives. Obviously, communications skills, programming abilities, and leadership or administrative skills are needed in addition to a sensitivity to the complex issues associated with students' growth and development.

USING A GENERATIONAL LENS

One of the most thought-provoking and unique perspectives that can help us understand our students better is the recent volume, *Generations:*

The History of America's Future from 1584 to 2069 by W. Strauss and N. Howe (1991). The following pages present the key elements of this analysis of groups of people using the generational lens proposed by Strauss & Howe. The material is considered noteworthy because of its ability to add to our understanding of students from another and different perspective. While not intended to describe only today's college and university students, their generational lens provides important insights to guide orientation planners in serving students. A preliminary word of caution seems in order. As with any schema, attempts to apply labels to large groups of people need to be read and appreciated for their overall contribution to understanding, while not losing sight of the existence and value of individual differences.

In the initial pages we are told that the authors propose "looking at the American lifecycle as it has actually been lived by each generation, from childhood through old age" (1991, p. 32). The following key concepts are presented to help the reader understand the observations and predictions offered about college students.

Generations of people, from the 17th century to the present, are viewed as "people moving through time" (1991, p. 32). Members of each generation are perceived as sharing a peer personality: "a generational persona recognized and determined by (1) common age location; (2) common beliefs and behavior; and (3) perceived membership in a common generation" (1991, p. 64). Throughout American history, a recurring cycle of four distinct peer personalities, always appearing in the same repeating order, can be identified. For Strauss and Howe, these are: idealist, reactive, civic, and adaptative (p. 74). Central to their theory is the linking of age with societal events, which they believe produces a cohort-group. For them, a generation is defined as "a special cohort-group whose length approximates the span of a phase of life and whose boundaries are fixed by peer personality" (1991, p. 60). Within each generation are four separate life phases:

ELDERHOOD (age 66–87). Central role: *stewardship* (supervising, mentoring, channeling endowments, passing on values).

MIDLIFE (age 44–65). Central role: *leadership* (parenting, teaching, directing institutions, using values).

RISING ADULTHOOD (age 22–43). Central role: *activity* (working, starting families and livelihoods, serving institutions, testing values).

YOUTH (age 0–21). Central role: *dependence* (growing, learning, accepting protection and nurture, avoiding harm, acquiring values) (1991, pp. 60–61).

Another key concept is Social Moment: "an era, typically lasting about a decade, when people perceive that historic events are radically altering their social environment" (1991, p. 71). An example offered is the 13-year period from 1932 when Franklin Roosevelt was elected until the end of World War II in 1945. Within this time frame or social moment, America's "social landscape" was "visibly rearranged . . . from the function of government and the organization of the economy to man's relationship with technology and the U.S. role in world affairs" (p. 71). Two types of social moments are noted: SECULAR CRISES, "when society focuses on reordering the outer world of institutions and public behavior; and SPIRITUAL AWAKENINGS, when society focuses on changing the inner world of values and private behavior" (p. 71). The authors have determined that "Social moments normally arrive in time intervals roughly separated by two phases of life (approximately forty to forty-five years), and they alternate in type between secular crises and spiritual awakenings" (p. 71).

Each of the four cyclical and repeating generations named above can now be understood in greater depth:

1. A dominant, inner-fixated IDEALIST GENERATION grows up as increasingly indulged youths after a secular crisis; comes of age inspiring a spiritual awakening; fragments into narcissistic rising adults; cultivates principle as moralistic midlifers; and emerges as visionary elders guiding the next secular crisis.
2. A recessive REACTIVE GENERATION grows up as underprotected and criticized youths during a spiritual awakening; matures into risk-taking, alienated adults; mellows into pragmatic midlifer leaders during a secular crisis; and maintains respect (but less influence) as reclusive elders.
3. A dominant, outer-fixated CIVIC GENERATION grows up as increasingly protected youths after a spiritual awakening; comes of age overcoming a secular crisis; unites into a heroic and achieving cadre of rising adults; sustains that image by building institutions as powerful midlifers; and emerges as busy elders attacked by the next spiritual awakening.
4. A recessive ADAPTIVE GENERATION grows up as overprotected and suffocated youths during a secular crisis; matures into risk-adverse, conformist rising adults; produces indecisive midlife arbitrator-leaders during a spiritual awakening; and maintains influence (but less respect) as sensitive adults. (1991, p. 74).

Returning to our focus on college students and orientation programs, we are ready to ask what Strauss and Howe can contribute to our understanding? Individuals born between 1961 and 1981, now 15 to 34 years of age, are members of a REACTIVE cohort described above and are members of the thirteenth generation or "13ers." The previous generation, members of the Boom Generation, are those born between 1943 and 1960 and who are currently 35 to 53 years old. In 2013, Boomers will be 70 to 87 years old and 13ers will be 31 to 51 years of age.

Among the more striking of the 19 facts presented in Strauss and Howe's description of the 13th generation are these:

- The 13th generation is the most aborted generation in American history. After rising sharply during the late 1960s and early 1970s, the abortion rate climbed another 80 percent during the first six years (1973 to 1979) after the Supreme Court's *Roe v. Wade* decision. Through the birthyears of last-wave 13ers, would-be mothers aborted one fetus in three.
- Parental divorce has struck 13ers harder than any other American generation. In 1962, half of all adult women believed that parents in bad marriages should stay together for the sake of the children; by 1980, only one in five thought so. A 13er child in the 1980s faced twice the risk of parental divorce as a Boomer in the mid-1960s.
- No other generation has ever grown up in families of such complexity. In 1980, just 56 percent of all dependent children lived with two once-married parents, another 14 percent with at least one previously married parent, 11 percent with a stepparent, and 19 percent with one parent. One in five had half siblings. The likelihood of children receiving support payments from the noncustodial parent declined from the Boomer to 13er childhood eras.
- A sampling of teachers who taught Boomers in the mid-1960s and 13ers in the mid-1980s was asked to compare the two, in forty-three measures of aptitude and achievement. The score: Boomers 38, 13ers 4, with one tie. The teachers scored Boomers higher in all academic skills, communications ability, and commitment to learning. Thirteeners outscored Boomers in negotiating skills, consumer awareness, adult-interactions skills, and "defenses to prevent extreme dependency on parents and authorities."
- As teenagers, 13ers are committing suicide more frequently than any generation since the Lost (those born between 1883 and 1900). In 1976, the child suicide rate rose above the previous record, set in 1908. Through the 1980s, roughly 5,000 children under age 18 committed suicide each year, the largest number and proportion ever recorded for that age bracket.
- Already, 13ers have become the most heavily incarcerated generation in American history. From Boom to 13th, the proportion of youth in jail rose by roughly one-third for whites, blacks, women and men. The average length of a sentence has risen 12 percent during the half-dozen years in which 13ers have entered the adult criminal justice system. . . . (1991, pp. 324–328)

Current undergraduate students and the freshmen of the next few years are 13ers. "No other generation in living memory has come of age with such a sense of social distance—of adults doing so little for them and expecting so little from them" (Strauss & Howe, p. 323). The challenges for orientation professionals are enormous. Adjustment to higher education needs to include opportunities to foster the development of trust and interdependence, perhaps more so now than ever before. Orientation programs planned for the freshman adjustment period may need to include a different emphasis on student growth than before and will demand greater understanding and sensitivity on the part of professionals.

According to Strauss and Howe, future college and university attendees, born since 1982, may well be members of the CIVIC generation cited above. The tone seems to change as facts about these youngest of people are presented. These are the individuals who "in green coats and yellow blouses (uniforms) are the vanguard of America's MILLENNIAL GENERATION. Cute. Cheerful. Scoutlike. Wanted." (p. 335). "Its birthyears will stretch to and probably just beyond the year 2000, the end of the second millenium" (p. 335). Consider the following:

- First-wave Millennials, born after the great 1960s and 1970s plunge in American fertility rates, have the lowest child-to-parent ratio in American history. They arrived at a time when only 2 percent of all kids under age 18 live in families with five or more kids—just one-fourth the population of first-waver 13ers.
- In contrast to 13ers . . . Millennial babies frequently arrive to parents who want them desperately. The abortion rate peaked in 1980 and has since shown a gradual decline.
- The early 1980s marked a decisive turnaround in public attitudes toward public schools: the beginning of 'quality education' as a political issue; the first year most parents approved of performance of their local school districts; and the first of seven straight years in which teacher salaries increased faster than inflation—after seven straight years of real salary decline.
- The poverty rate for children under six peaked in 1983 (at 24.6 percent) and thereafter has gradually declined. The U.S. divorce rate peaked in 1981; the homocide rate against children age 1–4 peaked in 1982. (p. 341–342)

ISSUES FOR THE PRACTITIONER

As one of the initial student affairs specialty areas experienced by new students, the orientation program has the opportunity and the potential to significantly affect student adjustment and future success. Participation in orientation activities is linked to student satisfaction and persistence. Additionally, research data suggest that the entire four-year undergraduate experience can be significantly affected by the efforts of orientation professionals and their programs.

Now more than ever, professionals need to have their practice grounded in student development theory and a familiarity with research literature that describes the new student. Entering students' values, perceptions, needs and concerns are the basis of a course in Bowling Green's graduate curriculum entitled, "The Freshman Year Experience." Other preparation programs might consider offering a similar course for future student affairs professionals. Committed to student development and assisted by paraprofessionals, members of an institution's orientation team comprise one of the more influential groups on campus because of their ability to foster student growth and development through intentional interventions.

The following trends or issues will be a part of the orientation professional's agenda for the next few years:

- With the emphasis on student learning and new attempts to reintegrate the extracurriculum, more and more institutions will require entering students to participate in orientation programs whether they be fashioned from the week-long or freshman seminar models.
- While the increasing use of technology helps to make procedures such as registration easier for students, its greater use removes the opportunity for personal interaction within institutions. Professionals will need to put greater emphasis on the concepts of mattering and belonging using them as cornerstones of future programs.
- The need for an extended program of support through small groups, facilitated by peers and staff/faculty, beyond the first few weeks, seems to be in evident. Such programs may be needed not only during the first semester but into the second as well.
- More attention needs to be given to the more traditional issues of adjustment like homesickness than is being done presently. The suitcase college or university phenomenon may result now more from some new students' needs to reconnect with a loved pet at home than the lack of planned activities on campus or student apathy.
- With increased attention on assessment, accountability, and learning, institutions will expect that orientation professionals utilize skills to design and complete more evaluation and other research activities than ever before.
- Fewer students residing on campuses in the future will create new challenges for orientation professionals. New methods of communication may be necessary to assist new students with building a sense of identity as well as commitment to learning and higher education.

REFERENCES

Anderson, E. (1985). Forces influencing student persistence and achievement. In L. Noel, R. S. Levitz, D. Saluri, & Associates (Eds.), *Increasing student retention* (pp. 44–61). San Francisco: Jossey-Bass.

Apps, J. (1978). *Study skills for those adults returning to school.* New York: McGraw-Hill.

Baker, R. W., & Siryk, B. (1980). Alienation and freshman transition into college. *Journal of College Student Personnel, 21,* 437–442.

Beal, P. E., & Noel, L. (1980). *What works in student retention.* The American College Testing Program and the National Center for Higher Education Management Systems. Iowa City: ACT.

Bennett, M. E. (1938). *The orientation of students in educational institutions.* Thirty-seventh Yearbook (pp. 163–166). NSSE, Part I, Public-School.

Bergman, I. B. (1978). Freshman orientation in the college classroom. *Journal of College Student Personnel, 19*(5), 363–364.

Bookman, G. (1948). Freshman orientation techniques in colleges and universities. *Occupations, 27,* 163–166.

Brinkerhoff, D. B., & Sullivan, P. E. (1982). Concerns of new students: A pre-test—post-test evaluation of orientation. *Journal of College Student Personnel, 23*(5), 384–390.

Brown, R. (1972). *Tomorrow's higher education: A return to the academy.* The American College Personnel Association.

Brubaker, J. S., & Rudy, W. (1958). *Education in transition.* New York: Harper.

Butts, T. H. (1971). *Personnel service review: New practices in student orientation.* Ann Arbor. (ERIC Document Reproduction Service No. ED 057 416).

Caple, R. B. (1964). A rationale for the orientation course. *Journal of College Student Personnel, 6,* 42–46.

Chandler, E. M. (1972). Freshman orientation—is it worthwhile? *NASPA Journal, 10,* 55–61.

Chickering, A. (1972). Education and identity. San Francisco: Jossey-Bass.

Chickering, A., & Havinghurst, R. J. (1981). The life cycle. In Chickering & Associates (Eds.), *The modern American college* (pp. 16–50). San Francisco: Jossey-Bass.

Chickering, A., & Reisser, L. (1993). *Education and identity.* (2nd ed.). San Francisco: Jossey-Bass.

College Entrance Examination Board. (1985). Trends in adult student enrollment. New York: Office of Adult Learning Services, National Center for Education Statistics, U.S. Department of Education.

Cohen, R. D., & Jody, R. (1978). *Freshman seminar: A new orientation.* Boulder: Westview.

Copland, B. (1989). Adult learners. In M. L. Upcraft et al., *The freshman year experience* (pp. 303–315). San Francisco: Jossey-Bass.

Council for the Advancement of Standards for Student Services/Development Programs. (1986). *CAS standards and guidelines for student services/development programs.* Iowa City: ACT.

Council of Guidance and Personnel Associations. (1943). Recommendations, *Occupations, 21,* 46–48.

Creamer, D. G., & Kramer, T. (1978). An in-class orientation method. *Journal of College Student Personnel, 19*(3), 287–288.

Crocker, L. G. (Ed.). *Advice to freshmen by freshmen.* Ann Arbor, MI: G. Wahr.

Cross, K. (1970). *Occupationally oriented students, 5*(3). Junior College Review.

Dannells, M. (1986). *Orientation director's manual,* NODA.

Doermann, H. J. (1926). *Orientation of college freshmen.* Baltimore: Williams & Williams, p. 162.

Doman, E. F., & Christian, M. G. (1976). Effects of a group life seminar on perceptions of the university environment. *Journal of College Student Personnel, 17*(1), 66–71.

Drake, R. W. (1966). *Freshman orientation in the United States colleges and universities.* Colorado State University, Fort Collins. (ERIC Document Reproduction Service No. ED 030 923 [a]).

Drake, R. W. (1966). *Review of the literature for freshman orientation practices in the United States.* Fort Collins: Colorado State University. (ERIC Document Reproduction Service No. ED 030 920).

El-Khawas, E. (1985). *Campus Trends, 1984.* Washington: American Council on Education. NODA.

Emme, E. (1933). The adjustment problems of college freshmen. Council of Guidance and Personnel Associations. Recommendations. *Occupations, 21,* 46–48.

Feldman, K. A., & Newcomb, T. M. (1969). *The impact of college on students.* San Francisco: Jossey-Bass.

Fitts, C. T., & Swift, F. H. (1928). *The construction of orientation courses for freshmen, 1888–1926.* Berkeley: University of California Press.

Fitzgerald, L. E., & Evans, S. B. (1963). Orientation programs: Foundations and framework. *College and University, 38,* 270–275.

Flum, M. E. (1989). *The relationship of selected variables to transfer student academic performance at the University of Maryland.* Unpublished master's thesis, University of Maryland, College Park.

Forest, A. (1982). *Increasing student competence and persistence: The best case for general education.* Iowa City: ACT.

Forrest, D. V., & Knapp, R. H. (1966). Summer college orientation programs. *Journal of College Student Personnel, 7*(1), 47–49.

Foxley, C. H. (1969). Orientation or dis-orientation. *Personnel and Guidance Journal, 48,* 218–221.

Gardner, D. H. (1936). *Student personnel services. Evaluation of higher education institutions.* Chicago: University of Chicago Press, p. 235.

Gordon, V., & Grites, T. (1991). Adjustment outcomes of a freshmen seminar: A utilization-focused approach. *Journal of College Student Development, 32,* 484–489.

Goodale, T., & Sandeen, A. (1971). The transfer student: A research report. *NASPA Journal, 9*(4), 248–263.

Goodrich, T. A., & Pierson, R. R. (1959). Pre-college counseling at Michigan State University. *Personnel and Guidance Journal, 37,* 595–597.

Gordon, V. N., & Grites, T. J. (1984). The freshman seminar course: Helping students succeed. *Journal of College Student Personnel, 25*(4), 315–320.

Greenfeig, B. R., & Goldberg, B. J. (1984). Orienting returning adult students. In M. L. Upcraft (Ed.), *New Directions for Student Services: No. 25. Orienting students to college* (pp. 79–92). San Francisco: Jossey-Bass.

Guber, S. K. (1970). Four approaches to freshman orientation. *Improving College and University Teaching, 18*, 57–60.

Harrison, C. H., & Varcoe, K. (1984). Orienting transfer students. In M. L. Upcraft (Ed.), *New Directions for Student Services: No. 25. Orienting students to college* (pp. 93–106). San Francisco: Jossey-Bass.

Hall, B. (1982). College warm-up: Easing the transition to college. *Journal of College Student Personnel, 23*(3), 280–281.

Herron, D. (1974). Orientation effects on student alienation. *Journal of the National Association of Women Deans, Administrators and Counselor, 37*(3), 107–110.

Higginson, L. C., Moore, L. V., & White, E. B. (1981). A new role for orientation: Getting down to academics. *NASPA Journal, 19*(1), 21–28.

Hirschorn, M. W. (1988). "Students over 25 found to make up 45 percent of campus enrollments," *Chronicle of Higher Education,* March 30, 1988, A35.

Holland, A., & Huba, M. E. (1989). Psychosocial development among student paraprofessionals in a college orientation program. *Journal of College Student Development, 30*, 100–105.

Holohan, C. K., Curran, L. T., & Kelley, H. P. (1982). The formation of student performance expectations: The relationship of student perceptions and social comparisons. *Journal of College Student Personnel, 23*, 366–367.

Jackson, G. S., & Seegan, R. B. (1978). Ongoing orientation for freshmen. *Journal of College Student Personnel, 18*(2), 145–146.

Justiz, M. J., & Rendon, L. I. (1989). Hispanic students. In Upcraft et al., (1989). *The freshman year experience.* San Francisco: Jossey Bass, pp. 261–276.

Kamm, R. B., & Wrenn, C. G. (1947). Current developments in student-personnel programs and the needs of the veteran. *School and Society, 65*, 89–92.

Keil, E. C. (1966). College orientation: A disciplinary approach. *Liberal Education, 52*, 172–180.

Klostermann, L. R., & Merseal, J. (1978). Another view of orientation. *Journal of College Student Personnel, 19*(3), 86–87.

Knode, J. C. (1930). *Orienting the student to college with special reference to freshman week.* New York: Bureau of Publications, Teachers College, Columbia University.

Knoell, D. M., & Medsker, L. L. (1965). *From junior to senior college: A national study of the transfer student.* Washington, DC: American Council on Education.

Knott, J. E., & Daher, D. M. (1978). A structured group program for new students. *Journal of College Student Personnel, 19*(5), 456–461.

Krall, J. K. (1981). New student welcome day program. *Journal of College and University Housing, 11*(2), 320–333.

Kramer, G. L., & Hardy, H. L. (1985). Facilitating the freshman experience. *College and University, 60*(3), 242–252.

Kramer, G. L., & Washburn, R. (1983). The perceived orientation needs of new students. *Journal of College Student Personnel, 24*(4), 311–319.

Kramer, G. L., & White, M. T. (1982). Developing a faculty mentoring program: An experiment. *NACADA Journal, 2*(2), 47–58.

Lange, A. J., & Gentry, R. F. (1974). Uni-prep: An innovative program to university orientation. *NASPA Journal, 12*(2), 90–95.

Levine, A. (1980). *When dreams and heroes died.* San Francisco: Jossey-Bass.

Lowe, I. (1980/April). *Preregistration counseling: A comparative study.* Paper presented at the California College Association Conference, Monterey, CA.

McCann, J. C. (1967). Trends in orienting college students. *Journal of the National Association of Women Deans, Administrators and Counselors, 30*(2), 855–889.

Medsker, L. L. (1960). *The junior college.* New York: McGraw-Hill.

Miller, T. K., & Jones, J. D. (1981). Out-of-class activities. In A. W. Chickering & Associates (Eds.). *The modern American college.* San Francisco: Jossey-Bass.

Miller, T. K., & Prince, J. (1976). *The future of student affairs.* San Francisco: Jossey-Bass.

Miville, M.L., & Sedlacek, W. E. (1995). Transfer students and freshmen: Different or parallel experiences? *NASPA Journal, 32,* 145–152.

Moore, L. P., Pappas, E. K., & Vinton, J. C. (1979). An organizational model for orientation programs. *NASPA Journal, 17,* 40–45.

Morison, S.E. (1936). "The histories of the universities." Lectures delivered at the Rice Institute, Apr. 3–4, 1935. *The Rice Institute Pamphlet,* 1936(b), 23, 211–282.

Mueller, K. H. (1961). *Student personnel work in higher education.* Boston: Houghton-Mifflin.

Murray, J.L., & Apilado, M. (1989). Design and implementation of a holistic orientation program for small colleges. *NASPA Journal, 26*(4), 308–312.

O'Banion, T. (1969). Experimentation in orientation of junior college students. *Journal of College Student Personnel, 10*(1), 12–15.

Pervin, L.A. (1967). Satisfaction and perceived self-environment similarity: A semantic differential study of student-college interaction. *Journal of Personality, 35,* 623–624.

Prola, M., & Stern, D. (1984). The effect of a freshman orientation program on student leadership and academic persistence. *Journal of College Student Personnel, 25*(5), 472–473.

Ramist, L. (1981). *College student attrition and retention.* College Board Report, No. 80–81. Princeton, NJ: College Entrance Examination Board.

Riesman, D. (1961). Changing colleges and changing students. *National Catholic Education Association Bulletin, 58,* 104–115.

Ross, M. (1975). College orientation: A three-way street. *Journal of College Student Personnel, 16*(6), 468–470.

Rothman, L. K., & Leonard, D. G. (1967). Effectiveness of freshman orientation. *Journal of College Student Personnel, 10,* 12–15.

Sagaria, M. A. (1979). Freshmen orientation courses: A framework. *Journal of the National Association of Women Deans, Administrators and Counselors, 43*(1), 3–7.

Sandeen, A., & Goodale, T. (1972). Student personnel programs and the transfer students. *NASPA Journal, 9,* 179–200.

Sanford, N. (1962). Developmental status of the freshman. In N. Sanford (Ed.), *The American College.* New York: Wiley.

Santee, R. T., & Davis, B. G. (1980). The summer threshold program: An experiment in preparatory education. *Evaluation Review, 4*(2), 215–224.

Schmidt, D.K., & Sedlacek, W.E. (1972). Variables related to university student satisfaction. *Journal of College Student Personnel, 13,* 233–237.

Shaffer, R. H. (1962). A new look at orientation. *College and University, 37,* 272–279.

Smith, G. C. (1984). Integrating academic advising with ongoing orientation programs. *NODA Journal, 3*(1), 9–12.

Strang, R. (1951). Orientation of new students. In C. G. Wrenn (Ed.), *Student personnel work in college* (pp. 274–292). New York: Ronald.

Strauss, W., & Howe, N. (1991). *Generations: The history of America's future, 1584 to 2069.* New York: William Morrow.

Striffolino, P., & Saunders, S.A. (1989). Emerging leaders: Students in need of development. *NASPA Journal, 27*(1), 51–58.

Sturtz, S.A. (1971). Age differences in college student satisfaction. *Journal of College Student Personnel, 12,* 220–222.

Tautfest, P. B. (1961). An evaluation technique for orientation programs. *Journal of College Student Personnel, 3*(32), 5–28.

Terenzini, P. T., & Pascarella, E. T. (1977). Voluntary freshman attrition and patterns of social and academic integration in a university: A test of a conceptual model. *Research in Higher Education, 6,* 25–43.

Tinto, V. (1985). Dropping out and other forms of withdrawal from college. In L. Noel, R. Levitz, D. Saluri & Associates (Eds.), *Increasing student retention* (pp. 28–43). San Francisco: Jossey-Bass.

Tricket, E.J., & Moos, R.H. (1975). Social environment of junior high and high school classrooms. *Journal of Educational Psychology, 65,* 93–102.

Twale, E.J. (1989). Social and academic development in freshman orientation: A time frame. *NASPA Journal, 27*(2), 160–167.

Upcraft, M. L. (Ed.). (1984). *Orienting students to college.* New Directions for Student Services, No. 25. San Francisco: Jossey-Bass.

Upcraft, M. L., Gardner, J. N., & Associates. (1989). *The freshman year experience.* San Francisco: Jossey-Bass.

Upland, M. L., Finney, J. E., & Garland, P. (1984). Orientation: A context. In M. L. Upcraft (Ed.), *New Directions for Student Services: No. 25. Orienting students to college* (pp. 5–26). San Francisco: Jossey-Bass.

Upcraft, M. L., & Farnsworth, W. M. (1984). Orientation programs and activities. In M. L. Upcraft (Ed.), *New Directions for Student Services: No. 25. Orienting students to college* (pp. 27–39). San Francisco: Jossey-Bass.

Varcoe, I. E., & Harrison, C. H. (1983). Programs that work in transfer orientation. University Park, PA: The Pennsylvania State University.

Wall, H. W. (1962). A counseling program for parents of college freshmen. *Personnel and Guidance Journal, 40,* 774–778.

Wolfe, J.S. (1993). Institutional integration, academic success, and persistence of first-year commuter and resident students. *Journal of College Student Development, 34,* 321–326.

Chapter 10

RESIDENCE HALLS

JOHN H. SCHUH

On residential college campuses that primarily serve traditional students (aged 18–24), student housing plays an integral role in the experiences of students. As Blimling (1993) observed: "At the core of any established student affairs organization at a residential college is a strong residence hall program. Life outside the classroom is amplified here. It provides more opportunities to influence student growth and development in the first year or two of college than almost any other program in student affairs. Although educational opportunities are offered through a variety of student affairs programs and departments, none are as pervasive in scope or have the potential to influence as many students as residence halls do" (p. 1).

In the best situations, students will gain tremendously from living in campus residence halls, but in the worst, their experiences could detract from their academic work.

This chapter discusses selected topics concerning residence halls including the history and purpose of residence halls, organizational patterns and staffing, residence hall programming, the influence of residence halls on students, selected legal issues, and the future of residence halls at colleges and universities. The reader should note that the administration of residence halls is a very complex matter, and a number of very important issues will not be described as they are beyond the scope of this chapter. Among them are marketing facilities and programs, financing and construction of residence halls, and maintenance and renovation of facilities. Additionally, many excellent reference sources not mentioned in this chapter are available through the Association of College and University Housing Officers-International (ACUHO–I), the American College Personnel Association (ACPA) and the National Association of Student Personnel Administrators (NASPA).

HISTORY

Three approaches characterize the development of student housing in the United States. The first, adapted from colleges in England, tried to bring students, faculty, and tutors together in a residential environment. This approach attempted to integrate learning inside and outside the classroom while efforts were made to provide an environment which fostered learning.

As the 19th century progressed, the Germanic Influence on American higher education and on housing and campus life provided a striking contrast to the English residential system as modified in the U.S. The German approach did not provide for student housing, and in fact, was not concerned with students' lives outside the classroom.

Shortly before the turn of the 20th century, interest was rekindled in residence halls. While a few institutions attempted to implement the English model, more commonly U.S. colleges and universities emphasized the housing, feeding, and social life of students. The goal of integrating the curriculum with residential living was not achieved and may have been impossible (Brubacher & Rudy, 1958), given the differences in the types of facilities and students who attended American colleges compared with their English counterparts. Follow the evolution of housing philosophy through this brief discussion of the history of the American student housing movement.

The Colonial Period

Like the legal system, the language, and many other aspects of American culture, the initial model of "early American higher education was patterned after the colleges of Oxford and Cambridge" (Frederiksen, 1993, p. 168). Certain factors, however, made the higher education scene in the colonies different from the English model. Residential colleges in England contributed formally and informally to students' education, while the early American dormitories were more a place to eat and sleep. "The sparseness of the resultant barracks-like dormitories was not designed to foster the characteristic close and well-built social life of the English college" (Brubacher and Rudy, 1976, p. 41).

Colonial students were perceived as young men with souls to be saved, and therefore, a profound, religious influence permeated the colleges (Fenske, 1980) and "religion dominated student life" (Brubacher &

Rudy, 1976, p. 42). These early colleges were directed by presidents who were "almost without exception gentlemen of the cloth. Governing boards, too, abounded with clerics" (Fenske, 1980, p. 8). Parents supported having their students closely supervised by the college, giving rise to the concept of *in loco parentis* (having the college serve as surrogate parents to very carefully supervise all the activities of the students, both inside and outside the classroom) (Frederiksen, 1993).

Among the problems that emerged in early residence facilities were food riots, gambling, drunkenness, vandalism, and destruction. Discipline was a recurring problem. "The tendency was to house students together in a residential dormitory of one sort or another whenever possible. The aim was to foster among all students a common social, moral and intellectual life. Early experiments met with decidedly mixed results" (Lucas, 1994, p. 111).

Because of poor living conditions, disciplinary problems, and the like, relationships between American students and their faculty were never as close as those in England. Students' relationships with faculty were often adversarial rather than tutorial. This modified English residential concept framed the American approach to campus housing until about the Civil War (Frederiksen, 1993).

Mid to Late 19th Century Developments

Two developments occurred in the 1800s that negatively influenced the development of student housing in the United States. The first of these was the Germanic Influence on American higher education. From about 1850 to 1890, many faculty from American colleges and universities pursued graduate education in Germany. They were exposed to a philosophy of higher education that was characterized by intellectual impersonalism (Appleton, Briggs, & Rhatigan, 1978) and viewed students as responsible for managing their own housing, food, and social life. "A number of educators returned from German universities in the mid-19th century and popularized the German belief that housing students was not the responsibility of the institution" (Frederiksen, 1993, p. 169). Among these were President Wayland of Brown and President Tappan of Michigan. Wayland " . . . argued an enforced residential pattern encouraged the spread of disease, fostered unsanitary habits, reinforced the disinclination of students to exercise . . . (and) diverted funds needed for building up libraries and classrooms" (Lucas, 1994, p. 126).

Recurring financial problems, the second development which hindered the development of student housing, plagued higher education and resources were not readily available to support residential construction and operations. As a result, "Dormitories built in the early nineteenth century continued in operation, but many of them had been allowed to fall into semi-decay" (Cowley, 1934, p. 712).

While Harvard and Yale continued their house systems during this time of disinterest and disfavor toward student housing, the rest of the country exhibited much less interest in the idea of housing students. Toward the end of the 19th century, a countervailing trend developed concerning student housing with the result being that colleges and universities revived their interest in student housing. The founding of the University of Chicago dramatically contributed to the rebirth of interest in student housing (Brubacher & Rudy, 1958). William Rainey Harper, the first president of the University of Chicago, based on his experience as a faculty member at Yale, insisted that housing for students be an integral part of the Chicago campus. As the University of Chicago became an outstanding educational institution, it served as a model for others.

Two other factors led to a revitalization of student housing toward the end of the 19th century. The first was that several private colleges were founded for women and these institutions valued student housing. Their rationale for housing focused primarily on providing close supervision of these young women. Alumnae of women's colleges attended graduate school at larger universities and carried with them the traditions of their residential, undergraduate experiences. As larger universities began to admit women, concern for women's housing became an important agenda item for administrators. Ultimately, separate residential facilities were developed to house men and women. The other contributing factor to the attractiveness of student housing was the development of campus life outside the classroom. Intercollegiate sports, debating societies, and student publications encouraged students to spend their out of classroom time in various extracurricular activities (Brubacher & Rudy, 1958). Living in campus housing became more convenient for those students who wished to participate in such activities and consequently, the demand for housing increased.

Early 20th Century

While Harper organized residence halls at Chicago, Woodrow Wilson unveiled his quadrangle system for housing students at Princeton. Although this plan ultimately failed, due to alumni opposition (Brubacher & Rudy, 1976), Wilson was highly regarded as a leader in higher education and his approach influenced many of his presidential colleagues (Brubacher & Rudy, 1958).

Fueled by private funds, construction of residence halls was undertaken at perhaps the fastest rate in the American history up to this time (Frederiksen, 1993, citing Cowley). The Great Depression decreased residence hall construction in the 1930s. Such diverse institutions as the University of Idaho, Michigan State College, and Virginia Polytechnic Institute constructed housing with state assistance (Fredericksen, 1993). Similarly, the development of the Public Works Administration allowed colleges to borrow funds from the federal government to construct housing on their campuses (Frederiksen, 1993). By 1939, three-fourths of institutions examined for accreditation by the North Central Association reported making efforts to enhance their student housing facilities (Brubacher & Rudy, 1976).

Post World War II

Campus life changed dramatically during the years following World War II since so many young people who might have gone to college were involved with the war effort. Many veterans returned to complete their education and housing, especially for married students, was in short supply. Apartment style housing was constructed to accommodate married students (Schneider, 1977). This, in itself, was an oddity because previously, most of those who attended college as undergraduates had been single students, 18 to 22 years old. Institutions of higher education needed to exercise great flexibility in meeting the needs of these new and older students.

During the late 1960s, student housing was increasingly criticized for its restrictive rules governing student life. Institutional policies did not permit students to entertain guests of the opposite sex in their living quarters, and women generally had to return to their residence hall by a certain time each evening or face disciplinary action. Students vigorously questioned these policies and, where possible, left the residence halls, or brought legal actions against institutions. As a result, institutions relaxed parietal rules, often dropping requirements that students live on campus and making it possible for students to live under conditions similar to those of their peers who lived off campus.

Toward the middle and latter part of the 1970s, students began to return to campus residence halls because of economic conditions and the widespread indifference of students to any cause except earning a degree and finding a job (Fenske, 1980a). Inflation hindered the American economy, and on-campus living became particularly convenient and economical for students. Students returned to residence halls in large numbers, and as the 1980s unfolded, a number of campuses experienced shortages in the number of available spaces for student housing.

Moving into the 1990s, student housing faced yet another set of challenges related to the student as consumer. Students in today's environment expect more services than ever before, including such former "luxuries" as cable television, access to computers in their rooms, a wide variety of meal plans, and a cornucopia of choices at each meal. Increasingly, security has become a vexing issue, as students expect a maximum of freedom with a minimum of supervision while being guaranteed that their personal safety is assured. As Frederiksen concluded, "The administration of student residential facilities and residence life policies presents a real challenge to housing professionals in colleges and universities throughout the United States" (1993, p. 174).

MISSION AND PURPOSE

Ask a number of student affairs administrators what they think the purposes of residence halls are and you may well might receive a variety of answers. Among these might be to provide for a good fiscal operation, to keep physical facilities in good repair, to provide activities for students to participate in outside of class, to keep order, and perhaps to provide for student growth. This section describes different perspectives on the purposes of student housing.

When reviewing the purpose of student housing, or any unit within student affairs, the best place to start is to examine the mission of the institution within which student housing operates. Lyons (1993) reminds us that "The most important factor that determines the shape and substance of student affairs is the mission of the institution" (p. 14). Consequently, the institutional mission will determine not only the role of student housing, but its relative importance, and the amount of attention and resources it receives from senior administration and faculty. The Council for the Advancement of Standards (CAS) described the contribution and role of student housing to the institution's mission. "The residential life program is an integral part of the educational program and academic support services of the institution" (CAS, 1988, p. 21).

In practical terms, at a small liberal arts college where virtually every student lives on campus, housing will be inextricably linked to the educational experiences of virtually all students. At a residential college, the mission would include language that describes a living learning environment for all students enrolled in the college. Quite the opposite would be true of a commuter university with a small residential population. Here the residence halls will assume a far less central role in the life of the university and its mission may not describe the campus providing as a residential learning environment for students. The purposes of student housing have evolved over the past thirty years as the following paragraphs will illustrate.

In 1961, three objectives for student housing were suggested: (1) the physical accommodation of students; that is, a place needed to be provided where students could eat and sleep, and that should also be convenient to classrooms and the library; (2) promoting academic learning; and (3) aiding in the personal development of students (Mueller, 1961). In addition, she indicated that two minor objectives of residence halls were good public relations, especially with parents, and the supervision and control of student conduct.

Riker and DeCoster (1971) identified five general objectives for student housing in building block fashion. These ranged from providing satisfactory physical facilities to developing opportunities for individual growth and development. They concluded, " . . . the overall objectives of student housing are interrelated and interdependent" (p. 5).

Over time educational or developmental objectives for the residential living experience have received even more emphasis. In the 1990s, Schroeder and Mable proposed that " . . . the challenge for residence halls is to place a renewed emphasis on promoting student learning through integrating residence hall learning opportunities with the goals and priorities of undergraduate education" (1993, p. 15). To complement this overarching goal, Winston and Anchors (1993) recommended that residence halls address the following objectives:

1. Assisting students in becoming literate, liberally educated persons;
2. Promoting students' development in becoming responsible, contributing members of multiple communities;
3. Advocating commitment to the ideals of altruism and social justice;
4. Endorsing the cultivation of a healthy lifestyle, both physically and psychologically;
5. Encouraging students to examine their spiritual life;
6. Challenging students to confront moral and ethical issues (pp. 40–41).

While there has been considerable debate over the years about which functions of student housing are more important than others, in the final analysis the consensus of opinion probably reflects an integrated approach. The physical environment and programmatic offerings are inter-related and each contributes substantially to the advancement of the residence hall system. Students cannot be expected to be interested in learning opportunities unless they live in adequate physical facilities. If adequate guidelines for community living are not established, it is possible that facilities will not be respected and may be abused. All members of the housing staff contribute to the vitality of the system—the residence hall director, the custodian, the food service worker, the resident assistant and the senior administrator. It should be remembered that housing exists within the framework of an institution's mission, and that mission will define the role of housing.

ADMINISTRATION AND ORGANIZATION

Six contextual factors have been identified as influencing the organizational structure of a student housing department (Upcraft, 1993). They are (1) the size of the institution, (2) its mission, (3) the characteristics of the student body, (4) the class mix of resident students, (5) the institution's position on requiring students to live in campus housing, and (6) the racial and ethnic mix of resident students. To these might be added the institution's philosophy regarding the extent to which housing is regarded as an auxiliary service, a student service, or both.

The most common organizational arrangement is for student housing to report to the senior student affairs officer (Stoner, 1992). Other patterns include having housing report to the senior business officer, or having typical residential life functions report to student affairs and the business functions report to the senior business officer. Indiana University and Michigan State University, two institutions with large residential populations, are examples of the latter arrangement. Still another arrangement is for the director of housing to report to both the senior student affairs and senior business affairs officer.

According to Upcraft (1993), having housing report to the senior student affairs officer is desirable. In the final analysis, however, he concluded that the decision on the reporting arrangement depends " . . . on the values of the leadership of the institution" (p. 194).

STAFFING PATTERNS

While titles of various residence hall staff positions may vary from campus to campus, the functions performed remain fairly consistent across most campuses. As the size of the housing department increases, additional staff will be added at the administrative level. Consequently, housing departments on large campuses will have a variety of services provided by a large number of highly specialized staff.

The undergraduate student living on a residence hall floor and providing direct service to students usually is called a resident assistant or resident advisor (RA). At times this person has the title of resident counselor, although providing advice and referral are more typical of this person's responsibilities than actually entering into counseling relationships with residents. Commonly an upperclass student, the RA is responsible for working with students individually and in small groups, assessing student needs and planning programs, advising the floor government, handling certain administrative matters, and enforcing university rules and regulations.

There is probably no more difficult position in student affairs work than that of the RA, because, quite literally, RAs are expected to live where they work. They are always on call and deal with many problems that can be very challenging. Additionally, since RAs are paraprofessionals, they need a great deal of support in terms of training and supervision. Winston and Fitch conclude that "Effective RA programs require the commitment of substantial resources by the housing program" (1993, p. 340). Many senior student affairs officers began their careers as these front line members of the student affairs team.

Generally, larger residence halls will have assistant residence hall directors who are graduate students at the master's level. They supervise RAs, handle student conduct problems, organize more complex programs and offer general supervision and staff training in the absence of full-time professional staff. Since these staff often are enrolled on a full-time basis in a graduate program, they are " . . . neither fish nor fowl, neither paraprofessional nor professional, but some amalgam of the two" (Astin, 1993, p. 318).

The professional staff person in charge of the residence hall often is called a head resident, resident director, hall director, or building manager. Typically, this person has a master's degree in student affairs, counseling or a related field and the position is considered entry-level in the student affairs field. Some residential systems use graduate students to supervise buildings. This works best when the size of the buildings is small and substantial supervisory resources are available to provide leadership for hall directors.

Beyond the individual residence hall, a variety of administrative positions may exist to provide overall direction for the housing department. In larger housing systems, it is common to find an area director responsible for a group of residence halls. Hall directors report directly to the area director, who frequently has several years of full time experience in addition to a master's degree. In a smaller system, hall directors may report to an assistant director of housing or an assistant dean for residential life. This person has overall responsibility for residence life programs on campus, including such activities as coordinating the RA selection and training program, advising the all residence hall student government and judicial board, and selecting, training and supervising the hall directors. A person at this level usually has held several positions before moving into a situation where he or she coordinates an entire campus residence life program which often requires a master's degree and in the case of a larger system, a doctorate.

Particularly in larger institutions, other central office administrators may include an assistant director for operations, who is concerned with the managerial aspects of student housing including room assignments, budget preparation and management, and the various business aspects of student housing such as purchasing, personnel and summer conferences. There also may be an assistant director working with physical facilities, supervising maintenance and housekeeping, working with the campus physical plant, preparing long range repair and rehabilitation plans, and serving as project administrator for major construction projects.

Food service, more appropriately termed "dining services," usually is provided in one of two ways. Smaller campuses frequently contract with a private company to provide food service. Other campuses, particularly those with a larger resident population, tend to have a food service that is provided by the campus or by the housing department itself. Traditionally, campus philosophy, resources, and facilities will be factors to be considered when determining whether or not the campus provides its own food service or contract with a private vendor. Regardless of how food service is provided (self-operated or contractor), the contribution of this segment of the operation is crucial to student satisfaction. Underscoring this observation, Fairbrook (1993) noted, "Today's college or university food service directors are not merely cafeteria managers. They can be vital members of the student affairs team, . . . dedicated to furthering students' overall development into educated, well-adjusted, and well-informed citizens" (p. 246).

The typical entry-level professional position for a person contemplating a career in student housing is as the director of a fairly large building, 500 students or more, or a director of a complex of smaller buildings. Entry-level positions require a master's degree in student affairs, counseling, higher education, or a related field. Some experience as a graduate assistant or resident assistant is highly desirable since there are subtleties to this work that are difficult to understand without direct operating experience in a student residence hall. Entry-level positions frequently require that the staff person "live in," meaning that they have an apartment in the building or complex for which they are responsible. While this living arrangement is not always highly desirable from the perspective of privacy, it does provide an excellent opportunity to work directly with students and paraprofessional staff in meaningful ways.

PROGRAMS AND SERVICES

The number and variety of programs available to the typical residence hall student are virtually limitless. On any given campus, programs can range from social to recreational, from cultural to academic. Providing sufficient programming, in a quantitative sense, rarely is a problem in a residence hall environment. Making programming meaningful to students, and linking residence hall programs to student needs is another matter.

A number of conceptual frameworks are available from which one may plan residence hall programs. Among these are student development theories, intervention models and campus ecology models. One of the best frameworks is the dimensions of intervention for student development model developed by Morrill and Hurst (1980). This model identified three specific types of programming: (a) remedial programming; (b) preventive programming; and (c) developmental programming.

Remedial programming refers to those programs which emphasize issues where something has gone wrong and the problem needs to be addressed. An example of this might be where international students have experienced subtle forms of discrimination within the residence hall because of their religious customs. Educational workshops might be designed for all students where the specific customs are explained. Moreover, some emphasis might be placed on the religious discrimination that, in part, was responsible for many people leaving their homelands to come to the U.S.

Preventive programming includes programs that are implemented because student problems or issues are predictable. Morrill, Hurst, and Oetting (1980) for example, providing programs which help ease the transition from home to the university setting (Morrill, Hurst, & Oetting, 1980). Such programs are designed to minimize homesickness, roommate conflicts, and academic problems.

Developmental programming sessions are those designed to foster student growth. These programs include leadership development, volunteer opportunities, and social programs. Their goal is to promote the growth and development of students desiring to enhance their skills and abilities.

Most educational programs can be fit into one of the three categories in the taxonomy above. Using this framework as a guide, program planning can be undertaken to meet the needs of students, assuming that their interests and needs have been assessed appropriately. However other program development models also would be appropriate to consider in providing a framework for programming. Among these are the campus ecology manager model (Banning, 1989), a health and wellness model (Mosier, 1989), a program planning model (Barr & Cuyjet, 1991) and the student service program development model (Moore and Delworth, 1976). Which model among these or others is chosen is less important than having a logical framework that provides the desired results consistently (Schuh, and Triponey, 1993).

Before describing programs which are currently of wide interest among residence hall administrators, it may be helpful to review reasons why some programs fail. Hurst and Jacobson (1985) identified several reasons why programs may not be effective.

At times, professional staff members plan programs around topics that are of interest to them without measuring student need or interest. For example, staff interested in issues related to East European cultures, plan programs focusing on that area, regardless of whether or not students have interests or needs concerning issues related to East European cultures.

Secondly, professional staff knowledgeable in a specific area tend to develop programs to showcase their area of expertise. To illustrate, staff having undergraduate majors in physical education, may plan programs related to recreational sports and nutrition, even though students in this hypothetical situation already are required to take courses in these areas. In effect, these programmers repeat what their residents have learned in the classroom.

Thirdly, a crisis emerges on campus and programs are planned quickly to help deal with the crisis. Often what happens is that the program focuses on the chaos created by the crisis, rather than dealing with the underlying causes of the problem. For example, we frequently address instances related to racist behavior rather than working on the underlying causes of bigotry.

Issues become popular within professional associations, and after attending a conference, staff members plan programs on their campus because they know the programs were successful on another campus. Without understanding why the program was successful at another institution, and not realizing that programs are not automatically transferable from one campus to another, staff may plan programs used at an engineering school dealing with using computer technology for their own campus, with an emphasis on fine arts, where computer capability may be more modest.

At other times, programs are developed to meet the political needs of the campus or simply because special interest groups have pressured us to do so. Neither is a good reason to implement a program. Programs should be designed to meet the needs of our students after these needs have been assessed carefully and thoughtfully.

Finally, we plan particular programs because we have always planned these programs. Student needs and interests change over time. In the late 1960s there was considerable interest in political issues on many of our campuses. Since then, the campus climate in many cases has changed to the extent that student needs and interests are quite different. We need remain current about changing student needs and values and plan our programs accordingly.

Selected Programs

As mentioned earlier, the number and range of programs that one might find in residence halls on a particular campus is large. Rather than provide an exhaustive listing of programs, suggestions are provided about program development. In addition, a few programs which illustrate contemporary programming efforts.

Chickering and Reisser (1993) made several recommendations to enhance student development along the lines of their seven vector psychosocial theory. Among their suggestions are the following:

1. Incorporate learning activities into living units;
2. Adapt existing halls to allow for a balance of interaction and privacy and to permit a more personalized environment;
3. Enhance community by building new units that are small enough to allow maximum participation but large enough to allow more experienced students to induct newer ones into the culture;
4. Improve the "fit" and diversity by placing students carefully;
5. Use regulations, policies, and hall management strategies as tools for fostering autonomy, interdependence, and integrity. (p. 402)

"There is very clear evidence that residence halls and campus activities have a positive impact on retention and personal development, but only if institutions support and structure student participation to positive ends" (Upcraft, 1989, p. 154). Toward that end, a number of programs have been developed which address the needs of first year students, such as the programs at Miami University (Kuh, Schuh, and Whitt, 1991). Zeller and Mosier (1993) recommended that programs be designed which help new students develop skills, provide a sense of connectedness to the university and balance students' needs for autonomy, security, and interdependence. One way of accomplishing these objectives is through the use of a four phase model which includes (recruitment, orientation, involvement, and academic support) and involves "complementary partnerships among academic affairs, student affairs, and residential life staff" (Zeller, Kanz and Schneiter, 1990, p. 14). What is particularly useful to remember about this program is that it symbolizes the vanguard of contemporary educational programming with such features as collaboration across institutional divisions (student and academic affairs), clearly articulated goals, careful attention to entering students, and outcomes related to student learning. Programming in the future will continue to emphasize such features.

Another excellent example of programming is the integration of fitness, wellness, and recreational programming described by Hoelting and Navarro (1994). Current thinking emphasizes providing this kind of programming in the residence facility rather than leaving such programming to the recreational sports staff. In this example, additional equipment was added to the inventory in the residence center, and fitness programming for women as well as men became part of the overall portfolio of activities. Complementing the equipment were diet and nutrition initiatives to supplement the actual workout programs developed by students. The value of this approach was described by Hoelting and Navarro (1994) "Combined with a wellness life-style, the fitness centers can impact the students' well-being during their college years and beyond" (p. 7).

A third example of a programming trend is illustrated by the collaboration between counseling centers and residence life departments (Black, 1993; Schuh & Shipton, 1985). These departments work together to deliver programs to students in addition to providing support and assistance for the residence hall staff. This kind of programming represents another contemporary approach to program development in that in an era of shrinking resources, collaboration and sharing are very common. It is unlikely that higher education in the foreseeable future will receive large infusions of additional resources. Consequently, sharing of assets and resources is one way that new programs can be developed to meet students' needs.

The common elements of these programming initiatives illustrate contemporary approaches to programming. Collaboration between departments (the counseling programs), integrating various elements within the housing department (the exercise example), and bringing academic programs into the residence hall (the programs for first year students) are features of effective programs. Programs are most effective when developed from a conceptual framework related to the growth of students and careful attention is paid to needs assessment. Program development in the future will feature these elements.

Applying Student Development

Before leaving the topic of programming, it is useful to provide some illustrations of how specific programs can be incorporated into an overall plan for fostering student development in the residential environment.

In this case, student development refers to " . . . specific outcome goals resulting from attending college and living in college residential facilities" (Winston & Anchors, 1993, p. 40). As was the case with having a model for program planning, what is crucial here is that a theory of student growth and development serve as the basis for plan programming. In this case, a programmatic framework described by Winston and Anchors (1993) provides the structure for these examples.

Cognitive Learning. Verbal skills: residence hall newsletter, radio station, library. Rationality: hall government and judicial board. Esthetic appreciation: art collection or contest, painting of murals, talent show, photo contest, dark room. Intellectual tolerance: speakers' series, international living learning center.

Emotional and Moral Discipline. Psychological well-being: counselor in residence, structured group experiences; Religious interests: consultation with campus ministers; Citizenship: student government, community volunteer projects, fund raising projects for charities; Personal self-discovery: assessments conducted and interpreted by counselors in residence.

Practical Competence. Health: wellness programs, exercise and dance facilities, diet and nutrition workshops; Leisure skills: various workshops and programs, outdoor recreation programs, clubs; Practical affairs: Cooperative residence hall, service projects, volunteer programs.

By no means is this list of categories or programs complete, but it provides ideas of how student development can be fostered through residential programs. Every example has been implemented in residence halls under the supervision of the author. By tying the goals of programs to developmental outcomes, a richness of meaning is given to the residential living experience. This meaning, in turn, differentiates living in campus residence halls from living in off campus facilities.

A Practical Example. Tom is a freshman student who lives in Greene Hall. He has chosen a major in finance but has no practical experience handling the funds of an organization. Sally, the Greene Hall Director, knows that the hall council's former treasurer resigned because she took an RA job at the last minute and is aware of Tom's concern about having no practical experience in handling an organization's funds. Sally suggests to Tom that he apply to the Hall Executive Council to become the Treasurer. At the next meeting the Hall Executive Council interviews the candidates and selects Tom. Tom spends the balance of the year as the Hall Council Treasurer gaining the practical experience he lacked.

In this example, Sally works with Tom in identifying an area where he needs to improve his skills. This can be framed by applying Chickering's theory of psychosocial development. The first vector, Developing Competence, has three elements: intellectual competence, physical and manual competence, and interpersonal competence (Chickering & Reisser, 1993). Tom's work as treasurer will improve his intellectual competence by engaging in active learning as the treasurer.

Other more complex examples of applying student development theory occur virtually on a daily basis in the residential setting. Student development theory helps residence hall staff understand how students change and grow, and serves as a guide in structuring interventions. Whether the presenting circumstance is simple or complex, student development theory can be extremely useful in framing educational responses in helping students learn.

THE INFLUENCE OF RESIDENCE HALLS ON STUDENTS

Numerous studies have been conducted to determine the influence of residence hall living on students. Evidence reported in these studies and published over a 20-year period concluded that students benefit substantially from living in campus residence halls.

Chickering (1974) compared commuting students with resident students and found that while resident students start from a favored position compared to commuters, the residential experience accelerates the differences between these two groups. Such factors as family background, finances, and high school academic record distinguish resident students from commuters. "Commuters and residents begin their college careers with an unequal start which strongly favors the residents. The gap between them grows. Residents have access to, find and are forced to encounter diverse experience and persons who spurt them on their way" (Chickering, 1974, p. 85).

Another example of research on this question is found in the work of Astin. In 1985, he concluded that " ... simply by virtue of eating, sleeping, and spending their waking hours in the college campus, residential students stand a better chance than do commuter students of developing a strong identification with and attachment to undergraduate life" (p. 145).

More recent studies reiterate the benefits of residential living to students. Pascarella and Terenzini (1991), concluded " ... residential living is positively, if modestly, linked to increases in aesthetic, cultural, and intellectual values; a liberalizing of social, political, and religious values and attitudes; increases in self-concept, intellectual orientation, autonomy, and independence; gains in tolerance, empathy, and ability to relate to others; persistence in college; and bachelor's degree attainment" (p. 611). Astin pointed to other benefits of living on campus, including " ... the attainment of the bachelor's degree, satisfaction with faculty, and willingness to re-enroll in the same college" (1993, p. 367).

Why does the preponderance of evidence suggest that living on campus, be it in a residence hall, fraternity, or sorority house, have such a positive influence on students? There are several reasons.

Applying Astin's theory of involvement as an interpretive framework, it is clear that merely by residing on campus, students have greater opportunities to become involved in campus life, through leadership opportunities, recreational sports and cultural activities. These opportunities ultimately are translated into greater student growth and development.

Additionally, the environment created in a campus residence contributes to student learning by providing opportunities for students to experience diversity, to be challenged by their peers, and to learn from one another. The responsibility of residence educators is to maximize the learning opportunities available. That means finding ways of encouraging students to become involved with faculty, assume leadership positions, and participate in the myriad of activities and programs available both not only in the residence hall but on the campus at large. Chickering summarized the effects of residential living on students this way, "By applying developmental principles in programming, governance, architectural design, size of units, and matching of students, college administrators can amplify the positive aspects of residential living" (1993, p. 276).

SELECTED LEGAL ISSUES

Early in a career in student affairs, one finds that the work environment is full of challenges, some of which may not be settled anywhere other than in a court of law. Students, parents, and others will hold staff legally responsible for their decisions and actions (Owens, 1984). In light of the above, a brief introduction to several legal issues follows.

Staff should understand that they should not function as their own attorney. Staff should, however, have " . . . an understanding of the legal aspects of their work and their relationships to students . . . " (Gehring, 1991, p. 379). When legal advice is needed, it should be sought through appropriate channels on campus. The campus may have an office of legal counsel, or it may have an attorney on retainer. Regardless, when it is concluded that legal advice is needed, do not hesitate to use your campus protocol for seeking advice!

It is also important to realize the difference in working in a public, private, or independent institution. Public institutions are more fully regulated than private ones, and those working in public institutions are more fully constrained by the federal constitution than those employed in private institutions (Kaplin & Lee, 1995). The Fourteenth Amendment to the U.S. Constitution prescribes that states must respect all the rights of citizens outlined in the Constitution; this amendment does not apply to private citizens or institutions (Young, 1984). Consequently, private institutions have more latitude in promulgating rules and regulations, and that while due process in disciplinary situations is absolutely guaranteed in public institutions, private institutions are not held to the same standard (Kaplin & Lee, 1995).

Fire and Safety Procedures

Perhaps the greatest danger to the safety of students living in a residence hall is fire (Schuh, 1984). While most states have laws and regulations regarding fire fighting equipment, smoke detectors, fire drills, and the like, it is critical that residence life staff become conversant with these laws and regulations, and follow them explicitly. Routine inspections should be held and staff should work closely with physical plant personnel to ensure that all equipment is functional. Failure to engage in these safety procedures will result in tremendous legal exposure to the campus.

Additionally, if the campus is located in a high crime area, or there is concern that students' physical safety may be threatened, resident students should be informed of ways to minimize such risks as soon as they move into a residence hall. If a series of criminal acts occur on the campus or in the residence halls and the institution fails to take steps to rectify the situation or notify students, the institution, through its administrators, could be held liable (*Duarte v. State,* 1979).

Physical Facilities

Usually at inopportune times (late at night or during the weekend), something will happen to render physical facilities inoperable or dangerous. This could be anything from an elevator breaking down to a violent act of weather resulting in making the physical facility unusable. No one can predict with absolute certainty when a snow storm, heavy rain, or flood will ravage the campus. During times such as these, resident staff will need to take steps to make sure that students are protected from injury or possibly death.

When a resident staff person becomes aware of a problem, it should be reported to the appropriate individual and repairs should be made. To protect staff and the institution, make sure that potential problems such as icy sidewalks or slippery hallways are corrected immediately. Anticipate problems that might arise such as an elevator that has been balky for the past day or two, and report any problems as soon as they are discovered. To protect the institution, "Documented, periodic inspections with follow-up maintenance requests are essential in avoiding negligence" (Gehring, 1993, p. 363).

Duty to Warn

One must accept the duty to warn a potential victim of a threat. The most famous case that addresses this point is *Tarasoff v. Regents of the University of California* (1976) which involved an individual threatening to do harm to a student who was away from the campus. When the student returned, she was murdered. The court found that the person receiving the information concerning the threat had an obligation to warn the potential victim. If this kind of information is received, even if the information is supposed to be confidential, the intended victim should be notified as well as campus or local police departments. The concept of privileged communication rarely is extended to student affairs practitioners and staff are held responsible if a potential victim is not warned and becomes a victim.

Program Supervision

A wide variety of programs occur in or are sponsored by the residence halls. Most require little or no risk on the part of participants. Some programs, however, require a certain amount of participants skill or involve the consumption of alcoholic beverages. In these two instances, the risk of problems occurring increases.

For programs requiring participants to master certain skills or the use of complicated equipment, the most successful strategy for the program planner is to consult a person on campus who has expertise in the skill area, or in the use of the equipment. For example, when developing an excursion program involving mountain climbing, someone should be contacted in the physical education department to learn how best to prepare participants for the activity. An expert consultant might be hired to help with the supervision of the activity as well. Activities involving trampolines, skate boards, amateur boxing, or tugs-of-war need to be planned with great care since serious injuries might result (Miller & Schuh, 1981). Additionally, any activity involving water sports should be supervised by an individual holding a current Red Cross certification as a lifeguard.

Activities involving alcohol can result in tragedy, especially if automobiles are involved in transporting students to and from an event where alcohol will be consumed. A prudent strategy is to hire licensed, public carriers to provide transportation whenever alcohol is part of an event off campus.

To minimize risk, be knowledgeable about state laws. If students are under the legal drinking age, they should not be allowed to consume alcoholic beverages. The institution should never be a part of sponsoring illegal activities. As mentioned above, transportation should be provided through common carriers such as buses. The amount of alcohol purchased should be realistic. Planners should purchase an amount which will be commensurate with the number of participants anticipated. Food and alternative beverages should be provided. Before planning an event where alcoholic beverages will be available, the campus alcohol information center or health center should be consulted for information about program planning with alcohol.

Simply getting up in the morning and going to work involves some risks. The key to protecting oneself, students, and institution is to employ risk management strategies which minimize the likelihood of potential risks becoming real disasters.

PROFESSIONAL ASSOCIATIONS

Several professional organizations extend membership to residence hall staff. Three objectives of professional organizations are " . . . to advance understanding, recognition, and knowledge in the field; to develop and promulgate standards for professional practice; to serve the public interest; and to provide professionals with a peer group that promotes a sense of identity" (Nuss, 1993, p. 365).

The principle professional association comprised of housing officers, defined as any person who works with student housing on campus, and in some cases off-campus, is the Association of College and University Housing Officers-International (ACUHO–I). ACUHO–I was organized in 1949 at the University of Illinois and membership is by institution. Thus, all members of a housing department which holds membership in ACUHO–I are eligible to participate in the organization's activities and use ACUHO–I's services. Ten regional associations sponsor conferences in addition to the annual ACUHO–I conference and the association has expanded its presence aggressively in Europe and Asia during the past few years. The ACUHO–I annual conference is held in the Summer, typically in either June or July.

The American College Personnel Association (ACPA) is another professional organization having a direct interest in student housing through its Commission III. This Commission is comprised of ACPA members responsible for student housing, residence hall programs, staffing issues and so on. Membership in ACPA is on an individual basis and no additional fees are charged for commission affiliation.

In addition, professional development opportunities are offered by state groups or associations affiliated with ACPA. Typically, they will offer an annual state-wide conference or drive in workshops for members. ACPAs annual conference is held in March.

Housing officers may also hold membership in the National Association of Student Personnel Administrators (NASPA). Membership in NASPA is individual and by institution. Although sometimes perceived as an organization for senior student affairs officers, NASPA welcomes members regardless of their professional responsibilities. Its annual conference is held in March and conferences within the seven NASPA regional associations are scheduled throughout the year.

One other organization worthy of note, the National Association of College and University Residence Halls, Inc., is a student association designed to promote student involvement in college residence halls. NACURH holds national and regional conventions which are attended by students to improve their skills in student government, programming, and to strengthen networks with their colleagues regionally and nationally.

THE FUTURE

What does the future hold for residence halls? Planning for developments as we move toward the beginning of the 21st century is a challenge. More than likely, future students will view privacy as the norm, requesting and expecting to live in situations where they do not have roommates. Currently, two students are housed in every room and the expectation is that roommates will become compatible partners. The roommate model was adopted at a time in history when families had more siblings and sharing one's bedroom was the usual condition. Future students may not be willing to live in a situation where their privacy is limited.

When resident students live alone, more efforts will be required on the part of residence staff to encourage students to interact with each other. Isolation and alienation are possible without programs and activities encouraging students to socialize and work together. The residence hall environment, in such a situation, could promote depression. Community building will be more difficult. Thus, strategies will have to be devised that motivate students to leave their individual living spaces and to spend time with others.

The use of computers and cable television will increase as teaching media. Necessary equipment should be provided to make it possible for students to learn in their rooms. The ability to access computing networks, libraries, and learning resource centers will be part of the well equipped student room. Cable television hookups in a student's room will be required and therein lies a danger. As each room becomes more of a locus of learning, the possibility of isolation and depression increases. Our role will be to bring students together in meaningful ways in an effort to fight depression, isolation, and boredom, plus encourage them to engage in collaborative learning experiences (Bosworth & Hamilton, 1994).

Obviously residence halls are being expected to provide more academic support facilities. Libraries, computer terminals, offices for academic advisers and classroom space will all be very much a part of future residence halls. As more classes are offered in residence hall, students should be encouraged to form study groups and may be assigned to specific residence halls based on their prospective major or area of career interest. Some of these activities are already a part of residence hall responsibilities; however, it is clear that they will also be part of the future.

Hand-in-hand with greater academic opportunities will be a strong emphasis on providing programs allowing faculty and students to interact in the residential situation. As our concerns about greater isolation of students are defined, one way to respond to these feelings is to design programs facilitating more faculty and student interaction. This may require increasing or expanding a faculty fellow program, more faculty/student research projects, and perhaps additional faculty- or guests-in-residence positions.

Demonstrating student learning also will be a challenge for the future. The Student Learning Imperative (ACPA, n.d.) reminds us "Student affairs professionals must seize the moment by affirming student learning and personal development as the primary goals of undergraduate education" (p. 4). It is highly likely that future residence halls will be full partners in enriching the learning environment on campus and that administrators will be called upon routinely to demonstrate the impact of the residential experience on students.

Participation in residence hall student government is becoming more complicated. Student government budgets are now larger and the demands placed on student government leaders by their constituents and university administrators make service in student government appear less attractive. Moreover, substantial numbers of students work to pay their college bills and do not have time for student government responsibilities. Incentives must be developed to attract students to become involved in student government leadership positions. Combining a room assignment and providing office may be one arrangement. Perhaps a scholarship program could be established to assist those student government leaders who must forego part time work because of their responsibilities. The point is, student government service is becoming a burden to students, and mechanisms should be found to make involvement in this type of activity more attractive.

On some campuses, occupancy rates of residence halls and associated financial concerns will be a problem for administrators. Many residence hall systems were designed to resolve a housing shortage caused by the attendance of the baby boom generation, while today there is an oversupply of capacity. Competition with off-campus housing developments is causing problems at some institutions, especially when off-campus accommodations are newer and more luxurious. As a result, we may be very close to rather difficult financial times for many institutions. Austere budget management will be the normal operating procedure for institutions in the foreseeable future.

One solution to financial problems may lie in the privatization of residence halls. Private companies may serve as contractors to operate campus residence halls or in some situations may construct and manage residence halls. Generally, this approach removes much of the financial exposure of the residence hall operations from the campus, but it also means that the institution loses control other than what the contract with the company provides. Nonetheless, privatization may be more common in future years.

It is entirely possible that students of the future will demand more services. Academic support activities have been identified earlier in this section, but we may also be moving into a closer relationship with off-campus vendors to provide services to our students. These might include convenience markets, if the students do not operate them as a government or service project, barbershops and beauty salons, and dry cleaning are a few examples. As these kinds of services are added to the auxiliary enterprises portfolio, administrators will need to be careful not to create problems for the institution in its relationships with local businesses. One approach is to operate the new service as a concession under contract to a private firm, rather than the institution operating the business by itself. A number of colleges and universities already use this approach in providing food service, bookstores, and banking services. More recreational facilities will be expected by students, including aerobics rooms, exercise areas, and weight rooms. Instead of considering these as amenities or luxuries, administrators might be better served by considering them essential to the well-equipped residence hall.

Many residence halls were built to provide housing to accommodate the baby-boom generation, now the parents of incoming students. As a result, these facilities in many cases are old, tired, and perhaps obsolete. Renovation is a tremendous financial challenge facing housing officers. Blimling (1993) characterized it this way, "After thirty years or more of service, even with good maintenance, most buildings should be renovated. . . . To find the funds, room rental charges have to be increased, fund reserves depleted, or money appropriated from educational programming funds. None of these are appealing options" (pp. 11–12).

While students demand an environment free of regulations and supervision, they expect to be safe and secure in their residence facility. It is difficult to provide these dimensions since a natural tension exists between a lack of supervision and presence of safety. In the final analysis, issues related to crime and security will continue to become more difficult in the future. "Residence life professionals must move campus security issues to a higher priority within their organizations and attack the problem aggressively" (Janosik, 1993, p. 514). While technology can be used to deal with this issue in some respects, such as installing keyless door locks and television cameras to monitor hallways, institutions often have chosen not to address safety and security issues as forthrightly as they should.

Finally, residence hall staff of the future will be faced with a variety of challenges. On the one hand, they will have to carefully market their facilities because of the competition raised by off-campus housing developments for traditional college students. On the other hand, they will have to be prepared to work with students who are not used to sharing living space. These students may see little value in leaving the relative comfort of their single rooms with computer and television and thus may be less likely to participate in student activities. Special skills will be necessary for residence staff members to do their jobs effectively. The challenge, then, seems to be to identify ways that staff can stay current, facilities remain attractive, and students find the living experience satisfying. Residence halls meeting these challenges will be recognized as pacesetters in the 21st century.

REFERENCES

American College Personnel Association (ACPA). (1994). *The student learning imperative: Implications for student affairs.* Washington, DC: Author.

Appleton, J. R., Briggs, C. M., & Rhatigan, J. J. (1978). *Pieces of eight.* Portland, OR: NASPA.

Astin, A. W. (1985). *Achieving educational excellence.* San Francisco: Jossey-Bass.

Astin, A. W. (1993). *What matters in college.* San Francisco: Jossey-Bass.

Banning, J. H. (1989). Creating a climate for successful student development: The campus ecology manager role. In U. Delworth, G. R. Hanson, and Associates,

Student Services: A Handbook for the Profession (2nd ed.) (pp. 304–322). San Francisco: Jossey-Bass.

Barr, M. J., & Cuyjet, M. J. (1991). Program development and implementation. In T. K. Miller, R. B. Winston, Jr., and Associates, *Administration and Leadership in Student Affairs* (pp. 707–7339). Muncie, IN: Accelerated Development.

Black, R. J. (1993). Facilitating a positive relationship between housing and counseling center staff. *Journal of College Student Development, 34,* 441–442.

Blimling, G. S. (1993). New challenges and goals for residential life programs. In R. B. Winston, Jr., S. Anchors, & Associates, *Student housing and residential life* (pp. 1–20). San Francisco: Jossey-Bass.

Bosworth, K., & Hamilton, S. J. (1994). Editor's notes. In Authors (Eds.), *New Directions for Teaching and Learning Sourcebook: No. 59. Collaborative learning: Underlying processes and technologies* (pp. 1–3). San Francisco: Jossey-Bass.

Brubacher, J. S., & Rudy, W. (1958). *Higher education in transition.* New York: Harper.

Chickering, A. W. (1974). *Commuting versus resident students.* San Francisco: Jossey-Bass.

Chickering, A. W., & Reisser, L. (1993). *Education and identity* (2nd ed.). San Francisco: Jossey-Bass.

Cowley, W. H. (1934). The history of student residential housing. *School and Society, 40* (1040, 1041), 705–712, 758–764.

Duarte v. State, 151 Cal. Reptr. 727 (Ap. Ct., Fourth District, Division 1, 1979).

Fairbrook, P. (1993). Food services and programs. In R. B. Winston, Jr., S. Anchors and Associates. *Student housing and residential life* (pp. 232–247). San Francisco: Jossey-Bass.

Fenske, R. H. (1980). Historical foundations. In U. Delworth & G. R. Hanson (Eds.), *Student services: A handbook for the profession* (pp. 3–24). San Francisco: Jossey-Bass.

Fenske, R. H. (1980a). Current trends. In U. Delworth & G. R. Hanson (Eds.), *Student Services: A handbook for the profession* (pp. 45–72). San Francisco: Jossey-Bass.

Frederiksen, C. F. (1993). A brief history of collegiate housing. In R. B. Winston, Jr., S. Anchors and Associates, *Student housing and residential life* (pp. 167–183). San Francisco: Jossey-Bass.

Gehring, D. D. (1991). Legal issues in the administration of student affairs. In T. K. Miller, R. B. Winston and Associates, *Administration and leadership in student affairs* (pp. 379–413). Muncie, IN: Accelerated Development.

Hoelting, F., & Navarro, R. Residence hall fitness centers' affects on students' strength and conditioning. *The Journal of College and University Student Housing, 24*(2), 3–7.

Hurst, J. C., & Jacobson, J. K. (1985). Theories underlying students' needs for programs. In M. J. Barr & L. A. Keating (Eds.), *Developing effective student services programs* (pp. 113–136). San Francisco: Jossey-Bass.

James, E. J. (1917). College residence halls. *The Journal of Home Economics, IX*(3), 101–108.

Janosik, S. M. (1991). Dealing with criminal conduct and other deleterious behaviors. In R. B. Winston, Jr., S. Anchors and Associates, *Student housing and residential life* (pp. 501–516). San Francisco: Jossey-Bass.

Kaplin, W. A., & Lee, B. A. (1995). *The law of higher education* (3rd ed.). San Francisco: Jossey-Bass.

Kuh, G. D., Schuh, J. H., & Whitt, E. J. (1993). *Involving colleges.* San Francisco: Jossey-Bass.

Lucas, C. J. (1994). *American higher education: A history.* New York: St. Martin's.

Lyons, J. W. (1993). The importance of institutional mission. In M. J. Barr and Associates, *The handbook of student affairs administration* (pp. 1–15). San Francisco: Jossey-Bass.

Miller, T. E., & Schuh, J. H. (1981). Managing the liability risks of residence hall administrators. *Journal of College Student Personnel, 23,* 136–139.

Moore, M., & Delworth, U. (1976). *Training manual for student services program development.* Boulder, CO: WICHE.

Morrill, W. H., & Hurst, J. C. (1980). Preface. In W. H. Morrill & J. C. Hurst (Eds.), *Dimensions of intervention for student development,* (pp. IX–X). New York: Wiley.

Morrill, W. H., Hurst, J. C., & Oetting, E. R. (1980). A conceptual model of intervention strategies. In W. H. Morrill & J. C. Hurst (Eds.), *Dimensions of intervention for student development,* (pp. 85–95). New York: Wiley.

Mosier, R. (1989). Health and wellness programs. In J. H. Schuh (Ed.), *Educational programming in college and university residence halls* (pp. 122–138). Columbus, OH: ACUHO-I.

Mueller, K. H. (1961). *Student personnel work in higher education.* Boston: Houghton-Mifflin.

Nuss, E. M. (1993). The role of professional associations. In M. J. Barr and Associates, *The handbook of student affairs administration* (pp. 364–377). San Francisco: Jossey-Bass.

Owens, H. F. (1984). Preface. In H. F. Owens (Ed.), *Risk management and the student affairs professional* (n. p.). NASPA Monograph No. 2, NP: NASPA.

Riker, H. C., & DeCoster, D. A. (1971). The educational role in student housing. *The Journal of College and University Student Housing, 1*(1), 3–6.

Pascarella, E. T., & Terenzini, P. T. (1991). *How college affects students.* San Francisco: Jossey-Bass.

Schneider, L. D. (1977). Housing. In W. T. Packwood (Ed.), *College student personnel services* (pp. 125–145). Springfield, IL: Charles C Thomas.

Schroeder, C. C., & Mable, P. (1993). Residence halls and the college experience: Past and Present. In C. C. Schroeder, P. Mable, and Associates, *Realizing the educational potential of residence halls* (pp. 3–21). San Francisco: Jossey-Bass.

Schuh, J. H. (1984). The residential campus-high risk territory! In H. F. Owens (Ed.), *Risk management and the student affairs professional,* (pp. 57–82). NASPA Monograph No. 2, NP: NASPA.

Schuh, J. H., & Triponey, V. L. Fundamentals of program design. In R. B. Winston, Jr., S. Anchors and Associates, *Student housing and residential life* (pp. 423–442). San Francisco: Jossey-Bass.

Stoner, K. L. (1992). Housing as an auxiliary enterprise. *The Journal of College and University Student Housing, 22*(1), 16–21.

Tarasoff v. Regents of the University of California, 551 P. 2d 334 (Cal. Sup. Ct., 1976).

Upcraft, M. L. (189). Residence halls and campus activities. In M. L. Upcraft, J. N. Gardner and Associates. *The freshman year experience* (pp. 142–155). San Francisco: Jossey-Bass.

Upcraft, M. L. (1993). Organizational and administrative approaches. In R. B. Winston, S. Anchors and Associates, *Student housing and residential life* (pp. 189–202). San Francisco: Jossey-Bass.

Winston, R. B., Jr., & Anchors, S. Student development in the residential environment. In R. B. Winston, Jr., S. Anchors and Associates, *Student housing and residential life* (pp. 25–64). San Francisco: Jossey-Bass.

Winston, Jr., R. B., & Fitch, R. T. (1993). Paraprofessional staffing. In R. B. Winston, Jr., S. Anchors and Associates, *Student housing and residential life* (pp. 315–343). San Francisco: Jossey-Bass.

Young, D. P. (1984). The student/institutional relationship: A legal update. In H. F. Owens (Ed.), *Risk management and the student affairs professional,* (pp. 15–31). NASPA Monograph No. 2, NP: NASPA.

Zeller, W. J., Kanz, K., & Schneiter, K. (1990). Creating partnerships with academic affairs to enhance the freshman year experience. *The Journal of College and University Student Housing, 20*(1), 14–17.

Zeller, W. J., & Mosier, R. (1993). Culture shock and the first-year experience. *The Journal of College and University Student Housing, 23*(2), 19–23.

Chapter 11

STUDENT ACTIVITIES

Edward G. Whipple

HISTORY

Student activities has always been a part of college life; however, what constitutes "student activities" has taken different forms since the beginning of America's system of higher education history. Presently, students are able to choose from a variety of activities which include: lectures, films, social events, fraternity and sorority life, student organization involvement, student government participation, cultural programs, and artist series.

Early American higher education, however, did not offer students such an array of extracurricular activities. In colonial colleges which focused on religion as the foundation of student life, student activities were driven by regular prayer, church attendance on the Sabbath, and activities influenced by the study of religion. As early as 1719 at Harvard, groups of youths gathered to read poetry, discuss issues of life, and enjoy beer and tobacco. A movement away from more "pious" activities was attributed to the academic class system, a unique feature of American higher education which perpetuated competition among students and led to hazing within certain types of student activities.

Horowitz (1987) described the beginning of college life which originated in the late 18th and early 19th centuries:

All over the new nation colleges experienced a wave of collective student uprising, led by the wealthier and worldlier undergraduates. College discipline conflicted with the genteel upbringing of the elite sons of Southern gentry and Northern merchants. Pleasure-seeking young men who valued style and openly pursued ambition rioted against college presidents and faculty determined to put them in their place. In every case, the outbreaks were forcibly suppressed; but the conflict went underground. Collegians withdrew from open confrontation to turn to covert forms of expression. They forged a peer consciousness sharply at odds with that of the faculty and of serious students and gave it institutional expression in the fraternity and club system (p. 11).

Among early student activities, the literary society played a major role in campus life until the latter part of the 19th century. The original purposes of these societies was to provide opportunities for public speaking and discussions of literature (particularly modern), political science, and history. These groups soon became competitive in nature and developed strong student loyalty. As literary societies grew, they took on different characteristics depending on the student's family social status and rank. As more students joined these societies, college and university administrators recognized their importance to student life. Societies were correctly recognized as being more than a mere extracurricular phenomenon. They came to be the center of interest on the campus, a powerful student-financed and student controlled educational enterprise that paralleled, some feared even threatened, the narrow and traditional classical academic program of the old-time college (Sack, 1961).

Literary societies eventually evolved into Greek letter organizations. The first national Greek letter organization, Phi Beta Kappa, was founded in 1776 at the College of William and Mary as essentially a literary society. Greek letter social organizations (fraternities) began with the Union Triad—Kappa Alpha Society (1825), Sigma Phi (1827), and Delta Phi Society (1827) (Anson & Marchesani, 1991, 11). With increasing numbers of Greek letter social organizations appearing on college campuses, antagonism appeared on the part of many members of the campus communities. This antagonism and strife lessened after the Civil War. The period immediately preceding the Civil War and after saw the rise of women's Greek letter social organizations (sororities) as well as the rise of professional fraternities in fields such as medicine, law, and engineering.

Student government began during the days of early Greek letter social organizations in the early 19th century. At the University of Virginia, Thomas Jefferson believed that students needed to be motivated by pride and ambition, rather than fear. He supported a student governing board to enforce university regulations, a function that had previously been a faculty responsibility. His plan was not successful due to the state legislature's failure to establish the proposed governing board, the inability of the Virginia students to handle the responsibility, and the honor code that bound many of the students from providing evidence against each other (Brubacher & Rudy, 1976).

After the Civil War, literary societies declined in importance as other forms of student organizations and athletics grew in popularity. Literary societies finally declined as institutions' curricula were expanding. More pronounced after the Civil War was the emergence of a "different" America:

> Students came to represent a broader group than heretofore and some of them were lacking in any serious intellectual or preprofessional interest. Others were coming to college mainly as a prelude to an active career in business and finance. This was the era of the emergence of modern American, when strong-willed entrepreneurs were constructing a vast industrial plant and creating the economic basis for a complex urban society. The goals that were being pursued by the ambitious young men of the country were, more than in ante-bellum times, predominantly materialist, tangible, pragmatic ones. The attitude of such young people was very often likely to be one of profound anti-intellectualism (Brubacher & Rudy, 1976, p. 120).

This anti-intellectualism quickly provided an atmosphere on campus for the emergence of clubs, fraternities, intercollegiate athletics, and publications. In many cases, these activities were based on a philosophy antithetical to the institution's academic mission. In addition, a more radical student government movement emerged at Illinois, Vanderbilt, Pennsylvania, Chicago, Vermont, and Bates.

Also after the Civil War, faculty tended to "pull in" and not be as concerned with student life outside the classroom. With faculty hesitant to become involved with students, the fraternity became a natural place for socializing. These organizations tended to meet developmental needs not being met by the literary societies and toward the end of the 19th century also provided living accommodations. For students who attended strict religious institutions, Greek letter social organizations provided a release from rules and regulations pertaining to behavior. Also, the fact that fraternities and sororities were secret in nature was appealing to students who sought to challenge college authorities (Brubacher & Rudy, 1976, p. 128).

As the country moved into the 20th century, students not interested in fraternity or sorority life, or who could not afford it, established other types of student organizations. Thus, campus life took on a different focus with the emergence of nonsecret organizations. These included clubs which were academic in nature—English, foreign language, history— and included faculty membership. Other clubs governed solely by students such as religious groups, music interest clubs, and special sports clubs were started.

The first student union facility was constructed at the University of

Pennsylvania in 1896. As the campus community saw the importance of the student union and the activities associated with it, the number of unions built after World War I increased rapidly (Stevens, 1969). Along with the buildings came various programming efforts designed to meet the needs of the institution and surrounding community. Campus unions attempted to develop activities which were tied to the academic mission of the institution. These activities included cultural events, speakers' series, lectures, and music events. The union truly became, on many campuses, the "living room" or "hearthstone" of the institution (Packwood, 1977).

After World War I, administrators were concerned about the lack of connection between the extracurricular aspect of student life and the academic mission of the particular institution. There was a concerted effort on the part of administration and faculty to integrate the two. "As administrators shifted from confrontation to accommodation, they officially recognized student organizations. . . . As deans of men and women cooperated with leaders of student society in planning events and enforcing codes of conduct, the apparent distinctions between institutional goals and those of college life faded" (Horowitz, 1987, p. 119).

Prior to World War II, administrators worked to more clearly define the goals of students' activities. The importance of the college environment, particularly as it impacted the students' education, was being recognized. Hand (1938) wrote:

> Thus we see that every experience makes a difference. It either helps a little or hinders a little. This means that proper self-activity—or the right kind of experiences—will result in right learnings; that wrong self-activity—or the wrong kind of experiences—will result in wrong learnings. As a corollary, it follows that the college, since it is an educational institution dedicated to right learnings, can legitimately support or permit only those student activities which result in desired learnings (p. 2).

With the return of the GI's from World War II, the complexion of college and university campuses changed dramatically. Increases in the number of women and older men provided new opportunities for student activities. Fraternity and sorority life was dominant as it retained its commitment to achievement in college life (Horowitz, 1987). During the 1960s, with the decline of *in loco parentis*, institutional priorities changed the relationship between the institution and its students. Extreme cultural currents, the civil rights movements, and new left radical groups all influenced the college campus. These movements provided an air of student independence on campuses. Thus, students became more autonomous in their program choosing, both in and out of the classroom. For example, the need to associate in traditional student activities, such as a fraternity, sorority, or student government, became unpopular. Consequently, membership nationally declined in traditional student activities programs, particularly the Greek letter social organizations.

The evolution of graduate student personnel preparation programs in the late 1960s and early 1970s also influenced student activities. Professionally prepared student affairs practitioners worked with students to promote campus environments with more positive working relationships among faculty, staff, and students. During this period of change, faculty became involved in student organization advising, special interest clubs flourished, residence halls became more attuned to the living-learning environment, and student unions provided well designed programs covering a variety of extracurricular areas. Leadership and volunteerism emerged as popular out-of-class activities for students.

Since the 1980s, the college campus has become much more diverse than the century prior. Numbers of older students, international students, minorities, women, and veterans caused changes in how student affairs professionals provide student activities. What is the future for student activities? After the conservative movement of the 1980s and the student's focus on a career and salary, it appears that more students are attempting to balance their collegiate experience with their noncareer involvement. Today, the opportunity for participation in extracurricular activities is seen by many employers as important to future success in the job market. For whatever reason, many students are seeking ways through student activities to enhance their academic experience.

DEFINITION

Student activities traditionally encompasses out-of-class programs including student organization advising, leadership development, student union programming, Greek letter social organizations, student government, and special institutional events (e.g., Homecoming and Parents' Weekend). In addition, many campuses have a student programming organization, often connected with the student union to plan events such as cultural programs, concerts, or a speakers' series. The array of opportunities for programs is great and varies from campus to campus. Higher education literature, however, does not provide for a definition of student activities.

Instead it identifies specific objectives for a student activities program. For example, Mueller (1961) stated that a student's development is enhanced by activities that are successful in "complementing classroom instruction or enhancing academic learning; developing social interaction; providing for a profitable use of leisure time; and encouraging better values and higher standards" (p. 275). Successful student activities programs today still encompass these objectives which enhance learning outside the classroom, provide for relationship and community building, allow for social interaction, and promote a value-based developmental experience. Traditional student activities programs are not in as much demand as they once were. Today's college students are more focused on careers and financial concerns than ever before. Student participation in personal activities and special interest groups continues to grow, at the expense of more traditional, organized activities such as student government, Greek letter social organizations, and student union programming. More students are engaged in activities which have a direct impact on their job opportunities and future careers.

"Campus-community activities" might be a more appropriate term today given the magnitude and variety of programming (Saddlemire, 1988). Programs can be both student sponsored and sponsored in conjunction with faculty, administration, and community members. During the last decade, students' interests have turned more toward service and volunteer work, either on the campus or in the community.

Need

Involvement in student activities is crucial to the development and growth of a student. Student activities, according to Miller and Jones (1981), is an essential part of a student's educational development. Williamson (1961) and Chickering and Reisser (1993) stress the development of the whole student and the importance of educating the intellectual, social, emotional, and physical aspects of college students. A thorough understanding of students, their developmental needs, and the value of involvement is crucial. Jacobi, Astin, and Ayala (1987) wrote:

> A principal concept in {student development} theory is that of student involvement, the time and the physical and psychological energy that the student invests in the academic experience. The more students are involved in the academic experience, the greater their learning and growth and the more fully their talents are likely to

develop. The less they are involved, the less they learn and the greater the chances they will become dissatisfied and drop out" (pp. 17–18).

Staff must be able to evaluate effectively students' needs and where students are developmentally in order to provide meaningful programs. Staff must be directed toward, and committed to, the growth and development of students. They must have the resources to assess and enhance programs. In addition, a philosophy should define the thematic rationale of activities, not a particular activity program. Within that rationale, activities are designed to meet the programming goals of a specific population (Mills, 1989).

Purposes

The Council for the Advancement of Standards (CAS) for Student Services/Development Program (1986) stated that the "purposes of the student activities program must be to complement the academic program of studies and enhance the overall educational experience of students through development of, exposure to, and participation in social, cultural, intellectual, recreational, and governance programs" (p. 91). The mission of the CAS Standards encourages student activities programs to operate in an environment which focuses on the development in areas which expand to the campus community and society; to provide for individual growth both cognitively and effectively; to experience diversity in its many forms; to be informed about the institution and its policies; to assist in the development of an institution spirit; and to work toward providing leadership learning opportunities.

Schmidt and Blaska (1977) identified six functions of student activities: (1) academic, (2) intellectual, (3) social, (4) group, (5) full student development, including personal and moral, leadership and democratic, and (5) campus and community. Comprehensive student activities programs tend to incorporate these functions in various ways in their program development and implementation.

Recent research has focused on the "learning purpose" of involvement in student activities. For example, student activities can aid in values development. Brock (1991) indicated that programming strategies can be designed to provide students with values and growth opportunities. Student activities also can assist students in clarifying ethical decision making. Boatman and Adams (1992) provided five ethical systems which reflect different leadership values and contents. These frameworks can be integrated into leadership training modules and used as a basis for what students need to learn while practicing ethical leadership.

Thus, student activities is not merely a respite from the classroom. Effective activities programming provides its own classroom. Student learning, leadership development, and campus and community involvement are all enhanced when the purposes of student activities are understood and incorporated in a comprehensive program.

ADMINISTRATION OF STUDENT ACTIVITIES

Student activities administration takes different forms, depending on an institution's mission, history, size, student demographics, funding levels, and public or private status. Common emphases, though, are found in an activities program. These include student organization advising, leadership education, student union activities and programming, concerts, speakers series, Greek affairs, and all campus special events. Also, on many campuses student government advising functions are found in the student activities administrative organization.

Research indicates there is no common or preferred model for administering student activities (McKaig and Policello, 1979). What is crucial, however, in determining the administrative organization is the assurance that it meets the needs of a particular campus student population. Upcraft (1985) wrote that an activities program broad in scope and with a variety of offerings enhances student retention and increases student satisfaction. Key to providing programs which aid in retention is the ability to administer effectively the program.

Effective program development is also a key to student retention. Student activities program planners must offer programs which reflect the priorities of the Student Affairs organization and the institution. Styles (1985) indicated that effective program planners should pay particular attention to specific areas which impact effective programming. Areas applicable to the student activities programmer include: research, assessing special populations' needs, balancing bureaucracies, managing power and influence, internal evaluation, and accountability (pp. 203–205).

One of the major factors which determines the focus of a student activities program is if the program is tied to the institution's student union. If there is a link, the administration of the student activities program most likely would be handled using a central staffing pattern. If a link does not exist, specific programs may be the responsibility of other Student Affairs offices, such as a Dean of Students Office or Office of Student Life. Depending on the size of the institution, the staff member responsible for directing student activities may report to the senior student affairs officer, or in cases where the activities program is part of the union operation, may report to the Director of the Union. Three sample organization models are:

Private Liberal Arts Institution of 1,600 Students

The administrator responsible for student activities carries the title of Director of Student Activities and the Union, and reports to the SSAO. The Director has an Assistant Director who serves in a support capacity for all responsibilities under the Director. Given the size of the campus and its liberal arts focus, the activities program is a comprehensive one, including all student union programming, cultural events, concerts, speakers series, leadership training, student organization advising and services, and Greek affairs.

Public Urban Institution of 4,000 Students

At this institution, the Director of Student Activities also carries the title of Director of the Union. The Director reports to the Dean of Students, who reports to the Vice President for Student Affairs. Staff support typically includes an Assistant Director, who has the primary responsibility for the Student Union operations. The programming responsibilities are primarily the Director's. These responsibilities are student union programming and all campus events (i.e., concerts, Homecoming, major speakers). Additional staff support is provided by graduate assistants. Greek affairs, student organization advising, and leadership training are the responsibilities of staff in the Dean of Students Office.

Public Institution of 20,000 Students

At this institution, the Director of Student Activities reports to an Associate Vice President for Student Affairs who is also Director of the Student Union. The Director of Student Activities has distinct programming areas, each administered by an Assistant Director of Student

Activities. Programming areas include Student Union programs, Greek affairs, leadership and student organizations, and multicultural programs.

Sandeen (1989) wrote about the issue of administrative responsibility for activities programming and the student affairs staff's need to seek a balance between control and freedom. He advised program planners to be sensitive to issues of other important campus constituencies, including the president, students, faculty, external groups, and other student affairs staff. In formulating policy for campus activities, administrators should consider the following:

The educational mission of the institution
The priorities of the president
The social and educational needs of the students
Legal considerations pertinent to the institution
The willingness of faculty to participate
The support of the student affairs staff
Student participation in establishing and revising the policy
The establishment of a faculty-student policy council to review the policy and its application

The needs (for example, concerts, child care, cooperative living groups) of special student groups (Sandeen, 1089, p. 67).

The key to successful administration of a student activities program is dependent on the student activities staff's ability to work with different constituencies, particularly students. Williamson's (1961) advice is still pertinent today regarding the different roles one must play in working with students during their extracurricular time. Williamson stated that staff may be asked to:

- Advise when asked by students regarding their own voluntary activities.
- Serve as a joint partner with students concerning programs and activities which are both voluntary student activities and also an organized part of the university's program.
- Serve as a consultant in determining what suggestions and reactions students may have to the institution's own programs.
- Serve a leadership role, suggesting and urging adoption of new objectives by an organization.
- Serve as a technical consultant, having expertise superior to that

possessed by students and improving programs geared to students' own objectives and achieved through their own activities (p. 223).

In addition, successful student activities staff need to understand clearly the context in which the activities programs lies at a particular institution. They must be cognizant of the "larger picture" and sensitive to the many variables which affect the student environment. Also, successful staff work collaboratively with other student affairs staff to ensure a strong student activities program.

STUDENT DEVELOPMENT AND STUDENT ACTIVITIES

Importance

Why is it important for the student activities administrator to have knowledge of student development theory? Student development theory provides insight into the importance of providing both educational activities in and out of the classroom to assist in the development of the whole student. If one of the purposes of higher education is to prepare students to be informed and responsible citizens, then not only the academic, but also the extracurricular experience, is important. Gardner (1989) emphasized the developmental aspect of the extracurricular:

> The opportunities for individual growth will be numerous and varied for all members . . . [O]n the playing field, and in group activities in and out of school and college, they will learn teamwork. Through volunteer and intern experiences outside of school they will learn how the adult world works and will have the experience of serving their society (p. 80).

The need for student affairs staff to be grounded in student development theory is increasingly important as research shows the tremendous impact of the extracurricular experience. Because students spend the vast majority of their waking day out of class, the emotional, social, moral, physical and mental impact of campus activities are significant (Feldman and Newcomb, 1969; Pascarella and Terenzini, 1991; Astin, 1993; Chickering and Reisser, 1993). In addition, the influence of the peer group is significant. Astin (1993) stated:

> Perhaps the most compelling generalization from the myriad findings summarized . . . is the pervasive effect of the peer group on the individual's development. Every aspect of the student's development—cognitive and affective, psychological and behavioral—is affected in some way by peer group characteristics, and

usually by several peer characteristics. Generally, students tend to change their values, behavior, and academic plans in the direction of the dominant orient of their peer group (p. 363).

Astin's research also indicated that satisfaction with campus is influenced directly by the degree of involvement. For example, students who were involved in activities with other students (e.g., sports, student organization involvement, attending campus events, socializing) were more pleased with their collegiate experience. Furthermore, the impact of association makes a dramatic difference regarding students' success in college and their retention. According to Upcraft (1985), "There is considerable evidence, however, that active participation in the extracurricular life of a campus can enhance retention" (pp. 330–331). Types of student activities which do have a positive impact on retention include establishing close friends, participating in orientation programs and activities, belonging to student organizations, involving oneself in social and cultural activities, attending lectures, using campus facilities, and generally participating in extracurricular activities (Upcraft, 1985).

According to Wilson (1966), more than 70 percent of what a student learns in college comes from outside the classroom. Kapp (1979) concluded that around 80 percent of traditional age undergraduates participate in at least one or more of seven extracurricular activities, including cultural, social, political, and religious events. Kuh, Schuh, Whitt, and Associates (1991) posed the question of what students learn from these extracurricular activities? The importance of participation in student activities is central to their work, *Involving Colleges* (1991). Based on their research on college and university campuses they concluded that:

- Orientation participation positively impacts social integration and institutional commitment and then indirectly impacts the student's satisfaction with the institution and his or her desire to persist;
- Involved students are more positive about their undergraduate experience, including their social life, living environment, and academic major. The college participation, according to the research, is important to the student's job success after graduation;
- Participation in extracurricular activities allows for the opportunity to gain leadership, decision-making, and planning skills which are transferable to the job market;
- Involvement allows for learning about mature, intimate interpersonal relationship;
- The opportunity for leadership work in activities translated in to more active community and civic leaders after graduation; and
- The research indicates that the only factor which predicts adult success is participation in extracurricular activities (pp. 8–9).

The importance of student activities to promote association and involvement cannot be emphasized enough. The challenge for the student activities professional is to provide the experience necessary for positive growth and development. Activities based on an understanding of student development theory are crucial.

Using Student Development Theory

How can student development be utilized effectively in programming? To facilitate this learning and development, program planners must be aware of the different theories and how they can translate these theories into practice. Learning and development are dependent on the type of environment in which an activity takes place (e.g., workshop, meeting, program, policy) and the type of outcomes are desired.

Historically, student affairs has been criticized for not basing program development on student development theory. Hurst and Jacobson (1985) wrote that the lack of a theoretical or conceptual foundation has been due to the personal interests of professional staff, the skill or knowledge of professional staff, emerging crises, professional fads, political expediency, special interest groups, and tradition (pp. 117–118).

Given the importance of the student's extracurricular experience and the time devoted to it, it is critical that student affairs staff use student development theory to facilitate learning and development. Those involved in student activities programming must be knowledgeable of appropriate theories and related issues which pertain to student development. These include learning theory, group dynamics, student demographics, educational philosophy, institutional governance, supervision, and organizational development (Marine, 1985; Kirkland, 1987). An understanding of different student developmental theories provides for more effective program design and delivery.

The central question is "How does a student activities program meet the needs of the 45-year-old, divorced mother of three who is returning to college to complete a degree while at the same time attempting to provide for the 18-year-old, first time, college freshman?" Student activities practitioners must be cognizant of the developmental needs of both the 45-year-old and the 18-year-old. These two types of students are very different in what they expect from an extracurricular program. Miller and Jones (1981) identified ways in which an institution can become responsive to the different needs of students. They showed how student development theory can aid program planning in eight areas, including self-direction, social relations, leadership, volunteer service, and cultural preparation.

PROGRAMS

Student activities encompasses a wide variety of programs. There are, however, certain programs which tend to be common to most college and university campuses. These include student government advising, student organization services, Greek letter social organization (fraternity and sorority) programming, student union activities, multicultural programs, leadership development, and volunteer activities.

Student Government

Student government is an important part of campus life. For many student affairs staff, student government poses a problem. Most often, this problem centers on the relationship between the institution and the student government. If student affairs staff do not understand that important relationship (which is different than the relationship between any other student organization) serious problems can occur. In many cases, the student government president has direct access to the institution president; thus, it is crucial that the SSAO and the administrator who is the liaison to the student government be aware of that relationship. Student affairs staff should act in a strong supportive capacity with student government, ensuring that appropriate educational opportunities are available, such as leadership training and special workshops, to assist student government members' development. In addition, staff should continually keep the student government leadership aware of its role as "the voice of the students" and its legal, moral, and ethical responsibilities to represent students to the administration in a constructive and mature manner.

In a survey of student government advisors, Boatman (1988) found six characteristics of a strong student government. These are: (1) student leaders understanding the institutional structure and the relationship of student groups to student government; (2) the direct and regular access of student government leaders to top administrators and faculty in both a professional and social setting; (3) a mutual respect and common view of the institution by student government leaders, their advisors, and institutional representatives; (4) a positive working relationship between the student government and the student press; (5) a high degree of student participation and retention in student government elections, activities, and meetings; and (6) training student government leaders to analyze the institution's structure and implementing need change as well as being appointed to institutional committees.

Boatman also noted that the qualities of a student government advisor should include those of honesty, openness, strong interpersonal communication skills, and the ability to deal with a range of opinions and feelings. In addition, advisors should be resources to students with respect to the institution's history, culture, policies, politics, and current issues, as well as have credibility with, and access to, top administrators. While student government participation may advance student opinions and concerns on campus, at least one study indicated that involvement in student government activities had no short-term or long-term impact, either positive or negative, in students' postcollege lives (Downey, Bosco, & Silver, 1984). This same study did show, however, that those involved in student government reported greater satisfaction with their lives during their college years.

Student Organization Services

On many campuses, there is a student affairs practitioner who works with student organization registration, advising, and educational programming. With the ever-changing membership of student organizations, and at times, the lack of consistent advising, staff support is important to help students become more stable and less threatened by leadership changes. Other than student governing bodies and Greek letter social organizations, most student groups on campus do not receive much attention. Such groups include honor societies, religious organizations, academic clubs, sports clubs, and special interest groups. For many students who belong to these organizations, membership is their link to student life.

Campuses should provide their student organizations with meeting and work space and, depending on the size of the institution and the goals of the particular student organization, office space. Mail boxes, in a central location, can aid in the communication efforts in addition to providing important community building among student groups.

Staff should be instrumental in providing educational programs for student organization leaders and their members. These may include sessions on resources available at the institution, financial management, membership recruitment, publicity, motivating members, and fund raising techniques. Many campuses, either during new student orientation or early in the school year, sponsor a student organizations' fair, which allows for new and current students to learn more about the opportunities for campus involvement outside of class.

Because of the wealth of talent among campus faculty, student affairs staff should be encouraged to utilize faculty to provide programs. Besides using the expertise, it allows faculty members to work with students in a setting different than class, and helps to strengthen the ties between academic and student affairs. The student activities practitioner should take any opportunity to involve faculty.

Cooper and Porter (1991) recommended that student organizations co-sponsor various programs with the institution's general student programming board, if the institution has one. Co-sponsorship may include sharing funds, personnel, and communication resources to produce a program. Advantages of co-sponsorship are that the potential for multicultural programming is enhanced, student leadership and programming skills are developed, publicity for both groups can be favorable, and synergy develops between the two organizations.

Greek Letter Social Organizations (Greek Affairs)

For campuses with Greek letter social organizations, administrative support may come from a Student Activities Office, Dean of Students Office, Office of Student Life, or Housing Office.

The Greek Affairs area is undoubtedly one of the most controversial student activities programs. There has been continual debate, almost since the start of Greek letter social systems in the late 19th century, about the value of fraternities and sororities on college campuses. Critics have claimed that fraternities and sororities are exclusionary, sexist, and gender specific and that their existence is contrary to the values colleges and universities hope to convey to students (Maisel, 1990). Administrators have questioned the relevance to campus life as well as the relationship between a Greek system and the institution.

Institutional emphasis on and influence of fraternity and sorority life varies from campus to campus. Kuh and Lyons (1990) found that fraternities and sororities were less divisive at institutions where there were also strong residence life programs and other involvement opportunities for students. In urban institutions, fraternity and sorority members were the key to maintaining campus tradition and held many of the student leadership roles. At larger institutions, Greek letter social organization members tended to provide important community service, but at the same time promoted activities that could be construed as demeaning and even dangerous.

On a number of campuses today, the value of fraternity and sorority life remains the subject of debate and research. Institutions have established "blue ribbon" committees to review Greek life, with these committees recommending either elimination of Greeks from campus or a significant change in the relationship between the host campus and the fraternities and sororities. Campuses such as the University of Southern California, the University of Alabama, Bowling Green State University, Denison University, and Gettysburg College have, or are studying the role fraternities and sororities play on campus.

Faculty, particularly, have been critical as to what they perceive as anti-intellectualism among fraternity and sorority members. While chapters may have some of the most outstanding scholars on campus, they also may have some members in grave academic difficulty (Winston and Saunders, 1987).

Values and attitudes of students impact their view of learning. Baier and Whipple (1990), in a study of Greek values and attitudes, found that the Greek system appears to provide a "safe harbor" for those who seek conformity, family dependence, social apathy, and extensive involvement in extracurricular activities. The Greek system also "provides a 'legitimate' campus subculture for students to associate with others who are affluent, have relatively undefined academic and vocational goals, and place a higher priority on social life than intellectual pursuits" (p. 52).

Because of the debate on many campuses regarding the value of fraternities and sororities, it is important that staff have a well defined plan for working with students affiliated with these organizations. A thorough understanding of the value of fraternity and sorority life as it relates to an institution's academic mission is crucial for students to realize, if Greek letter social organizations are to succeed. The Council for the Advancement of Standards for Student Services/Development Programs (1986) specified the following six goals of a fraternity and sorority advising program:

1. Promoting the intellectual, vocational, social, recreational, and moral development of students;
2. Providing training in leadership skills and other personal and social skills;
3. Promoting student involvement in extracurricular activities and community projects;
4. Providing training in group processes, including the development of esprit de corps;
5. Promoting Greek life as a productive and viable lifestyle on campus; and,
6. Promoting an appreciation for different lifestyles and cultural heritages (p. 45).

Challenges for student affairs professionals who advise fraternities and sororities are many. Anderson (1987) stated that the roles the advisor must fulfill to meet the challenges of Greek Affairs include: (1) programmer, (2) institutional representative, (3) counselor, (4) administrator and manager, (5) researcher and evaluator, (6) organization development consultant, (7) public relations person, (8) conflict mediator and manager, and (9) role model.

A knowledge of a variety of management techniques to deal with the many issues associated with Greek life is also necessary for a Greek advisor. Cufaude (1990) suggested eight management strategies for Greek advisors:

1. Maintain a high level of visibility by attending Greek meetings and workshops;
2. Establish regular lines of communication with all involved constituencies, such as parents, alumni, and faculty members;
3. Focus efforts where results are likely to be best, such as upon pledges;
4. Establish clear expectations of behavior;
5. Incorporate fraternity and sorority members into campus leadership development programs;
6. Establish a university advisory board for Greek-letter organizations;
7. Create assistantship or paraprofessional positions to aid in advising fraternities and sororities; and,
8. Set clear, attainable goals.

Student affairs staff, to be effective, must help students understand their role on campus and the responsibilities that role entails. Programs should be designed to encourage a sense of community between the Greek system and the rest of the institution. In addition, it is critical that the Greek advisor work to establish effective lines of communication among the chapter leadership, alumni, campus administration, and the international and national Greek organizations. The communication linkage with these constituencies can prove invaluable in working with different issues which arise.

Current issues involving Greeks provide for continual challenges. These issues include substance abuse, hazing, poor community relations, and an insensitivity to diversity issues.

Substance abuse problems are an issue for both the institution and Greek members. Arnold and Kuh (1992) found that alcohol was an integral element of group life for fraternities, regardless of institutional size. In addition, alcohol and hazing were identified as key elements in socializing new members to the group. They concluded that national staff and institution officials were not as effective in addressing these issues and effecting positive changes as were the members themselves.

Hazing continues to be a problem for both men's and women's groups. National and international organizations and institutions aggressively have provided educational programs and intervention techniques to combat the mentality which promotes hazing. Unfortunately, the problem continues within many chapters with alcohol abuse, most often serving as the precursor to hazing incidents. The challenge for staff working with fraternities and sororities is to continue to focus on substance abuse and hazing education without alienating students who are tired of hearing about it.

With many fraternity and sorority chapters housed off campus, community relations are often stretched. Good relations with neighbors and the surrounding community are important for the success of any Greek system. Many Greek letter social organizations are attempting to nurture those relationships through educational programs involving member chapters about the responsibilities inherent in living in a community. Interfraternity and Panhellenic Councils, in some communities, have worked with local governments to address issues and concerns.

Fraternity and sorority members have been criticized for lacking tolerance for minority differences, religious choice, and sexual preference. Programs should be encouraged which promote diversity in membership and a realization of the importance of valuing differences. Some Greek governing boards have established human relations committees that work to promote, through programming, more sensitive and tolerant committees. Students need to understand that the acceptance of others can lead to the strengthening of their own group. Student affairs staff should continually look for educational opportunities to create a sensitivity and understanding among all students.

Fraternity and sorority life can add much to a campus and provide a positive experience for many students. It is, however, important that staff work to establish procedures whereby the institution can evaluate the positive campus contributions Greek letter social organizations and these organizations can make in turn. Evaluation of support services provided by the institution and national or international organization is also necessary.

Student Union Activities

On many campuses, the student union is the "community center of the college, for all members of the college family—students, faculty, administration, alumni and guests" (Packwood, p. 180). Depending on the student affairs administrative organization, much of the student activities advising for campus programming may come from the union staff. In any case, the student union should be an important gathering place for students and afford an array of activities. Both social and academic activities should be promoted with a goal of contributing to the overall campus community.

The CAS Standards and Guidelines for Student Services/Development Programs for College Unions (1986) stated that the goals of the union are " . . . to maintain facilities, provide services, and promote programs that are responsive to student developmental needs and to the physical, social, recreational, and continuing education needs of the campus community" (p. 21). In addition, the CAS Standards indicate that the program "should include a balanced variety of activities, such as art, performing arts, music, cinematic arts, games and tournaments, outdoor recreation, lecture and literary events, crafts and hobbies, social and dance events . . . " (p. 21). These activities can offer an important link to all of student life and strengthen the times with academic life.

Student activities have played an important role in student development since the first student union was built. Fagan (1989) emphasized the need for varied programming if student growth is to occur. For example, passive programming efforts such as posters and videotapes can introduce topics such as substance abuse, acquaintance rape, AIDS, and racism. Other types of programs, such as a speakers' series, social events, or festivals, can engage students in a more active learning process.

Levitan and Osteen (1992) believed that union activities programming must meet the needs of today's student. They address changes in programming which is affected by the ever-changing media world, technology, leadership programs, need for interpersonal and relationship skill building, an increased emphasis on volunteerism and service, and changing student demographics. Trends of importance to student union activities programs include:

- Changing demographics and the need to incorporate and embrace opportunities those changes bring;
- Changing student involvement patterns, impacted by demands of work, family life, study, and the need to be involved;
- Defining the role of the college union in the twenty-first century;
- Emerging leadership programs which must include cross-cultural understanding and global perspectives, ethical decision making, and handling change in organizations;
- Working to help students learn healthy interpersonal relationship skills;
- Assisting and supporting students in volunteer and community service opportunities; and,
- Managing the technological changes impacting institutions (p. 25).

Multicultural Programming

As the student population on campuses becomes more diverse, the need for multicultural programming increases. Students, faculty and staff are demanding programs which meet the diverse needs of all members of the campus community. Student Affairs staff increasingly will be called upon to provide the expertise to promote multicultural programming. They must be able to define multiculturalism for their programs and widen their views of acceptable student leadership behaviors. Kuh and Schuh (1991) wrote,

> If colleges and universities are to be modes of interactive pluralism, at least three conditions must be met: institutions must change in fundamental ways to accommodate and take advantage of the contributions of students from historically underrepresented groups; opportunities must be available for students to live in and learn about their subcommunity of choice, whether it be based on race, ethnicity, gender, academic interests, or life-style orientation; and boundaries between students subcommunities must be permeable, allowing and encouraging positive interaction and learning (pp. 300–301).

Student activities programs have an opportunity, through the variety of interactions with students, and the learning that occurs within a group, to promote multiculturalism. Students can be provided the opportunity, structure, and reinforcement for replacing stereotypes with personal knowledge for learning to view differences for their qualities, importance, and potential to create growth. Staff should avoid the common mistakes of (1) trying to program for diverse constituencies without including input from the target groups, (2) assuming that all students within a particular culture are alike, (3) making multicultural programming the responsibility of one committee only, and (4) assuming that ethnic artists hold the greatest appeal for that particular ethnic group.

Student Affairs staff must look at ways to redefine campus norms which have served as barriers to the integration of minority students into campus life. Sardo (1990) encouraged reexamining institution rules and student organization bylaws, co-programming, bringing minority student leaders into all-white organizations, cross-group advertising in publications, and posting of activities notices where minority students will see them. In addition, faculty and staff need to develop their understanding of the verbal communication styles of minority students.

Intercultural learning is becoming increasingly important on the college campus. As students become more familiar with each other's culture, the ability to program and participate becomes much easier for them. Leppo (1987) provided strategies for the student affairs practitioner to assist students in working through the different stages of awareness. He encouraged staff to step in when cultural differences create conflict within student organizations or when student groups plan activities that could be construed as offensive to other cultures. He believed the goals should be to move beyond simple awareness to the point where differences are celebrated.

In working to develop effective multicultural programming, student affairs staff, in conjunction with student organizations, must work to change organizational structures to (1) eliminate barriers to inclusion, (2) modify hierarchies that perpetuate majority viewpoints, and (3) recreate program and advisory boards to encourage diverse representation.

Leadership Development

Leadership development directly impacts the quality of student life on a campus. When student leaders are well versed in the basics of leadership, student activities will be more organized and developed, and in many cases, the process of that development will impact positively on an organization's members. A student's effectiveness to lead an organization depends, in many cases, on the success of the student organization. Miller and Jones (1981) emphasized the need for leadership development:

> What is needed beyond participation . . . is some type of leadership training that does away with much of the trial-and-error learning so common in student leadership activities. Systematic training, supervision, and consultation are necessary components to be added to student leadership programs if effective leadership development is to result. It is fine to give students the opportunity to become involved, but it is essential to aid them in developing the skills and competencies necessary to become socially responsible leaders (p. 663).

Some institutions have a staff member devoted solely to leadership development activities. Other institutions incorporate leadership training into the various program offerings, with the staff member responsible for each program handling the leadership education aspect.

Leadership development can take place in different environments. Seminars and workshops can be offered on specific topics. For example, a session on how to recruit members may be offered to all student organizations. A program on improving communication skills could be provided for fraternity and sorority executive officers. Nolfi (1993) emphasized that a leadership development program should highlight training, education, development, and experiential learning. She indicated a leadership advisory committee is beneficial to assist in assessing students' needs and available resources.

On some campuses, a student affairs office will sponsor credit and noncredit courses. For example, specific leadership training courses, for credit, are available to fraternity and sorority presidents and student government leaders. Credit courses are often available for freshmen and sophomores focused on beginning leadership skill building, with the purpose of preparing them to assume campus student leadership roles.

Recognizing the changing demographics of campuses, leadership training should be viewed from other than the traditional age student's point of view. Rather than campus-focused programs, Fisher and Sartoelli (1992) promoted developing student leadership programs which recognize students' on-campus involvement and reflect the beliefs that the needs of traditional and nontraditional students overlap, that leadership comes in many styles, and that leadership development is a future-oriented process. They emphasized maturity and personal development in place of skills normally associated with leadership.

Volunteer Activities

Volunteer activities are a vital part of a student activities program. Participation in a service organization helps prepare students for volunteerism in their community after graduation. Student affairs staff can aid in supporting volunteerism by explaining the civic responsibility it supports. These activities are valuable also because they help students learn about themselves and the world around them.

On a college campus, there are student organizations with the sole mission of service. In addition, many student organizations have "service" as part of their mission. These organizations include fraternities and sororities, honor societies and student government. Examples of service activities might include fund raising for the Heart Association, Cancer Society, or AIDS Awareness or spending a day working with disadvantaged youth or cleaning up a city park. Given the nature of volunteer or service organizations, it is important that staff work to help members understand the group's mission to establish clear goals and expectations for participation. Also, they should communicate continually the goals and benefits of the organization to the campus community. It is easy for these groups to lose focus if strong student leadership and committed advising are not present. The rewards of a volunteer group's efforts are sometimes not readily seen and members who desire "quick gratification," and may lose interest in participation.

Volunteer organizations or service clubs are valuable to a campus culture because of the positive impact participation makes. Astin (1993) found that "participation in volunteer work also has a positive correlation with a variety of attitudinal outcomes: commitment to developing a meaningful philosophy of life, promoting racial understanding, and participating in programs to clean up the environment" (p. 392).

Research on student development supports the importance of peer influence on college students (Pascarella and Terenzini, 1991, Astin, 1993; Chickering, 1993). Peers helping peers, in a volunteer or service setting, can also be extremely beneficial for students. Eight benefits to the peer helper identified by Delworth, Sherwood, and Casaburri (1974) include:

- Satisfaction and self-esteem obtained from "getting involved."
- Increased feelings of self-worth and confidence.
- Increased confidence in specific skill areas.
- Increased interest in their own educational experience.

- Increased contacts with key members of the college community.
- New work experiences providing increased understanding of particular careers.
- Skills and references of general value for future work or education.
- Advanced skills that may be directly applicable to employment after college.

Service learning can be integrated into leadership and campus activities. Delve and Rice (1990) promoted a model where administrators can integrate community service opportunities for student organizations with goals of emphasizing the advantages of different leadership models. They focus on linking community service and leadership development opportunities so student organization members can develop as "servant-leaders." "Moving a student from an understanding of charity to an understanding of justice often requires a parallel move from the group to a sense of individualism that then translates back to the group and community. It is through this movement that students mature and develop as 'whole people' committed to the betterment of the society of which they are a part" (Rice, p. 64). The integration process includes retreats and workshops, credit and noncredit leadership courses, orientation programs, and recognition.

Rubin (1990) discussed ten principles that should characterize effective service and learning programs. Such a program

1. engages people in responsible and challenging actions for the common good.
2. provides structure opportunities for people to reflect critically on their service experience.
3. articulates clear service and learning goals for everyone involved.
4. allows those with needs to define those needs.
5. clarifies the responsibilities of each person and organization involved.
6. matches service providers and service needs through a process that recognizes changing circumstances.
7. expects genuine, active, and sustained organization commitment.
8. includes training, supervision, monitoring, support, recognition, and evaluation to meet service-learning goals.
9. ensures that the time commitment for service learning is flexible, appropriate, and in the best interests of all involved.
10. is committed to program participation by and with diverse populations (pp. 117–120).

STUDENT ACTIVITIES ISSUES AND TRENDS

The issues of the 1990s are becoming the trends for the 21st century. Changing demographics, legal concerns, and funding problems will all be on higher education and student activities' agendas into the next century.

Changing Student Demographics

Adult Learners

At many institutions across the country, the impact of changing demographics is affecting the focus of student activities programs. "Nontraditional" students are fast becoming "traditional" students. The increase of adult learners, particularly women, is changing the makeup of student affairs programs and services and thus it is crucial for the student affairs staff to be aware of adult learners' needs and motivations. Ringgenberg (1989) submitted that:

> Returning students and women students need child-care facilities, support groups for themselves and their families, a common gathering ground, and social, recreation, cultural, and educational programs that meet their interests. Programming for a family is a great deal different from programming for the traditional-age student. For example, tastes in music and comedy can be extremely different. However, failure to provide family programming could isolate these students from campus (pp. 33–34).

Most adults returning to college, or attending for the first time, matriculate to accomplish specific objectives, to develop social contacts and relationships with others, or to learn for the pleasure of acquiring knowledge. Their developmental needs are different according to whether they are in early or middle adulthood, the mid-life transition phase, or later life. Within these phases are different levels of ego development, intellectual development, and moral development. Bennett (1992) wrote that the adult learner moves through three phases: Moving In, Moving Through, and Moving On. Student affairs staff should provide appropriate support for each phase. The Moving In phase is an opportunity for staff to provide a supportive atmosphere as the adult student makes the transition to college life. During the Moving Through phase, the support should be provided to help the student succeed (i.e., programs to meet social needs and efforts made available for involvement in student organizations). Finally, the Moving On phase should provide students with support for programs dealing with finding a job, such as resume writing and interviewing techniques, and researching graduate programs.

The challenge for student affairs staff is to provide student activities for adult learners that meet these developmental needs. Moore, Miller, and Spina (1989) stated there are two important roles for student affairs staff in working with adult learners and student activities: advocate and programmer. The advocate helps returning adults make the transition into college life by bringing them together through organizational activities, providing a common meeting place, and by encouraging that office hours be made available after the normal work day hours. Programmers can provide events for students, such as informal "return to learn" seminars focusing on transition to college issues and distribute communication, such as a newsletter, to help students be aware of campus events.

Gay, Lesbian, and Bisexual Students

On many campuses there is a student organization for gay, lesbian, and bisexual students. Unfortunately, given many campus climates, these students do not feel a part of the mainstream of student life. Student affairs staff can improve their quality of life for these students by developing programs to meet their needs. Scott (1988) wrote that institutional policies should be responsive to the needs of these students by including sexual orientation in the institution's statement of nondiscrimination; training student activities staff to work with gays, lesbians, bisexuals; and taking steps to handle verbal and physical harassment.

Campus environments are different in their acceptance of gay, lesbian, and bisexual students. Good (1993) provided five programming stages for student affairs staff, depending on the institution's level of readiness. The first stage is programming focused on reducing hate crimes and teaching students to appreciate diversity. The second stage develops programs to promote a positive self-identity for gay, lesbian, and bisexual students. The third stage aggressively establishes a place for students on campus and allows them to share their experiences with the college community. Stage four moves from the external environment faced by the students to personal adjustment issues. Finally, the fifth stage should provide for an environment wherein students can feel comfortable within the campus community and which helps them affirm who they are.

International Students

"International students contribute in several ways: by providing cultural diversity; by sharing their values, life experiences and world views; by serving as resources in the creation of a more cosmopolitan learning environment; and, of course, by achieving laudatory scholarship and study in classrooms, laboratories, and libraries" (Willer, 1992, p. 194). As more international students arrive at institutions across the country, it is important that they are accommodated not only academically, but also socially. Willer (1992) stated that it is not solely the responsibility of the international student services office on a campus to care for international students. It is everyone's responsibility to ensure that international students are successfully being integrated into the campus community. In addition, there is a great benefit international students provide to American institutions in their efforts to educate all students for living in a global society. "International students contribute in several ways: by providing cultural diversity; by sharing their values, life experiences and world views; by serving as resources in the creation of a more cosmopolitan learning environment; and, of course, by achieving laudatory scholarships and study in classrooms, laboratories, and libraries" (Willer, p. 194).

Student affairs staff should work closely with the staff responsible for administering the international students' program on the campus. Activities can be planned not only for international students, but for American students as well that promote common goals. The benefits which arise from the interactions and relationships formed are important to the personal development of all students. The challenge for staff is to acknowledge and balance the activities which are important to promoting international students' cultural, ethnic, or religious backgrounds with those activities which help assimilate them into the culture of the campus. The dilemma for the activities staff is how to create an environment where students share a sense of purpose and unity while still accepting and appreciating diversity.

Legal Issues

Like the university at-large, those in student activities are faced with a myriad of legal issues when developing student programs outside the classroom. While it is clearly not possible to discuss all the legal relationships and implications in depth here, college officials should be aware of the potential legal ramifications that may exist when implementing certain decisions relating to student activities.

Four primary legal relationships exist between students and their respective institutions. These four relationships are (1) constitutional,

(2) statutory, (3) constitutional, and (4) torts (Gehring, 1993). With respect to student activities, all four relationships can and will likely be formed between students and the institution as a result of decisions made by both college officials and student leaders.

For public institutions and those private institutions where state action is involved, the First Amendment must be taken into account before planning an activity or denying a student the opportunity to hold an event on campus. A decision to invite a controversial speaker to lecture on campus, to show an x-rated movie at the university theater, to deny a student group the opportunity to march on campus, or to hold a meeting at a campus building, will typically force the institution to balance the interests of the First Amendment with college officials' and students' desire to have a campus free of obnoxious and disrespectful speech. The First Amendment protects most speech, including controversial, offensive, or obnoxious speech. All speech, however, is not protected. If speech is obscene, represents a clear and present danger, constitutes fighting words, or will incite others to imminent, lawless action, the institution may be able to restrict the person's speech. While restrictions on a student's freedom of expression may be considered under only the most extraordinary of circumstances, student leaders and college officials should provide outlets to contrary opinions or activities when certain controversial events occur on campus.

As for tort liability and statutory concerns, universities will often find that such a relationship will exist with students, employees, and guests of the University. A tort is broadly defined "as a civil wrong, other than a breach of contract, for which the courts will allow a damage remedy" (Kaplin, 1995, p. 89). Fenske and Johnson (1990) noted that in the collegiate setting, tort law has been most often applied in negligent cases relating to personal injuries sustained while attending an activity sponsored by student group or the institution, while transiting university property, or while on a class field trip. Higher education institutions have a duty to protect their students and other invited guests from known or reasonable foreseeable dangers.

With respect to fraternities and sororities, the problems associated with hazing, alcohol, and physical defects of university premises have continually resulted in civil lawsuits being brought by students or their families for tortuous behavior. Thus, colleges should regularly check to see that (1) hazing or violent rivalries among fraternities are not occurring; (2) university premises (e.g., fraternity and sorority houses and residence halls) are safe from physical defects, and (3) no near-misses have occurred that forewarn the university of possible future injuries (Gulland & Powell, 1989).

Criminal statutes relating to uses of alcohol (e.g., social host liability and underage drinking) and proscribing hazing will create a legal relationship not only between the students and the institution, but students and the state as well. Thus, college officials and students need to be cognizant of the criminal and civil statutes that may apply to them. Finally, it is axiomatic that the relationship between an institution and a student is contractual in nature. Contracts may be explicit or implicit, written or oral. As such, institutions should be careful as to how they draft their student handbooks, brochures, and catalogues, since courts, depending upon the circumstances, may view these documents as creating a contractual relationship between the institution and the student. As is clearly evident, the law pervades the entire college campus, including action relating to student activities. Thus, when appropriate and possible, competent legal counsel should be sought to advise college officials and students on how best to stay clear of liability.

Funding Issues

On most campuses, funding of student activities programs is derived from nonstate dollars. The most common term for the funding source is a "student activity fee" or "general fee." On some campuses, student activities may be funded from both state dollars and nonstate dollars, depending upon which administrative office is coordinating the programs. With the increasing scrutiny of state budgets, and the continual evaluation that many institutions are doing regarding expenditures, it is important that student affairs staff be aware of the ever changing budget situation. One of the benefits for students in extracurricular involvement is the opportunity to work with budgets. Staff should educate students about federal, state, and budget issues and the impact that these issues have on student activity programs.

Floerchinger and Young (1992) provided suggestions for working with the volatile budget problems all higher education programs, including student activities, face. These suggestions are (1) co-sponsoring programs with other on-campus or off-campus organizations; (2) using local student, staff, and faculty talent in developing low-cost programs as opposed to hiring outside speaker or consults; (3) using computer linkages and videos for training rather than bringing in expensive outside trainers; (4) increasing emphasis on cooperative buying and cost sharing with other campuses; (5) improving professional and student skills in negotiating contracts and analyzing student interests; (6) developing grant-writing skills for student activities professionals; (7) analyzing office functioning and expenditures for waste; (8) encouraging volunteerism; (9) enhancing the prospect of students becoming supportive alumni; and (10) gaining a better understanding of the lobbying process before the state and federal government.

PROFESSIONAL ORGANIZATIONS

Student affairs staff who work in student activities have the opportunity to join several national/international organizations which promote activities programming. These are the Association of College Unions-International (ACU–I) and the National Association of Campus Activities (NACA). Both provide for professional development and for student activities programming ideas.

The Association of College Unions-International was founded in 1914. The purpose of ACU–I is to help college unions and student activities improve their programs and services and to contribute to student growth and development. There are approximately 1,000 members institutions from urban and rural campuses, four-year and two-year schools, large universities, and small colleges. Association members are located also in Canada, Australia, France, Great Britain, New Zealand, and Japan. The Association is divided into 16 geographical regions. At the regional level, there is the opportunity for participation of students as well as union and activities staff in ACU–I programs, activities, and leadership position. Besides regional activities, including conferences, there is an international conference and national workshops and seminars.

ACU–I publishes a magazine six times a year and provides updated information on the union and student activities areas. There is a monthly newsletter containing announcements, current news about student activities and union operations, and employment announcements. ACU–I's headquarters are in Bloomington, Indiana.

The National Association of Campus Activities was founded in 1968. Its purpose of NACA is to provide its members with educational and informational services in the area of campus activities programming. NACA provides members with services such as cooperative buying, educational programs and services, talent showcases, trade publications, and national and regional conferences and workshops. Over 1,100 institutions and 550 firms representing all 50 states and Canada are members. NACA features a national convention, regional conferences, summer and winter workshops, state meetings, educational projects, a resource library, numerous publications, and professional development services.

The Association publishes a magazine nine times a year, containing educational articles, news, reports, evaluations, and advertising of interest to institutions and other members. There is also a Membership Directory & Buyers' Guide which provides information about campus activities. Headquarters for NACA are in Columbia, South Carolina.

ENTRY–LEVEL EMPLOYMENT QUALIFICATIONS

While there are no set qualifications for student affairs staff who work in student activities, there are preferred qualifications. An individual should have had an active undergraduate student experience in student activities, preferably including leadership positions. This could be holding membership in a fraternity or sorority, serving as a member of the campus student government, planning concerts for campus events such as Homecoming, or actively participating in a special interest student organization. The opportunity for a prospective student activities practitioner to have had contact with not only students during his or her undergraduate years, but also the chance to interact with faculty and administration on a regular basis is beneficial.

Many institutions, when seeking student activities staff, prefer an individual from a graduate student affairs or higher education preparation program. At the master's level, a generalist background is important. Potential staff should take advantage of the breadth of courses available to them in their graduate work. Assistantships in a student activities area, such as student union activities, student activities programming, Greek affairs, or student organization advising, can be valuable. In addition, a prospective student activities practitioner should take the opportunity to participate in practica which offer experiences in different student activities settings. Preferred qualifications also include excellent organizational skills, verbal and written skills, and the ability to relate well with a variety of populations (students, faculty, staff, community, alumni, and parents).

REFERENCES

Anderson, J. W. (1987). Roles and responsibilities of Greek advisors. In R. B. Winston, Jr., W. R. Nettles III, & J. H. Opper, Jr. (Eds.), *Fraternities and sororities on the contemporary college campus* (pp. 75–86). San Francisco: Jossey-Bass.

Anson, J. L., & Marchesani, R. F. (Eds.). (1991). *Baird's manual of American college fraternities.* Indianapolis: Baird's Manual Foundation, Inc.

Arnold, J. C., & Kuh, G. D. (1992). *Brotherhood and the bottle: A cultural analysis of the role of alcohol in fraternities.* Bloomington, IN: Indiana University, Center for the College Fraternity.

Astin, A. W. (1993). *What matters in college?* San Francisco: Jossey-Bass.

Baier, J. L., & Whipple, E. G. (1990). Greek values and attitudes: A comparison with independents. *NASPA Journal, 28,* 43–53.

Bennett, L. G. (1992, September). Keeping adult students on the move. *ACU–I Bulletin, 60,* 4 ff.

Boatman, S. (1988, April). Strong student governments and their advisement. *Campus Activities Programming, 20,* 58.

Boatman, S., & Adams, T. C. (1992, April). The ethical dimension of leadership. *Campus Activities Programming, 24,* 62–67.

Brock, C. S. (1991, December). Ethical development through student activities programming. *Campus Activities Programming, 24,* 54–59.

Brubacher, J. S., & Rudy, W. (1976). *Higher education in transition.* New York: Harper & Row.

CAS Standards and Guidelines for Student Services/Development Programs. (1986).

Chickering, A. W. & Reisser, L. (1993). *Education and identify (2nd ed.).* San Francisco: Jossey-Bass.

Cooper, J. E., & Porter, B. E. (1991, April). Co-sponsorships: Bridging the gap among student organizations. *Campus Activities Programming, 23,* 42–46.

Cufaude, J. (1990). Strategies form a Greek advisor: Maximizing the Greek's co-curriculum's potential. *NASPA Journal, 28,* 82–90.

Delworth, U., Sherwood, G., & Casaburri, N. (1974). Student paraprofessionals: A working model for higher education. *Student Personnel Series, 17.* Washington, DC: American College Personnel Association.

Devle, C. I., & Rice, K. L. (1990, Summer). The integration of service learning into leadership and campus activities. In C. I. Delve, S. D. Mintz, & G. M. Stewart (eds.), *Community service as values education.* San Francisco: Jossey-Bass.

Downey, R. G., Bosco, P. J., & Silver, E. M. (1984). Long-term outcomes of participation in student government. *Journal of College Student Personnel, 25,* 245–250.

Fagan, A. F. (1989, January). The college union: The living room of the campus. *ACU–I Bulletin, 57,* 35–37.

Feldman, K. A., & Newcomb, T. M. (1969). *The impact of college on students.* San Francisco: Jossey-Bass.

Fenske, R. H., & Johnson, E. A. (1990). Changing regulatory and legal environments. In M. J. Barr, M. L. Upcraft, & Associates, *New futures for student affairs: Building a vision for professional leadership and practice* (pp. 114–137). San Francisco: Jossey-Bass.

Fisher, V. D., & Sartorelli, M. B. (1992, March). Leadership programs: Building bridges between non-traditional and traditional students. *Campus Activities Programming, 24,* 41 ff.

Floerchinger, D., & Young, K. E. (1992, Summer). The money crunch: Is it killing campus activities? *Campus Activities Programming, 25,* pp. 29–36.

Gardner, J. W. (1989, Fall). Building community. *Kettering Review,* 73–81.

Gehring, D. D. (1993). Understanding legal constraints on practice. In M. J. Barr and Associates, *The handbook of student affairs administrators* (pp. 274–299). San Francisco: Jossey-Bass.

Good, R. T., III (1993, Summer). Programming to meet the needs of the lesbian-gay community. *Campus Activities Programming, 26,* 40–44.

Gulland, E. D., & Powell, M. E. (1989, May). Colleges, fraternities and sororities: A white paper on tort liability issues. Research Report, Covington & Burling.

Hand, H. C. (1938). *Campus activities.* New York: McGraw-Hill.

Horowitz, H. L. (1987). *Campus life.* Chicago: The University of Chicago Press.

Hurst, J. C. and Jacobson, J. K. (1985). Theories underlying students' needs for programs. In M. J. Barr, L. A. Keating, and Associates (Eds.), *Developing effective student services programs* (pp. 113–136). San Francisco: Jossey-Bass.

Jacobi, M., Astin, A., & Ayala, F. (1987). *College student outcomes assessment: A talent development perspective* (ASHE–ERIC Higher Education Report No. 7). Washington, DC: Association for the Student of Higher Education.

Kaplin, W. A., & Lee, B. (1995). *The law of higher education: A comprehensive guide to legal implications of administrative decision making (3rd ed.).* San Francisco: Jossey-Bass.

Kapp, G. J. (1979). *College extracurricular activities: Who participates and what are the benefits?* Doctoral dissertation, University of California, Los Angeles. (University Microfilms, No. 80-01, 378).

Kirkland, R. (1987, September). Moving from philosophy to practical: Student development theories can help in the transition. *ACU–I Bulletin, 55,* 23–27.

Kuh, G. D., Schuh, J. H., Whitt, E. J., & Associates (1991). *Involving colleges.* San Francisco: Jossey-Bass.

Kuh, G. D., & Lyons, J. W. (1990). Fraternities and sororities: Lessons from the College experiences study. *NASPA Journal, 28,* 20–29.

Leppo, J. (1987, April). Multicultural programming: A conceptual framework and model for implementation. *Campus Activities Programming, 19,* 56–60.

Levitan, T., & Osteen, J. M. (1992). College union activities and programs. In T. E. Milani, and J. W. Johnston (Eds.), *The college union in the year 2000.* San Francisco: Jossey-Bass, pp. 11–25.

Marine, J. (1985, February). The college union's role in student development. *ACU–I Bulletin, 53,* 22–23.

Masiel, J. M. (1990, Fall). Social fraternities and sororities are not conducive to the educational process. *NASPA Journal, 28,* 8–12.

McKaig, R. N., & Policello, S. M. (1979). Student activities. In G. Kuh (Ed.), *Evaluation in student affairs* (pp. 95–103). Washington, DC: American College Personnel Association.

Miller, T. K., & Jones, J. D. (1981). Out-of-class activities. In A. W. Chickering and

Associates (Eds.), *The modern American college* (pp. 657–671). San Francisco: Jossey-Bass.

Mills, D. B. (1989). In D. C. Roberts (Ed.), *Designing campus activities to foster a sense of community* (pp. 39–48). San Francisco: Jossey-Bass.

Moore, L. V., Miller, D., & Spina, D. (1989, May). Returning adult students need staff to serve as advocates, programmers. *ACU–I Bulletin, 57,* 27–28.

Mueller, K. (1961). *Student personnel work in higher education.* Boston: Houghton Mifflin.

Nolfi, T. (1993, November). Designing a student leadership program. *ACU–I Bulletin, 61,* 4–10.

Pascarella, E. T., & Terenzini, P. T. (1991). *How college affects students.* San Francisco: Jossey-Bass.

Ringgenberg, L. J. (1989). Expanding participation of student subgroups in campus activities. In D. C. Roberts (Ed.), *Designing campus activities to foster a sense of community* (pp. 27–37). San Francisco: Jossey-Bass.

Rubin, S. G. (1990). Transforming the university through service learning. In C. I. Delve, S. D. Mintz, & G. M. Stewart (Eds.), *Community service as values education* (pp. 111–124). San Francisco: Jossey-Bass.

Sack, S. (1961). Student life in the nineteenth century. *Pennsylvania Magazine of History and Biography,* 270–273.

Saddlemire, G. L. (1988). Student activities. In A. L. Rentz & G. L. Saddlemire (Eds.), *Student affairs functions in higher education* (pp. 261–283). Springfield, IL: Charles C Thomas.

Sandeen, A. (1989). Freedom and control in campus activities: Who's in charge? In D. C. Roberts (Ed.), *Designing campus activities to foster a sense of community* (pp. 61–68). San Francisco: Jossey-Bass.

Sardo, R. C. (1990, December). Redefining the norms: A campus activities approach to multiculturalism. *Campus Activities Programming, 23,* 36–40.

Schmidt, M. R., & Blaska, B. (1977). Student activities. In W. T. Packwood (Ed.), *College student personnel services* (pp. 153–178). Springfield, IL: Charles C Thomas.

Scott, D. (1988, March). Working with gay and lesbian students. *ACU–I Bulletin, 56,* 22–25.

Stevens, G. (1969). The college union—past, present and future. *NASPA Journal 7,* 16–21.

Styles, M. (1985). Effective models of systematic program planning. In M. J. Barr, L. A. Keating, & Associates (Eds.), *Developing effective student services programs* (pp. 181–211). San Francisco: Jossey-Bass.

Upcraft, L. (1985). Residence halls and student activities. In L. Noel, R. Levitz, D. Saluri, & Associates (Eds.), *Increasing student retention: Effective programs and practices for reducing the dropout rate* (pp. 319–344). San Francisco: Jossey-Bass.

Willer, P. (1992). Student affairs professionals as international educators. In D. McIntire, & P. Willer (Eds.), *Working with international students and scholars on American campuses* (pp. 161–167). Washington, DC: National Association of Student Personnel Administrators.

Williamson, E. G. (1961). *Student personnel services in colleges and universities.* New York: McGraw-Hill.

Wilson, E. K. (1966). The entering student: Attributes and agents of change. In T. M. Newcomb and E. K. Wilson (Eds.), *College peer groups* (pp. 71–106). Chicago: Aldine.

Winston, Jr., R. B., & Saunders, S. A. (1987). The Greek experience: Friend or foe of student development? In R. B. Winston, Jr., W. R. Nettles III, J. H. Opper, Jr., (Eds.), *Fraternities and sororities on the contemporary college campus* (pp. 5–20). San Francisco: Jossey-Bass.

Chapter 12

STUDENT FINANCIAL AID

Michael D. Coomes

From the rather meager beginnings of a single £100 scholarship program, student aid in the United States has grown to incorporate dozens of federally-funded programs, hundreds of state programs, and countless institutional and private programs with resources in excess of $41 billion ("The Nation: Students," 1995). In 1995, more than 6 million students received over $27 million in federal financial assistance to help them in meeting their college costs (U.S. Department of Education, 1994c). Student aid and its administration by campus aid officers, state and federal bureaucrats, and corporate business men and women has become an increasingly important part of postsecondary education.

HISTORY

As is the case with many aspects of higher education, student aid in the United States starts with Harvard College. In 1643, Lady Ann Radcliff Mowlson bequeathed to Harvard College £100 for the "yea(rly) maintenance of some poor scholler" ("Scholarship & beneficiary aid," in Godzicki, 1985, p. 15). The scholarship, funded through the gifts of alumni and other generous benefactors, employment opportunities for needy students, and tuition remission constituted the student aid programs prior to the Civil War (Fenske, 1983). These programs of funded grants, tuition remission, and student employment established a number of trends, e.g., providing aid to the needy, multiple sources and types of aid, and institutional commitments of student assistance, that would influence the development of student aid programs sponsored by the states and the federal government.

Comprehensive, far-reaching, federal involvement in higher education is primarily a modern phenomenon (Coomes, 1994; Fenske, 1983). During the Depression, the National Youth Administration (NYA) was created (Brubacher & Rudy, 1976). The National Youth Administration was the first major program of direct federal aid to students. The NYA was followed in 1944 by the Serviceman's Readjustment Act, more commonly known as the G. I. Bill. Like other programs that preceded it (NYA) and were to follow, the G. I. Bill was enacted for noneducational reasons: to reward the veterans of the Second World War for their service and to ease the burden on a fragile economy that a substantial increase in the number of employable men would represent (Rivlin, 1961).

In 1958, prompted by the 1957 launching of the Sputnik satellite and by a number of national reports outlining the nation's need for improved scientific and technical education, Congress passed the National Defense Education Act (NDEA). The NDEA authorized funds for colleges to improve the teaching of modern foreign languages, created a graduate fellowship program, and authorized funds for the dissemination of scientific information. The cornerstone of the act was a student loan program for students planning teaching careers or pursuing programs in science, mathematics, or modern foreign languages (Conlan, 1981). In addition to creating the first program of generally available federal student aid, NDEA moved the federal government toward guaranteeing opportunity for education, and established the precedent for making students and not institutions the primary beneficiaries of federal education funds (Conlan, 1981).

The next major piece of student aid legislation, the Higher Education Act of 1965 (HEA), was an outgrowth of a growing national concern for the welfare of the underprivileged. The HEA created the Supplemental Educational Opportunity Grant and Guaranteed Student Loan programs and transferred the College Work-Study to the Office of Education (Moore, 1983). Enacted in a watershed year for federal domestic legislation, HEA "embodied for the first time an explicit commitment to equalizing college opportunities for needy students through grants and through such programs as Talent Search designed to facilitate access for the college-able poor" (Gladieux, 1983, p. 410).

The final pieces of the federal student aid puzzle were set in place when the Education Amendments of 1972 created the Basic Educational Opportunity Grant (BEOG) and the State Student Incentive Grant (SSIG) programs in 1972. The BEOG program was intended to serve as the foundation for a student's financial aid package, and its creation established that "students, not institutions, are the first priority in federal support" (Gladieux & Wolanin, 1976, p. 225).

The passage of the Middle Income Student Assistance Act in 1978 extended participation in the federal student aid programs to the children of middle class families. Not only would the traditional recipients of student aid, the financially disadvantaged, be able to attend their choice of postsecondary institution, but now middle income students would be able to as well (Finn, 1985). The Education Amendments of 1980 further expanded the federal student aid programs and created a new loan program, the Parents Loan for Undergraduate Study (PLUS).

Student aid legislation during the 1980s and early 1990s focused on the rising costs of federal student aid and on program efficiency issues. During the Reagan and Bush administrations, efforts were focused on reducing federal involvement in higher education and on limiting funding, not on creating new programs. While only one student aid program (i.e., Social Security Educational Benefits) was eliminated, constant efforts to reduce funding for the federal student aid programs resulted in very modest program growth (Coomes, 1994; Eaton, 1991).

The federal student aid programs were reauthorized again in 1992. It was anticipated that the 1992 reauthorization would result in extensive changes in the student aid programs (Parsons, 1994); however, political disagreement resulted in a bill that contained only minor programmatic changes (DeLoughry, 1992). One such change was renaming of the guaranteed student loan program as the Federal Family Education Loan program. In 1993, the Student Loan Reform Act of 1993 created the Federal Direct Student Loan program. Also in 1993, the National Community Service Trust Act created a program that connected participation in community service with funding for postsecondary education.

In addition to federal involvement, the states have been involved in the creation and implementation of student aid programs. Many of the early state aid programs were created to assist students of high ability. The creation of state aid programs based on financial need with the intention of equalizing opportunity occurred concurrently with the development of the federal role in student aid (Marmaduke, 1983). Nineteen state aid programs existed prior to the 1969–1970 academic year and by 1979 the remaining thirty-one states and seven territories had instituted programs (Marmaduke, 1983). A major impetus for the development of state grant programs was the creation of the SSIG program in 1972 which provided federal matching funds intended to encourage states to create their own grant programs. In addition to state scholarship programs, state governments also fund loans and student employment programs.

PHILOSOPHY AND PURPOSE

Student aid has traditionally lacked a consistent philosophy. This is particularly the case at the federal level where student aid has frequently been used to realize goals only tangentially related to higher education (Coomes, 1994; Hansen, 1991). Student assistance programs have been used to reward members of the military for their service; as means to encourage draft registration and community service; and as levers to force institutions to comply with a wide-range of consumer information requirements (e.g., placement and graduation rates, campus safety statistics). This lack of a clearly and intentionally developed philosophy has resulted in a system that is, at times, overly confusing, cumbersome, and replete with duplicative programs (Coomes, 1994). Nevertheless, if an intentional philosophy for student aid is not present, it is possible to discern a set of goals that have emerged over time as policy makers have attempted to develop programs to meet the financing needs of post-secondary students. Some of these goals, as identified by Finn (1985), are: to increase the supply of well-educated and highly skilled manpower in society; "to nurture extraordinary individual talent . . . ; to encourage the study of particular subjects or disciplines . . . ; to increase social mobility, foster equality of opportunity, and diminish the importance of private wealth; [and] to advance interests of members of designated groups judged to be deprived in part by lack of access to or participation in higher education" (pp. 2–3).

Since 1965, these last two goals have been the primary purposes of federal student assistance and are frequently interpreted as improved equity and increased access to postsecondary education opportunities. Realizing the goals of equity and access for needy students requires a delivery system that equitably establishes the student's, and where appropriate the family's, ability to pay; determines the student's cost of education; and provides a package of resources to meet their calculated financial need.

Needs Analysis, Budget Construction, and Packaging

According to Case (1993), needs analysis is predicated on a number of important principles. First and foremost among those is that the student and, if the student is a dependent student, the student's parent(s) have the primary responsibility for paying for the student's education. Independent students are also required to use their income and assets to meet necessary educational and living expenses. The determination of a student's family financial situation should be "an objective assessment of their present [financial] circumstance" (Case, 1993, p. 2). Financial contributions should be built on progressive assessment rates; those with greater financial resources are required to make greater contributions toward their educational costs than those with more meager resources. Finally, "needs analysis procedures recognize that part of family resources must be devoted to taxes, basic living costs, and other unavoidable expenses; other expenditures that are a matter of family choice are usually not included as allowance against available income or discretionary net worth" (Case, 1993, p. 2). Each of these principles can be, and frequently are, challenged by applicants for financial aid, and while arguments can be proffered, one central concept is unassailable: Need based financial aid should be awarded to those who cannot afford to attend college without that support. "Need" should not be confused with "want." Some families will be unwilling to tap their discretionary income and use those resources for educational costs; this does not make them financially needy. Discretionary income is just that, discretionary, and student aid policy makers believe the first use for discretionary income should be meeting educational costs.

Operationally, financial need is the difference between the student's cost of attendance and the student and/or families expected family contribution (EFC). Since 1992, the expected family contribution that must be used in establishing eligibility for the federal student aid programs has been calculated using a Congressionally mandated formula called the Federal Methodology (FM). Data used in the FM to calculate the EFC include, but are not limited to: student information (e.g., dependency status, student's year in college, student's marital status); parent's information for dependent students (e.g., family size; number of tax exemptions); family income, including both the parent's and the student's income; taxes paid; allowances for employment of both spouses in a two-parent family; an income protection allowance; medical and dental expenses; and family assets (e.g., savings; investments; but, as of the 1993–1994 award year, not home equity). Needs analysis raises a number of interesting and important philosophical questions: Should a needs analysis system "objectively" determine the family's ability to pay or should it be used as a means to ration limited student aid resources? What family resources should be included in determining the EFC? How should a student's dependency status be determined? Which data elements should aid officers be allowed to change "for cause" and how should aid officers employ their professional judgment in making changes to needs analysis calculations? Should individual institutions be required to use FM for determining student eligibility for need-based institutional funds? Readers wishing to explore the answers to these questions as well as philosophical reasons for, and policy implications of, needs analysis are directed to J. P. Case (1983, 1990, 1993); K. E. Case (1990); Davis (1990); Fisher (1990); Heffron (1990); and Wolanin (1990).

The second element of need determination is the establishment of the student's cost of attendance. For federal student financial aid programs, cost includes: tuition and fees, an allowance for room and board; and allowances for books and supplies, transportation, and miscellaneous personal expenses (U.S. Department of Education, 1995). Certain special allowances may be added to a student's budget if warranted. These include reasonable costs for study abroad, costs associated with cooperative education expenses, and costs incurred by disabled students for expenses related to their disabilities (U.S. Department of Education, 1995). While costs are rather rigidly controlled by statutory guidelines, student aid officers do have the authority to utilize their professional judgment to adjust the cost of attendance on a case-by-case basis if they feel that such an adjustment is warranted (U.S. Department of Education, 1995). Additional information on the process of constructing student budget can be found in *Constructing Student Expenses Budgets* (National Association of Student Financial Aid Administrators, 1993).

Few students receive only one type of aid; rather, most students receive a combination of grants, loans, and student employment funds, referred to as a financial aid package (Binder, 1983). Like the determination of the family/student's ability to pay and the establishment of realistic expense budgets, financial aid packaging is a complex process. Federal Pell Grants usually form the foundation of a student's financial aid package and Federal Supplement Education Opportunity Grants (FSEOG) and Federal Perkins loans must be awarded to exceptionally needy students (Berkes, 1989). Once Pell Grants, FSEOG, and Perkins loans have been awarded, remaining need can be met with a combination of Federal Work Study, institutional aid, loans from either the Federal Family Education Loan Program or the William D. Ford Federal Direct Loan Program, state assistance, and/or institutional aid. Students who receive funding from private sources (e.g., private scholarships) must have that aid included in their financial aid package. It must be remembered that, if a student is receiving need-based financial aid, the sum total of a student's financial aid cannot exceed the student's demonstrated financial need.

STUDENT AID PROGRAMS

Fundamentally, there are three types of student aid: grants, loans, and employment (Binder, 1983; Coomes, 1988; Dannells, 1977). This section will examine those three general aid types; discuss the typical funding sources for student aid programs; and describe the generally available federal student aid programs.

Grants are nonrepayable student aid resources or gift aid. Dannells (1977) identified five different types of gift aid: (1) Grants, which are nonrepayable awards based on financial need (e.g., Pell Grant, Ohio Instructional Grants; (2) Merit/honors scholarships which are based on the student's past performance, future promise, exceptional intellectual potential, or outstanding leadership abilities (Finn, 1985); (3) Graduate fellowships for graduate study (Dannells, 1977); (4) Tuition remission and subsidized tuition which is frequently awarded to the spouses or children of university employees (Finn, 1985); and (5) Service awards given to students for services rendered such as veterans benefits and funds earned by students who have participated National and Community Service Program (United States Department of Education, 1994c). Service awards are also made in anticipation of future services, e.g., athletic scholarships and performing arts scholarships (Finn, 1985; Mueller, 1961).

Loan funds require repayment and can be made to either the student or, where appropriate, the student's parent(s). The repayment of many loans is deferred until the student leaves school; however, some programs require repayment while the student is enrolled. Many student loans carry interest rates lower than the rates for other types of loans because the interest rate is subsidized by a lender, or by state or federal governments.

Most loans are made to pay general educational expenses and are awarded as part of the student aid package. However, many institutions maintain short-term loan programs that are intended to aid students in meeting emergency expenses.

Student employment funds may be either need-based or nonneed based. Although many students work while attending a postsecondary institution, only those jobs provided or arranged by the institution are rightfully considered student aid (Dannells, 1977). Student employment positions can exist in both on- and off-campus settings, and financial aid officers frequently attempt to place students in jobs that complement their academic interests.

Funding Sources

Funding for the various student aid programs comes from a variety of sources. In 1975 the National Task Force on Student Aid Problems identified the following sources of student aid: the federal government; state governments; postsecondary institutions; and private sources like corporations, service clubs, and philanthropic organizations (Binder, 1983).

The federal government is the largest source of aid for students. For the 1994 academic year, federal funding for student aid totaled an estimated $31.4 billion or 75 percent of all aid awarded ("The Nation: Students," 1995). Funding for the generally available student aid programs for the same year totaled an estimated $29.2 billion ("The Nation: Students," 1995). From the 1984 academic year to 1994 academic year, funding for generally available federal student assistance increased (in current dollars) by $17 billion or 158 percent (Knapp, 1992; "The Nation: Students," 1995). In recent years, the fastest growing and the largest federal programs have been the federal guaranteed loan programs. From the 1984 academic year to the 1994 academic year, funding for the federal guaranteed loan programs grew (in current dollars) by $13.6 billion or 179 percent (Knapp, 1992; "The Nation: Students," 1995). In 1994, guaranteed student loan funds accounted for 72 percent of all federally supported generally available aid and 51 percent of funds from all sources ("The Nation: Students," 1995).

All 50 states as well as Puerto Rico, the Virgin Islands, and the Trust Territories of the Pacific support some type of student aid programs (Marmaduke, 1983). State aid programs vary widely in terms of type (e.g., need-based and merit grants, loans, and student employment) and in terms of the amount allocated to those programs by state legislatures. Nationally, state supported aid totaled $2.9 billion in academic year 1994 ("The Nation," 1995). The vast majority of those funds came in the form of grants to students which totaled $2.1 billion ("The Nation: Students," 1995). From the 1984 academic year to the 1994 academic year state grant aid increased (in current dollars) by $1.3 billion (119 percent). Funding from individual states varies widely and is generally a function of the number of students enrolled in the state's postsecondary institutions. New York, with the oldest state supported grant program, awarded $666 million in state aid in 1993.

Like the other sources, institutions support the full-range of grant, loan, and student employment programs. In 1994, institutional awards totaled $8.1 billion ("The Nation: Students," 1995). The institutional sector provided the largest increases in student aid funding for the period 1983–1993. During that period, institutional support increased (in current dollars) from 13 percent of total aid to 19 percent, an increase of 46 percent (Knapp, 1992; "The Nation: Students," 1995). Much of that increase can be attributed to the need to off-set rapidly increasing costs of attendance coupled with stable funding for federal and state student aid resources (Knapp, 1992).

The Federal Student Aid Programs

This section will provide a broad overview of generally available federal student aid programs[1] as well as information on institutional and student eligibility. For more detailed program descriptions as well as detailed information on administering the federal student aid programs, student affairs practitioners are directed to the current editions of: *Counselor's Handbook for Postsecondary Schools* (U.S. Department of Education, 1994a); *The Federal Student Financial Aid Handbook* (U.S. Department of Education, 1995); and *The NASFAA Encyclopedia of Student Financial Aid* (Burns, 1984, updated annually).

---

[1] The federal government offers a wide range of programs to assist students with meeting their educational costs (e.g., Paul Douglas Teacher Scholarships, Reserve Officers Training Corp Scholarships, veterans benefits). However, for purposes of this chapter, discussion will be limited to generally available student financial aid programs administered by the Office of Postsecondary Education within the Department of Education.

Institutional Eligibility

For students to receive federal student financial aid, they must attend an eligible postsecondary institution. Institutions of higher education (e.g., colleges and universities); proprietary institutions (e.g., private, for profit educational institutions); and postsecondary vocational institutions are all eligible to participate in the federal student financial aid programs (U.S. Department of Education, 1995). Eligible participating institutions must comply with a wide range of administrative standards if they wish to continue to participate in federal financial assistance programs. Institutions must provide applicants with information on the types and amounts of student aid available at the institution; how eligibility is determined and aid is awarded; institutional degree programs; satisfactory academic progress standards; and instructional personnel and physical facilities (U.S. Department of Education, 1995). In addition, schools participating in the student assistance programs must comply with the requirements of the following protective policy laws: the Family Educational Rights and Privacy Act; the Student Consumer Information Act and its amendments, the Student-Right-to-Know and Campus Security Act and the Sexual Assault Victim's Bill of Rights; and the Drug Free Schools and Communities Act and its 1989 amendments (Gehring, 1994a). Participating institutions must also assure that the aid program is effectively managed, that counseling is offered to students, that adequate staff is available to meet student needs, and that they avoid excess loan default rates (U.S. Department of Education, 1995). As concerns over institutional fraud and abuse and consumer protection have grown, Congress has passed more laws that impact the management and operation of student aid offices. Some view these laws and their attendant regulations as placing an undue burden on institutions that has stripped institutions of their autonomy (Gehring, 1994b). Be that as it may, they are the law and institutions wishing to participate in the federal student aid programs must comply.

Student Eligibility

In addition to institutional compliance, students must meet certain criteria if they wish to receive assistance from the federal government. Students must be United States citizens or nationals, permanent residents of the United States or citizens of the Marshall Islands Federated States of Micronesia and Palua. Certain students who are noncitizens—

refugees and individuals granted permanent asylum in the United States—
are also eligible to participate in the programs (U.S. Department of
Education, 1995). To receive federal assistance, students must be enrolled
in an eligible program of study; possess a high school diploma or its
equivalent, or demonstrate the ability to benefit from a postsecondary
education; maintain satisfactory academic progress; generally not be in
default on a federal loan or owe a repayment of a federal grant; possess a
valid social security number; and if required, be registered with the
Selective Service System (U.S. Department of Education, 1995).

Federal Pell Grants

First authorized by the Education Amendments of 1972, and originally titled the Basic Educational Opportunity Grant (BEOG) program,
Federal Pell Grants were intended to serve as the foundation of a
student's financial aid award (Coomes, 1994). This need-based grant
program was envisioned by its creators as a quasi-entitlement program,
i.e., "grants were to be made to every student who was determined
eligible under a formula that assessed the family's ability to contribute
toward a student's cost of education" (Moore, 1983, p. 37). However,
appropriations for Federal Pell Grants have seldom been adequate to
fully fund the grant program. The gap between the amount of program
authorizations (e.g., the amount Congressional authorizing legislation
suggests is needed to fund the program at entitlement level) and program appropriations "grew during the 1980s and continues to grow in
the early 1990s" (Knapp, 1992, p. 3). A second major difference between
the Federal Pell Grant and other federal grants is its portability. Awards
are made directly to students who can use the award at any eligible
institution they choose to attend. The maximum amount of individual
grants is determined each year based on yearly appropriations from
Congress.

William D. Ford Direct and Federal
Family Education Loan Programs

In 1965, Congress created the Guaranteed Student Loan (GSL)
program, a program of subsidized low-interest loans (Coomes, 1994).
The program was reauthorized as part of the Higher Education Amendments of 1992 and renamed the Federal Family Education Loan Program (FFEL) (U.S. Department of Education, 1995). In 1993, the
Student Loan Reform Act created the William D. Ford Direct Loan

Program (U.S. Department of Education, 1995). The Direct Loan program was created to simplify the existing loan program and to reduce interest subsidies and default payments to lenders and guarantee agencies and thus the cost to the federal government.

Under the Direct Loan program students and/or parents apply directly to their institution for a loan and the institution determines eligibility for and the amount of the loan. Once approved, payments are made to the student and/or the parent through the institution. The Direct Loan program consists of four individual loans:

(1) Federal Direct Stafford Loans which are need-based, subsidized loans;
(2) Federal Direct Unsubsidized Stafford Loans which are available to students regardless of financial need. As an unsubsidized loan, interest accrues on the loan while the student is enrolled;
(3) Federal Direct PLUS Loans which are made directly to parents to aid them in meeting the costs of their dependent children's education. These are not subsidized loans; and
(4) Federal Direct Consolidation Loans which "combine one or more federal education loans into a new Direct Loan" (U.S. Department of Education, n.d., p. 3).

Loan limits vary depending on dependency level and year in school and interest rates vary by program (e.g., Direct Loans, Direct Plus Loans) and are adjusted each year.

The major difference between the William D. Ford Direct Loan Program and Federal Family Education Loan Program (FFEL) program is who makes the loans to students (U.S. Department of Education, n.d.). As indicated above, eligibility for Direct Loans is determined and funds are allocated by the student's institution. Under the FFEL program eligibility is determined by the student's institution, but funds are lent by private lenders like banks or credit unions, and repayment is made to those lending agencies. Students, and the parents of students, who attend institutions that do not participate in the Direct Loan program participate in the FFEL program.

Campus Based Programs

The campus based programs are the Federal Supplemental Educational Opportunity Grant (FSEOG), Federal Work Study (FWS), and the Federal Perkins Loan programs. All three programs are managed at the campus level. Funds for the three programs are allocated by the federal government directly to the institution and eligibility for awards and award amounts are determined by the campus aid officer. The federal government has established statutory limits on the amount of aid a student may receive from each of the campus based programs as well as general administrative responsibilities that apply to all three programs (U.S. Department of Education, 1995).

ADMINISTERING STUDENT AID

Sound Financial Aid Practice

The financial aid profession is founded on a set of good practices originally developed by the College Scholarship Service in 1953 (College Scholarship Service, 1989; Hart, 1989; Hart, 1991). Hart (1989) has also suggested that aid officers are directed in their professional practice by the National Association of Student Financial Aid Administrators Statement of Good Practices (National Association of Student Financial Aid Administrators, 1995b). The NASFAA Statement holds that financial aid administrators:

1. Shall make every effort to meet the demonstrated needs of all students at his or her institution to the extent funding will permit in an ethical manner.
2. Shall award all aid on the basis of demonstrated financial need except where funds are specified for recognition of special talents. Where aid is not based on need and represents a significant portion of institutional assistance, the aid administrator should make every effort to redirect such funds to assist those students with demonstrated need.
3. Shall exercise adequate controls to insure that need-based aid awards do not exceed documented need.
4. Shall recognize that the primary responsibility for financing postsecondary education rests with the student and his or her family. Financial assistance from institutions and other sources is only intended as supplementary to the efforts of the family.
5. Shall help students seek, obtain, and make the best use of all financial resources available.
6. Shall provide in all appropriate literature a clear statement of actual costs of attendance, which shall include both the direct and nondirect costs.
7. Shall inform the student of all conditions under which an award is granted at the time the offer is made.
8. Shall refrain from and discourage others from making any public announcements of the amount or type of financial aid awarded to a student in order to protect the confidentiality of the economic circumstances of the student and his or her family.

9. Shall respect the confidentiality of student records. Information should be released only on the written consent of the student and/or his or her family, and all policies and procedures should protect the student's right to privacy.
10. Shall oppose the administration of aid to accomplish disciplinary objectives.
11. Shall, when preparing funding requests, estimate needs honestly and fairly. (National Association of Student Financial Aid Administrators, 1995, p. 7)

Responsibilities and Roles

Johnstone and Huff (1983) have suggested that the financial aid administrator must fulfill the following responsibilities: serving students; informing the institutional community; promoting the program's efficiency; ensuring the program's integrity; and educating students and others. A similar list was developed by the College Scholarship service in 1973 and included the additional responsibility of research and professional development (College Scholarship Service, 1989).

The traditional roles for the student aid officer have been counseling and administrative management (Lange, 1983). Since much of financial aid administration involves the interpretation and communication of regulations, application processes, and award details to students and the management of personnel and programs, these two roles have maintained their centrality. However, the roles of student aid administrators have become more complex as the number of and types of students and programs has grown in the past 30 years (Gordon, 1994; Hart, 1991). "Today ... the financial aid world is full of individuals who emphasize computer savvy, legislation literacy, and numerical knowledge" (Gordon, 1994, p. 16). The most important trend that has shaped student aid administrators current role is the advent of technology. Other factors that have necessitated a changing role for student aid administrators include: increasing campus diversity necessitating "specialized counseling techniques and financial assistance programs" (Gordon, 1994, p. 16); increasingly complex and diverse student aid programs; customer needs and institutional enrollment management efforts (Gordon, 1994).

Structure and Staffing

Student financial aid offices are generally a part of one of the following institutional divisions: business and finance, student affairs, academic affairs, or enrollment management (Davis, Ross, Blanchard, & Bennett,

1983; Johnstone & Huff, 1983). Valid reasons exist for placing the aid office in any of those divisions, but the most reasonable placement would appear to be in either the student affairs division or the division of enrollment management. Johnstone and Huff (1983) provide an eloquent rationale for housing student aid in the student affairs division: "The office of financial aid reports to the dean of students or vice president for student affairs not merely because it is manifestly a 'helping' service but because it must have extensive communication with all the offices that deal closely with the out-of-classroom problems of students; also, it must share the basic 'helping' orientation traditionally associated with student affairs" (p. 249). The value of linking student aid to the enrollment management function of the university is examined in the section on practice paradigms. As is the case with many organizational decisions, the final disposition of the student aid office within the organization will be a result of institutional mission (DeJarnett, 1975), the personal preference and expertise of the aid administrator (Adams, 1975), historical accident, or institutional politics.

A 1987–88 study of student aid office staffing patterns disclosed that, like many other student affairs functional areas, the student aid profession is predominately female (Knapp, 1989). While the majority of student aid administrators are women (81 percent), they constitute only a small majority (53 percent) of senior student financial aid administrators (Knapp, 1989). The most prevalent title of the senior student financial aid administrator was Director (85 percent), while two percent of the respondents carried the title Vice-President/Dean. Student aid offices tended to be small; 12 percent of the offices responding to the survey indicated they only employed a single student aid administrator; 27 percent reported two full-time staff members; and 81 percent reported six or fewer staff members. Larger staffs tended to be found at larger institutions; the number of full-time staff members at public institutions with undergraduate enrollments over 30,000 ranged from four to thirty, with a median of 29.5 (Knapp, 1989).

Practice Models

Student financial aid administrators have not grasped student development as either a philosophical foundation for their work or as a guide to professional practice. Few direct applications of student development concepts to the field exist. One of the few attempts to connect student aid administration and student development theory has been proposed by Coomes (1992). In addition to providing an overview of the theoretical work of Chickering (1969) and Perry (1968), Coomes offered insights into the ways that those theories could help student aid administrators understand student behavior and suggested ways student aid practices could be effectively grounded in developmental theory. Perry's scheme was used to suggest a more educational response for students who are on financial aid probation (i.e., students who do not maintain satisfactory academic progress must improve their academic standing or relinquish their financial aid) by requiring them "to seek and document assistance from the institution's study skills or academic assistance center" (p. 28). Suggestions were offered for assisting students to develop a sense of interpersonal competence and for fostering a sense of purpose (Chickering, 1969, Chickering & Reisser, 1994) through student employment positions. Other applications included using Perry as a framework for more effective student debt counseling and for the development of financial aid publications.

In lieu of student development as a guiding rationale, many student aid administrators have embraced the concepts of the total quality movement (Chaffee & Sherr, 1992, Deming, 1986, Seymour, 1992). Starting in 1983, the Department of Education introduced the Institutional Quality Control Project "encouraging higher education institutions to engage in a self-verification/self-monitoring model of improving quality in the management of financial aid" (Gordon, 1991, p. 24). The Institutional Quality Control Project was originally intended as a means to encourage select institutions to more carefully shepherd federal student aid resources through the careful verification of student aid application information. Institutions which chose to participate in the program were given considerable autonomy in determining how they would implement institution specific verification procedures (Gordon & Hart, 1989; Hart, 1989). In addition to improving the student aid application verification process, participation in the project fostered a number of unanticipated benefits, including: increased emphasis on staff development activities, increased support from upper-level management for student aid activities and programs, improved services to students, and the development of a "culture of quality" within the financial aid office characterized by "pride in work, innovation, open communication and objective setting at all levels and in all departments" (Gordon, 1991, p. 25).

Lackey and Pugh (1994) outlined a number of important benefits of total quality management (TQM). Like Gordon, they noted the importance of building a "culture of quality" based on the "need to manage the reality of an interactive and constantly changing environment in order to constantly improve" (Lackey & Pugh, 1994, p. 7). According to Lackey and Pugh the effective implementation of TQM in a student aid setting requires the realization that TQM is not just the continuation of existing quality practices, but a change in thinking "based on achieving effectiveness through being good at the right things, rather than just being good" (p. 7).

Fundamental to the TQM philosophy is the idea of continuous improvement. Total quality management is not a goal, it is the means to an end and that end is improved customer satisfaction. Total quality management is presented as a process that is continually evolving. The emphasis is on long-term gains and the development of an office culture that supports customer satisfaction and operational efficiency.

Commitment from the staff who will be implementing TQM is critical. As noted by Gordon (1991), support from senior level administrators for the integration of TQM in organizational operations is important, but Lackey and Pugh contended it is less important than a clear commitment to those principles from mid-managers and office staff. "Admittedly, TQM implementation can go more smoothly with top management commitment. Our experience, however, suggests that applying TQM internally can help us provide better services without such overall support" (p. 9).

Total quality management is predicated on a customer focus. "TQM implies that the management approach in student financial aid services may shift from assigning staff time to assist students in accurately completing forms, to reducing the student's time in the delivery system by assuring quality processing and contact services" (Lackey and Pugh, 1994, p. 10).

Finally, TQM principles encourage employee participation in the identification of organizational goals and processes and in the effective and efficient delivery of services to students and customers. "In the TQM bottom-up type of organization, control is focused at the level of the employee who must be responsive to a variety of customer wants. Managers become facilitators, typically guiding teams of employees to serve customers in a manner consistent with organizational goals" (Lackey and Pugh, 1994, p. 10).

A third practice paradigm that is influencing the operation of many student aid offices is enrollment management (Hossler, 1984, 1986a, 1986b; Hossler & Bean, 1990a; Scannell, 1992). The definition of enrollment management, the reasons for its development, and suggestions for implementing enrollment management within an institutional setting are offered in this volume by Hossler. The financial aid office and the efficient delivery of student aid resources has important implications for student matriculation and persistence (Graff, 1986). The financial aid office must work with the offices of admissions to ensure that students receive all the aid for which they are eligible and that students "receive their awards in a timely fashion" (Hossler & Bean, 1990b, p. 8). By improving services to students and ensuring effective cooperation and communication between other service areas (e.g., bursar and registrar) the financial aid office can assist in the removal of structural barriers which may influence student persistence. Finally, the financial aid office has an important responsibility within the enrollment management paradigm to participate in the development of research on the relationship of student aid to student recruitment and persistence and the accomplishment of institutional objectives (Huff, 1989; Nelson & Fenske, 1983; Wilcox, 1991).

Enrollment management models similar to those described by Hossler (1984, 1986) appear to provide student aid offices with the most useful practice paradigm. Such an approach not only ensures that student aid is playing a critical role in the recruitment and retention of students but that it is supporting the overall mission of the institution. Total quality concepts would appear to provide the student aid administrator with a set of tools that can enhance office operations and improve services to the customer-student. Aid officers are encouraged to consider how to effectively wed concepts from enrollment management and total quality improvement to realize the goals of effective service and enhanced student recruitment and retention efforts.

PROFESSIONAL DEVELOPMENT

Professional Associations

The National Association of Student Financial Aid Administrators (NASFAA) was founded as the National Student Aid Council in October 1966 (Brooks, 1986). NASFAA had its roots in a number of organizations including the College Scholarship Service and its parent organization the College Board, Commission V of the American College Personnel Association, and a number of regional student aid officer associations (e.g., Midwest Association of Student Financial Aid Administrators). The development of NASFAA was a result of the increasingly complex nature of student aid brought about by the creation of such programs as the National Direct Student Loan and the Supplemental Educational Opportunity Grant and by the emergence of campus administrative units focusing specifically on the administration of student aid resources.

The National Association of Student Financial Aid Administrators "exists to promote the professional preparation, effectiveness, and mutual support of persons involved in student financial aid administration. NASFAA works with others in institutions of postsecondary education, government agencies, foundations, private and community organizations, and regional and state financial aid associations who are concerned with the support and administration of student financial aid" (National Association of Student Financial Aid Administrators, 1995b, p. 23). To realize this goal, the Association serves as a forum for the discussion of student aid related issues, sponsors research on student aid and its impact on students and institutions, offers a wide-range of training opportunities and materials for new and experienced aid officers, advocates on behalf of students and institutions with student aid policy makers, and facilitates the development of professional identity through publications and national conferences.

The National Association of Student Financial Aid Administrators maintains four classes of members; institutional members, affiliate members, constituent member, and student members (National Association of Student Financial Aid Administrators, 1995b). In 1995, NASFAA consisted of 2,992 institutional members, 28 affiliate members, 264 constituent members, and 8 student members for a total membership of 3292 (NASFAA, 1995a).

Structurally, NASFAA consists of the membership headed by a National Chairperson, a Board of Directors, and an Executive Committee. The work of the Association is conducted by a number of committees, task forces and administrative groups like the Association Governance Committee, the Needs Analyses Committee, the Membership Development Committee, the Task Force on the Development of Financial Aid Standards, and the Multi-Cultural Initiatives Committee (National Association of Student Financial Aid Administrators, 1995b). Like many other student affairs professional associations, the NASFAA membership has empowered a full-time management staff with the responsibility to oversee the day-to-day operation of the organization. That staff, based in Washington, DC, is headed by a president and consists of the following divisions: Finance and Administration, Communications, Governmental Affairs, Program Planning and Development, and Professional Development, and Training Contract (National Association of Student Financial Aid Administrators, 1995b).

The Associations two most important roles are advocacy and professional development. Since 1972, the Association has played an important role in shaping federal student aid policy. Brooks (1986) has commented that: "Its [NASFAA's] involvement with the higher education policy arena has moved from practically nil to a position of leadership within two decades" (p. 121). Because of the highly complex and technical nature of many of the student aid programs, NASFAA has carefully built and nurtured a reputation as the voice of expertise with many student aid policy makers. Few other student affairs associations can point to as successful a record in shaping and influencing federal education policy as can NASFAA.

Since its inception, NASFAA has recognized the need to foster professional development and training among its members. To assist in that process, NASFAA holds an annual national conference and conducts a wide-range of technical training programs. In addition to conferences, NASFAA supports training and professional development through a number of publications. The *NASFAA Encyclopedia* is one of the most comprehensive sources of information on the federal student aid programs available. General Association news, legislative and agency updates, and current events in the financial aid arena are covered by the bi-weekly *NASFAA Newsletter.* The *NASFAA Newsletter* is complemented by the *NASFAA Federal Monitor* which reprints relevant issues of the *Federal Register* as well as other documents focusing on legislation and regulation of the federal student aid programs. Research on student aid related issues is published three times a year in the *Journal of Student Financial Aid* and opinion and practice oriented articles see print in the Association's magazine the *Financial Aid Transcript.* In addition to print media, NASFAA utilizes electronic media like the NASFAA Hot Line and its own proprietary software, computing services, and data bases—the Postsecondary Education Network (PEN)—to keep members informed about programmatic changes, legislative events, and administrative decisions ("PEN," n.d.).

The work of NASFAA is complemented by six regional student aid associations (e.g., the Midwest Association of Student Financial Aid Administrators, the Western Association of Student Financial Aid Administrators). In addition each of the 50 states, Puerto Rico, and the District of Columbia have their own state associations of student aid administrators. Regional and state associations focus on issues of importance to their specific areas and ensure that student aid resources like newsletters, training meetings, and conferences are available to administrators who may not be able to take advantage of or participate in activities sponsored by the national association.

Entry Level Qualifications

Ryan (1983) has noted:

> The financial aid profession, unlike most other student service professions, has not established any preservice programs. Consequently, completion of such formal educational programs has not been required for admission to the profession. Instead, the financial aid profession has been responsible for establishing its own standards of professionalism and in-service training programs. (p. 211)

Entry level professional staff positions carry a variety of titles including Counselor at larger institutions and Assistant Director at smaller institutions. Prior experience working in financial aid appears to be more important in hiring entry level professionals than does education level. Most entry level positions require a minimum of a bachelor's degree with a master's degree preferred. A 1987–1989 survey of student financial aid personnel disclosed that only 20 percent of student aid counselors had earned either master's, professional, or doctoral degrees; 66 percent of all counselors held at least a bachelor's degree (Knapp, 1989). Since financial aid administration combines counseling, programmatic oversight, financial management, and technological expertise, no single type of degree is essential; entry level professionals can hold degrees in college student personnel, business, or the liberal arts. Most hiring officers seek well-rounded individuals with prior experience in the financial aid field. As Reisinger (personal communication, July 19, 1995) noted: "While extensive training will have to occur [for] any new person in the office, it helps to have someone who knows what needs analysis is, and who just needs to be trained in the University policies rather than an entire course on what is financial aid and how . . . it works." Relevant experience for entry level professional is frequently gained through graduate internships, employment in related fields (e.g., banking), or quite often through undergraduate student employment in a student aid office.

With the exception of a strong orientation toward quantitative work and a need for attention to detail, the personal and professional qualities necessary to be an effective student aid administrator are similar to those for other student affairs professionals. New professionals must be adaptable, open to learning about the institution's and profession's philosophy and mission, able to get along with others, willing to participate in on-going professional development and training, self-reliant, and able to tolerate a high level of stress and ambiguity. Henning (personal communication, July 19, 1995) summarized the qualities he looks for in hiring a new professional:

> A new professional should demonstrate a sincere interest in assisting students and have some understanding of developmental theory as it applies to young adults. The ability to multi-task is crucial, as is the ability to effectively counsel. Good presentation skills are desired, as much computer knowledge as possible is required, and all new professionals should have a desire to participate in professional associations.

ISSUES AND TRENDS

The issues and trends facing student aid policy makers and administrators are the same issues and trends facing higher education in general. These include demands from the public and their elected representatives for increased accountability, rising costs, limited resources, a rapidly changing student clientele that is becoming increasingly diverse on a number of dimensions (e.g., race and ethnicity, socioeconomic status, academic perpetration and ability), the technological revolution, and declining public confidence in the value of a postsecondary education.

In 1988, Coomes identified the following issues as having particular salience for the student aid field: (1) Overregulation, (2) Changing student populations, (3) Student debt levels, (3) Limits on access to postsecondary education brought about reductions in aid for the neediest students (see also Kean, 1995), (4) A growing financial need gap, and (5) Deficit reduction. Many of those issues are currently salient and will continue to shape student aid policy and administration in the future. To the list could be added such issues as alternative financing plans for postsecondary education, e.g., increased support for merit scholarships (Allan, 1988; Massa, 1991) or college savings and prepayment plans (College Entrance Examination Board, 1988); program complexity; the credentialling and professional preparation of student aid administrators (Russo & Woolridge, 1991; Shelley, 1988; Stillwagon, 1991); student loan default issues (Bennett, 1990); increasing technological demands, and fiscal accountability (Hansen, 1991). Three of these issues, deficit reduction, programmatic complexity, and the paradox of technology, warrant closer attention.

Deficit Reduction

A perennial problem with student aid programs has been adequate funding (Coomes, 1988). Institutions, states, and the federal government face significant demands on financial resources. The mid-term election of 1994 resulted in the election of a fiscally conservative Congress that has set deficit reduction as one of its primary goals. As a major item in the federal budget, the federal student assistance programs are logical targets for budget reductions. Most likely targets for the budget-cutting ax are the student loan programs; some Congressional proposals in 1994 suggested cutting an estimated $12.4 billion over five years from the Federal Direct and Federal Family Educational Loan Programs (Martin, 1995). Interventions to realize those savings include the elimination of the in-school interest subsidy for the two programs and/or the elimination of the Direct loan program which is perceived to be a duplication of the FFEL program. Other deficit reduction proposals have included proposals to eliminate the SSIG program, and some of the campus-based programs like the Federal Supplemental Educational Opportunity Grant or the Federal Perkins Loan (Martin, 1995).

In 1995, the NASFAA Board of Directors responded to the push for deficit reduction by approving two resolutions. The first of those resolutions outlined a set of principles which should be maintained in the federal loan programs (e.g., allowing institutions the choice of participating in either the Direct Loan of FFEL program). The second resolution opposed eliminating the interest subsidy for need-based federal loans. The resolutions stated:

The Board of Directors is fully cognizant of the budgetary problems which confront the United States and is supportive of Congressional efforts to reduce the federal deficit. . . . The Board of Directors wishes to express its desire to help Congress achieve responsible deficit reduction; however, the Board remains steadfast in its belief that the federal student financial aid programs have not over the past 15 years contributed to the nation's deficit. . . . Therefore, the Board of Directors encourages Congress to maintain its current investment in the federal student assistance programs. (Martin, 1995, p. 10)

Deficit reduction has been an on-going concern since the mid-1980s; how it will be realized, and the role the federal student assistance programs will play in that process remains to be seen.

Programmatic Complexity

If the student aid system is not broken, then it is certainly badly damaged. The system is overly complicated, rigid and confusing to students and parents (Hansen, 1991). Multiple programs exist and program goals are unclear. Of particular concern to policy makers has been the student aid delivery system (Fitzgerald, 1991). The Education Amendments of 1992 corrected some of the problems of the student aid delivery system by instituting a single application and needs-analysis process for all federal need-based student aid programs. However, institutions and states, may use other methods for determining eligibility for their resources. Fitzgerald (1991) has suggested a number of ways to simplify and integrate needs analysis, reduce regulations, and streamline the application process. The latter task is particularly important as the complexity of the application (the Free Application for Federal Student Aid contains 105 data elements) and the application process itself certainly deters some students and families from applying for and, therefore, receiving assistance. Suggestions for streamlining the process include moving away from paper application to electronic data entry and updating existing application data, rather than submitting completely new applications each year (Fitzgerald, 1991). Extensive discussion of using total quality management principles to improve the entire federal student aid delivery process have been offered by the Panel on Quality Improvement in Student Financial Aid (Fesco, 1993). As is the case with office operation, the use of TQM principles may provide quittance for necessary reforms leading to simplification of the student aid delivery system.

The redundant nature of the federal student aid programs must also be addressed. As noted earlier, the federal student aid programs developed over a period of 35 years and were created to respond to a wide-range of policy imperatives. It is time to look at the entire system with an eye toward simplification. Program duplication is a problem (Can three federal loan programs be justified?). However, simplification raises one important concern. For a number of years, eliminating program duplication has been proffered as a way to reduce governmental funding for student aid. Fiscal concerns are valid, but the needs of students who want to attend postsecondary education would support not less funding for student aid but additional funding. Simplification coupled with adequate financial support for student would be in the best interest of individual students, postsecondary institutions, and the nation.

The Dilemma of Technology

The highly quantitative, formalized, and routinized (Hage & Aiken, 1970) nature of much of student aid work (e.g., needs analysis, student data verification, student aid packaging) makes it a student affairs area particularly appropriate for the application of technology (Thompson, 1992). The complexities of the student aid programs and the numbers of students applying for and receiving assistance makes it nearly impossible, even at small institutions, to administer the student aid programs without the use of a wide-range of technological resources (Gordon, 1992; Hart, 1991; Thompson, 1992). The advent of technology in student aid has not come without attendant costs. Sears (1994) contended that student aid administrators have become technocrats who are more interested in "information than ideas" and who have the responsibility to "hone ideas and rearrange facts as the political process unfolds in new and different ways" (p. 18). Many aid administrators have become more "process-oriented," attending to the demands of programs rather than "client-services oriented," attending to needs of students (Gordon, 1994). An unfortunate side-effect of this process and program orientation is the perception that student aid officers are bureaucratic information managers interested more in regulatory compliance and legislative interpretation, than educators interested in meeting the needs of students. Technological applications in student financial aid have traditionally been targeted at information management systems designed to at increases efficiency and effectiveness (Gordon, 1992). Once student aid offices put into place state-of-the-art information management systems, and if those systems remain relatively stable (an outcome that will be determined to a significant degree by minimizing changes in student aid programs), then student aid administrators will be able to turn their attention to utilizing technology to improve services to students.

REFERENCES

Adams, F. C. (1975). Administering the office of student work and financial assistance. In R. Keene, F. C. Adams, & J. E. King, *Money, marbles, or chalk: Student financial support in higher education* (pp. 214–228). Carbondale, IL: Southern Illinois University Press.

Allan, G. (1988, Summer). No need for no-need. *Journal of College Admissions, 120,* 23–26.

Bennett, M. A. (1990, Winter). The future is now? *Student Aid Transcript, 2* (4), 8–9.

Berkes, J. (1989, Spring). A guide to packaging principles. *Student aid transcript, 2* (1), 10–12.

Binder, S. F. (1983). Meeting student needs with different types of financial aid awards. In R. H. Fenske, R. P. Huff, & Associates, *Handbook of student financial aid: Programs, procedures and policies* (pp. 149–168). San Francisco: Jossey-Bass.

Boyd, J. D., & Henning, G. E. Using student aid in recruiting and admissions. In R. H. Fenske, R. P. Huff, & Associates, *Handbook of student financial aid: Programs, procedures and policies* (pp. 307–329). San Francisco: Jossey-Bass.

Brooks, S. (1986). *NASFAA—The first twenty years: An organizational history of the National Association of Student Financial Aid Administrators, 1966–1986.* Washington, DC: National Association of Student Financial Aid Administrators.

Brubacher, J. S. & Rudy, W. (1976). *Higher education in transition: A history of American colleges and universities, 1963–1976.* New York: Harper-Row.

Burns, R. K. (1984). *The NASFAA encyclopedia of student financial aid.* Washington, DC: National Association of Student Financial Aid Administrators.

Case, J. P. (1983). Determining financial need. In R. H. Fenske, R. P. Huff, & Associates, *Handbook of student financial aid: Programs, procedures and policies* (pp. 124–148). San Francisco: Jossey-Bass.

Case, J. P. (1990, Spring). Is simpler always better? Principles, politics, and budgets. *Journal of Student Financial Aid, 20* (2), 40–45.

Case, J. P. (1993). *Professional judgment in eligibility determination and resource analysis.* (NASFAA Monograph No. 9). Washington, DC: National Association of Student Financial Aid Administrators.

Case, K. E. (1990, Spring). Principles, politics, and budgets. *Journal of Student Financial Aid, 20* (2), 35–36.

Chaffee, E. E., & Sherr, L. A. (1992). *Quality: Transforming postsecondary education* (ASHE–ERIC Report No. 3). Washington, DC: ASHE–ERIC.

Chickering, A. W. (1969). *Education and identity.* San Francisco: Jossey-Bass.

Chickering, A. W., & Reisser, L. (1993). *Education and identity* (Rev. ed.). San Francisco: Jossey-Bass.

College Entrance Examination Board. (1988). *Invitational conference on college prepayment and savings plans.* New York: Author.

College Scholarship Service. (1989). *Manual for student aid administrators: 1990–1991 policies and procedures.* New York: College Entrance Examination Board.

Conlan, T. J. (1981). *The federal role in the federal system: The dynamics of growth. The evolution of a problematic partnership: The Feds and higher ed.* Washington, DC: Advisory Commission on Intergovernmental Relations.

Coomes, M. D. (1988). Student financial aid. In A. L. Rentz, & G. L. Saddlemire (Eds.), *Student affairs functions in higher education* (pp. 155–184). Springfield, IL: Charles C Thomas.

Coomes, M. D. (1992). Understanding students: A developmental approach to financial aid services. *Journal of Student Financial Aid, 22* (2), 23–31.

Coomes, M. D. (1994). A history of federal involvement in the lives of students. In M. D. Coomes & D. D. Gehring, (Eds.), *Student services in a changing federal climate* (*New Directions for Student Services, No. 68,* pp. 5–27). San Francisco: Jossey-Bass.

Dannells, M. (1977). Financial aid. In W. T. Packwood (Ed.), *College student personnel services* (pp. 51–91). Springfield, IL: Charles C Thomas.

Davis, J. S. (1990, Spring). Barriers to implementation of general need analysis for all federal financial aid programs. *Journal of Student Financial Aid, 20* (2), 45–50.

Davis, J. S., Ross, J., Blanchard, S. G., & Bennett, R. (1983). *A profession in transition: Characteristics and attitudes of the financial aid administrator Fall, 1981.* Washington, DC: National Association of Student Financial Aid Administrators.

DeJarnett, R. P. (1975). The organization of student support programs in institutions of higher learning. In R. Keene, F. C. Adams, & J. E. King, *Money, marbles, or chalk: Student financial support in higher education* (pp. 206–213). Carbondale, IL: Southern Illinois University Press.

DeLoughry, T. J. (1992, April 22). College officials say politics and budgetary constraints doomed reauthorization bill's promise of reform. *The Chronicle of Higher Education,* pp. A29, A34–A35.

Deming, W. E. (1986). *Out of crisis.* Cambridge, MA: Center for Advanced Engineering Study.

Eaton, J. S. (1991). *The unfinished agenda: Higher education in the 1980s.* New York: Macmillan.

Fenske, R. H. (1983). Student aid past and present. In R. H. Fenske, R. P. Huff, & Associates, *Handbook of student financial aid: Programs, procedures and policies* (pp. 5–26). San Francisco: Jossey-Bass.

Fesco, R. S. (Ed.). (1993). *Quality in student financial aid programs.* Washington, DC: National Academy Press.

Finn, C. E., Jr. (1985). Why do we need financial aid? or, Desanctifying student assistance. In College Entrance Examination Board, *An agenda for the year 2000: Thirtieth anniversary colloquia proceeding* (pp. 1–23). New York: College Entrance Examination Board.

Fisher, F. J. (1990, Spring). Toward the use of a single needs analysis (or virtue may be more than its own reward). *Journal of Student Financial Aid, 20* (2), 6–34.

Fitzgerald, B. K. (1991). Simplification of need analysis and aid delivery: Imperatives and opportunities. In J. P. Merisotis, (Ed.), *The changing dimensions of student aid* (New Directions for Higher Education, No. 74, pp. 43–63), San Francisco: Jossey-Bass.

Gehring, D. D. (1994a). Protective policy laws. In M. D. Coomes & D. D. Gehring, (Eds.), *Student services in a changing federal climate* (*New Directions for Student Services, No. 68*, pp. 67–82). San Francisco: Jossey-Bass.

Gehring, D. D. (1994b). The federal university. In M. D. Coomes & D. D. Gehring, (Eds.), *Student services in a changing federal climate* (*New Directions for Student Services, No. 68*, pp. 93–110). San Francisco: Jossey-Bass.

Gladieux, L. E. (1983). Future directions of student aid. In R. H. Fenske, R. P. Hage, J., & Aiken, M. (1970). *Social change in complex organizations.* New York: Random House.

Huff & Associates, *Handbook of student financial aid: Programs, procedures and policies* (pp. 399–433). San Francisco: Jossey-Bass.

Gladieux, L. E. & Wolanin, T. R. (1976). *Congress and the colleges: The national politics of higher education.* Lexington, Mass.: Lexington Books.

Godzicki, R. J. (1975). A history of financial aids in the United States. In R. Keene, F. C. Adams, & J. E. King, *Money, marbles, or chalk: Student financial support in higher education* (pp. 14–21). Carbondale, IL: Southern Illinois University Press.

Gordon, L. E. (1990/1991, Fall/Winter). Cultivating a quality culture. *Student Aid Transcript, 3* (3), 24–25.

Gordon, L. E. (1992, Summer). The computing generation gap. *Student Aid Transcript, 5* (1), 7–9.

Gordon, L. E. (1994, Spring). Sounding board: From counselor to technician. *Financial aid transcript, 6* (2), 16–17.

Gordon, L. E., & Hart, T. (1989, Winter). Verification—100% or less: Use of the Quality Control Pilot Project. *Journal of Student Financial Aid, 19* (1), 63–65.

Graff, A. S. (1986). Organizing the resources that can be effective. In D. Hossler, (Ed.). *Managing college enrollments: New Directions for Higher Education, No. 53* (pp. 89–101). San Francisco: Jossey-Bass.

Hansen, J. (1991). The roots of federal student aid policy. In J. P. Merisotis, (Ed.), *The changing dimensions of student aid* (New Directions for Higher Education, No. 74, pp. 3–19). San Francisco: Jossey-Bass.

Hart, N. (1989, Winter). Assessing our ethics. *Student Aid Transcript, 1* (4), 18–19.

Hart, N. K. (1991). Constant response to change: The role of the financial aid office. In J. P. Merisotis, (Ed.), *The changing dimensions of student aid* (New Directions for Higher Education, No. 74, pp. 65–73), San Francisco: Jossey-Bass.

Heffron, M. (1990, Spring). Philosophy behind needs analysis methods. *Journal of Student Financial Aid, 20* (2), 37–39.

Hossler, D. (1984). *Enrollment management: An integrated approach.* New York: College Entrance Examination Board.

Hossler, D. (1986a). *Creating effective enrollment management systems.* New York: College Entrance Examination Board.

Hossler, D. (1986b). Enrollment management and its context. In D. Hossler, (Ed.).

Managing college enrollments: New Directions for Higher Education, No. 53 (pp. 5–14). San Francisco: Jossey-Bass.

Hossler, D., & Bean, J. P. (Eds.) (1990). *The strategic management of college enrollments.* San Francisco: Jossey-Bass.

Hossler, D., & Bean, J. P. (1990). Principles and objectives. In D. Hossler & J. P. Bean, (Eds.), *The strategic management of college enrollments* (pp. 3–20). San Francisco: Jossey-Bass.

Huff, R. P. (1989). Facilitating and applying research in student financial aid to institutional objectives. In R. H. Fenske, (Ed.), *Studying the impact of student aid on institutions* (*New Directions for Institutional Research, No. 62,* pp. 5–16). San Francisco: Jossey-Bass.

Johnstone, D. B., & Huff, R. P. (1983). Relationship of student aid to other college programs and services. In R. H. Fenske, R. P. Huff, & Associates, *Handbook of student financial aid: Programs, procedures and policies* (pp. 237–257). San Francisco: Jossey-Bass.

Kean, T. H. (1995, Winter). A crisis of access is coming to campus. *Student Aid Transcript, 6* (4), 16–17.

Knapp, K. (1989). *Salary and staffing patterns in financial aid offices: 1987–1988.* Washington, DC: National Association of Student Financial Aid Administrators.

Knapp, L. G. (1992). *Trends in student aid: 1982 to 1992.* Washington, DC: The College Entrance Examination Board.

Lackey, C. W., & Pugh, S. L. (1994, Winter). With TQM, less is more for students. *Student Aid Transcript, 6* (2), 7–11.

Lange, M. L. (1983). Factors in organizing and effective student aid office. In R. H. Fenske, R. P. Huff, & Associates, *Handbook of student financial aid: Programs, procedures and policies* (pp. 221–236). San Francisco: Jossey-Bass.

Marmaduke, A. S. (1983). State student aid programs. In R. H. Fenske, R. P. Huff, & Associates, *Handbook of student financial aid: Programs, procedures and policies* (pp. 55–76). San Francisco: Jossey-Bass.

Martin, D. (1995, May 8). Letter to the members. *NASFAA Newsletter, 27* (7), 7–10.

Massa, R. J. (1991, Spring). Merit scholarships and student recruitment: Goals and strategies. *Journal of College Admission, 131,* 10–14.

Moore, J. W. (1983). Purposes and provisions of federal programs. In R. H. Fenske, R. P. Huff, & Associates, *Handbook of student financial aid: Programs, procedures and policies* (pp. 27–54). San Francisco: Jossey-Bass.

Mueller, K. H. (1961). *Student personnel work in higher education.* Boston: Houghton-Mifflin.

National Association of Student Financial Aid Administrators. (1993, April). *Constructing student expense budgets* (NASFAA Monograph No. 9). Washington, DC: Author.

National Association of Student Financial Aid Administrators. (1995a). *NASFAA Commission and committee handbook.* Washington, DC: Author.

National Association of Student Financial Aid Administrators. (1995b). *NASFAA national membership directory.* Washington, DC: Author.

Nelson, J. E., & Fenske, R. H. (1983). Strategies for improving research, projections, and policy development. In R. H. Fenske, R. P. Huff, & Associates, *Handbook of student financial aid: Programs, procedures and policies* (pp. 285–306). San Francisco: Jossey-Bass.

Parsons, M. D. (1994). *Power and politics: A study of power in the higher education policy arena.* Unpublished doctoral dissertation, Indiana University, Bloomington.

PEN: "We're cruising down the information superhighway of life with PEN". (n.d.). Washington, DC: National Association of Student Financial Aid Administrators.

Perry, W. G., Jr. (1968). *Forms of intellectual and ethical development in the college years: A scheme.* New York: Holt, Rinehart, & Winston.

Rivlin, A. (1961). *The role of the federal government in financing higher education.* Washington, DC: Brookings Institute.

Russo, J., & Wooldridge, C. (1991, Spring). Graduate courses that help you grow. *Student Aid Transcript, 3* (4), 9–10.

Ryan, D. R. (1983). Staffing the aid office and improving professional expertise. In R. H. Fenske, R. P. Huff, & Associates, *Handbook of student financial aid: Programs, procedures and policies* (pp. 194–220). San Francisco: Jossey-Bass.

Scannell, J. J. (1992). *The effect of financial aid policies on admissions and enrollment.* New York: College Entrance Examination Board.

Sears, K. R. (1994, Spring). Sounding board: How we evolved. *Financial aid transcript, 6* (2), 18–19.

Seymour, D. T. (1992). *On Q: Causing quality in higher education.* New York: American Council on Education/Macmillan.

Shelley, R. (1988, Fall). Credentialing: What is there to lose? *Student Aid Transcript, 1* (3), 24–25.

Stillwagon, R. C. (1991, Spring). Adventures in graduate education. *Student Aid Transcript, 3* (4), 8.

The nation. (1995, September). *Chronicle of Higher Education: Almanac Issue, 42* (1), 8.

The nation: Students. (1995, September 1). *Chronicle of Higher Education: Almanac Issue, 42* (1), p. 12.

Thompson, K. (1992, Summer). Adventures in automation. *Student Aid Transcript, 5* (1), 10–11.

U.S. Department of Education. (1994a). *Counselor's handbook for postsecondary schools.* Washington, DC: United States Government Printing Office.

U.S. Department of Education. (1994b). *Direct loans: A new way to borrow.* Washington, DC: United States Government Printing Office.

U.S. Department of Education. (1994c). *Financial aid from the U.S. Department of Education: The student guide, 1995–1996.* Washington, DC: United States Government Printing Office.

U.S. Department of Education. (1995). *The federal student financial aid handbook.* Washington, DC: United States Government Printing Office.

U.S. Department of Education. (n.d.). *All about direct loans: William D. Ford Federal Direct Loan Program; 1995–1996.* Washington, DC: United States Government Printing Office.

Wilcox, L. (1991). Evaluating the impact of financial aid on student recruitment. In D. Hossler, (Ed.), *Evaluating student recruitment and retention programs* (*New Directions for Institutional Research, No. 70,* pp. 47–60). San Francisco: Jossey-Bass.

Wolanin, T. R. (1990, Spring). A political perspective on need analysis. *Journal of Student Financial Aid, 20* (2), 50–52.

Chapter 13

STUDENT HEALTH

Josh Kaplan, Edward G. Whipple, and Jeanne Wright

HISTORY

Student health care has been a part of American higher education since the beginning days at Harvard. However, from the 1660s until the mid 1850s, the health of students was viewed as the responsibility of the student with institutions assuming no responsibility nor expressing any concern about it. Depending on students' socioeconomic class, they were expected to seek aid from medical personnel in surrounding communities or were left to turn to the charitable nature of a local citizen who might offer financial assistance (Farnsworth, 1965 as cited in Saddlemire, 1988).

The gymnastic period of higher education, starting about 1825, was an opportunity to introduce German and Scandinavian methods to promote physical exercise to American college and university campuses (Packwood, 1977). At Amherst College in 1859, Dr. Edward Hitchock, labelled the father of college health by Boynton (1962) was the first professor of hygiene to provide student health services. The philosophy that guided his practice and treatment of students was that the "body and mind should work together harmoniously and (he) offered health education lectures on such topics as tobacco use, skin care, and venereal disease (VD) (Saddlemire, 1988, p. 185). Later, in 1861, Amherst created the first comprehensive department of hygiene and physical education. The college provided for annual examinations, instruction on hygiene, regular physical exercise, and statistics on student illness and treatment (Boynton, 1971).

Concerns among the faculty for campus living conditions, the potential threats from contagious diseases and an interest in promoting mental health led to the creation of faculty committees which began inspecting student living quarters. As athletic programs grew in size and stature, teams were provided with what today is known as a "team doctor" who also began to treat nonathletes as well. Student infirmaries were soon created to care for students unable to remain in their rooms. Princeton University claims the first higher education infirmary in 1893, followed by the first student health service in 1901 at the University of California (Boynton, 1962).

The American College Health Association (ACHA), founded in 1920 as the American Student Health Association, has been instrumental in promoting health education, medical services, and addressing current health-related issues. The ACHA's latest Recommended Standards and Practices for a College Health Program (1991) list the following as general characteristics of a college health program: community responsibility; ethical principles; patient and provider—shared responsibilities; student participation; sexuality education, counseling, and health; mental health, counseling, and psychotherapy services, college health clinicians; support staff; dental health; athletic, sports, and recreation medicine; and physically challenged students.

Student health services grew slowly until the 1960s. During this period, there was a focus on public health care and prevention. Students frequently turned to other health sources than their campus service for information and help with VD, drug use, mental health issues, and contraception. Consequently, college health centers were made more comprehensive as reflected in the following areas of recommended programs suggested by the ACHA in 1977: "(1) outpatient and inpatient services, (2) mental health, (3) athletic medicine, (4) dental services, (5) rehabilitation/physical medicine, (6) preventive medicine, (7) health education and promotion, (8) environmental health and safety, and (9) occupational health" (Saddlemire, 1988, p. 187). The need for colleges and universities to establish and provide health care for their students was evident:

> The mission for health centers remained relatively unchanged until the late 1960s and early 1970s, when the social and cultural revolution sweeping our nation altered forever the way colleges and universities dealt with students. The sexual liberation movement, the popularization of drug and alcohol use on campuses, and an aggressive new student activism brought change to the student health agenda. These new issues demanded new approaches: drug and alcohol treatment and education programs; specialized services, such as women's clinics offering gynecologic and contraceptive services; and many others. And during this period, students became much more vocal in expressing their discontent with campus agencies or services that were not meeting their needs. All of these

forces served as catalysts leading to the health centers that we see on today's campuses (Bridwell & Kinder, pp. 481–482).

Today, college and university student health services are affected by many of the issues facing health care in the United States. Citing the increasing complexity of higher education campuses, the American College Health Association wrote in College Health 2000: Strategies of the Future (1991):

> Higher education, and more specifically college health, can be effective only to the degree that those in the field remain responsive to the needs of the larger community in which they operate. College and university campuses, reflecting changes occurring throughout the nation, are becoming increasingly rich in their diversity. Campuses are becoming more heterogeneous environments with respect to ethnicity, age, and religious preference, and more open with respect to sexual orientation. Health services must increase their sensitivity and assume leadership in understanding the issues and special needs of the many different populations comprising the campus community (p. 1).

MISSION

The ACHA's *Recommended Standards for a College Health Program* (1991) furnish a guide for providing health services for students, and health and safety services for the institution. The standards are based on several important assumptions: (1) that physical and mental health have an important impact on social issues; (2) that college health services can play a major role in encouraging students to attend to these issues; and (3) that college students are particularly receptive to education and self-exploration. It is essential that the scope of health services extend beyond treatment of illness, to encompass disease prevention and health promotion. Further, health services must meet the special needs of diverse student populations, including international students; single parents; returning students; gay, lesbian and bisexual students; the physically and mentally challenged; and students with special health needs.

Disease prevention and health promotion require a broad range of activities. Health services must contribute to the development of policies for immunization requirements, policies on alcohol and other drug abuse, policies on suicide and homicide threats, and policies on sexual harassment and assault. Health services should participate in planning emergency responses, and in programs to deal with potential health hazards associated with sanitation facilities, chemistry and biology labs, and food service. Health services must support intercollegiate athletics, intramurals, recreational athletics and physical education by developing programs for prevention, conditioning, early recognition of injury, treatment and rehabilitation. Health education programs should address alcohol and other drug abuse, nutrition, sexuality issues, prevention of sexually transmitted disease, and stress management. Clinical counseling and psychotherapy services must be used for prevention, in addition to early intervention and treatment, through outreach and educational programs.

A college health service responds to illnesses that encompass all of medicine. Many problems are minor, but severe problems occur as well. For example, in a single year a typical college health service might see students with cancer, serious infections, endocrine disorders, neurologic and psychiatric disease, all potentially severe. Fingar (1989) reported that in one year, a single college health physician saw 5,748 patients, with 505 different diagnoses. However, 50 percent of the visits were accounted for by just 23 diagnoses. When diagnoses, which are very specific, were grouped, 70 percent of visits were accounted for by the following thirteen groups: respiratory infection, routine gynecological exams, gynecological disorders, viral infection, urinary disorders, dermatitis, joint pain, conjunctivitis, sprains, psychological disorders, abdominal pain, ulcer/gastritis, superficial injury.

ADMINISTRATION

A college health service may provide care to students only, or may serve an entire university community, including faculty, staff, and dependents. The range of health care services may vary widely as well. Smaller health services may provide only first aid and referral. At the other end of the spectrum are comprehensive clinics that provide a pharmacy, radiologic imaging, laboratory, physical therapy, and care by medical and surgical specialists. Factors that predispose toward more comprehensive services include a larger student body, a residential campus, and lower availability of services in the immediate surrounding community.

The extreme variation in size and services is reflected in a diversity of administrative structures and staffing arrangements. Most often the health service is housed within the Division of Student Affairs. Larger health services usually employ one of the following as director: an administrator, a physician, or a psychologist. Many smaller health services are directed by a nurse. The director should have authority to administer the college health program and also to participate actively in the development of institutional policies effecting health and safety (American College Health Association, 1991).

Staffing needs can be estimated from a study of the ten largest public and ten largest private American universities (Patrick, 1988). For each 10,000 students, public institutions averaged 3.2 physicians and 23.2 total health service staff, while private institutions averaged 4.1 physicians and 31.5 total staff. These staffs provided an average of 2.0 visits per student per year at public institutions, and 2.5 visits per year at private institutions.

Most often, college health services are financed primarily by prepaid or mandatory student fees. This approach serves to maximize preventive care and assures access to treatment without financial barriers (Kraft, 1993). A 1991 Blue Cross/Blue Shield survey of 400 college health services revealed that 85 percent of their funding was prepaid; 46 percent from general fees and 39 percent from student health fees. Another 5 percent of the funding was derived from fee-for-service income; the remainder coming mainly from insurance, with very small amounts from other miscellaneous sources. The average annual budget was $102 per full-time student, $81 at commuter schools and $128 at residential campuses.

EMERGING ISSUES

Trends

Few endeavors are more precarious than attempting to predict the future. In 1987, the ACHA described the following areas it believed would require continued attention in the future: (1) student health; (2) insurance plans; (3) seeking grant money from AIDS research; (4) collaboration with such national associations as ACPA, NASPA and ACUHO–I; and (5) sharing reports with colleges and universities from various task forces on alcohol and substance abuse, minority and student involvement, and health goals for the American society (Blom, 1987). Two other major trends in student health services of the future were identified as an increasing role for preventive services and an increasing role for psychological support services (McGinnis, 1987 as cited in Saddlemire, 1988). In the area of preventive services, optimism was expressed for multiple new vaccines, better contraceptives, better blood pressure medication, and definitive dietary and exercise packages. So far, for the most part, these predictions have not been fulfilled. Dietary advice, the treatment of high blood pressure, and contraception remain essentially unchanged. Women now have injectable contraceptives available; this is perhaps more convenient, but risks, efficacy, and side effects remain unchanged. The new vaccines for hepatitis A and chicken pox will not revolutionize health care; vaccines for AIDS and tuberculosis, which would, do not appear imminent. As for an increasing role for psychological support services, the anticipated improvements in risk factor identification, motivational tools and neuro-pharmacology have not yet come to pass. In fact, traditional therapies are being subjected to increasing scrutiny by health insurers who are demanding proof of efficacy.

With the understanding that conjecture may be a better term than prediction, there are some current trends in medicine that seem noteworthy. Antibiotics have revolutionized health care in the last fifty years, but the emergence of bacteria resistant to antibiotics threatens to reverse these gains. In recent years, bacteria have been developing resistance faster than new antibiotics can be developed, and some are now resistant to all known drugs. Probably most worrisome is the appearance of multiple drug resistant tuberculosis. This could become the great epidemic of the next decade.

Gene Research

Research into genetics seems on the threshold of providing the next revolution in therapy. Genetic diseases, such as cystic fibrosis, infectious diseases including AIDS, metabolic disorders such as diabetes, and even cancer may soon be treated by insertion of custom designed genes (Lancet, 1995).

Technology

Electronic communication over the Internet has already allowed improved communication among health care providers and patients, other providers, and reference materials. The next decade should see expansion of this networking process, with particular emphasis on using the Internet for health education, and providing specialist consultation to remote sites by "telemedicine."

Health Care Reform

The area where change is having the greatest effect on college health services is not in technology but rather in the business of health insurance and health care delivery. Skyrocketing health care costs have become a major national issue. As recently as 1993, it seemed likely that there would be significant changes in health care delivery based on federal health care reform. In 1996, it appears that legislative reform will occur primarily at the state level, if at all. But regardless of what happens in the state and national legislatures, market forces will almost certainly continue to produce sweeping changes in American health care delivery. Student health services, which have been somewhat sheltered so far, can expect to be dramatically affected, and have already started to prepare.

The driving force behind marketplace reform is the desire of employers to reduce, or at least limit, the cost of providing employee health care. Early approaches included fee schedules, mandatory second opinions, close scrutiny of catastrophic cases ("case management"), and increasing demands for documentation of the need for tests and treatment. More recently, growing numbers of employee insurance plans are embracing managed care approaches that limit the choice of provider. The basic concept is simple: insurers, representing large numbers of patients, are able to negotiate with health care providers. In return for directing patients to specific providers, insurers can negotiate discounted rates, and may in some cases even impose standards of care. One structure is a preferred provider organization (PPO) of independent providers who may be associated with several plans. Another is a health maintenance organization (HMO) whose staff serve only HMO clients.

How does this affect student health services? Traditional indemnity insurance plans coordinate well with student health services. Such plans usually pay for tests and hospital care, and typically have deductibles that apply to office visits, so that students do not object to the prepaid health fee that covers office visits. Now, however, students are often covered by insurance with managed care components that restrict their choice of provider. Tests done at the student health services may not be reimbursed. And the plan may even cover office visits, but only when provided by designated providers or clinics. These plans pose problems for both the student and the student health service. From the student's perspective, there may not be adequate access to care. The student is required to obtain primary care not from the student health services, but instead from providers that are off campus, and possibly out of town. Moreover, these providers may not provide the appropriate focus on prevention and education issues, such as alcohol and drug abuse, sexually transmitted disease, and eating disorders. From the health services' perspective, there is decreased utilization and decreased opportunity to pursue its mission. Further, students who cannot be reimbursed for tests or treatment provided at their health services, and who cannot be referred to specialists by their health services, are going to resist paying student health fees. This is a threat to the health services' continued existence.

Many of the concerns of both payers and consumers are addressed by the traditional student health model. Student health services are nonprofit, usually provide service on a prepaid basis, and use salaried providers. These features allow universal access without financial barriers, remove financial incentives to provide unnecessary care, and remove profit incentives to inappropriately limit care. However, this model health care delivery system is far from comprehensive. Many student health services do charge for laboratory and radiology services, and for pharmaceuticals. Others simply do not provide these services. And with few exceptions, student health services do not provide specialty care or hospital care. What is needed is a system that incorporates the student health model into a comprehensive health care program, under the new rules of managed care.

It is perhaps easier to say what should happen rather than what will happen. Insurers should make provisions for students to have access to health care while they reside at school. Students should have access to plans that meet their unique needs for education and preventive services. Whether this will happen will depend on how well student health services adapt to the new rules. One way for student health services to survive is to form alliances with groups of specialists and with hospitals, in order to be able to offer students comprehensive care plans. Another approach is to subcontract with an HMO to provide primary care services to those HMO members who are students. Student health services are already taking steps to prepare for the inevitable changes.

Education Health service directors are attending conferences and workshops, hastily acquiring knowledge about managed care and the medical marketplace. At the 1995 annual meeting of the American College Health Association (ACHA) representative programs included "How College Health Services Can Be Competitive in the Changing Marketplace," "Managed Care: Concepts and Issues," and the somewhat apocalyptic "Change Now: Make Dust or Eat Dust."

Accreditation. Health services are, in unprecedented numbers, seeking formal accreditation. There are two major accrediting bodies for outpatient health care facilities: the Joint Commission on Accreditation of Healthcare Organizations (JCAHO) and the Accreditation Association for Ambulatory Health Care (AAAHC). Accreditation, while not required by law, may be valuable in negotiation with insurers or HMOs; accreditation also provides demonstrable evidence of quality when a school considers outsourcing student health. The accreditation standard that requires a formal quality assurance program is usually the one that requires the most change; the 1995 ACHA meeting devoted three hours to programs on how to prepare for accreditation, and five hours to programs on how to implement a quality assurance program.

Advocacy: The ACHA has implemented an organized response, the scope of which is illustrated by the following partial list: The president of ACHA has written to the Nation's Vice Presidents for Student Affairs soliciting support for college health. ACHA has hired a consultant to lobby congress and the Clinton Administration. ACHA has created a national network of state ACHA representatives to share information and coordinate state level lobbying efforts. ACHA has also drafted a proposed amendment for inclusion in federal legislation. ACHA's board of directors has endorsed the QSHP, a qualified student health plan-proposal of Grace and Beckley (1994):

> Under the QSHP proposal, student health services and student health insurance plans would be combined, and would have to meet minimum standards. HMO's and other insurers would be able to enroll their members in QSHPs, and employer contributions to QSHPs would be tax deductible for the employer. Implementation of the QSHP proposal would require changes in several federal laws.

AIDS/ARC/HIV

Acquired immune deficiency syndrome (AIDS) and AIDS related complex (ARC) are caused by infection with the human immunodeficiency virus (HIV). These conditions are of particular concern in college health. AIDS is virtually 100 percent fatal; there is no cure. Prevention is possible by eliminating the behaviors that allow transmission of the virus, primarily unprotected sexual intercourse and sharing of needles used for drug abuse. Unfortunately, there are numerous moral, ethical, and legal obstacles to an effective prevention program. Among the issues of particular concern are homophobia, moral objections to condom use and to sex education, irrational fears of infection from casual contact, and issues of privacy.

To address these serious and complex issues, the American College Health Association established the Task Force on AIDS in 1985, chaired by Richard P. Keeling, M.D. This Task Force produced a special report, *AIDS on the College Campus* (1989), which provides guidance to colleges and universities in responding to this epidemic. The report provides thoughtful and comprehensive guidelines for establishing a general institutional response, as well as specific policies on housing, educational programs, testing and screening, confidentiality, use of recreational facilities, and medical care.

WELLNESS

Wellness as a concept and program emphasis has been an important element of student health services. From the beginning, the goal has been to foster a positive attitude toward gaining those competencies and skills that will assist individuals in protecting their own health and possibly preventing serious health problems (Farnsworth, 1965 as cited in Saddlemire, 1988). Educational programs aim to acquaint people with the health hazards and risks associated with such everyday factors as obesity, inadequate nutrition, insufficient exercise, drug and alcohol use, and high levels of stress. Comprehensive prevention program planning initiatives among not only colleges and universities but public health and community agencies as well, access to larger databases for wellness policies and programs, Internet connections to global information, and evolving research on holistic therapies have greatly influenced college health prevention practices.

Healthy People 2000 (United States Department of Health and Human Services, 1990), a national effort to guide prevention practices, identifies age-related goals and objectives to decrease preventable illness, injury, and disability. Its framework clearly outlines the challenges facing the higher education community in the 1990s in the areas of health promotion, health protection, and preventive services. Health promotion strategies include physical activity and fitness, nutrition, tobacco, alcohol and other drugs, family planning, mental health and mental disorders, and violent and abusive behavior. Health protection strategies include unintentional injuries, occupational health and safety, health and environmental health, food and drug safety, and oral health. Health preventive services include strategies aimed at maternal and infant health, heart disease and stroke, cancer, diabetes, HIV infection, sexually transmitted and infectious diseases. Research suggests that two-thirds of all deaths in the United States are attributable to preventable factors (Steenbarger, 1995). College health prevention practices must creatively implement policies, programs, and services to impact positively the health status of students.

As the number of higher education health and wellness issues continues to escalate, it is unlikely that revenues will increase to support expanded programming. The national investment in prevention programming is only a small portion of the total health care cost. Less than 5 percent of the total annual health care costs are aimed at prevention practices (McGinnis, 1993). Cost-effective measures which will yield effective outcomes among a diverse population will continue to be the challenge that confronts wellness program planners. Maintaining a variety of active and passive interventions which can be adapted to gender and various cultural backgrounds is imperative (Ford, 1994).

Student affairs leaders continue to strive toward the development of social and cultural settings which empower students to develop to their fullest potential (Rhoads, 1995). The institution and surrounding community environment can be extremely influential in fostering healthy normative behaviors. In order to enhance health behaviors in a college or university setting, supportive social environments and accessible facilitative services are needed to reduce death and disability. Fabiano (1994) contrasts the traditional health education model with the community-action, service-learning model. Traditional models include educational programs which are aimed at influencing an individual's health behaviors without considering the social/environmental influences. The community-action, service-learning model that provides an active interaction of problem-solving within social, cultural, and political systems will continue to increase individual's ability to successfully adopt positive lifestyle changes. Student life staff and health services staff can work closely with members of the university community and outside community members to generate ideas for fostering environments which are conducive to supporting healthy behavioral change. For instance, dining unit managers can provide heart-healthy menu items while student nutrition peer educators provide nutritional informational activities to promote these selections. In addition, local merchants can work with student affairs personnel in providing campus and city-wide wellness events.

Peer education programs will continue to be an integral part of university wellness programming of the future. In order to accomplish wellness objectives, peer educators will need to be selected, recruited, trained, and evaluated carefully to determine if their talents, skills, and preparation are appropriate to the specific activity and program (Keeling, 1993). For example, at Bowling Green State University, each year approximately 50 students are recruited and selected (through an application and interview process) to function as wellness consultants in the Center for Wellness and Prevention. After completing a semester training course for academic credit, each consultant may apply for specific job responsibilities. Twelve job responsibilities have been designed to complement programming needs as well as the wellness consultants' interests and academic majors. For example, psychology majors assist with referrals using active listening skills, journalism majors assist with promotion, and dietetics majors assist with nutritional consultations. This procedure has greatly increased volunteer retention rates, while at the same time enhancing program delivery.

Information on wellness continues to evolve. Perhaps the increase in both immuno-deficiency diseases and unexplained chronic conditions has necessitated the movement toward a biopsychosocial model with an interactive exchange among all types of individuals. Psychoneuro-immunology and holistic therapies are relying on research which stems from a better integration of medical and psychological resources. The institution can play a primary role in facilitating the coordination of holistic strategies to address wellness issues through such varied areas as international programs, medical schools, nutritional studies, and psychology departments. The institution also continues to serve as a pioneer in the wellness field through increasing student and staff access to the "information highway." On-line, self-help organizations with interactive forums, health issues bulletin boards and health and wellness-related informational services flourish on the Internet.

Surprisingly, the same technology which expands wellness horizons also limits expansion into other wellness dimensions. Although technology has expanded access to information, in many cases it has decreased contact with nature and the amount of leisure time available. In the last ten years, Americans have lost 15 percent of their leisure time (Powell, 1991). In order to maintain or achieve a high level of well-being, a variety of individualized wellness strategies are needed to continually assist with rapid adaptations to ever-changing life stresses.

In this decade, there will continue to be a need to deliver programs which are broader than basic health issues. People will continue to be dissatisfied with programs which only promise symptom control through medical management, but will investigate wellness programs which facilitate an improved quality of life. Core issues concerning violence prevention and substance abuse will need to be addressed within their social context. The future of college and university wellness programming depends on a greater integration of resources, stronger collaborations, holistic approaches targeting diverse needs, attention to expanding informational systems, and dynamic interactions with social, cultural, and political systems which influence health choices.

ADDITIONAL SERVICES AND CONCERNS

This chapter has provided only an overview of college health. *Recommended Standards for a College Health Program* (1991) provides information about additional services. These recommendations address care for international students, athletes, and physically challenged students. They also address additional services including dental, pharmacy, laboratory, diagnostic imaging (x-ray), emergency, surgery, occupational health, and inpatient infirmaries.

The American College Health Association not only identifies additional areas of concern for college health, but also serves as an authoritative source of information and advice. The 1992 *ACHA Publications Catalog* lists a number of special publications. Among them are

General Statement of Ethical Principles and Standards
Statement on AIDS and International Education Issues
Suggestions for Implementing the Drug-Free Schools and Campuses Regulations
    of 1989
Statement on Tobacco Use on College and University Campuses

Recommendations for an Institutional Prematriculation Immunization Requirement
Recommended Standards: Alcohol and Other Drug Use, Misuse, and Dependency
Standards on Student Health Insurance
Position Statement: Health Insurance for Foreign Students
College Health 2000 . . . A Perspective Statement and Strategies for the Future
Healthy Campus 2000: Making it Happen

Additional resources for learning about the breadth of concerns of college health personnel are the *Journal of American College Health,* the annual meetings of the American College Health Association, and an internet user group, SHS, which is served by a listserver at the address <listserv@utkvml.utk.edu>.

REFERENCES

American College Health Association, Committee on Standards for College Health. (1991). *Recommended standards for a college health program.* Linthicum, MD: American College Health Association.

Boynton, R. E. (1962). Historical development of college health services. *Student Medicine, 10,* 354–359.

Boynton, R. E. (1971). The first fifty years: A history of the American College Health Association. *Journal of the American College Health Association, 19,* 269–285.

Bridwell, M. W., & Kinder, S. P. (1993). Confronting health issues. In M. J. Barr and Associates, *The handbook of student affairs administration* (pp. 481–492). San Francisco: Jossey-Bass.

Editorial, (1995, March 25). Lancet, pp. 739–740.

Fabiano, P. (1994). Personal health into community action: Another step forward in peer health education. *Journal of American College Health, 43,* 115–121.

Fingar, A. R. (1989). Patient problems encountered at a student health service. *Journal of American College Health, 38,* 142–144.

Ford, D., & Goode, C. (1994). African American college students' health behaviors and perceptions of related health issues. *Journal of American College Health, 42,* 206–210.

Grace, T. W., & Beckley, S. T. (1995). The QSHP proposal: 10 questions most often asked. *Journal of American College Health, 44,* 43–49.

Keeling, R. P. (1986). *AIDS on the college campus (ACHA Special Report).* Linthicum, MD: American College Health Association.

Keeling, R., & Engstrom, E. (1993). Refining your peer education program. *Journal of American College Health,* 41, 255–257.

Kraft, D. P. (1993). College health: A model for our nation's health. *Journal of American College Health, 42,* 77–78.

McGinnis, M. J. (1987). A health campus—forecasting from the 1990 health objectives for the nation. *Journal of American College Health, 35,* 158–170.

McGinnis, M. J. (1993). Actual cause of death in the U.S. *Journal of the American Medical Association, 270,* 2207–2211.

Packwood, W. T. Health. In W. T. Packwood (Ed.), *College student personnel services* (pp. 298–339). Springfield, IL: Charles C Thomas.

Patrick, L. (1988). Student health, medical care within institutions of higher education. *Journal of the American Medical Association, 260,* 3301–3305.

Powell, D. R. (1991). Crystal-clear vision prediction for the future of health promotion. *Health Action Manager* (January), 6–7.

Rhoads, R., & Michael, A. (1995). Student affairs practitioners as transformative education: Advancing a critical cultural perspective. *Journal of College Student Development, 36,* 413–421.

Saddlemire, G. L. (1988). Health services. In A. L. Rentz, & G. L. Saddlemire (Eds.), *Student affairs functions in higher education* (pp. 185–202). Springfield, IL: Charles C Thomas.

Springer, L., Terenzini, P., Pascarelli, E., & Amaury, N. (1995). Influences on college students' orientations toward learning for self-understanding. *Journal of College Student Development, 36,* 5–17.

Steenbarger, B., Conyne, R., Baird, M., & O'Brian, J. (1995). Prevention in college health: Counseling Perspective. *Journal of American College Health, 43,* 157–162.

United States Department of Health and Human Services. (1990). *Healthy people 2000: National health promotion and disease prevention (DHHS Publication No. PHS 91-50213).* Washington, DC: U.S. Government Printing Office.

AUTHOR INDEX

SUBJECT INDEX

A

Academic advising, 88–102
  academic model, 93, 94
  administrative model, 95
  application student development theory, 97
  beginning of, 89
  centralized model, 94
  components characteristic of, 93
  definition, 88
  description, 92–93
  entry-level qualifications, 98
  faculty advising, 92–93
  faculty model, 93
  future considerations, 100–102
  historical development, 89–91
    early systems, 89
    professional associations, 90–91
    use of ACT, 91
  institutional configurations, 91–92
  issues, 98–100
  multiple advisors for a student, 99–100
  practice models, 93–96
  purpose of, 92
  specialized, 99
  staffing, 96
  student or peer advisors, 96
  tasks associated with, 93
  uses of, 73
Academic evaluation, definition, 198
Academic misconduct, definition, 198
Accreditation Standards for University & College Counseling Centers, 165–166
Acquired immune deficiency syndrome, 373–374
Admissions management
  admissions officer (*see* Admissions officer)
  Deans of, 60
  definition of, 56–57

emergence of, 59
enrollment management (*see* Enrollment management)
historical development, 57–62
marketing techniques, 59, 61–62
purpose of, 57
role accreditation in, 60
role of today, 61–62
Admissions officer
  history of, 57–59
  image of, 57–59
  of today, 59
  roles of, 57–58
Adult learners, 255–256, 323–324
  factors in returning for higher education, 255–256
  need for orientation programs, 256
  phases levels ego development, 323–324
Aesthetics, definition, 6–7
African Americans in higher education, 218–219
  Brown v. Board of Education and, 219
  Civil Rights Act of 1964 and, 219
  growth after Civil War, 218–219
  problems in 1960s on campus, 222–223
AIDS Related Complex, 373–374
AIDS/ARC/HIV, 373–374
American College Health Association, 164, 366, 367, 369
American College Personnel Association (ACPA), 40, 41, 46–47, 52, 163, 200, 269
American College Testing Program (ACT), 91, 94
American Council on Education, 42–43
American Counseling Association, 163
American Home Economics Association, 39
American Personnel & Guidance Association (APGA), 40
American Psychological Association (APA), 163

PHYSICAL EDUCATION RECONCEPTUALIZED
Persons, Movement, Knowledge

Published 2001, 276 pages
Saul Ross

PROCEDURES FOR STRUCTURING AND SCHEDULING SPORTS TOURNAMENTS
Elimination, Consolation, Placement, and Round-Robin Design (3rd Ed.)

Published 2000, 192 pages
Francis M. Rokosz
$29.95—spiral

SYMPATHETIC VIBRATIONS
A Guide for Private Music Teachers

Published 2000, 190 pages
Amber Esping
$32.95—spiral

EMOTIONAL AND BEHAVIORAL PROBLEMS IN THE CLASSROOM:
A Memoir

Published 2000, 122 pages
Herbert Grossman
$19.95—paper

TEACHING THE ENGLISH LANGUAGE. (2nd Ed.)

Published 2000, 166 pages
John H. Bushman
$29.95—paper

MEDIA AND LITERACY:
Learning in an Electronic Age - Issues, Ideas, and Teaching Strategies. (2nd Ed.)

Published 2000, 244 pages
Adams, Dennis & Mary Hamm
$43.95—hard
$31.95—paper

ISSUES IN SOCIAL STUDIES
Voices from the Classroom

Published 2000, 222 pages
Cameron White
$46.95—clothbound
$31.95—paper

HUMAN SERVICES AND THE FULL SERVICE SCHOOL
The Need for Collaboration

Published 2000, 128 pages
Robert E. Kronick
$18.95—paper

CHILDREN WITH SPECIAL NEEDS
A Resource Guide for Parents, Educators, Social Workers, and Other Care-givers

Published 1999, 234 pages
Karen L. Lungu
$51.95—cloth
$38.95—paper (displayed)

STUDENT DISCIPLINE AND CLASS-ROOM MANAGEMENT

Published 1999, 126 pages
Jack Campbell
$31.95—hard
$19.95—paper

BEHAVIOR MANAGEMENT STRATEGIES FOR TEACHERS
A Student Workbook

Published 1999, 142 pages
Joan C. Harlan & Sidney T. Rowland
$23.95—spiral

EFFECTIVE TEACHING
Preparation and Implementation (3rd Ed.)

Published 1999, 266 pages
Gilbert H. Hunt, Timothy J. Touzel & Dennis G. Wiseman
$49.95—cloth
$34.95—paper (displayed)

Charles C Thomas • Publisher, Ltd.
2600 S. First Street, Springfield, IL 62707
Call 1-800-258-8980 or 1-217-789-8980
or Fax 1-217-789-9130
Complete catalog available at www.ccthomas.com •
books@ccthomas.com

TEACHING AND TESTING IN READING
A Practical Guide for Teachers and Parents

Published 1999, 164 pages
Charles H. Hargis
$40.95—hard
$28.95—paper